The Letters of Gertrude Bell

By

Gertrude Bell

(Volume II 1917-1927)

The Echo Library 2006

Published by

The Echo Library

Echo Library
131 High St.
Teddington
Middlesex TW11 8HH

www.echo-library.com

This volume has been proof read by
Gemma Williams
Freeman Williams - Language Solutions
The College Business Centre
Uttoxeter New Road
Derby DE22 3WZ
Tel: 01332 869342 & 869343
Fax: 01332 869344
www.freemanwilliams.co.uk

First Published 1927

Please report serious faults in the text to complaints@echo-library.com

ISBN 1-40680-053-8

CONTENTS

XVI	1917 Bagdad	01
XVII	1918-1919 Bagdad	24
XVIII	1920 Bagdad	49
	1. Major General Sir Percy Cox, G.C.M.G., Etc.	67
	2. H.E. Sir Henry Dobbs, K.C.S.I., Etc.	95
XIX	1920 Bagdad	104
XX	1921 Bagdad	118
XXI	1921 Bagdad	133
XXII	1922-1923 Bagdad	151
XXIII	September 1923 to June 1924 Bagdad	177
XXIV	July 1924 to December 1924 Bagdad	202
XXV	1925 Bagdad-England	210
XXV	1926 Bagdad	233
XXVII	Conclusion	249

CHAPTER XVI
1917

BAGDAD

To F.B. & H.B.
April 15th, 1917.

We are within two hours of Bagdad and I'm free to admit that coming up this river gives one a wholesome respect for our lines of communication. This is the 9th day we've been at it, tying up for a few hours at night but steaming 17 or 18 hours a day notwithstanding. It's well that it wasn't a month later for already the temperature is 90 and on a crowded ship it's hot. We passed Kut before sunrise, but I got up to see it—poor tragic little place—it's shelled walls and shattered palm trees catching the first flash of day. It is quite empty still, but we are going to clean it out and build it up as soon as possible.

We anchored last night just above Ctesiphon. I know the river banks well, for I've ridden up them more than once. Our big camps are the only unfamiliar objects. It's exactly three years to-day since I last set out from Bagdad across the Syrian Desert on my way back from Arabia.

To H.B.
BAGDAD, April 20th.

Such an arrival! Sir Percy made me most welcome and said a house had been allotted to me. I went off to see it and found a tiny stifling box of a place in a dirty little bazaar. It was absolutely empty—what furniture I had was with my heavy luggage and not yet landed, and I hadn't even a boy, as I had left my servant to look after the heavy luggage. Fortunately, like a good traveller, I had not parted from my bed and bath. These I proceeded to set up and further unpacked my box which had been dropped into the Tigris, and hung out all the things to dry on the railings of the court. It was breathlessly hot. I hadn't so much as a chair to put anything on, and when I wanted water for washing I had to open my front door and call in the help of the bazaar. Fortunately they responded with alacrity. I dined with Sir Percy, armed myself with a loaf of bread for breakfast and returned to my empty house to sleep. By good luck my servant turned up late that night, so that there was someone to water tea for me next morning.

I confess, however, that after having done my hair and breakfasted on the floor I felt a little discouraged. It was clear that something must be done at once, and I proceeded to hunt for one. The first thing I tumbled on to was a rose garden with three summer houses in it, quite close to the Political Office and belonging, fortunately, to an old friend of mine, Musa Chalabi. I decided at once that this was the thing, but a kitchen had to be built and a bath room, and sunblinds to be put up—a thousand things. I got Musa Chalabi to help me and summoned in an old man, a servant whom I've known for ages, and after five days work I'm in—'tant bien que mal' and it promises very well. My old man

Shamao has engaged me a cook and the Englishman who runs all the supplies Col. Dixon is my faithful friend, having been charged by the I.G.C. to look after me. And my roses I must tell you are glorious. Oh, but it is hot! I'm longing for my thin summer clothes. I wonder when they will reach me here.

Meantime all my acquaintances and friends have flocked in to see me. I've visited the Naqib, the head religious man and an ally of many years' standing, and have been received with open arms. And it is all wildly interesting—War Office telegraphing for signed articles from me, etc., etc. I'm going to have an exciting summer. Sir P. gives me lots of thrilling things to do and is the kindest of chiefs. Bagdad is a mass of roses and congratulations. They are genuinely delighted at being free of the Turks. The rest for another time, I am so busy.

To H.B. & F.B.
BAGDAD, April 27th, 1917.

I'm never here, that's the pity of it, but I intend, when I write my War Office articles, to retire here solidly for the afternoons; otherwise I'm so terribly interrupted by visitors. I love seeing them and they are most useful for purposes of information, but they eat up the hours. I have the most amusing reunions with gentlemen I met at Hayil and Najaf and Heaven knows where besides. It's immense fun, and also it's a great pride to be provided with so many acquaintances. But the heat! It's 90 in my coolest room to-night after dinner, and of course that's nothing really. Next month it will be 10 degrees hotter at least. My programme is to ride from 6 to 7:30, come in and have a bath and breakfast and then straight to the office. I don't get away till past 7 or sometimes nearly 8. Very shortly I shall begin the day an hour earlier and try to come in at 7 for dinner. I'm conscious of an unworthy rejoicing at the material comfort of existence. At Basrah one could get nothing—lived on tinned milk and butter for a year, and at last I lived without them because one grew so sick of tinned things. Here I have fresh milk and butter and sour curds every day. A bowl of sour curds is my lunch, and it's the nicest possible meal in this weather, that and a cup of Arab coffee. And then masses of roses everywhere. My duties are of the most diverse kinds. We are very shorthanded. I take on everything I can to spare Sir Percy—interview representatives of innumerable creeds, keep an open door for tribal sheikhs and messengers from the desert whose business I discover and send up in brief to Sir Percy, and then behind all this there's my real job, the gathering and sorting of information..Already the new tribal maps and tribe lists are getting into shape, and the first big batch of confidential notes on Bagdad personalities will be issued to our Political Officers to-morrow—that's not bad going. Presently all the new surveys will begin to come in and I shall have the revision and correction of the place names, a thing I like doing because in the first place it's so nice to get them right, and in the second it teaches me so much geography. The head survey man is an enthusiast, and gives me a free hand. And then I'm going to be Curator of Antiquities or at least I'm going to show the Revenue Commissioner all the old buildings and scraps of buildings that are left here, and he has promised to keep guard over them. . . . It's a thousand times more interesting than Basrah, you understand. To-day there arrived by miracle two charming black satin gowns from Marthe which makes me hope that my new cotton gowns may presently arrive also. I'm very badly in need of them. It's almost too hot already for unwashable clothes, even in the evening. I shall rejoice when I hear that muslin gowns are on their way. . . .

Oh if it were as near the end in France! Is Maurice still out of it? Every time a post comes in I dread to hear that he has gone back.

[Maurice (now Colonel Bell, C.M.G.) had gone to the front in the beginning of 1915 in command of the 4th Battalion, Green Howards. He was invalided home the following year and then had a command in England.]

To H.B.
BAGDAD, May 3rd, 1917.

. . . . Please will Mother have sent to me by post six pairs of thin white thread stockings, and the same of brown—rather dark brown.

The days melt like snow in the sun. But it's just as well, for I've been realising this evening that if I weren't so very busy I should be very lonely. To-day I was in the office from 8:30 to 8, and had scarcely anything to show for it by reason of the reams of odds and ends that take up all the time. I can't write any of the interesting and pre- occupying things, so you must put up with small change. I spent a couple of hours yesterday before breakfast inspecting an exquisite 14th century mosque and a tomb of the same date and seeing what repairs were immediately essential. The two learned men who dwelt in the respective mosques were my enthusiastic guides. I took the Revenue Commissioner with me, Mr. Garbett. We must have a trained architect out as soon as possible. Fortunately Mr. Storrs from Cairo (Sec. to the High Commissioner) is on his way up on a short visit. He'll give me a hand over getting out the man I want and over several other things.

The Bishop of Nagpur wants me personally to conduct him to Babylon, which I'm well qualified to do I may say! I hope the plan will materialize. I would like to go back there, though it will make my heart ache a little. They were all so kind to me, the German excavators, and no war can put an end to the affectionate esteem in which I hold Koldewey.

We have not got nearly enough clerks and typists, one never seems to roll the stone finally to the top of the hill—it rolls back for want of mechanical appliances. I suppose it will all straighten out in time, meanwhile it's laborious. Thank Heaven my house is finished, so that I don't have to begin the day by interviewing carpenters and bricklayers— it was the last straw! Still on the whole, in spite of the rush and scramble, it's so deeply interesting that one doesn't bother about a straw more or less.

To F.B.
BAGDAD, May 11th, 1917.

This week's post is drifting in—a very welcome one from Moll announcing the sending off of my summer clothes. The patterns are charming—it's to be hoped they'll wash. But Lord how glad I shall be to have them. My present appearance is that of a hobbledehoy in straitened circumstances who has outgrown her wardrobe—only it's my gowns which have diminished (from much washing) not I who have increased. The event of the week has been the arrival of Mr. Storrs from Egypt. He's here for a fortnight. He brings a perfect hurricane of fresh air from outside and I'm jigged if we shan't send him back on the wings of a similar storm which will blow open their eastern-facing doors and windows. An admirable plan it is having such interchanges. I've taken him round to all my religious dignitaries and learned men, who delight in him and his Arabic also—the comfort it is to go about in the company of a Father of Tongues! Unfortunately I'm too busy to go about with him much, but such interludes are very reviving and the result is I've applied and outlined a reasonable scheme for the Government of this country—'pas dégoûté!' which I really think may be useful as something to bite upon. There's nothing like a spice of audacity.

. . . . I'm getting to be rather a dab at Arab politics—but it doesn't make them seem the easier. We've shouldered a gigantic task, but I can't see what alternative there was.

This is how I pass my days : I'm out riding before 6, sometimes through the gardens by the river bank, sometimes round the old line of the city wall, a gallop in the desert and home through the bazaars. Occasionally I inspect an ancient monument on the way back—I did so this morning. A bath and breakfast and so to the office before 9. I'm there till after 7. I have a cup of coffee and a bowl of sour curds at 12:30 and tea with Sir Percy at 4—it's the only time I peaceably see him. People drop in all day. Occasionally one has a clear hour or two—generally there's a lull between 12 and 2 and one tries to straighten out all the information one has acquired. But the end of the day finds me with two or three unfinished things and no hope of getting at them the day after. They are piling and piling up and I can't think when I shall be able to clear them off. That's the only bother—there's always just a bit too much to do. I come back to dinner in my garden at 8 and I generally go to bed at 9:30, at which time I begin to fall asleep. It's gloriously cool still but that must certainly end in a day or two.

I must tell you I love Bagdad, and the people are so outgoing—partly propitiatory no doubt, but they are glad to have us.

To H.B.
BAGDAD, May 18th, 1917.
. . . I couldn't possibly come away from here at this moment. It's an immense opportunity, just at this time when the atmosphere is so emotional; one catches hold of people as one will never do again, and establishes relations which won't dissolve. It is not for my own sake, but because it greases the wheels of administration—it really does, and I want to watch it all very carefully almost from day to day, so as to be able to take what I hope may be something like a decisive hand in final disposition. I shall be able to do that, I shall indeed, with the knowledge I'm gaining. It's so intimate. They are beyond words

outgoing to me. What does anything else matter when the job is such a big one? Incidentally I may tell you—so that you won't be surprised when you see me—that this summer will turn my hair quite white. it is one of the results of this climate. However, that won't matter to gentlemen like one I had in to-day, who was so holy that he couldn't look an unveiled woman in the face! It didn't prevent him from desiring to have a long talk with me on his private affairs, and at the end I'll admit be tipped me a casual wink or two, just enough to know me again. General Wauchope has been here, Mr. Philby has come up from Amarah, he's so quick and intelligent. . . There never was anything quite like this before, you must understand that—it's amazing. It's the making of a new world. You see I couldn't come away. The W.O. has telegraphed for a series of signed articles on Mesop. and Asia Minor. I shall have to set about them, but it's a wide order.

I never get through my work, but that's better than having no work to get through. Only it makes my letters scrappy. And I feel so ashamed when I get splendid screeds from you two who are just as busy. It's not really hot yet, seldom up to 100, but it must begin soon. I ride daily in the early morning on my love of a pony, and keep fit thereby. I really must have another copy of Amurath; will you please send me one. It's in great request, there being nothing else so modern. It is 8 o'clock, and I have been in the office uninterruptedly since 9, with 20 min. for lunch!

To H.B. & F.B.
BAGDAD May 26, 1917.
. . . . The post brought me a letter from Mother this week—and also, what do you think? Two muslin gowns! I hope they are swallows, so to speak, announcing all my summer clothes. But I regret to say that one of them which according to Moll's pattern was intended for me to wear in the evening was no more an evening gown than it was a fur coat, and won't do at all for that purpose. It's rather a blow, for I had a vision of some nice trailing muslin gowns with floating sleeves, and far from it. However, I shall just have not to dine out when it gets hot. It really hasn't reached that yet. We're almost through May and the breeze has never slackened. It's wonderful. Of course you would think it warm in England—it's got to 100, but that is nothing here.

[Gertrude's disappointment expressed in this letter about the evening gown is explained by the fact that the fashion in London dresses had changed and that there were no 'trailing muslin gowns with floating sleeves.']

Mr. Storrs leaves next week. He has done us an infinite amount of good. One becomes so provincial seeing no one from outside. The great event in our circles is the arrival of Fahad Bey, paramount sheikh of the Amarat, an almighty swell and an old friend of mine. I stayed with him in the desert three years ago on my way back to Damascus. I hope that with his help we shall get a move in among the tribes. Anyhow, it's a great 'coup' getting him to burn his boats and come in to us. We had the most tenderly affectionate meeting I assure you. Now I'll tell you a sweet story. There came in a couple of old sheikhs, hopelessly ragged and very sorry for themselves, for their tribe happens to be just in the borderland and first they had been harried by the Turks and then by us, and finally making the best of a bad business, they had sought refuge with us, and we, after our truly idiotic manner, had clapped half their followers into gaol, and they couldn't find them, so they came to me and I said I would ask Sir Percy what could be done. At that they almost wept with gratitude and declared that they would forthwith send me a beautiful mare. But I said no, it was a kind thought, but I could not take presents and therewith I went down to talk to Sir Percy. When I came back I found them with their two old heads together and as soon as they saw me they said, "Khatun—if you won't take the horse we're going to send u—a gazelle!" The gazelle hasn't materialized yet, and I rather hope it won't, for gazelles eat everything including your most important papers, but wasn't it nice of them to hit on such small change for mares. The great pleasure in this country is that I do love the people so much.

We revel in fruit here. The excellent oranges are nearly over, but the apricots have come in in masses and small sweet greengages, and now the good little melons have begun. Next we shall have grapes and figs—truly a bountiful country. I'm. loving it, you know, loving my work and rejoicing in the confidence of my chief. One morning last week when I was out riding I paid a very early call on my way home on the son of a celebrated old warrior a Circassian whom I knew in the old days. And I found, too, a great man of letters, a native of Bagdad, who is writing leaders for me which I send to the Egyptian papers, and we sat round and sipped tea and coffee and talked and I went away feeling that I really was a part of Bagdad. You know I'm growing into it terrifically fast— taking root; what do you think of it? I don't think I shall ever be able to detach myself permanently from the fortunes of this country. But I don't bother to look ahead. It's enough that my job is here now. But it's a wonderful thing to feel this affection and confidence of a whole people round you. There are so few of us, you see, that each one is absolutely salient and each is a focus for so many hopes and fears. But oh to be at the end of the war and to have a free hand!

To H.B. & F.B.
BAGDAD, June 1, 1917.

Dearest Parents, I had finally to take desperate steps to cure the above mentioned cold. I lay flat on a bed in a draught in my nice cool room in the office for 3 days and saw no one, and curious as the treatment seems it has now restored me to rude health. I told you about Fahad Bey, didn't I. We had a conference with him one morning, in which he ended by describing the powerful effect produced by a letter from me last autumn—I wrote to him from Basrah. "I summoned my sheikhs" he wound up (I feeling more and more of a person as he proceeded) "I read them your letter and I said to them, Oh Sheikhs,"—we hung upon his words—" This is a woman—what must the men be like!" This delicious peroration restored me to my true place in the twinkling of an eye. We took him to see an exhibition of flying yesterday, to his immense delight. He said he had never enjoyed anything so much. He even ventured into an aeroplane—so that he might tell the Arabs, he explained; but once there he turned to me anxiously and said "Don't let it go away!"

Oh my dearest ones it's so wonderful here—I can't tell you how much I'm loving it.

To H.B.
BAGDAD, June 8, 1917.
I must write to you because I've been reading with profit your papers on dumping and the future of trade. The former appears to me to be unanswerable and the latter both brilliant and moderate. My compliments.

I'm completely recovered—no further bulletins will be issued. But I've retained the excellent habit of sleeping for an hour after lunch, which, though a terrible waste of time, brings a remarkable increase of energy. I'm busy at spare moments with the W.O. articles of which I told you. I've written 4 and I think they will run to 7. It's no light task in the midst of so many other things. They are as good a plea as I can make for the Arab race and I want people to listen. Frankly, who knows if I don't? Life has been 'égayée' by the coming of a harmless old lunatic from the Syrian side of the desert. The motive of his journey was as follows: he met in the desert a woman of stupendous stature and luminous countenance. On being questioned she declared that she was the sun, but this reply did not, apparently, satisfy our friend and pressing her further she admitted that she was the British Government. Thereat he resolved to come straight to Kokus (Sir Percy Cox) seeking the sun, as he reasonably explained.

The word Kokus is rapidly passing into the Arabic language, not as a name but as a title. You are a Kokus, just as once upon a time you were a Chosroes or a Pharaoh. I'm currently described as a Kokusah, i.e., a female Chosroes. Isn't it delicious!

To F.B.
June, 1917.
I've been dining out frequently. Sir Percy and I dined with General Cobbe. Next evening I dined with General Gunning. The matron of the hospitals was of the party, a nice woman. And it's so pleasant to meet a woman. My chief female friend is the Mother Superior of the Dominican Convent, a charming French woman from Touraine. She comes in often to the office to see me on business of one sort and another, and I have often, to my great pleasure, been able to help her. It's something to be a " Kokusah"" you see. Last night—to continue— I dined with the head of the police, Major Gregson, and spent the evening talking to a General called Edwardes. Let me announce to you the arrival of 2 charming hats, for which many thanks to Moll, your chiffon veils, brown stockings. Of the gowns 2 arrived a fortnight ago and no more since.

The gazelle has materialized and now inhabits my garden. It lives chiefly on the little wizened dates which fall at this season from the unripe bunches on my date trees, and on cucumbers both of which for a child of the desert must be acquired taste. But it seems to flourish on them. It is a darling little animal. I'm on the look out now for a mongoose.

To F.B.
BAGDAD, June 22nd, 1917.

Ramadhan began last night and everyone is fasting. We keep Ramadhan in state here with big guns at sunset and an hour before dawn. I was awakened today by the latter. It is to warn people that they must hasten with their last possible meal. And as I lay wondering over it all I was aware of a bright light through my garden. I sleep on the roof of My central Summer House, and looked up to see a blazing palm leaf fire in the still hot air near my gardener's tent. It was his wife cooking the last meal which must be eaten while it is light enough to distinguish a white thread from a black. Strange isn't it? to be so much in the midst of it all—strange and delightful for I love it.

It has become to me more than a second home now—it's a new life a new possibility of carrying on existence. Only I'm afraid of my personal perspective melting. I'm so flattered, so absurdly over-estimated by my chiefs in England by my colleagues, and of course the Arabs.—If I become too egregious do call me smartly to attention. It is so immensely difficult to preserve the values . . .

The sand flies are outrageous to-night. I stop in every sentence to engage them in mortal combat but they carry out a strategic retirement after inflicting some casualties. The flying ants are as numerous but they don't bite Heaven be praised. Still I hate the way they cock their tails in the air.

No more muslin gowns! I have telegraphed to Basrah to make enquiries.

To H.B.
BAGDAD, June 29th, 1917.

All my colleagues are enchanting to work with—they make our collaboration delightful, and best of all is Sir Percy's kindness and consideration. He treats me with what I can only describe as an absurd indulgence. Anything that I want done—anything reasonable—he puts at once into execution. This week, really to please me he has rushed through this arrangement for a local Arabic newspaper for which we have all been longing. We have been held up till now for lack of paper, but it would have dawdled on through many official stages but for my great desire for it. Mr. Philby is official editor and my principal friends in Bagdad, Arab friends, have posts on the staff, and we bring out this first number with a flourish of trumpets on July 1st. We are going to make a great splash. It is called The Arab because it is the first paper published under the new order of Arab liberty. I have, as indeed I ought to have, with the opportunities I am given, a growing sense of mastery in my own work, of familiarity with country people and conditions which is very enjoyable.

There is always an immense amount to learn, but one knows how to learn which is the main thing.

To F.B.

June 30th, 1917

May I ask you to oblige very kindly with 4 shirts? 'Crèpe de chine' if you please, 2 ivory and two pink. I enclose some advertisements of Harrods which look nice, specially the cross one.

I should also be very grateful if Lizzie could find and post me a green silk woven jacket thing with silver buttons.

TO H.B. & F.B.
July 6th, 1917.

I have no letters from you as yet by this mail, but oh my parents, everything is blotted out by the fact that I have two muslin gowns from the L.S.C. Now isn't that great? I was beginning to wonder what I should do and whether I should ask the nuns to make me some clothes and one really hasn't energy to bother about these things now, for its damned hot. I can't conceal it from you. I'll try not to repeat that observation. You may take it as a marginal note passim in my letters for the next two months. I've been very unsociable this week for I've been writing—I have written my five articles on Turkey after dinner. I can't well get the time by day for these things in the press of other work. I've been arranging and getting out the mass of tribal stuff collected since I've been here and have now got all the tribes to the N. and N.E. alphabetically tabled and beautifully typed in many copies for Members and all generals with whom I'm friends. It's really a great work and most useful—to judge by the use we make of it at our office, and I'm busy with this huge confusion of the Euphrates tribes I hope to have reduced to a similar order by the end of next week. I've seen every Sheikh when he has come in to pay his respects to Sir Percy and got this information about his tribe direct from him so that this body of stuff I have is not a bad beginning. . . . I don't know whether it is a scientific truth but its undoubtedly in accordance with facts—full moon nights are by far the hottest and the stillest. Two nights ago I was completely defeated. I tried to work sitting outside in my garden after dinner, but after half an hour the few clothes I was wearing were wringing wet and I so much exhausted by a day similarly spent that I went to bed helplessly and fell asleep at once on my roof. I hadn't been asleep long when I woke up to find the Great Bear staring me in the face. I lie looking north. It was very strange to see the Great Bear shining so brilliantly in the full moon of Ramadhan and while I wondered half asleep what had happened I realized that the whole world was dark, and turning round saw the last limb of the moon disappearing in a total eclipse. So I lay watching it, a wonderful sight the disc just visible, a dull and angry copper colour. In the bazaar a few hundred yards away everyone was drumming with sticks on anything that lay handy, to scare away the devil which hid the moon, and indeed they ultimately succeeded, for after a long, long time the upper limb of the moon re-appeared and the devil drew slowly downwards, angry still with deep red tongues, and wreaths projecting from his copper coloured body and before I had time to sleep again the Ramadhan moon had once more extinguished the shining of the Bear.

But as for people who read of these things in their almanacs and know to a minute when to expect them, I think nothing of them and their educated sensations.

We've got our treaty settled with my friend Fahad of the Anazeh.

To H.B.
BAGDAD, July 13th, 1917.

We have had a week of fierce heat which still continues, temperature 122 odd and therewith a burning wind which has to be felt to be believed. It usually blows all night as well as all day and makes sleep very difficult. I have invented a scheme which I practise on the worst nights. I drop a sheet in water and without wringing it out lay it in a pile along my bed between me and the wind. I put one end over my feet and draw the other under and over my head and leave the rest a few inches from my body. The sharp evaporation makes it icy cold and interposes a little wall of cold air between me and the fierce wind. When it dries I wake up and repeat the process. This evening Sir Percy and I went out motoring at 7 but it was too hot. The wind shrivelled you and burnt your eyeballs. They say it does not last very long like this— inshallah! at last the sand-flies have given up the ghost. Also you get an immense satisfaction out of iced lime juice and soda, usually rather an anaemic drink. There is a pleasant hour just after dawn when I usually ride. My room in the office I shut up all day long and have it sluiced out with water two or three times a day. By these means I keep the temperature just under 100. Yes, that's what it is like.

To H.B.
BAGDAD, July 20th, 1917.

I shall undoubtedly revert to the weather, so I may as well begin with it. We've not had the temperature under 116 by day for a fortnight. At night it drops to 82 just for the dawn hour. My room at the office is 99 all day, by dint of keeping it hermetically shut. Yesterday I went in the evening to one of the big hospitals, to see General Gunning. I went into the first ward to ask my way. It happened to be the ward where they treated the acute heat stroke cases, men with a temperature of 109 and 110—the latter don't often live. You don't consciously suffer with fever like that, but it is awful to see and hear. To-day there hasn't been a flicker of air. Mr. Philby and I motored a little after sunset — the dust hung in the streets like a dense fog, and in the desert it lay in mysterious wreaths, marking, I suppose, the track of some motor or cart. People here say they haven't had such a burst of heat as we had last week since 1882, but now I imagine, it's normal, and we have six weeks more of it to wear through. Well! . . .

There came in the other day a tribesman who had been my guide on the last four days into Najaf when I came up from Hayil. They were the worst days of all the road, and he served me well. He is a grave silent man, well known in the desert. Twice to my knowledge he saved me from being stripped to the skin— on one occasion, though accursed of their two parents, the Iraq tribes had surrounded my caravan and couched the camels before they saw him. On his rebuke they left us. I had sent word to him that I was here and bidden him to come. Besides the usual present from Sir Percy which they all get when they come for the first time, I gave him Rs. 100, and clothed him. He stood solemnly while I flung round him a thick cloak, heavily woven with gold—such wear in this heat!—and draped an orange coloured silk kerchief over his head. I owed him a costume in return for that which remained on my back thanks to him. Another nice thing happened this week. One of my Damascenes who came down with me to Nejd, has turned up here. He heard I was at Basrah, "and I come to your service," he said. Sir Percy is delighted to have him; we shall put him to use.

The hot silence has been broken by 20 big gun shots, which announce the end of Ramadhan. Even I hear them with thankfulness. It has been oppressive to think of people thirsting through these long days.

A Reuter says that Edwin has gone to the India Office. It's splendid. He will be my chief, you realize. Won't that be fun. I wish you would go and see Sir A. Hertzel, the Permanent Under-Secretary. He is a friend of mine, and an ally.

To H.B.
BAGDAD, July 27, 1917.

Another week—it's less hot. I don't think we're likely to have a second bout such as we've had. It has caused as many casualties as a battle and what is tantamount to another breakdown in the hospital arrangements. I have a long letter from Beatrice [Lady Brownrigg]—will you please thank her for it if you're seeing her. . . I can't pick up the thread where I dropped it two and a half years ago; I can't. And it becomes more, not less difficult. Oh if one could look forward and see a time when thought should stop, and memory, and consciousness, I'm so tired of struggling on alone.

Still I'll do it, as you know. At least it's easier here than in England.

On the feast day after Ramadhan Sir Percy and I paid the Naqib a congratulatory visit. Our personal relations with him are useful as well as pleasant. Sir Percy is so charming with the people of the country, grave and kind and attentive. I don't wonder they respect and trust him. He never himself realizes how strong his personal hold is, but we count it one of our best assets. The satisfaction that it is to work for a Chief who is always at the height of the situation . . . .

I paid another before breakfast call yesterday, on the Jamil Zadah family, some of my oldest friends here. They are landowners, very rich, upright, honest people, staunchly pro-English. Their friendship is worth having. I sat for a long time talking to Abdul Rahman Effendi, the head of the house, —and then with him and his wife and sisters whom I also visited—I knew them before—and came away with a warm sense of cordial and even affectionate companionship. It's when one gets that that one gets the best that can be had. Abdul Rahman's friendship takes also an agreeably tangible expression! He sends in weekly a great basket of fruit from his estate—at this season it's filled with huge white grapes.

Oh and! more muslin gowns came last week:—a red letter week! That makes 7.

To H.B.
BAGDAD, August 3, 1917.

I must tell you I've been on the sick list this week and am not off it yet. Having survived the heat I caught cold with the first chill morning and a cold in this country reduces me at once to a state of maddening and unconquerable feebleness. It's no good forgetting it; —one has to knock under. So for 4 days I've done absolutely nothing and am still much as before, confound it. But the first day when I was lying in my comparatively cool room in the office and cursing, in came Col. Willcox to pay me a friendly call—I could have embraced him, his visit was so opportune. So now he comes regularly to see if I have pneumonia or consumption—but I never have. Well, he told me some interesting things about the heat wave and its consequences. (It began on July 10 quite suddenly with a temperature of 112 and ended on July 20 with a temperature of 122). In between it was frequently over 120. He notes that 115 is the limit of human endurance. The moment the temp. rises above that point, heat strokes begin, and when it drops below, they end. We could have saved many lives if after the crisis was over there had been any cool place to put the men in. But there wasn't and after fighting through the heatstroke they died of heat exhaustion. I suppose if we had had masses of ice we could have made cool places, but ice was lacking. It happened once or twice that we well people went without it because the hospitals needed all there was. I don't think I shall stay through the whole of next hot weather unless there is any very strong reason for it. I shall come to England for a month and return in September. But who knows what we shall be all doing by then. I don't believe we shall still be fighting. Some way or other peace will have to come about.

To H.B.
BAGDAD, August 10, 1917.

I've had rather a slack week getting gradually better and I now consider that I'm returned fit for duty....

The worst of the extreme physical weariness which is apt to attack one in this climate is the mental weariness, not to say desperation, which accompanies it. You feel as if you never again would lift a finger without exhaustion and for all the iron and arsenic you are taking three times a day you're persuaded you'll not get well—not that you want to get well, far from it. However I hope I'm through it now for the moment....

The thermometer rarely goes much over 110 and is sometimes below that.

The truth is that we are living in a rather exasperated state, concerning which I refer you to Edwin, to whom I have just been writing a long letter on Mesopotamian economics.

I've invested in a cock and four hens, for to lay me eggs, but so far without any very marked success. They don't lay many more eggs than my gazelle, or to be exact, they've laid exactly one more. I never liked hens and I'm contemplating the conversion of these into roast chicken. On the other hand the dates in my garden are ripe and very good. The fresh date is a thing apart.

To H.B.
BAGDAD, August 31st, 1917.
    I am coming out of hospital to-morrow. I am perfectly sound but very slack. I don't suppose I shall be much better till the weather begins to cool down, which it ought to do in the latter half of Sep. It is still damnably hot.
    There have been some very good articles in the Spectator lately on War Economies, sound common sense about attempts to fix prices and regulate markets. Will you tell St. Loe [Strachey] if you see him that I've found them most useful as propaganda. Every economic mistake that could be made has been made here, with the result that all trade is at a standstill and food prices have quadrupled. I turned up a document the other day in which one of these announced blandly that he felt no anxiety at the rise in the cost of living, because nothing would be easier at any moment than to fix a maximum price. As a cure for scarcity. I ask you! Doesn't it rouse 'Höhnisch' laughter.

To H.B.
BAGDAD, September 3, 1917.
    I didn't go to Samarra after all, doom struck out, as the poet says, like a blind camel and he caught me straight and full. For with my box and bedding packed, my dinner almost carried to General Lubbock's hospitable board—I was going to dine with the Father of Railways. On my way to the train—I began to feel curiouser and curiouser and anyhow very certain that I had fever. And then Col. Willcox drifted in (Providence always directs the angelic man to my door just when I want him) took my temperature and shattered my plans—I held out for two miserable days in my own house, too achy and above all too headachy to stir, and then came into hospital with a temperature of 102. Sandfly fever. Everyone has it. I don't know how I've escaped it so long. They don't know what it is really; they haven't caught its microbe yet. But you get your money's worth out of it, if only from the intolerable headache. Quinine is no good. They give you febrifuges and phenacetin and feed you only on slops, all of which things being unfit, so to speak, for human consumption, you find yourself pretty ragged when at last the devil thing goes.
    I'm really over the thing—it's gone. But there's no doubt I shall feel cheap for a bit and as soon as I can I shall go away for a fortnight. Col. Willcox is very keen that I should do this and I think it will be salvation. It's so beautifully cool now that one can go anywhere. They are extremely kind to me in this hospital. They treat me as if I were a Major General.
    Damnable as sandfly fever is it isn't a matter for the smallest anxiety so please feel none, you and Mother. I feel ashamed of behaving like this.

To F.B.
BAGDAD, September 6, 1917.
    There's one thing I forgot to answer in some old letters from you and

Father. Please, please don't supply information about me or photographs of me to newspaper correspondents. I've said this so often before that I thought you understood how much I hate the whole advertisement business. I always throw all letters (fortunately they're not many in number) asking for an interview or a photograph straight into the waste paper basket and I beg you to do the same on my behalf. . . .

I've been five days out of hospital and I feel much better though still rather weak in the knees and imbecile in the mind. But another day or two will put me right. My quiet leave hasn't been quite as peaceful as might have been wished for the second night after my return I found a large wasp in my bed. I found him by the simple process of lying on him, upon which he retorted after his kind. The next night when I came back from the office I went to look at my pony and found him having a bad fit of colic. We had some restless hours doctoring him and walking him about, and finally he recovered.

It's still very hot, but the temperature is falling, though very slowly. The nights are quite pleasant, but in the middle of the afternoon it's usually about 112. I won't deny that when you come to September here you feel you've reached about the limit of human endurance. I shan't stay through the whole of next summer.

To H.B.
BAGDAD, September 15, 1917.

I've got a day out with the week and find suddenly that it is Saturday morning and mail day instead of Friday as I fondly hoped. Fortunately the most important letter—to Bridget [Richmond)—I wrote last night. I asked the kind Red X Commissioner, Major Stanley, about your launch. He says it is the best on the river, never sick or sorry. I went to a party this week—the first party I've been to since Delhi. There was a regatta on the Tigris and G.H.Q. entertained us all at tea. I think, by the way, I was one of the hosts, since we're included in G.H.Q. I didn't see much of the regatta because there was a glaring sun on the river, even at 5 p.m. but I sat under an awning and talked to all the Major Generals and felt that I was seeing life. It resulted in my going to tea next day with General Marshall, he commands the 3rd Corps, a very interesting man whom I had just met as he passed through Basrah last summer and hadn't seen since. I went to see some carpets and china which he had bought, very pretty and I should think one or two of the rugs very good, but I know less and less about rugs I find. He is coming to see two of mine which are also rather pretty. But I no longer buy any on account of the War Loan—that was a little burst when I came to Bagdad. It's really getting cooler; my room at the office is never above 91 and these last two days I haven't needed a punkah till 10 o'clock. It's so blessed. A propos of the Red X I can't tell you how beneficent they are here. I get my money's worth—or yours—out of them, for Major Stanley is always supplementing my needs with various odds and ends otherwise unprocurable. However, as I served them for a whole year I feel less reluctance in sponging on them for comforts. I'm much better, almost quite well. Its time too. This country is a desperate place for recovering from anything. You go staggering on feeling like a worm long after there has ceased being anything the matter with you. But it's all the more pleasurable when at last the worm begins to turn.

To H.B.
BAGDAD, September 21, 1917.
    We are having deliciously cool weather, between 70 and 80 and quite cold at night. I want nothing better but I think the moment of sudden transition is rather trying even if it is enjoyable. One doesn't know how to adapt oneself at first. I had an afternoon out this week—General Cobbe and I went to Kadhimain, 2 or 3 miles above Bagdad, a sheikh town with a very sacred mosque. I remember last time I was there, in 1909 it must have been, how I hurried past the gateway of the mosque with a sidelong glance into the courtyard. Turbaned gentlemen did us the honours and escorted us well within the gates to the very edge of the courtyard. Except as an unexampled privilege there wasn't much in it, for it's all the worst modern work, gimcrack and hideous, with tiles 30 years old already peeling from the walls and no loss either. Nevertheless I was vastly entertained, having been nowhere since I came to Bagdad.
    Kermit Roosevelt turned up this week with letters of introduction to me and to Sir Percy. We both liked him—a very pleasant creature, quite unostentatious. He is serving here as an engineer and has three brothers in the American army in France. They are doing their bit, aren't they? I still dine out of doors, but I sit indoors afterwards, with all doors and windows open. It's most pleasant. I'm longing to begin riding again and indeed I did begin a few days ago, but it wasn't a great success—I felt too tired afterwards. So I shall be very prudent and wait a little longer. It isn't a time of year to play pranks; nearly every one has little goes of fever when the heat begins to drop. I've escaped that luckily. My dear love to all my family. I write indifferently to you and Mother as the letters are equally to you both.

To F.B.
BAGDAD, September 25, 1917.
    I'm writing this week because I'm going to Samarra for a day or two. It will be very nice and I think it will do me good for I've not been very flourishing this last month since I came out of hospital and it will be a pleasant change of air and scene. I haven't stirred out of Bagdad since I got here in April. But it's amazing how unmonotonous it has been. . . .
    To think that I've been nearly two years without a maid! But I'm exceedingly tidy, thanks to your good supply of clothes. Oh would you please send me a pair of plain tortoiseshell combs. There's a lizard walking about my walk and catching, I suppose, sand flies. God prolong its existence!

To H.B. & F.B.
BAGDAD, October 12, 1917.

I'm better and going to-morrow to the Convalescent Hospital, a mile down stream from Bagdad. . . .

Maurice doesn't sound very flourishing, which worries me. I do hope he'll come back to R'ton now to set about his own work. It's very difficult not to feel a growing depression. Perhaps I'm rather influenced by being so slack still and certainly the last two months have been horrid. However I expect the winter will set me right and I shan't stay here all through next summer, war or no war. It wouldn't be profitable. -

I can match you at food—we've had no butter all the summer and when we have it it's turned and I would rather be without it. I've forgotten what potatoes taste like—the meat is almost too tough to eat., chickens ditto milk turned—how sick one gets of it! Bread I never eat what one gets is fairly good, quite good indeed, but that doesn't affect me—much. Its all right when one's well, but when one's feeling rather a poor thing one does hate it all.

Well,well—I daresay I'll write from Samarra in a different key.

To H.B. & F.B.
OCTOBER 18th, 1917.

Yesterday came your telegram through Admiral Hall enquiring after my health. I'm afraid you will be rather agitated when you come to hear that I've been ill again which I haven't told you in my present reply. But I'm now very nearly well of my fever which I don't suppose I should have had if I hadn't been rather run down before. I've been for the last 6 days at the Convalescent Hospital, a delicious place on the river about 2 miles below Bagdad. They have taken immense care of me and I've got well with great rapidity. In 3 days' time I'm going up to Samarra for a week to stay with Gen. Cobbe. I hope to return in far more flourishing health than I've been since August and since the cold weather is now definitely beginning and the winter climate is delicious I'm as well here as anywhere. Whatever happens I shall not stay here all through next hot weather. I spend my days very peacefully, breakfasting in bed, reading and doing a little work afterwards. I spent this morning in Bagdad getting warmer clothes from my house and doing various odd jobs. The mail had just come in. Bless you both. I can't tell you what it is to have your love and sympathy always with me. . . .

I might be able to see Mrs. Taggart's grandson if he's at Bagdad. I'll try anyhow.

[Mrs. Taggart was a woman at the Clarence ironworks, a very old friend.]

It's bad hearing that there's no more parcel post to Mesop. You don't seem to be aware—indeed I only knew of it by letters of congratulation received this mail from Sir Reginald Wingate and others—that I'm a C.B.E. I am, however. It's rather absurd. . . .

I have a delightful letter from Beatrice Chamberlain which I really must answer, but time is too short this week.

To H.B.
BAGDAD, October 18th, 1917.

You know your friendship is more to me than anything. What a thing it is to be able to talk of friendship with one's parents. Those who haven't got it don't know what it means.

I'm much better. Even after my rackety morning at Bagdad I don't feel a bit tired, and I've been writing letters all this afternoon. But oh, I do long to be back at work! However, I'll be patient this time and take the Samarra time to get really well in.

To F.B.
BAGDAD, October 26th, 1917

Thank you for your congratulations—I don't really care a button about these things. As for Samarra, I've no luck with it, for just as I was starting—actually stepping into the launch to go and dine—with General Lubbock on my way to the station, came a telegram from General Cobbe putting me off. Turks had heaved into sight and there was a possibility of active operations. They've since heaved out of it again, and I may after all go up presently, but I've ceased to believe it. I'm very much enjoying being back in the office though I'm not much more than a half timer as yet. Still I'm getting better every day. The weather is delicious but it is extraordinary how one feels the cold. My room at the office is now under 70, but after sunset I sit wrapped up in a thick coat and add to it a woollen comforter to walk home in. It's a way the human frame has of showing resentment for having been called upon to endure a temperature of 122. I find that this is the season for gardening operations; I've some vegetables, peas, lettuce, onions and a local sort of mustard and cress—the latter I've not only sown but eaten. And in order not to be too utilitarian, I've bought 7 Pots of geraniums and 4 of carnations besides sowing carnations and eschscholtzia. I wish I had snapdragon seeds. A clump of chrysanthemums is coming into bloom, and my rose trees are flowering. Everything comes to life when the summer is over, even the washed out European. And one forgets at once how infernal it was. I hope my bijou residence won't prove too damp in winter; it's so nice being quite away by oneself. Anyhow it's particularly pleasant now.

The shirts haven't arrived but I expect they'll turn up and I've enough to go on with for the moment. And oh I'm so sorry to bother you, but would you send me 8 pairs of white thread stockings—they will go by letter post at the worst, and they'll arrive just about the time the warm weather begins again. Those I have are worn out beyond mending.

To H.B.
BAGDAD, November 2, 1917.

You sent me a lot of interesting pieces which I read with much satisfaction and agreement. I always feel when I read your works such an admiration for your style as well as your matter. It's so lucid and so pointed, so entirely unstrained. I hand on some of your works to Sir Percy who reads them with grave attention, not unmixed with surprise. It is all new to him.

For my part I'm quite well. I've even taken to riding again of an early morning, with great profit to my health and spirits. It's ideal now at that hour. The sting has gone out of the sun which has become a cheerful and companionable luminary. Samarra is off for the present. . . .

We have now got a judicial Officer, Mr. [now Sir Edgar] Bonham Carter from the Sudan. A highly trained man with a very level head is just what we want and I do welcome him sincerely.

To H.B.
BAGDAD, November 9th, 1917.

No mail as yet this week. Happy to tell you I'm much better and have felt to-day quite a zest in life—for the first time. Partly, I think, because yesterday I spent the whole day, nearly, out-of-doors, for Sir Percy and I motored to Baquba. It was 6 years since I went along that road—I say 6 years because it was in 1911, but really it's a lifetime—when I was on my way to plan Rasawan palaces at Qasr-i-Shirin, over the Persian frontier. I remember it as a long and tedious day's ride; we did it yesterday in 2 hours. It's 32 miles of bumpy desert road. Baquba is a nice little place set in palm gardens and olive groves on the Diala. I looked at my camping ground near by the river bank and tried to remember the sort of person who pitched tents there, but I couldn't. I hadn't been out of Bagdad since April, nor Sir Percy since March, so you think what a pleasant sense of irresponsible holiday it gave both of us. I only wished we could have gone on further. I am beginning some nice new jobs. One is the taking over of the editorship of Al Arab, the vernacular paper we publish. I'm full of schemes for making it more alive by provincial correspondents and a local news-writer. I feel certain my public will take more interest in hearing that Ibu so and so was fined for being out without a lantern after dark than in the news that an obscure village in Flanders has been bombed. Père Anastase, the sub-editor comes weekly to read our leading articles, which I censor. He's an Arab from the Lebanon, straight out of Chaucer —all the same; very learned in his own tongue, he speaks and writes French like a Frenchman. . . .

In my garden there's the most gorgeous mud pie I've ever been privileged to see. It's not, however, for frivolous persons; we're busy mending my roofs against the rainy season, and mud is what you do it with. I'm credibly informed that when there's a high flood my garden is under water and that objects from the house I inhabit have been observed to float down the neighbouring street. It's a gloomy thought. I don't know whether to wish for a dry season for my comfort, or to hope for the rain which is essential for our next harvest. If I'm obliged to move out I shall no doubt manage to get a lodging for the necessary two months. Sir Percy would put me up, In any case, but I do very much prefer living alone. It's a comfort to get away from the office and think of other things which it is morally impossible to do if you remain in the place you've worked in all day.

TO F.B.
BAGDAD, November 15th, 1917.

You all sound over-strained. I don't know how you can be anything else. You know we are out of that atmosphere here; I often feel ashamed of escaping it, but it is so. There are not the perplexities and the worries that assail you in England, and then the work is all of one kind and runs naturally along its own groove.

I have quite recovered and have polished off a lot of things that had got into arrears. We have all moved into winter quarters in the office, out of dark, cold rooms into sunny ones. It is strange to welcome the sun again. My room is charming, warm and comfortable, with some delightful rugs which I've bought here on the floor, and all the new maps of Mesopotamia pinned up on the walls. Maps are my passion; I like to see the world with which I'm dealing, and everyone comes round to my room for geography.

To F.B.
SAMARRA, November 22nd, 1917.

I wrote to you last week the day before I was to come up here with the I.G.C. We all dined that evening with Col. Dixon, the Director of Local Resources; the C. in C. was to have been there also but sent a message at the last moment to say he wasn't well. At the beginning of dinner Colonel Willcox was called away—an urgent case of illness, it didn't occur to anyone to ask who it was. Next morning before breakfast the I.G.C. came to my house and said that our departure must be postponed, the C. in C. was dangerously ill of cholera and was not expected to live. I flew round to Sir Percy—it was still very early—and found that he had not yet been informed. It was almost incredible to us all. There had been a little cholera in the town for some weeks past, nothing very serious but very widely distributed. There were a few cases among the troops and one officer had died last week. We had all been inoculated and thought no more about it. Certainly the last person likely to fall a victim was the C. in C. who saw no Arabs and scarcely ever went into the town. He had been at the entertainment at the Jewish school the night before, but we all went there, drank coffee and ate cakes and no one else was any the worse. So there it was—where he got the infection it is impossible to say. He rallied in the afternoon and was distinctly better next morning, well enough to receive a telegram from his wife and dictate an answer. Then his heart failed, he became unconscious and died in the evening. The I.G.C. came in after dinner and told me. It has had for him a tragic ending, the conquest of Bagdad, and yet how fortunate it is when the man dies before the name. There is a splendid sentence in Ammianus's Marcellinus history of that other conqueror who was mortally wounded, N.E. of Ctesiphon,—the Emperor Julian, and "praised the Almighty God that he should die in the midst of glory fairly earned." General Maude was, I should think, a greater Commander, but the epitaph might be his . . . . .

. . . It's a wonderfully picturesque little walled town with the golden dome of the shrine closing the vista, incongruously enough, in the narrow tumble-down streets....

Oh, there is such a good smell of rain—the first rain, this dry year, since February. If only we have a good plash of it, it will mean a good harvest next spring. An early rain is the most important thing in this country; it sets all the desert growing and starts cultivation—the people can't begin to plough till it comes.

To her Family.
SAMARRA, November 30th, 1917.

I'm still here though I wanted to go back a day or two ago. The Corps Commander (my kind host) insisted however on my staying till the end of the week to "complete the cure." I'm really most briskly well and longing to get back to work. I'm going back to Bagdad the day after to-morrow. Col. Willcox came up this morning for a change (it's looked upon as a health resort, Samarra) and brought me a bag of letters. I was rather pining for news of you. It's a great comfort to think of Maurice back at home but what with household and industrial difficulties, present or ahead, you don't any of you seem to be having an easy time. We score over you now in weather—day after day of bright sun and exhilarating N. wind. It's perfect and in this empty desert one gets the best of its advantages. I've been out all day, usually riding the whole morning and motoring somewhere in the afternoon—if you can call it somewhere when it's just desert with the scoring of old canals and mounds of dead villages far out in what is now uninhabited wilderness. It's almost impossible to picture what the country must have been like when it was irrigated by loop canals from the Tigris and (to judge by the village mounds) thickly peopled ten miles out on either bank of the river. It is now cultivated only in the low ground by the river edge, a mile, perhaps, deep on one bank or another, but after last week's rain (we had 18 hours of it) the people are all busily ploughing and the turned up earth looks a live brown instead of a sandy yellow.

To F.B.
BAGDAD, OFFICE OF THE C.C., December 7th, 1917.

I wish to announce the arrival of 6 pairs of white and ditto of brown stockings which I found here when I got back a week ago....

I was very glad to get back. I plunged at once into a mass of accumulated work and have scarcely lifted my eyes from maps and files. But the pleasure of being well and able to work the whole day long! The truth is that one can't do without that narcotic. To be idle means having time to think and no thoughts are bearable......

The new régime promises well. I haven't seen General Marshall since I came back but he gives signs of being sympathetic towards our side of the game. It's as well, for we were running fast on to rocks, in my opinion. We are now in the middle of operations on our R. flank which seem to have been very successful so far, and that's very encouraging too, though I don't believe we can accomplish anything very dramatic while the Turk holds off as far as he can. The presence of an enemy is an essential element in battle. And we can't walk after him indefinitely because an army walks on its stomach. Vigorous steps have been taken to ensure a good harvest next spring—but that is not till the middle of April and meantime we are going to be hard put to it to get the civil population fed. This morning I was riding in the desert, out on the Diala road, when I met Arabs from the Diala bringing in donkey loads of brushwood to sell. As soon as I had opened the conversation with a God-save-you they began to tell me how hungry they were out there, and I to explain what we were doing to bring the hunger to an end. I expect they don't usually live in the lap of luxury, those mean tribes on the Diala river, but with prices what they are they must be well pinched this year. We had a very bad harvest this year, what with lack of rain and neglect of canals. They are all being dug out now, seed corn distributed and advances given in money. But it is a big job. To-night it's warm and windy, we might have rain.

My dear pony which I bought up from Basrah is lame. But kind Captain Lupton, who is at the Remounts, has let me send it up to be blistered and meantime he has let me have a charming little mare, a little pocket mare which I feel sure would be up to nobody's weight but my diminished stones, so I'm harming no one. But what she lacks in height she makes up in spirit and we had a delightful gallop this morning out on the Diala road—road, I call it but it's just desert—with the sun rising and a warm wind in our face. It's everything to see a little of the world outside of a morning I see plenty of the world inside—a succession of callers all with some axe or another to grind and one's task generally being to remove the grindstone gently out of their reach!

To -
BAGDAD, December 13th, 1917.
. . . . My only news of the outer world is derived from the egregious Reuter and that not good, and one begins to consider what the end will be. Till the Americans can bring in great reinforcements—and can they across all the seas?—it's clear that we shall be put to it to hold our own. It's like the first year of the war over again. Well, it's no good guessing, and we know too little even to guess. Here war is at an end, but administration goes on apace. We are taking hold of the Euphrates valley to the S.W. and getting into lands unmapped and tribes little known. I want to go down there at the end of the month. Meantime I'm puzzling over Euphrates geography and writing a sketch of it as best I can. It's the sort of job which is almost impossible to do in the office, where one is constantly interrupted, and I generally bring home books and maps and work at it after dinner. The days fly and the weeks hurry after them; it's terrible to think that we're nearly at midwinter. The desired rain hasn't come but we have had a week of delicious cold. The water basin in the middle of my garden has been iced over the last two mornings. It's amazingly invigorating. Yesterday I was out in the desert at dawn in a frosty air which was quite delicious, even though I came in after nearly an hour's brisk riding, with numb hands and feet. I went

one afternoon to see the Remount establishment outside the town. Capt. Lupton presides over it. A clearing place with the horses playing about in great paddocks under the palm trees, and a model farm attached where they grow their own maize and barley and vegetables. Capt. Lupton offered me a very handsome Arab mare if the General (Holdsworth) consented. I met the latter next day in the street and he approved the suggestion. So, in the official phrase, I'm issued with her—Heaven prosper me for writing such horrible English.

To -
BAGDAD, December 21st, 1917.

Bagdad, and, indeed, most of Mesopotamia is immobilized by mud. My daily walk to and from the office is a real feat of gymnastics, but, as I stumble and reel through the swamp which was once a road, I return thanks for the rain which has gone far to assure next year's harvest. We had about 24 hours of it. I woke after the first night to find my garden a lake, from which emerged a few islands, but I had been provident enough to construct a brick causeway between my bedroom and sitting room—they are at opposite ends of the garden—and along it I was able to get to breakfast high and dry. The water has vanished to-day and a smoothly hard bed of mud remains. I'm rather disgusted to see in Army Reuter Orders that on the days when we thought the weather so shockingly cold the max. temp. was never below 52. One loses all sense of proportion about climate.

The new régime has ordered the force to take a holiday on Sunday afternoon, and in obedience to their decree I dragged Sir Percy out riding last Sunday. The immortal baked clay preserves the trace of human habitation when all else has returned to the dust it was; as soon as the canal dries up, the village is deserted, the roaming Arab pulls out the roof beams and breaks up the doors for firewood, the mud walls disintegrate and nothing remains but the imperishable pot. You may break him up as much as you choose, but unless you take a hammer to him and reduce him systematically to powder, he will continue to bear witness to the household which he served. Usually this rough peasant pottery is undatable; you know it isn't of yesterday, however, when you find masses of it in places which have not been irrigated for the last 400 years.

To H.B.
BAGDAD, December 29, 1917.

I am very glad to hear that Maurice is better and congratulate Mother on her pleasant nights with Zeppelins. . . . On Xmas Day I dined with General Stuart Wortley, a Ladies' Dinner, the other guests being matrons and nurses, a quite agreeable evening, but I've crept, on the whole, into a very long shell and seldom care to be pricked out of it by anybody's pin. Also I've got a temporary (let's hope) anaemia of the brain which makes me work so slowly that I never get through my jobs and bring work home every night to finish after dinner. Incessant interruption at the office adds immensely to the fatigue of putting together reports or compiling information. I've no sooner got hold of the thread than it's broken by someone with a petition or a complaint or what not, and my slow mind must laboriously gather it up again. Perhaps a fortnight's absence in the Euphrates will make me a littlie less imbecile. There are times when I can scarcely find words to talk or write in French, much less in Arabic. And memory is a lost art. Though half-witted I'm physically well. I've liked this cold weather and not felt cold as I did last year, though it's much colder here than in Basrah. But it's the general sense of being too much driven through not working quickly enough—because I can't—which is tiresome. I would like to take a month off, learn Arabic and see people —but the awful amount one would have to catch up at the end of it deters me. I'm almost reluctant to go away because I know what a task it will be to write the next fortnightly report when I have to look everything up instead of jotting it down as it happens. But I very much like doing the fortnightly reports, which are the record of our work here, and though I haven't leisure to do them as well as they should be done, they will still be valuable.

Did I tell you of a visit I paid to the home for Armenian girls? Over 100 of them have been collected here, from all places and of all ages. There's an American fund to provide for them. Some had lived for months with the Arabs and were tattooed like Beduin women, some had just borne children and some were such children themselves that they could not remember whence they came. The Beduin coming down to our frontiers from the north bring hundreds of these girls with them. One woman when she first saw the Tigris burst into tears. "Ah," she cried, "the mass of water here! and my sister died in the desert of thirst." And ah! the rivers of tears, the floods of human misery that these waifs represent. What is life worth in this age of violence?

I write every week and if you don't get letters it is not because I don't send them.

CHAPTER XVII
1918-1919

BAGDAD

To F.B.
KARBALA, January 3rd, 1918.

I'm having a little holiday which is very pleasant and beneficial. I was beginning to feel terribly caged and stale and, though I haven't stepped out of the cage very far, or for very long, it's agreeable to be knocking about a tiny corner of the world again. It's a corner so full of associations. So many times I've come over the Bagdad-Karbala road after long desert expeditions, with a sense of accomplishment, and, at the same time, with that curious sense of disappointment which one nearly always feels with the accomplished thing. The best time, I think, was when I came back with the plan of Ukhaidir in my pocket—the worst when I came up from Arabia. I find myself forever stepping back into a former atmosphere—knowing with my real self that it has all melted away and yet half drugged with the lingering savour of it, and chiefly what I miss is the friendly presence of my good Fattuh, who smoothed all the way of travel and is now where? dead, I fear. I hear there are no men left in Aleppo; all have been taken for the war and Turkish soldiers have a poor chance. However—I'll tell you of my adventures, very modest ones, not like the old days. I left Bagdad on the 31st, a beautiful sunny morning, and motored out to Musaiyib on the Euphrates. We spun over the first three-quarters of the road, but the last eight miles, over low ground, unspeakably muddy, were not so advantageous to motors. We stuck once badly and I called in some 10 or 15 Arabs who were removing the mud from one part of the road to another—that seemed to be the extent of their activities—and made them haul us out. . . .

[The fortnight's holiday takes her motoring through familiar places full of memories.]

Yesterday, I motored out along the sandy road, the very familiar road, to Karbala, and reached Major Pulley's house about midday. He had put me up close at hand in Col. Leachman's house, the latter being out in the desert with the Arabs, my very own Arabs, Fahad Bey's tribe, but I can't go to them. And then out through mud and swamp on to the edge of the Syrian Desert, which lifted its yellow shoulder in front of me in a manner so inviting that I could scarcely bear to turn away from it. . . . I had tea in my own house before a wood fire and afterwards received a visit from one of the desert merchants one of the Agail who had somehow heard I was here. I knew one of his brothers in Damascus and another in Bagdad. They come, like all Agail, from Central Arabia, and we sat talking desert gossip for a long time—until I felt again that I could scarcely bear to be so close and not to go in to the tribes. What a welcome Fahad Bey would give me. He's about 2 days away.

To H.B.
HILLAH, January 16th, 1918.

    I wrote to you almost at the beginning of my fortnight's holiday and now that I've come almost to the end of it I'll begin another letter. I get back to Bagdad to-morrow and feel very much like one going back to school. I'm not sure that it's a good plan to get out of the cage for a fortnight and enjoy the illusion of days that were almost like a former existence. Certainly I've never realized more keenly than I do now the chains and bonds which war draws about one. I wrote from Karbala, didn't I? I spent three days there, saw many people, was greeted by friends from the desert and had the wildest desire to escape into it and be heard of no more. . . .

    On my way home yesterday I stopped at Babylon, having been asked by Sir Percy to advise about the preservation of antiquities. 'Tempi passati' weigh very heavy there—not that I was thinking of Nebuchadnezzar, nor yet of Alexander, but of the warm welcome I used to find, the good company, the pleasant days spent with dear Koldewey—it's no good trying to think of him as an alien enemy and my heart ached when I stood in the empty dusty little room where Fattuh used to put up my camp furniture and the Germans and I held eager conversation over plans of Babylon or Ukhaidir. What a dreadful world of broken friendships we have created between us.

To F.B.
BAGDAD, January 25th, 1918.

    Yesterday I went all over the Civil Hospital with the Municipal doctor, Capt. Carey Evans—he is a son-in-law of Mr Lloyd George. He is doing his work with real intelligence and is full of schemes for the future. . . . . Medical organization is of the very first importance, not only because there is so much to be done but also because it is so deeply appreciated. It is an invaluable political asset if you choose to look at it from that point of view. Hospitals and dispensaries are the first things the people ask for, and they flock to them, men and women, and don't hesitate to undergo operations or any treatment you please. Capt. C. E. says the standard of vitality is much higher than in Europe; the people here pull through operations which he would not dare to attempt at home. Their nervous system is much more solid. They don't suffer from shock . . . . .

To H.B. and F.B.
BAGDAD, January 31st, 1918.

    I have your letters. Also Father's very good and wise piece about Capital and Labour, which I read with profit. A remarkable writer, there can be little doubt.

    . . . . The price of living here is enormous, and, though I'm rationed, a great many of the necessaries of life have to be bought, such as soap, rice, eggs and sugar, and they are all at preposterous prices. This also means that one has to raise wages. Kind Musa Chalabi, my landlord, has got me out of difficulties with regard to my gardener's family. There have been living in a single mud room, my gardener, his aged father and mother, two brothers, a wife, a sister and all of them came piteously to me for help and support. I couldn't help feeling that my garden was overcrowded, but, with feeble compassion, I didn't like turning them out into the mud. But there came a day when they quarrelled, and I called in Musa Chalabi as arbitrator. He arbitrated with some vigour and the aged father and mother, together with other members of the family, have found other lodgings. I relinquish any personal share in their fortunes.

I found some irises and some verbenas in a market garden which I used to frequent here, and transferred them to my flower beds. They were very dear, but the joy of them will be worth the price. I have a few pots of violets which provide a tiny bunch for my writing table. Their little blue faces are very friendly and cheerful. I now pursue a happy plan of going out riding or walking every afternoon, generally alone but sometimes in company. . . . There is a great bend in the Tigris below the town which is my favourite resort. It makes a huge peninsula full of gardens and cornfields, and almost empty of soldiers, and there I go and remember that I am really part of Mesopotamia and not part of an army of occupation. The spring is there and colour and life and sound have come with the rains, the sound and colour of the reviving world. We had a tidy drop of rain this week, enough to make 2 days of mud, but we want more. Heaven send it! We are barely up to 2 in. yet and I'm afraid we shall not get our average 6.

The days I don't ride I generally find myself in the bazaar a mildly expensive form of exercise. To-day, after I had been to see additional houses taken on for the Armenian refugees, I dropped into the new shop of an old acquaintance—he used to have a much nicer poky room in a khan—and came away with a very charming Chinese bowl, a little copper incense burner 300 years old (it has a dated Arabic inscription, a thing I can never resist) and a metal water bottle, not old, but such a good shape. All these metal water jars are lovely, traditional shapes which you may see in any 16th Century Persian miniature. The bowl was cheap for it's good Chinese stuff—no bowl would have been cheaper, but there! even the bowl and the verbenas don't run extravagance into a high figure.

I rather fear that my friend Thomas Effendi (he's an Armenian) will send me round a pair of rugs to-morrow. Let's hope they won't be good. Talking of rugs, I'm hatching a plan which, though it isn't directly concerned with rugs, touches their place of origin. I have been thinking about schemes for the summer and am rather inclining towards a 3 months' travel in Persian mountains, I should take tents and might very likely land up in Teheran ultimately, and home by Ispahan. The journey home takes at least five weeks, four of them through heat and the monsoon, whereas I can motor in 2 days to Kirmanshah and reach at once a temperate climate. Then motor through great hills to Urumiah perhaps, which is a paradise. Col. Willcox gives the plan his warm approval from a health point of view, but it's great drawback is that I shan't see you this summer. At any rate, when you get this letter, you might telegraph and say what you think, and meantime I'll consider things more closely. I like the Persian idea much better than Baluchistan, for to get there one still has the terrific journey down river and across the Indian Ocean—terrific in June or July heat. It's the thought of getting into camp once more, and being out of doors among mountains that attracts me and also the possibility of being away from people for a while.

One of the worst drawbacks of the occupation, from the point of view of the inhabitants of the country, is the requisitioning of houses. I don't see what's to be done, for we haven't time to build and we must be lodged, but it's a terrible hardship to the luckless ejected ones . . . . . I have a clean sheet myself, for my house isn't a house and probably no one but me would think of living in it. (They would be wrong, for it is quite comfortable and the space and freedom of my garden are invaluable boons.) It's certainly very difficult to be popular rulers in war time.

With which reflexion I'll close, merely adding that I'm very well now and much less thin.

To H.B.
BAGDAD, February 8th, 1918.

It is getting quite perceptibly, but pleasantly warmer. I've begun to discard some of the innumerable wraps I wear by day and coverings by night. To-day, with the soft air blowing into my room, I thought of R'ton in February and wondered whether by chance it were snowing with you. . . . It is curious to find how many of the Bagdad notables are tribesmen, often only settled in the town for the last generation or two. Some sheikh builds himself a town house, sends his sons to school and starts them in a learned profession leading to Government employment. And at once they settle down into citizens. But the tribal links are unbroken. Any sheikh with business in the town looks by right to his kinsman's house for entertainment in the matter of daily meals—a pretty expensive duty it is—and if a member of the town family gets into trouble he will seek sanctuary with the tribe, safe in the assurance that he would never be given up. Several men I know fled to their tribe during the year before the Occupation, when the Ottoman hand was heavy on the Arabs of Bagdad. Most of these are now in our service and their tribal connection makes them all the more useful. We have a few really first-class Arab officials, just as we have found a few really first- class sheikhs who will assume responsibility and preserve order. There are not many of them, but such as there are, are invaluable. And we in our turn have an immense responsibility towards them. . . . We are pledged here. It would be an unthinkable crime to abandon those who have loyally served us. But there! if I write of Arabs I shall write all night.

To H.B.
BAGDAD, February 15th, 1918.

. . . . All the telegrams prepare me for a terrific assault in France. I've also got your address at the Horden meeting which is excellent. It is so full of ideas and of wise appreciations. When I feel stale I think of your wonderfully fresh mind. There's no doubt you are a very remarkable person and I say it quite without prejudice. . . .

The peace with the Ukraine is the worst thing that has happened, it seems to

me. I agree with Lady Macm[...]
shown Himself disappointingly [...]

Today I combined busin[...]
abbot of the French monks, a[...]
the buying of MSS. for the I[...]
traditional books, which is [...]
Office. You see, the first thi[...]
understanding of the things [...]
together in the parlour ove[...]
the heart of Bagdad; we h[...]
incredibly narrow crooke[...]
streets wind in and out c[...]
And so I am, you know; [...]
curious sense to have t[...]
that by long links of ass[...]
just taken, not to accomp[...]
for a Conference. He invited me to com[...]
most interesting, I'm not necessary and I think I had bette[...]
the weather)s so good and we can work. I shall have to go away in the su[...]
for reasons of health. I'm rather discouraged about Persia because people coming in from there give such terrible accounts of the destitution of the country. You can't travel in a place where there's nothing to eat. England, with Palestine on the way, is another idea, but anyhow there are 3 months still before I need decide. The truth is I have a great longing to see you. . . .

However many native lands I may have I've only one father and mother anyway and I'm therefore ever your devoted daughter.

To H.B.
BAGDAD, 22nd February, 1918.

You will get this letter quicker than all the others because Sir Percy carries it. He is coming home on a hasty mission and will probably only be in England a few days, but I have asked him to communicate with you on his arrival, because I feel sure you will want to see him. Also he will discuss with you my plans for the summer. . . . Anyhow, he will be able to tell you what it is like, and, if I can get home without an unreasonable delay, I think I will probably come. . . .

Springy's [Sir Cecil Spring Rice] death is just another piece of the old life gone—a life which I can't in imagination carry on into the future. . . .

Well now, I will finish by writing you an ordinary letter of my doings. . . .

On Monday afternoon, I had a funny, charming expedition. I borrowed a motor and took my old friend and landlord, Musa Chalabi, with his wife and daughter, to their garden outside Bagdad, five or six miles away. Musa's brother, Shakir, lives there and looks after the farming. It was a ramshackle place, with a couple of big single-storied mud-built houses; refuse heaps scattered around and even inside the courtyard; a dirty, smelly, Arab village, half tent, half reed hut under their walls; but the sun shone on the river bank and growing things and

ee most darling little children of Shakir's to
pies and the other wonders. . . . And then we
ladies were in the seventh heaven, never, I think,

has been an angel of kindness to me always, but he
e value of anything I've done here. . . . .

other story to tell. To-day there came in to see me one of my
ons of 1914. An Arab of the Dulaim tribe, who rode with me
hen I was going back to Damascus. He was a good guide, and I
ee his pleasant face again—as glad as one can be when one of these
n independent past rises up before one. He set me longing for the
he grass is springing there and the black tents flowing with milk, and
nd beast prosper.

To F.B.
BAGDAD, March 1st, 1918.

We had a day or two of wind and rain this week after which the world burst into loveliness. I rode directly after the rain through the gardens S. of the town and found them a vision of apricot and peach blossom and brilliant green cornfields. Everything grows together, fruit tree and palm and corn, with a marvellous luxuriance. If only it weren't going presently—and very soon—to be so infernally hot. I have been very busy this week, contributing some chapters to the review of administration here during 1917. It makes a most remarkable story, the truly remarkable part being the way the people have accepted it. The immense energy with which agricultural development has been pushed forward has been of incalculable political value. . . . There is nothing easier to manage than tribes if you'll take advantage of tribal organization and make it the basis of administrative organization. And our people, with their natural inclination to deal with men on their merits, at once establish familiar relations with sheikh and headman and charge them with their right share of work and responsibility. And the men so treated respond wonderfully well—but then they are men, they've got stuff in them and that's all that is necessary. . . . The European news is terribly bad and I see no prospect of an end. The strain on you at home is more than I like to think of. Don't you wonder often when you wake in the morning, how you are to carry on through the day? I wonder often enough how you bear it. . . .

Yesterday afternoon I went to see one of our new primary schools where the headmaster is a friend of mine. There wasn't a very large attendance. I went round the 3 classes and asked them questions. In the smallest class we held a kind of general intelligence examination and I began by asking who was king of England. One student of history (aged about 7) replied unhesitatingly Chosroes, and another with a better grasp of modern politics amended with Lloyd George. (I don't know whether Father will be able to bear that story!). . . . The roses in my garden will be out in a week or two and I'm eating my own lettuces, but I'm sorry to say the cabbages have burst into luxuriant yellow flower before they ever became cabbages, so to speak.

To F.B.
BAGDAD, March 6th, 1918.

I'm going away the day after to-morrow down Euphrates again to gather up the remaining threads of tribal information which I want in order to complete my monumental work on Mesopotamian tribes. So if I don't catch a mail next week you'll know why. I'm looking forward to it very much and I hope I shall be able to get the material I want, but it's a difficult job and if one thing's more certain than another, it is that all one writes on tribes is sure to be full of mistakes. One ought to live for a month or two in each district in order to understand them.

This afternoon I attended a small function, the opening of a Civil Dispensary in the heart of the town. It has been the darling wish of Capt. Carey Evans to have a dispensary on this side of the river, and it will be infinitely valuable. There's a ward with 6 beds besides accommodation for seeing outpatients. All the notables came, secular and religious; it was most gratifying as well as being most agreeable. I sat in a row with the Qadhi, the Mudir of Church Lands (Muhammadan), the judge of Appeal and so on and so on, and we had tea and talked and were pleased to see one another. The Grand Rabbi, the Prior of the Dominicans, the Mother Superior and representatives of other Christian denominations were there too.

That's not the only party I've been to, but the other was improvised. Mr. Bullard and I were riding last Sunday through the exquisite fruit gardens S. of the town and I insisted on paying a call on their owner. We found him in his orchards, a hale old man who owns 2 square miles, or thereabouts, of the richest gardens near Bagdad and plants his seedling potatoes with his own hands. He led us through his fruit trees, showed us where he was laying out a new orange grove and where transplanting spring onions. Apricot and peach, apple and greengage are all in white and pink flower, and the thick grass lines the water channels, as it does only in exceptionally good years. Therewith he took us to his house and gave us an excellent tea of fresh bread and butter —the latter a rare luxury—and preserved fruits. We sat on a wide wooden bench in his mud-built guest room and listened to his shrewd talk. As a sequel to the visit he sent me today a present of eggs and fresh beans, wrapped up in a red cotton handkerchief.

With Sir Percy away, I have even more visitors than before and most of my morning is taken up with interviews. The Naqib's water pipe has been the question of the hour. I may say it has devastated my prospect as well as swamping the Naqib's quarter, for nothing in this world will keep it in repair. Yet you can't treat it like an ordinary pipe, for it is a religious bequest and must therefore be approached with the utmost circumspection. At length the Naqib, after much heart searching, has agreed to let the Municipality be responsible for its upkeep and a load is slipping from my shoulders.

Yet it's because matters like this one have been so tactfully handled by Sir

Percy that all the notables come to tea at the Civil Dispensary. . . .

[In March she again leaves Bagdad to motor among the Sheikhs and] " got a lot of tribal stuff."

[I include here some extracts from letters written by Gertrude at this time to Mildred Lowther (daughter of Lord Ullswater) with whom her friendship had become very close during 1915 when Mildred helped in the work for tracing the wounded and missing.]

To Hon. Mildred Lowther.
March 6th, 1918.

I want to see you so very much, beloved Milly. I feel as if I had jumped into old age during the last two years. You would scarcely believe from outside I am the same person, but inside I am not changed.

To the same.
BAGDAD, March 18, 1918.

My Father eagerly desires me to leave this summer but I can't settle myself to making plans while the fate of the world swings in the balance.

To the same.
July 6th, 1918.

No, I'm not coming back yet, darling. Do not forget me. When I come back I shall want your help and understanding so much. It will be so difficult to pick up life in England I dread it. You must give me a hand as you did before.

It is too hot to write more. I shall go up on the roof and lie on a hot sheet while the sandflies drift through the meshes of the mosquito net— that's the Arabian night if the truth were known.

To H. B.
SAMAWAH, March 17th, 1918.

At Kufah while I was standing on the high point aforesaid I saw some black tents and camels in a hollow to the S. and presently the owners crept up to us and laid their difficulties before me. They were men of the Ghazzi, a semi-nomadic tribe near Nasiriyeh, and they had been out in the desert since October. Now they wanted to go back to their own people by the river for the summer, but when they got to Shinafiyah where they meant to cross the river, behold there were soldiers and people riding about and the devil's own puzzlement. And they wanted to know whether there was permission for their crossing or what was to happen to them if they might not come down to the river. I said their Sheikh was a friend of the Govt. and bade them go in peace where they liked, but they were not happy till I wrote them an order to say they might cross and continue on their way. With that they kissed my shoulder and departed reassured, I hope, but think what bewilderment all these strange happenings must cause to camel folk who don't know what the intention of the soldiers and the Govt. may be. Next day was disgusting, a high wind and terrific rain.

Fortunately my tent stood - (by a miracle) and my roof didn't leak much. There was nothing to be done but to continue sitting under it. I wrote up my tribal notes, and in the afternoon was visited by various sheikhs and saiyids and had some interesting talk, the net result of which was that they too were a little bewildered and anxious like the camel people. We have only been in effective occupation in these parts for the last three months; we are new and strange to them, and they to us. I've had in masses of sheikhs to see me and I think I've made a pretty good tribal register. . . .

It's immensely interesting seeing this bit of the Euphrates and making acquaintance with its inhabitants. No doubt I've only got the vaguest outline of what there is to know, but at any rate it is an outline of a very complicated bit of tribal country, concerning which we were, a few months ago, in complete ignorance. . . .

To F.B.
BAGDAD, March 28th, 1918.

. . . . A terrible cloud has fallen on our work here in the murder at Najaf of one of our Army Political Officers [this was Captain Marshall]. He was a brilliant creature—I personally was very fond of him, and spent a delightful afternoon with him three weeks ago when I was at Kufah. He had I thought a great future, and I do most bitterly regret him. . . .

This tragedy cast a great storm over the end of my journey, but I must tell you the remainder of my tale. I wrote to you from Samawah the day before I left. I came up the Hillah branch of the Euphrates in a motor launch from Samawah to Diwaniyeh. Capt. Goldsmith, a young Surrey officer, came with me for the first couple of hours, with a party of mounted police—for honour you understand, not for safety. I could have done with less but in spite of them all the ride over the desert green with aromatic plants was delicious. The smell of a desert in spring is like nothing in this world. Each night I held a levy of notables after dinner. The second night when I had listened to the praises of myself, my government and my host, I was fortunately relieved by the entrance of an aged worthy whose appearance and conversation I must describe to you. His face was black with age, his beard scarlet with henna; the black and red were enfolded in a gigantic white turban. As he entered we all gave him salutations which were repeated when he had sat down. Talk then flagged until he took up his tale. "As I came in," said he. "As I entered the very door, without a pen I composed a verse." "Without a pen!"—ejaculations of surprise and admiration fell from the company and we begged to be acquainted with the production. He raised his ancient bony hand as though he would bid the world listen, and in a cracked voice recited three times running, an egregious couplet to the effect that all had learned humanity from the high Government, and that the coming of the Khatun (me) had filled the universe with joy. After the third recital I felt it my duty to write it down—seeing that he had no pen. The rest of the hearers overflowed with praise and a general hope was expressed that "Please God" and with His help the Haji would that night be able to complete the ode so felicitously begun. But whether he did or he did not I don't know, for I fled from Diwaniyah in a motor very early before the notables were awake.

The I.G.C. has been up for a couple of days cheerful and cheering as ever. Also whom do you think I have seen? Driver Woodcock, Mrs. Taggart's grandson. I gave him some cigarettes and a book of mine, which he asked me for, and to-day I've got him some razors and things from the Red Cross.

I must tell you, I'm a person of consequence, for Father's launch is beating all records.

Father's letter of Jan. 15th came also with my last mail. I wish you wouldn't write me such splendidly long letters. Though I love them, Father's account of his week's work is really appalling. His billiard table groaning with his papers! I also got your wire about the Geog. Soc. Medal. It was an absurd thing to give me; they must have been hard up for travellers this year.

To her family.
BAGDAD, April 5th, 1918.

Mr. Bullard and I rode miles up the Tigris and dropped in to call on a charming old gentleman who owns a large garden by the river bank. We were received by his servants with enthusiasm and led out into the garden where we found Faik Bey budding orange trees. He then took us through his fruit garden and cornfields, out to the edge of the desert. It was all green and wonderful with the barley in the ear and deep grass under the fruit trees. So we went back with him to tea, which consisted mainly of dates and oranges. My other gardener host, Haji Naji, came in to see me this week. He was dressed in beautiful purple cloth and looked very imposing: "Do you sit here all day and work?" said he, inscribing imaginary epistles in the air with his forefinger. "Very laborious!" and he tapped his forehead to indicate his sense of my mental effort. "You must come out again to my garden and be happy among the fruit trees."

A raging south wind, which brought that night a wild storm of rain—rain which lasted intermittently for 3 days and that's unusual at this time of year—but very fortunate, for it keeps the world cool and fresh. On the second afternoon the rain held up a little and I, not being able to bear sitting in the office any longer, waded out through the mud and had tea with the French nuns, darling creatures, whom I found trembling with anxiety about the news of the battle—as who is not? . . . .

Behind all one's doings lies the terrible sense of these days in France. The first assault seems to have spent itself—at what cost!—and we now, with deep anxiety await news of the second.

Goodbye, my beloved family. . . .

To H.B.
BAGDAD, April 10th, 1918.

I am sending home 50 little black sheepskins in 5 parcels. My fur coat is in holes and some day they will do to make a new one, being both pretty and cheap.

The Willingdons are here on a short excursion from Bombay, staying with the C. in C. It is very nice having them, they are so cheerful and pleasant. If the hosts enjoy a party you may be pretty sure the guests are happy too. Among the latter were two wise men from Najaf, crowned with gigantic white turbans, and it was assuredly the first time in history that Najaf Ulama [the doctors of divinity, the learned clerics of Islam] had been seen at such a gathering. . . .

If I can concoct a suitable telegram I shall telegraph to you saying that if you want me to come home this summer you must make arrangements from your end. Women aren't allowed to cross the Medit., but I should think they'll make an exception for me. If I can't come to England I shall go on leave to Baluchistan.

To H.B.
BAGDAD, April 18th, 1918.

I've just got a four weeks' mail with your letters of Jan. 27, 31, Feb. 12 and 26, and Mother's of Jan, 30, Feb. 6, 20 and 23. It's an immense comfort to have them. Three days ago I telegraphed to you about plans, saying I doubted whether coming home was advisable. I received next day a wire from you approving all my plans of Jan. 31 - but Lord knows what they were! However, I've left it at that, because you will certainly see Sir Percy in a day or two and I shall have your final decision. My own feeling is that it's no good attempting to make plans while everything in France hangs in the balance. While things are very critical I don't want to leave this country for, naturally, it will make people here extremely jumpy as to their future—and I, in a small way, am one of the people who can help to comfort them. If I went, I fear they might think I was deserting them, and that would make them more nervous still.

Except for the fear of your disappointment if I can't come, I don't worry. I'm perfectly well, better than I've been for a year; and escape in the middle of the summer to high ground in Persia is always possible. Two easy days' motoring lands one 5,000 feet up, just think of it! So as regards health I'm all right.

First the accounts of Springy. I'm really glad he hadn't had long months of failing health, as I had feared. I do grieve so much over the loss of him. He did his part splendidly, none better. We've just had the Willingdons here. I saw a great deal of them and loved them both. The Chief insisted on my coming with them to Babylon. We had a delightful two days. We motored to Hillah, where we lunched. . . . We went to Babylon; this wonderful spring had clothed the ruin mounds in flowering weeds and cast a fresh beauty over the dust of palaces. I took them on to a high place, spread out a map, and told them all the long tale, down to Nebuchadnezzar, and then down to Alexander, who died there in the palace on the northern mound. The Willingdons were the most enchanting audience, so was the Chief, and one of the staff said that though he hated ruins (i.e., the staff man hated them) he really had liked Babylon. Lady W. and I agreed that I really had slung quite a good scalp on to my belt!. . . .

I jumped up at 6 and walked for an hour along Euphrates bank—the beloved river—under palms and willow trees, talked with the peasants who were driving their oxen up and down the long slopes of the water lifts, heard the Mesopotamian nightingale and remembered that these were the same sights and sounds that Nebuchadnezzar had known and even Hammurabi. Were they, I wonder, comforted and sustained by the eternal beauty of the earth and the simple country life of field and river? We motored that day to Birs Nimrud which is supposed to be the Tower of Babel, and I need not say isn't (because, partly, there wasn't one, and partly because the one there wasn't was not in that place —but I fear you'll fail to understand me!) and home to Bagdad. I motored always with Lord W. and told him all we had done—irrigation, agriculture, pacification of the tribes—with illustrations drawn from the country we passed through, and he was the most sympathetic listener. He is so delightfully full of interest and eager that I don't think he can have been bored, for if you care for administration it was a tale worth hearing.

To H.B.
BAGDAD, April 19, 1918.

This evening I have a telegram from Sir P. saying that you and he in consultation had agreed that I had better not come. I feared he would warn you that the journey is now very difficult and I think the decision is a wise one but I can't help feeling a dreadful tightening at the heart at the thought of not seeing you within measurable time. I do sometimes want you so much that I can scarcely bear it. You could always get me home by making the India Office or the F.O. telegraph that they want me and asking the Admiralty to give me facilities. We'll see how things turn; it may be easier in a month or two. I've almost forgotten about France in thinking of you and Mother and Maurice. . . .

This is becoming a sort of diary letter—it's because you are so much in my mind that I want to talk to you. To-day it has been positively cold. I was dressed in a silk coat and skirt and shivered so much that I had to get into a white serge gown which was fortunately hanging up in my dressing-room at the office. Amazing, isn't it? Last year we were grilling at this date.

I've brought out a work on Euphrates geography and tribes which has given satisfaction. I shall have to revise it now, for I learnt so much more when I was down the river last month, but at least it's a beginning. I must tell you that I know a great deal about the Euphrates and nothing about the Diala. That's the next task when I can get at it.

The nuns are making me a muslin gown—it will be a monument of love and care, for I really believe they lie awake at night thinking what new stitches they can put into it. I often go in to see them after tea; we sit on the balcony in their courtyard and talk of France and Bagdad. And then they all troop down in a body to the door to wave me farewell down their narrow, curling street—it's not 6 feet wide, nor are any streets wider in the heart of Bagdad. Yesterday I rode with the O.C. of one of the big hospitals, Col. Crossley, and think of it! he had been for 2 years at Richmond, had taught and examined many of our R. Cross detachments and been to our field day in 1912. . . .

Good-bye, darling Father. I think and think of you. However long I'm away from you, your love and Mother's is like the solid foundation on which all life rests. But I don't feel as if I could bear not seeing you for very much longer.

To H.B.
BAGDAD, May 4th, 1918.
Received June 22nd, 1918.

The river has been in great flood this week. We trembled for our sown fields, but it's a wonderful sight. The great wealth and bounty of water. All the little water courses flowed in spate through the fields and gardens, things grew as you watched them and the Mespot nightingales shouted through the orchards.

The event of the week was a tea party which I gave to the ladies of Bagdad in Sir Percy's house. I asked no one but the big people, mainly Moslems, and to my surprise they came in flocks. An Armenian family (Madame Sevian and her daughters, whom I like very much), the Mother Superior and some of the nuns came to help and it was an immense success. I've heard that the ladies said that not even in a Mohammedan house would so much care have been taken to exclude all males—it's odd isn't it, that the success of a party should depend on the absence of that element! One woman, the wife of the Director of Religious Bequests (Moslem of the Moslem), said as she went away that if only they could see one another and meet more in company life would be quite different. So now I'm concocting a scheme to hire the cinematograph for an evening and have a ladies' night. They never see anything or go anywhere, think of it!

To F.B.
BAGDAD, May 9th, 1918.

I've had a charming little jaunt of 5 days. I motored to Kamadi in about five hours and stayed there with General Brooking.

Next morning I motored on to Hit over a barren desert road which not even this year's rain can bring to life. We walked about Hit which is the strangest place, unlike any other in Mesop.—set on a high steep mound, made of some 6,000 years' of former Hits.... And then we went on into the edges of the desert, flower strewn, struck the Kubaisah road, where I met several dead people who were once me, riding on camels, and gave them greeting with mixed feelings—And so I came home to breakfast.

To H.B. & F.B.
BAGDAD, May 24th, 1918.

Will you forgive me if I write in pencil—it's not really a bit hot, but hot enough to make a fountain pen rather a nuisance; it dries up so fast. Here we are at the end of May and the temperature rarely over 100—it's wonderful. . . .

Oh dear, how much I would like to have you just for an hour to show you our office. I'm accustomed to it now, but it's a wonderful place. We occupy two big houses built round courtyards on the river. Capt. W. and I have rooms next door to one another on the first floor. Mine is all shielded with mats and blinds against the sun and is beautifully cool. It has a writing table and a big map table, a sofa and some chairs with white cotton covers and lovely bits of Persian brocade over them, 2 or 3 very good rugs on the brick floor and a couple of exquisite old Persian glass vases on top of the black wood bookcase. The walls covered with maps. It's a nice place. On the verandah, which runs round the inside of the court, sit our kavasses—office servants in khaki uniform—to fetch and carry files and papers for us, run messages and so on. They are mostly Arabs, some Persians, with immensely high bulbous felt hats. Opposite is the room of the Financial Adviser, Major May; the peacock mostly sits with him; and in between the map room, the cypher room, the room of the P.O. Bagdad, Captain Gillan, with a crowd of people waiting always to see him. In the next house all the clerks, British N.C.O.'s, capital men, Eurasians doing the confidential work (and they are first rate too), two vernacular departments, Arab and Persian—I love them all; they are so delightful to work with. But a medley, isn't it! And though I'm accustomed to it, I never quite get over the amusement and interest of it. I spend an entertaining time every morning learning Persian, which I've almost forgotten. But it comes back quickly, and during the first week I've already begun to chatter an amazing jargon, three parts Arabic, I'm afraid. I have the complete illusion of speaking Persian, for my teacher (one of our vernacular clerks) instructs me in Arabic and understands what I'm trying to say, but I fear the natives of Persia won't. However, it's great fun.

To her family.
BAGDAD, June 14, 1918.
   I've now got a Persian cook, who, besides being able to cook (an art none of my former cooks have possessed), knows no Arabic, so I'm forced to do my housekeeping in Persian, which amuses me—doubtless amuses the cook also at times. The nuns have made me some muslin gowns which are really quite nice—also cheap. The 'essayages' are not like any other dressmaking I've ever known. I go in after riding before breakfast and stand in practically nothing but breeches and boots (for it's hot) while the Mother Superior and the darling dressmaking sister, Soeur Renée, hover round ecstatically and pin on bits of muslin. At our elbows a native lay sister bearing cups of coffee. We pause often while the Mother Superior and Soeur Renée discuss gravely what really is the fashion. The result is quite satisfactory. Soeur Renée isn't a Frenchwoman for nothing
   My roses are flowering anew, rather dusty in the face, poor little things, but very sweet.

To H.B.
BAGDAD, July 5th, 1918.
   . . . Two splendid long ones from you. And the first and most interesting thing in them is your suggestion that you might come here next spring. I can't imagine greater pleasure than showing you this world of mine. I hate your not knowing what has meant so much to me.
   I'm going to Persia on Tuesday night. I really feel as if a judgment ought to

fall on me for doing anything so nice. It has been very hot this week. The temp. danced up one day to 118 and I can't keep my office under 100. I'm still very well, but I don't feel as if I could bear 3 uninterrupted months of it.

(The holiday in Persia was all that she had meant it to be. She writes from camp on her way to Kirmanshah.]

I jumped up at dawn and climbed to the top of the hills, 2,300 feet above the camp—a tough scramble up limestone rocks. But it was magnificent. The gentians and tulips were seeding—I send you some tulip seed which will you kindly give Hanagan—but the dianthus was still out, and gorgeous thistles and pediculatis—all the great garden of mountains. I came in at 10 to breakfast, a little footsore—I haven't walked for 4 years—but feeling like a new-born creature. It's about 100 in the tents at noon, but one doesn't feel it because there's a cool wind. The country is almost uninhabited here. I met a few woodcutters on the lower slopes this morning, with whom I stopped and talked, but from the top you can see no sign of human habitation—just mountain stillness. To-morrow I go on to Kitmanshah.

It's worthwhile to sit 2 years in an office in Mesop. in order to do this at the end with such enjoyment!

To H.B.
KERMANSHAH, July 13th, 1918.

It's a desert, this country; there's little difference between Persia and Mesopotamia, except that in the one the wilderness is set upright and in the other it's laid flat. We ran up 1,000 feet between steep and narrow mountain slopes. The road is a switchback, up and down over low passes, snow-blocked in winter. It's nothing short of a miracle that we can put it to use.

[She then goes to Gulahek, full of memories of her youth—and so back to Bagdad.]

To F.B.
BAGDAD, August 30th, 1918.

If Sir Percy had been here this winter I think they could have done quite well without me, but the moment I got back Capt. Wilson told me the staggering news that he had been appointed to Teheran. But his absence makes me feel that it wouldn't have been right for me to have been away this winter. But it is a disappointment, isn't it! I was looking forward so much to having him here after all these months. However, Capt. Wilson and I are excellent colleagues and the best of friends and I know I can do a good deal to help him by seeing people and being ready to sit and talk as much as they want. It will probably be my main job. But first I'm going to compile an Intelligence book on Persia, for which I've collected materials while I have been away, and I rather think I can make a passable bit of work. It's the sort of thing I love doing. I've rather lost my heart to Kurdistan, country and people. My Persian was enough to carry me through most interesting conversations— Persian is extraordinarily easy, you know, and I learnt more in that 3 weeks of riding through the country than I could have learnt in months of motoring. But it was hard work—unspeakably bad tracks and very hot in the middle of the day. There were many moments of deadly weariness which are not mentioned in my diary but remain in my memory. Still, I have come back extremely fit. We are now at what I think almost the worst moment of Bagdad, the stuffy autumn heat, temp. 104, and absolutely still and airless.

The two months in Persia have made me much more efficient—that's rather satisfactory. I have got roughly the hang of things there and can judge much better how they affect us here. Quite apart from the enjoyableness, it has been well worth doing.

To F.B.
BAGDAD, September 5th, 1918.

Why, yes, of course I wrote all the Arab of Mesopotamia. I've loved the reviews which speak of the practical men who were the anonymous authors, etc. It's fun being practical men, isn't it. Oh, I do so agree with you as to the great luck of having something to do during the war—no matter if it's much too much to do. It would be far greater suffering to stand outside it all. Father sends me the most delightful accounts of the Geographical Society meeting and dinner. How glad I am that it was he not I—firstly because he did it much better than I should have done it, thereby keeping up the credit of the family, and secondly because he liked it much better. I really should have been ashamed to receive that medal; it's far too great an honour.

I've had an uneventful week, but a busy one. Lots of people coming in to see me, and then lots of strings to pick up, and a report to write covering the whole time of my absence—fortunately not many things had happened—and then the Persian Intelligence book which is fairly under way. I've been making a Persian tribal map to-day and wishing I knew as much about Persian tribes as I do about Arab. Sir Percy goes to Teheran in 3 days' time.

To F.B.
BAGDAD, September 19th, 1918.

I must announce the good arrival of some gloves and a felt hat, just what I wanted, and General Cobbe tells me that Richard is bringing me some clothes, which is splendid. Woad is the only suitable wear at present. It's infernally hot, 113 and absolutely airless. I don't think I've ever felt the climate more. Also I've had a cold and though I'm taking every means to be better until the weather changes I don't look forward to much vigour. At sunset the dust and mist lie in thick bars over the world and you gasp for breath. When this reaches you I shall probably be shivering, so I write untrammelled—two l's?—by any fear of causing you anxiety.

We have had a tremendous function this week—a Durbar of Sheikhs held by the C. in C. It really was rather wonderful. We had all the leading men of the country, sheikhs and tribal saiyids, from Samawah to Tikrit—the Chief had seen the Basrah people there the week before. There were about 80 of them, only the very biggest from each district had been selected. The Durbar was held in the public gardens and all the notables of Bagdad attended to see it, an immense concourse. It was terrifically hot, but I fortunately was in the shade on the platform, with Consuls and distinguished foreigners, French and American, who happened to be here. At 5 o'clock the C. in C. came up in procession through the garden with all his Major-Generals behind him, very splendid it looked. The sheikhs filed past him by districts, each group introduced by its Political Officer and the Chief.

To H.B.
BAGDAD, November 28th, 1918.

    I am having by far the most interesting time of my life and thank Heaven I am now well and can grapple with it adequately. The Franco-British Declaration has thrown the whole town into a ferment. It doesn't happen often that people are told that their future as a State is in their hands and asked what they would like. They are all talking and mercifully they all come in to me with the greatest eagerness to discuss what they think. On two points they are practically all agreed, they want us to control their affairs and they want Sir Percy as High Commissioner. Beyond that all is divergence. Most of the town people want an Arab Amir but they can't fix upon the individual. My belief is (but I don't yet know) that the tribal people in the rural districts will not want any Amir so long as they can have Sir Percy—he has an immense name among them—and personally I think that would be best. It's an immense business setting up a court and a power. The whole situation requires very delicate handling. We can't be too wary at this moment when the public mind is so fluid that anything serves to divert it in one direction or another. I always speak quite frankly and they believe me, I think. They know I have their interests more deeply at heart than anything else and they trust me in the same sort of way that they trust Sir Percy.

    I'm so thankful to be here at this time, whatever happens I must remain till Sir Percy is brought back. We've telegraphed very fully, A. T. Wilson and I, and I think we have given a just view of the state of things. . . .

    . . . . I'm quite sure that I prefer Generals to Bps. Two days later I went with Generals Lubbock and Stuart Wortley to Baqubah to see the Nestorian refugees in camp. We have 80,000 of them; they tramped down from Urumiah to escape from the Turks. The camp is wonderful—like a huge town. Then I walked with my generals in the orange gardens on the other bank, made friends with one of the proprietors and came away laden with oranges. Baqubah oranges are certainly the most beautiful in the world. The gardens are an amazing sight now—5 and 6 huge yellow globes hanging clustered on & boughs—all the groves aglow with them.

To H.B.
BAGDAD, December 6th, 1918.

    We have had a day's rain this week and the world is pretty muddy. Luckily my first Tuesday party took place the day before. I had about 50 ladies, mostly Moslems—they flock now, and I shall get them all in time. We had tea in the garden and sat talking for nearly 2 hours most cheerfully. I talk Arabic perhaps not quite as well as French, but nearly. The younger men are trooping in now of a morning to give me their views on the political future.

A. T. Wilson and I spend a considerable part of our time laying down acceptable frontiers—by request. It's an amusing game when you know the country intimately, as I do, thank goodness, almost all of it. Was ever anything more fortunate than that I should have criss-crossed it in very nearly every direction.

To H.B.
BAGDAD, December 27th, 1918.
. . . . About Arab rule. In Mesopotamia they want us and no one else, because they know we'll govern in accordance with the custom of the country. They realise that an Arab Amir is impossible because, though they like the idea in theory, in practice they could never agree as to the individual. . . .

To F.B.
BAGDAD, January 3rd, 1919.
On the chance of an outgoing boat I make haste to write you and wish all yours a good new year. . . .

But more interesting was a lecture given one afternoon last week by Prof. Margoliouth. He lectured for 50 minutes by the clock on the ancient splendours of Bagdad in classical Arabic and without a note. It is the talk of the town. It's generally admitted that he knows more of Arabic language and history than any Arab here. . . .

To H.B.
BAGDAD, January 10th, 1919.
We have been having rather a difficult time here. The East is inclined to lose its head over the promise of settling for itself what is to become of it. It can't settle for itself really—we out here know that very well, because it might hit on something that certainly wouldn't simplify state government and that we can't allow in the interests of universal peace. But it is not going to be an easy job to hold the balance straight. I'm thinking of leaving in the last week of February, something like that.

Meantime I'm hard at work at the log book of Iraq Personalities, a gigantic task. I think I shall get it into shape by the end of this month. Further I'm seeing a great many people and incidentally a good many of the women. We have got a lady doctor. I'm taking her to see some of my friends and arranged a series of lectures for her in the home of a Pasha's wife. The ladies seem to be very keen about the classes.

The last day or two I've had a feverish cold—it is curious how everything turns to fever and knocks you out.

To H.B.
BAGDAD, January 17th, 1919.

I was deeply grieved about Beatrice [Chamberlain]; I've written to Mr. Austen. There were few people who were her equal in fair sanity and I realise now how much I always counted on her friendship. It's possible that I may come home a little earlier. A. T. Wilson shows signs of wanting someone at home who can help to give a guiding hand, if that's possible, keep him closely informed of how things are shaping and at the same time represent the experience we have gathered here. I really don't mind one way or the other myself. I should like to be back here in October, but we'll see what happens. I think on the whole I'm more useful here than in England, but just at this moment I might be able to help to keep things straight—if they'll let me. . . . We are having rather a windy time over self-determination. I'll tell you some day. I wish very much that Sir Percy were here. . . .

I flew with a young man last week—literally not figuratively. We flew for about three-quarters of an hour up and over the Tigris. For the first quarter of an hour I thought it the most alarming thing I had ever done and eagerly wished that that good young man would return to the ground. It was a windy day, the aeroplane wobbled a good deal. However, I presently became accustomed to it and was much interested and excited. I shall go up whenever I have an opportunity so as to grow quite used to it.

To F.B.
January 25th, 1919.

. . . . The best thing this week was a lecture of Prof. Margoliouths on Abbassid history. I asked him the other day what he thought of the Bagdadis, to which he replied, "You will I trust forgive me for quoting a sentence of the Prophet's of which I am often reminded by the people of Bagdad: seek the advice of women in order to do the contrary."

To F.B.
January 31st, 1919.

Col. Wilson telegraphed home this week saying he would like to send me to England more or less as his liaison officer while so much is under discussion there. My own view is that he will get no answer.

If we get a permanent form of Government established here by this time next year I think we shall be lucky. . . . . It is an immense job, the conversion of a military organisation into a civil administration, all the technical part of it is so overwhelming, forts, telephones, medical and sanitary organisation, etc.; and it means that you cannot demobilise wholesale as if you did there would be a sudden breakdown in all the functions of Government. I haven't anything to do with these things, but I can see how intricate they are. . . .

I have planted my garden most beautifully with hedges of chrysanthemums—it ought to be a sight next autumn . . . I'm sorry I shall not see the country here this spring it will be wonderful after such a winter of rain.

But I shall see you and I'm immensely looking forward to it. I can't quite believe yet that in 6 weeks or so I shall be in England. I expect I shall be pretty busy, you know. Anyhow I think it will be good for me to go away for a bit. I feel I've become very provincial. How can one help it when one's whole time and thoughts are given to one's province? But it is not a good plan to get quite out of touch. One is more useful here for knowing what the pulse is like at home. I would like to do some propaganda for my province—lectures perhaps, though my mind rather shrinks from the idea at this moment. The Geog. Soc. would perhaps be a good platform but it will probably be too late in the year for them—they don't, if I remember, have meetings after Easter. Heaven knows I shan't regret it personally; it's only that I want to advertise my province, you understand.

And do you know what I look forward to very much? A leg of mutton! That's not poetic, is it, but you should see and try to eat the meat I live on. I can't think what part of an animal it grows on. I must learn to cook mutton chops while I'm at home—and then see if I can't get them here.

[She goes to the Conference in Paris.]

To H.B.
HOTEL MAJESTIC, PARIS, March 7th, 1919.

You must have been surprised at not hearing from me before, but I've dropped into a world so amazing that up to now I've done nothing but gape at it without being able to put a word on to paper. Our Eastern affairs are complex beyond all words, and until I came there was no one to get the Mesopotamian side of the question at first hand. The magnates have been extremely kind. . .. They have all urged me to stay and I think for the moment that's my business. I'm filling up the time by getting in touch with the French and finding out for myself what their views are. . . . I would love above everything to come motoring with you but it depends on how busy I am seeing French people. If I can keep a day or two clear of course I'll come and in any case I'll manage to come to Boulogne and see you for an hour or two there. I hope you'll think I'm right to stay. I can't do anything else.

To F.B.
PARIS, Sunday, March 16th, 1919.

It will be quicker to send a letter by Father than to post it. I can't tell you what it has been like to have him for these two days. He has been more wonderfully dear than words can say, and in such good spirits looking so well. I can scarcely believe that three years of war have passed over his head since I saw him. . . . I'm deep in propaganda though I don't know that it does much good, I don't feel is if I can neglect the chance of doing something. Except for the interest of the things which lie in the melting pot I'm not really liking it much and I should be very glad to get away. But one has got to such a state of tension that I don't believe I could at this moment come quietly home and rest.

We had a very delightful lunch to-day with Lord Robert and T. E.

Lawrence—just we four. Lord Robert is I think the salient figure of the Conference and T. E. Lawrence the most picturesque. I spend most of my time with the latter and the former is unfailingly helpful.

I think that after A. T. Wilson has arrived and I've put him into touch with my friends, that I can leave matters in his hands. He comes next week, I hope. General Allenby arrives on Tuesday and Mr. Hogarth with him, so that we shall be in force. I can't write or think of anything else but what we are doing with the East—afterwards I wonder what I shall think about.

[On April 13th Gertrude starts for a motor tour with her father through Belgium and the north of France, Paris, then to Marseilles and so by sea for Algiers. Back via Paris in May.

Gertrude is in England for the rest of the summer and leaves again for the East in July.]

To H.B.
26th September, 1919.

. . . . We reach Port Said on the 28th so I'll begin to write to you. The weather beautiful, the ship excellent. And Marie [Delaere, her devoted maid] is proving an admirable traveller, and wonders why everyone who can doesn't do this all the time. For my part I've never been so well dressed on a ship for she digs into the boxes and produces a fresh costume daily.

[Gertrude writes from Damascus the account of her journey from Cairo,— of her halt in Jerusalem, where she stays with Lady Watson wife of the chief Administrator General Sir Harry Watson, and sees a good deal of Sir Ronald Storrs.

"There is practically no question but Zionism in Jerusalem."

From Jerusalem via Beyrout to Aleppo.]

To her family.
ALEPPO, October 17th, 1919.

I've been doing the usual thing here, seeing people, but the chief person I've seen is Fattuh. He looks older and as if he had been through an awful time as indeed he has. He has lost everything he had—he was beginning to be quite a well-to-do man and now he has only a horse and a small cart with which he brings in wood to sell in Aleppo. He was chiefly suspect because he was known to have been my servant. I went to see his wife—they live now in a tiny house which they have hired. He used to have two big houses of his own, poor Fattuh. I was very very glad to see him. He is preparing food for me to take on my motor journey and he still has some of my camp kit, cups and plates and things, so that I need not buy anything. We have had such happy times together—I called to mind joyous departures from Aleppo, and looking at his haggard face I said, "Oh Fattuh before the war our hearts were so light when we travelled, now they are so heavy that a camel could not carry us." He smiled and said, "Big lady, no, a camel couldn't carry you." My poor Fattuh.

To F.B.
BAGDAD, November 2, 1919.

    I have been to pay a visit of condolence on one of the big families, the head of which, an old friend of mine has died. I'm very sorry he's dead but I'm glad he won't have the opportunity of dying again so that I shall not have to pay another visit of condolence. . . . All the women of the family met me on the threshold of the harem, dressed in the blackest black, their hair cut short and tears streaming down their cheeks. N.B. He has been dead a month. They cried uninterruptedly for ten minutes and again at intervals whenever they remembered to do so. . . . I have also attended a meeting for the promotion of a Public Library for the native population. The scheme was started by the wife of one of the judicial Officers, Mrs. Forbes. She seems a nice woman. The proceedings were in Arabic and I made a speech. It was not extempore, I had been asked to do it the day before and had carefully prepared it with the aid of a native, for one has to make speeches in high falutin literary Arabic. Everyone else was much more high falutin. The chief man of letters recited an ode specially written for the occasion. It had an immense success. After any specially eloquent couplet the audience cried out "True, true," and sometimes "Repeat." . . . The enthusiasm lasted to the end and I made some valuable mental notes as to the right way of making further meetings agreeable to Bagdad audiences. The rules are quite different from ours. . . .

To F.B.
BAGDAD, November 9th, 1919.

    I've done very little this week except sit in the Office. I went to tea with the wife of Mustafa Pasha—she is the nicest of women. Also I went to tea with the Pachahji ladies whom I'm very fond of—he's the owner of my garden and lets me live in it. And I've been to a Jew tea party—you see I'm visiting all my acquaintances—and to a tea party of the wives of some of my colleagues, Mrs. Wilson, Mrs. Waller and Mrs. Bill, I liked them all. Brides come out in swarms to be married here. We've had two weddings in my service since I came. Mr. Bonham Carter dines with me to-night. He had a big function, to which I went as a P.O., for the opening of the new School of Law. Practically all the big people of Bagdad were present. Our greatest man of letters made a speech which it was a privilege to hear. He is a born orator and the rolling Arab periods are magnificent when he declaims them. . . . If only my furniture and crockery would come from Maples I could widen the circle of my dinner parties. I've telegraphed to Maples to ask when they were sent off. And when Marie is here she can look after the arrangements of my household and make it tidier and nicer, a thing I can't do when I'm at the office all day.

To F.B.
Monday, November 30th, 1919.

    Another thing came in to-day, quite as important as the post—two most beautiful Arab greyhounds sent to me by my old friend the paramount chief of the Anazeh, Fahad Beg. They had walked ten days down the Euphrates with two tribesmen to conduct them, and came in half starved. They are sitting beside me on my sofa as I write, after wandering about the room for half an hour whining. They are very gentle and friendly and I hope they will soon get accustomed to living in a garden instead of a tent. They are perfectly lovely and of course of the finest Arab breed. We have named them Rishan and Najmah—the feathered (that's because of his feathered tail) and the star . . . . .

I lead the life of a hermit, if a hermit could spend all his days in an office. Sir George has provided me with a pony on which I've been riding for three quarters of an hour after 4. I then come back to my house and work at my big Mesopotamian Report till dinner and after dinner until I go to bed. I can rarely get at it in the office because of constant interrupters. One day this week I went to a tea party in the house of a notable who is very far from being pro-British. His wife is a friend of mine and I think it's as well to conduct one's personal relations without regard to politics.

To-day I motored out with Sir George to pay a visit on my dear friend Haji Naji the owner of the best fruit gardens near Bagdad. He gave us coffee and delicious preserved nectarines and offered some very feasible suggestions as to the management of the police force, which here as everywhere is one of the most thorny questions. His gardens were looking lovely, the fruit trees just beginning to turn yellow in our late autumn.

I am sending you a copy of my Syrian Report. It is of course confidential but I have permission to let you have it, and I wish you would tell me what you think of it, I can't judge and nobody offers any criticisms except that on the whole they don't agree with my conclusions. Nevertheless I think I'm right.

To H.B.
BAGDAD, December 7th, 1919.
   . . . If you leave in the middle of February you should be here towards the end of March. But don't be later because by the end of April it may be quite hot. I must break to you that I shan't come back with you. I really can't go away from this country, with which I'm so closely identified, while it's going through such a crisis in its fortunes as all next year is sure to do. When you see the relations I'm on with the people you'll understand I feel sure. My idea is to go to George and Blanche [Lloyd] for a month or so in the middle of the summer, but we'll see about that later. . . .

I'm gradually getting my house furnished and its going to be very nice. Maple writes that my things were sent off in October. I ordered them in July! In the mean time I've bought a charming black cupboard and chest in the bazaar, very cheap too. Marie has been invaluable in making curtains and generally seeing to things. She is the greatest comfort! don't know how I did without her. Also my new cook—Oh father you'll love to see him. When he trails about in an abba he gives 'cachet' to my garden, I can tell you! Only, though he can cook a good deal and makes excellent cakes, he can't read or write and as his memory is deficient the morning accounts are a trial.

They run as follows:

G.B. Fallah! Mahdi! the accounts. I must go to the office.
M. Oh your servant, Khatun. I bought what's its name.
G.B. Well, what is its name.
M. Rice. Two krans.
G.B. Eight annas. What next?
M. Then I bought what's its name.
G.B. What? Fallah!
M. Bread, 6 annas.
G.B. Go on.
M. And then I bought what's its name.
G.B. Merciful God! What?
M. Sugar, two rupees.
G.B. Two rupees. Fallah!
M. And then—Khatun, I forgot the eggs yesterday, one rupee.
G.B. All right. Go on.
M. And then I bought meat, one rupee.
G.B. What next?
M. Wallah, I bought—Khatun shall I prepare for your Excellency this evening efter? (stew).
G.B. What you like. Finish the accounts.
M. On my head. And then what's its name.

    and so on, and so on till I'm hysterical between impatience and laughter. . . .

    By the way, will you please send my Syrian Report to George Trevelyan, confidentially. I think it would interest him after a talk he and I had in the Summer. . . .

    Do you know what they call me here? Umm al Muminin, the Mother of the Faithful, and the last person who bore that name was Ayishah the wife of the prophet. But you see why I can't leave.

    Would you let Milly see this letter?

    I wholly forgot to tell you the main feature of the week which was the Prophet's birthday, Sunni style, make no mistake, the Shiahs celebrate it a week later . . . . . The Pious Bequests Dept. gives an official celebration at Muadhdham, a much frequented Sunni shrine 3 miles above Bagdad. It consists of a square meal and prayers, and for the first time we were invited to the meal. I went and so did Frank Balfour with all his staff. It had rained heavily the night before—our long expected first rain which has come at last—and to motor out to Muadhdham was a ticklish business. The party began at 9 a.m. However we all arrived safely and found a gathering of all the men of religion sitting in the house of the Curator of the Mosque. We sat round and chatted for an hour or so, very pleasantly, and then we had a lunch of excellent Arab food, provided in incredible quantities. Some thought the hour 10:20 a.m., untoward, but I never mind how early I lunch. Then we all went back to our offices. I can't tell you how friendly and nice it all was; I loved it.

To H.B.
BAGDAD, December 16th, 1919.

Don't be later here than the middle of March—I don't think I would be able to meet you further away then Bastah. You must bring a camp bed with bedding which all does up in a Wolsey Valise. As for clothes, it is usually delicious here at that time, temp. rising towards 70 at midday, but we sometimes have rain which means that it would be colder. In mid April you must expect 80 or upwards. You are most likely to want here lightish woollen clothes or flannel, but a silk suit or two would not be amiss. A topee you must have—I advise a sun umbrella. . . .

I have had somehow rather a difficult week. First of all Allah afflicted me with a pain in my inside, but he has now taken it away. Next the Powers that be (on earth) got across the Sunni Vatican and they all tumbled in on me. It was very embarrassing because of course it is not my business and I'm always so dreadfully afraid of (a) misleading my visitors and (b) of annoying my colleagues whose job it is. If the latter weren't such angels (b) would be inevitable. It wouldn't have happened I think if Mr. Bonham Carter hadn't been away for a fortnight. First the Naqib sent round his son with a very special warning. Then next morning the door of my office opened and the room was filled with white turbaned Sunni Divines. I listened and begged them to betake themselves to Capt. Cooke, the Director of Pious Bequests, but no, they wouldn't go. If I hadn't been so bothered I could have laughed to find myself set up as an arbitrator of religious administration. However, all has turned out well. I sent for dear Cooke and after begging him to box my ears expounded the matter and he went straight to the Naqib to put things right. Meantime Mr. Bonham Carter, wisest of men has returned, thank heaven and I've got full absolution from him. What they (i.e. he) was doing was, I am convinced perfectly right, but by a series of accidents it hadn't been properly explained. And when that kind of thing happens they the Bagdadis always let off steam by coming to me.

. . . . We are in the middle of a very difficult situation which you will see in the papers—the seizing of Deir al Zor on the Euphrates by an Arab force. We don't yet know the rights of it.

To H.B.
Sunday, December 20th, 1919.

Mr. Bonham Carter dined with me one night and we had a delightful long croak about Arab things and politics. To-day we been riding with Major Bullard through Haji Naji's gardens. I delight in our strange winter landscape. The apricots and mulberries dropping golden leaves into the green carpet of the springing barley. . . .

Who so angelic as my two dogs who are curled up beside me on the carpets as I write. I'm beginning to persuade them that sofas and chairs are not meant for greyhounds. . . .

CHAPTER XVIII
1920

BAGDAD

To H.B.
BAGDAD, January 4th, 1920.
I'll tell you my life and times. On Xmas day I went to an enormous dinner party given by A.T. to all the Political Service and their wives. I came home early, when they began to dance. I dance no longer.

Next morning before eight I caught a special train for Babylon and went there with the Lubbocks and General Hambro and some others, I acting as guide. We had a delicious two hours there after which General H. and Captain Bacon, and his A.D.C. and I went on to Hillah. There we lunched with my dear Major Tyler, the P.O. The lunch was gorgeous because Major Tyler had told the leading citizen that I was coming and he had insisted on sending in the whole meal. The table groaned with delicious Arab foods, the chief dish being a stuffed lamb roasted whole with its tail in its mouth like a whiting. . . .

Here I parted with General Hambro and went on by motor to the other branch of the Euphrates where I found two young men, Captain Mann and Captain Wigan waiting with a launch to take me to the Camp of my host, Major Norbury, P.O. of Shamiyeh. . . . Next morning when I woke and stepped out of my tent into the bright sun and saw all the trees and things I wondered how anyone could live in Bagdad.

The camp was pitched quite near the little village which is the headquarters of the principal Sheikh of the district, Tbadi al Husain. So after dinner he invited us to his Mudhif, his guest house. Now a Mudhif you can't picture till you've seen it. It's made of reeds, reed mats spread over reed bundles arching over and meeting at the top, so that the whole is a huge, perfectly regular and exquisitely constructed yellow tunnel 50 yards long. In the middle is the coffee hearth, with great logs of willow burning. On either side of the hearth, against the reed walls of the Mudhif, a row of brocade covered cushions for us to sit on, the Arabs flanking us and the coffee maker crouched over his pots. The whole lighted by the fire and a couple of small lamps, and the end of the Mudhif fading away into a golden gloom.

We spent next day in camp. . . . It's a rice country and they have had this year a bumper crop. The yellow reed villages lay fat and comfortable in the winter sun, banked up with rice straw. The great golden heaps of rice were not all housed or shipped away but lay on the harvest floors. When we reached the Hor we got into tiny sajahs, the canoe-like boat, and rowed out by passageways through the reeds to the open water. There were thousands of duck, teal and other water birds. The osprey breeds here. The water was covered with the dying leaves of a small water lily on which buffaloes were peacefully browsing, standing belly-deep in the Hor. Of all incongruous diets for a buffalo water lilies are certainly the most preposterous. . . .

Next day we all went to Najaf . . . I am amused to find that my status in Najaf is rising. As a rule the great religious leaders, the Mujtahids, don't see me—I don't propose it. because they never look on an unveiled woman—but this time one of them, a first class Mujtahid, but an Arab, not a Persian, sent to ask me to come. He is an imposing figure. . . . . Najaf, mysterious, malign, fanatical, but drawing you with wonder and reluctance, by its beauty and unfathomableness.

The last time I had been there I was lunching with Captain Marshall who was murdered 8 days later. And we walked the same path round the town and said just these things about Najaf—alas, too truly. . . .

To F.B.
BAGDAD, January 12th, 1920.

First—and it clouds all other things—Reuter brings the news of Uncle Frank's death. I do grieve so much—there is a figure gone from our landscape, full of dignity and kindliness, which can never be replaced. When I remember how much I owed him, how many delightful experiences and how much sympathy, my heart aches with the thought that I didn't give him enough in return [this was Sir Frank Lascelles]. . . . . . And this country, which way will it go with all these agents of unrest to tempt it? I pray that the people at home may be rightly guided and realize that the only chance here is to recognize political ambitions from the first, not to try to squeeze the Arabs into our mould and have our hands forced in a year—who knows? perhaps less, the world is moving so fast—with the result that the chaos to north and east overwhelms Mesopotamia also. I wish I carried more weight. I've written to Edwin and this week I'm writing to Sir A. Hirtzel. I'm so sure I'm right that I would go to the stake for it—or perhaps just a little less painful form of testimony if they wish for it!

To F.B.
BAGDAD, January 25th, 1920.

I've telegraphed to Father saying I hope he'll come. I would love to show him my world here and I know if he saw it he would understand why I can't come back to England this year. If they will keep me, I must stay. I can do something even if it is very little to preach wisdom and restraint among the young Bagdadis whose chief fault is that they are ready to take on the creation of the world to-morrow without winking.

To F.B.
BAGDAD, January 25th, 1920.

I had an interesting day on Monday. First of all we had the formal opening of the Girls' School—our first. I had invited the important native ladies and to my pleasure the Mohammedans turned up better than I expected. Miss Kelly, the Directress of Education, had made the school look very nice. . . . I made a long speech in Arabic explaining the arrangements of the school and the way the children would be educated. The Muhammadan ladies took their share in it, chiming in with assent and approval. It was most exhilarating.

Then Mrs. Howell declared the school open after which we showed them round and then gave them tea. A most successful performance. That evening I had two young Arabs to dinner and a very interesting officer in the police service, Captain Morgan, to meet them. They came at 7 and stayed till 10:30 talking as hard as they could go, about education and the reform of religious endowments and all sorts of things. We were all on the most cordial terms when they left. I'm going to repeat the entertainment weekly, with different couples of my young men, the Arab young men I mean. I feel certain it's a good plan.

Next day Mrs. Leslie, the wife of the acting C. in C. came to tea, a most attractive woman. Then I had a tea party for my favourite monk, Père Anastase, he is exactly like a monk in Chaucer. . . .

I'm afraid there's going to be no rain. We have had practically none this winter, it's most serious. The birds are famished because there is nothing growing. It's not that I watch the sparrows falling to the ground—I wish I could, confound them. My interest in the matter is that they devour the seedlings in my garden and strip my carnations to the bone.

To F.B.
BAGDAD, February 1st, 1920.

I have been having rather an uphill week with a chronic cold that won't go. The result is that I feel too slack to amuse myself and I do nothing but write. Not a good plan as I feel so very tired at the end of the day. . . . The reason why I've been so busy is that people are beginning to come down the Aleppo road with news of Syria and Turkey, and I, having now rather a satisfactory network of informants, hear of the arrival of most of these and send for them. What with getting their information and writing it out my mornings have been pretty full. It's a distressing story which they bring. We share the blame with France and America for what is happening—I think there has seldom been such a series of hopeless tangles as the West has made about the East since the armistice. . . .

I have had two more little Arab dinner parties, both very friendly and successful. Sometimes we talk politics and sometimes we just talk about the country but anyhow we talk, exchange views and learn from one another. And it gives us the sense of being all part of the same game which is the main thing.

I have had to drop my India Office report—after writing two chapters on relations with the Kurds, a most thorny and difficult subject—for the annual reports are now coming in and I must read and digest them before I can complete my own chapters on administration. These will run to two or three chapters, after which a chapter on social and political conditions of which I've written half, and then a general revision of the whole will bring me to the end of the task. It has been a big job; I can't yet judge whether I have covered the ground satisfactorily.

Frank [Balfour] and I were agreeing this evening that we feel happier about the whole position here. We feel we are getting into closer touch, that antagonism is melting and cooperation growing. I hope we are right— it's a thing I don't think we can be mistaken about. He and I and the Howells dined at an immense Arab dinner party last week given by Fakhri Jamil in honour of the birth of a small cousin, the posthumous son of my poor friend, Abdul Rahman Jamil. . . . After dinner I went round to the women's quarters to see the new baby, 3 days old and the mother's up and walking about how they survive I can't think. I must tell you I am honorary head of the Jamil family—that's how the Jamil profess to regard me . . . . .

To F.B.
BAGDAD, February 14th, 1920.

I had a really delightful 3 days in Hillah, where I arrived feeling half dead and recovered steadily. I was staying with the Political Officer, Major Tyler, and all his staff, some 10 young men; great fun it was. Our job was to inspect the first beginnings of the land survey, the agrarian settlement which lies at the root of all our tribal problems—a gigantic task it's going to be, but if we get it done right it will mean agrarian peace for ever and a day. So we met the surveyors and looked at maps and boundary marks—heaps of earth in this country, not stones, for there are none. And then we rode back and half-way stopped and lunched at the mudhif of the chief sheikhs of the district. He had gathered in representatives of all neighbouring tribes concerned in the settlement, but being a poor man he had let it be understood that he intended to provide only for us and the Bani Hasan, his nearest neighbours. So when our great tray of foods had been set before us, another was laid in the end of the mudhif and the Bani Hasan summoned to it. The rest of the company contented themselves with cigarettes and coffee. After lunch there was a great talk—this is how business is conducted in the provinces, and there's no better council chamber than a sheikh's mudhif . . . It was a delightful scene. Our host had fought against us at Kut, having mobilized his tribe at the order of the Turks. "What was it like," I asked, "when you fought with the Turks?" "Khatun," he replied solemnly (that's what they call me—Madam), "we had nothing to eat. Mind you, they had plenty, but they gave us nothing." "Did you fight hungry?" I asked. "Wallahi no," he answered. "We returned home."

Next day Major Tyler and I motored to Diwaniyah. I hadn't been there for 2 years and I shouldn't have known the place again. Clean and tidy, with widened streets and a good hospital—it was a miracle. So is Hillah, which I spent the following morning in inspecting, after a couple of hours' talk with the two leading inhabitants. School, hospital, gaol, bazaars—like a rose, as we say in Arabic.

To F.B.
BAGDAD, February 29th, 1920.

It's too exciting to think that Father is already on his way here. It's also the first spring day after bitter cold and drenching rain, and being Sunday I'm not going to the office. I've installed myself in the verandah of my garden having brought all my work here for a good morning, which I shall begin by writing to you.

I took the whole Goschen family to Babylon this week. . . . They are charming people to take sight seeing because they are so much interested. . . . I'm very busy trying to get a private hospital for women of the better classes—they have already organised an excellent ward in the Civil Hospital for poor women. It was when we showed them this that the well born women asked if they would collect the money to pay for the building. It will cost, 'tout compris' Rs.45,000, and they must pay for it if they want it—an 8 bed hospital Of 4 rooms with a bathroom and nurses room, 6 rooms in all. We had an immense tea party at Aurelia Tod's whose house is more convenient than mine, being in the middle of the town. She did it beautifully for us. I explained the matter of the hospital to the ladies and they were all very enthusiastic. I am now sending a personal letter to 10 of the richest men in this town asking them each to give Rs. 3,000. The rest I think we should have no difficulty in collecting in small subscriptions.

To F.B.
BAGDAD, March 7th, 1920.
It's wonderful to think that by this time Hugo is back. I hope it will console you for Father's absence. I really do think it will do him all the good in the world to be away for a long spell, and the account he and you give me of his doings confirms that view.

I've just written a very long letter to Lord Robert giving an exhaustive criticism of the dealings of the Conference with Western Asia. . . . .

We've had torrents of rain and the world a sea of mud. . . . I went off at noon with the Hambros in a launch up river and we found a delicious place in the sun where it was dry and basked in the barley fields under palm trees. After which I made friends with the peasant proprietors and we had a long talk about the dealings of governments. They were darling people and when I went away they gave me five carrots and a fish, just caught. . . . And now my room is full of pots of wild mustard and green rye which we gathered in the fields and I'm reflecting on the recurring miracle of spring.

I told you about my hospital, didn't I? The Rs.3,000 subscriptions are beginning to come in. . . .

I went to tea on Monday with Saiyid Daud. He has a wonderful house, the finest I've seen here. You go out of a tiny narrow street into a big court with beautiful stucco rooms on the upper floor, ceilings of vaulted Persian stucco and looking-glass work 100 years old; and then into another still bigger court full of orange trees and Olives 40 feet high and lovely rooms and balconies, and best of all a stork's nest in the corner.

To F.B.
March 14th, 1920.
I'm glad it's not this week I was going to Basrah for I've had and have got

an unspeakable cold and feel as if my chest were a solid mass. I did not make it any better by going to Kadhimain yesterday and returning late, but the visit was worth making. I've been describing it to Lord Robert as a justification 'pro vita mea'—he cast up against me my love for the horrible Easterns—so to save trouble I'll tell you the same story.

It's a problem here how to get into touch with the Shiahs, not the tribal people in the country; we're on intimate terms with all of them, but the grimly devout citizens of the holy towns and more especially the leaders of religious opinion, the Mujtahids, who can loose and bind with a word by authority which rests on an intimate acquaintance with accumulated knowledge entirely irrelevant to human affairs and worthless in any branch of human activity. There they sit in an atmosphere which reeks of antiquity and is so thick with the dust of ages that you can't see through it—nor can they. And for the most part they are very hostile to us, a feeling we can't alter because it's so difficult to get at them. I'm speaking of the extremists among them; there are a few with whom we are on cordial relations. Until quite recently I've been wholly cut off from them because their tenets forbid them to look upon an unveiled woman and my tenets don't permit me to veil—I think I'm right there, for it would be a tacit admission of inferiority which would put our intercourse from the first out of focus. Nor is it any good trying to make friends through the women—if the women were allowed to see me they would veil before me as if I were a man. So you see I appear to be too female for one sex and too male for the other,

There's a group of these worthies in Kadhimain, the holy city, 8 miles from Bagdad, bitterly pan-Islamic, anti-British 'et tout le bataclan.' Chief among them are a family called Sadr, possibly more distinguished for religious learning than any other family in the whole Shiah world. A series of accidents led them to make advances to me to which I replied that if they would like me to visit them I should be delighted to honour myself . . . The upshot was that I went yesterday, accompanied by an advanced Shiah of Bagdad whom I knew well. I rather fancy he is secretly a free-thinker. We walked through the narrow crooked streets of Kadhimain and stopped before a small dark archway. He led the way along 50 yards of pitch-dark vaulted passage—what was over our heads I can't think—which landed us in the courtyard of the Saiyid's house. It was old, at least a hundred years old, with beautiful old lattice-work of wood closing the divan on the upper floor. The rooms all opened on to the court—no windows on to the outer world—and the court was a pool of silence separated from the street by the 50 yards of mysterious masonry under which we had passed. Saiyid Hassan's son, Saiyid Muhammad, stood on the balcony to welcome us, black robed, black bearded and on his head the huge dark blue turban of the Mujtahid class. Saiyid Hassan sat inside, an imposing, even a formidable figure, with a white beard reaching half way down his chest, and a turban a size larger than Saiyid Muhammad's. I sat down beside him on the carpet and after formal greetings he began to talk in the rolling periods of the learned man, the book-language, which you never hear on the lips of others. Mujtahids usually have plenty to say—talking is their job; it saves the visitor trouble. We talked of the Sadr family in all its branches, Persian, Syrian and Mesopotamian; and then of books and of collections of Arabic books in Cairo, London, Paris and Rome—he had all the library catalogues; and then of the climate of Samarra which he explained to me was much better than that of Bagdad because Samarra lies in the third climatic zone of the geographers. He talked with such vigour that his turban kept slipping forward on to his eyebrows and he had to push it back impatiently on to the top of his head. . . . And I was acutely conscious of the fact that no woman before me had ever been invited to drink coffee with a mujtahid and listen to his discourse, and really anxious lest I shouldn't make a good impression.

So after about three-quarters of an hour I said I feared I must be troubling him and I would ask permission to take my leave. "No, no," he boomed out, "we have set aside this afternoon for you." I felt pretty sure then that the visit was being a success and I stayed another hour. But I tackled this next hour with much more confidence. I said I wanted to tell him about Syria and told him all I knew down to the latest telegram which was that Faisal was to be crowned. "Over the whole of Syria to the sea?" he asked, with sudden interest. "No," I answered, "the French stay in Beyrout." "Then it's no good," he replied, and we discussed the matter in all its bearings. Then we talked of Bolshevism. He agreed that it was the child of poverty and hunger, "but," he added, "all the world's poor and hungry since this war." I said that as far as I made out the Bolshevist idea was to sweep away all that ever had been and build afresh. I feared they didn't know the art of building. He approved that. Then as I made signs of going, he said, "It is well known that you are the most learned woman of your time, and if any proof were needed it would be found in the fact that you wish to frequent the society of the learned. That's why you're here to-day." I murmured profound thanks for the privilege (with a backward glance at the third climatic zone), and took my leave in the midst of a shower of invitations to come again as often as I liked.

On my way home I went to see Frank Balfour who was in bed with a touch of fever and heard from him the afternoon's news which was that Faisal had been crowned king of Syria and Abdullah king of the Iraq. . . .

Tell darling Mrs. Wilson [Mrs. Gerald Wilson, of Mansfield, near Darlington] that the yellow hollyhock seeds have come and I've sown them in my garden and in all the gardens of my Arab friends. I may mention I've got daffodils in flower —the first daffodils seen in Mesopotamia.

To F.B.
BAGDAD, Sunday, April 10, 1920.

I'm leaving it to Father to describe an experience which I'm sure he'll do at length. This is only a word to tell you that it's wonderful having him. It is most interesting to see him sizing up our problems and he happens to have arrived at a very crucial time. I think we're on the edge of a pretty considerable Arab nationalist demonstration with which I'm a good deal in sympathy. It will, however, force our hand and we shall have to see whether it will leave us with enough hold to carry on here. . . .

What I do feel pretty sure of is that if we leave this country to go to the dogs it will mean that we shall have to reconsider our whole position in Asia. If Mesopotamia goes Persia goes inevitably, and then India. And the place which we leave empty will be occupied by seven devils a good deal worse than any which existed before we came.

With these few words, I remain your affectionate daughter.

To H.B.
BAGDAD, Thursday, 6th May, 1920.

It was a delightful surprise to have a letter from you this morning. I wonder how anyone can complain about anything when they have a father like you. I can't tell you what it was like to have you here. One takes for granted where you are concerned that no matter how unfamiliar or complex the things may be that you're seeing and hearing, you'll grasp the whole lie of them at once, and it's only when I come to think of it that I realise what it is to have your quickness of intelligence. Anyhow, I feel certain that you know the general structure here as well as we know it ourselves and I'm enchanted that you should, not only because it makes my job so much more interesting knowing that you understand it, but also because it's good for us all that you should be able to put in a word for us at home. . . .

Says Mizhir: "Some people have faces so heavy that they make the world dark; and some faces so light that everyone rejoices to see them." Hadhrat al Walid has a light face, God bless and preserve him.

To H.B.
BAGDAD, Sunday, 9th May, 1920.

With what different feelings I write to you now that you've been here! All the news seems to be of the utmost moment now you know all about it. The first and chief is Frank's engagement to Phyllis Goschen. I'm very very glad about it. I like her.

Captain A. L. Smith [Lionel] came to dine. We had a long and satisfactory talk about the education of Arabs. I'm not quite happy about what we're doing; nor is he. It's all very well to say we mustn't start secondary schools till we have really first-rate material, both in teachers and pupils, but we can't wait for that. We must get a move on and be content with second best, for the people here are so immensely keen to be provided with higher education and if we hold back they will think we are doing it on purpose to keep them back. You have to look at it from the point of politics as well as of education.

On Friday I went to tea with the ladies of the Jamil family to see my small "son," the little boy who was born after the death of his father, my friend Abdul Rahman. He's a quite beautiful baby. . . .

Rishan [her dog] is in terrible disgrace. First he jumped on to the pantry table and broke all the crockery on it, including my dear little Persian jam-pot. He was looking for something to eat of course. Next he thought fit to roll in a beautiful bed of nasturtiums and destroyed half of them. He was terribly beaten—by me—and goes about with an extremely penitent air.

Before all these unfortunate occurrences we were riding in the desert and the dogs had a magnificent stork hunt. Everyone was pleased; the dogs were wild with excitement and the old stork flapped along just over their heads and laughed aloud. . . .

To F.B.
BAGDAD, Sunday, May 23rd, 1920.
. . . . A.T. has been given a K.C.I.E.—I'm very, very glad. He well deserves it and I'm so specially glad of the recognition of his work by H.M.G. . . . .

Another very nice thing has happened this week—Fattuh has turned up, driving a man down from Aleppo. . . .

I am so glad to have my dear Fattuh. He wants to go back to Aleppo as soon as we can devise a safe way to get him back. His first words when he came in were, "Is His Excellency the Progenitor still with you?" I said, "How did you know he had been here?" "Oh," said Fattuh, "one of the Beduins in the desert told me that the Khatun was well and her Father was with her."

So I suppose it's the talk of Arabia. . . .

Next morning I rode out with Frank and Major Hay to Kadhimain to see the Shah make his pilgrimage there. We started about 6, a gorgeous morning—you can't think what it's like here in the early mornings, not hot and golden clear—getting to Kadhimain about 7. . . . I looked through the gateway of the mosque into the sacred court—Father knows the gate. The courtyard, into which we might not go, was full of rows of mosque servants in green turbans with groups of divines in white or dark blue turbans and long robes—it looked like a picture by Gentile Bellini. The Shah came up by launch. We rode down to the river where we found the mayor, Saiyid Jafar (with whom Father had tea) and two other magnates. We waited there under palm trees—the landing stage was just opposite the Sunni town of Mua dhdham. The river ran blue and silver, the air was like liquid gold, the gardens and houses of Muadhdham glittered on the opposite bank, with the tall minaret of the Sunni shrine rising out of them—what a setting for a king's pilgrimage, I thought. . . .

It's Ramadhan and everyone is fasting. I had my first Ramadhan party last Thursday evening. Five young Arabs came and 5 of my colleagues. We had very interesting talks about the Turkish treaty. After the Arabs had gone, towards 11, we all had a cold supper in the garden. I'm going on with these parties and I hope they'll be a success. . . .

Another petition story of Frank's: A gentleman who was harbourmaster at Port Sudan sent in a request that he might be granted a week's leave, as his wife was about to be delivered of a buoy.

The more you think of it, the nicer it is.

To H.B.
BAGDAD, June 14th, 1920.
I have your letter from Aden and a word from Mother also tell her, the

shoes from Yapp, most welcome. Did I ever announce to her the arrival of my linen riding habit? It's perfect, I've wired for another, 'wegen' the wash. But though linen habits are essential we're having a remarkably cool year. It has rarely been 110 as yet. I've become such a salamander that this is the sort of temp. I like.

We have had a stormy week. The Nationalist propaganda increases. There are constant meetings in mosques where the mental temp. rises a great deal above 113. The extremists are out for independence without a mandate. They play for all they are worth on the passions of the mob and what with the Unity of Islam and the Rights of the Arab Race they make a fine figure. They have created a reign of terror; if anyone says boo in the bazaar it shuts like an oyster. There has been practically no business done for the last fortnight. . . .

I've written 3 articles at the request of A.T. about the League of Nations and the Mandate. Both A.T. and Sir Edgar are much pleased with them and they are to be published here in English and Arabic.

Major Clayton has arrived to take a job here. He is Sir Bettie Clayton's brother. I like him particularly.

To H.B.
BAGDAD, Sunday, June 20th, 1920.

Ramadhan ended. . . . On Friday morning I rode out before breakfast round the suburbs of Bagdad where I knew people would congregate, and saw the whole world making merry over the great feast of Islam, "Id-al-Fitr," the festival of fast breaking. There were numberless booths of sweetmeat sellers, merry-go-rounds with children swinging in them, groups of women all in their best clothes, and the whole as little revolutionary as anything you can imagine. The East making holiday. . . .

On Sat. morning when I got to the office, Ghallal (head Kavass, you remember) met me with beaming smiles and told me Sir Percy had come. I went to the Mess and found him breakfasting with Lady Cox and Major Murray, and I felt as if a load of care had been lifted. To-day, according to my custom, I didn't go to the office. Sir Percy sent me a note in the afternoon saying that he wanted to come and have a talk. He came after tea. We talked a great deal about how to bridge over the next 4 crucial months till he comes back. H.M.G. have telegraphed to him to return to England at once and he leaves to-morrow. Though, of course, I hate his going, I'm thankful that he will be there to appeal to. For I can write everything to him as I can do to no one else, he being my real Chief, and he will be able to take direct action. At 7 he went to see the Naqib taking me with him. It was touching to see the Naqib's joy. We sat in the courtyard—it was fearfully hot and stuffy—and had an hour's talk. . . . It has been such an infinite comfort to be able to talk of public affairs here without committing an indiscretion, as I can to him. Lady Cox also has been most friendly and affectionate. I'm going to keep the parrot while she is away. I should feel easier in my mind if I were quite sure Rishan wouldn't look upon it as a species of chicken and eat it. . . .

To H.B.
BAGDAD, June 27, 1920.

.... I haven't made any plans for myself yet. Frank is going in July to be married. It will leave us rather short-handed here. Things are quieting down and there's a promising scheme in the wind. ... In this flux there's no doubt that they turn to us. The old brick of a mayor constantly drops in while I'm having breakfast just to talk things over with the Khatun! There's no particular point in it except that he likes it. Yesterday he said that he much regretted Frank's going on leave. "But after all, you'll be here to tell Major Bullard who people are and what they're worth." That sort of remark makes it rather difficult to go away, doesn't it. Meantime I'm very well, though the temp. is up to its summer 115. . . .

We've come to the conclusion that my report must be got out as soon as possible and Sir Percy has taken the first half home with him. He shall have a lot more this week, and there's now only half an administration chapter and the last political chapter to finish. The last I should like to keep by me for another month, by which time I may have got something satisfactory to end on. But we must publish something to show what the work here has been, and please will you do as much propaganda as you can.

Don't forget to go on loving me.

To H.B.
BAGDAD, Sunday, June 14th, 1920.

The political tide ebbs and flows and we don't get much further. The mayor dropped in while I was breakfasting a few days ago, as his habit is, and told me that several of the leaders had approached him and asked whether if they accepted the mandate they could be sure that we really meant to set up an Arab Govt. He replied that they might be certain of it and that he was ready to go further into the matter with them at any time, but so far they have done nothing more. . . .

This morning I rode out before breakfast to see H. Naji and found a large party of people with him. We talked long about the Political situation, they pointing out a good many of our errors, more of omission than of commission. They were extremely reasonable and had my full sympathy. We all agreed that there was no reason why the mandate shouldn't work with goodwill on both sides. Haji Naji, who is heart and soul with us, took a wise part in this conversation. . . .

I'm quite well and it's not particularly hot, seldom up to 110. As long as I don't have fever or something silly I shall be all right, and I see no reason why I should have anything. . . .

To H.B.
BAGDAD, Sunday, July 11th, 1920.

A.T. has got permission from home to begin active preparation for the calling of a constituent assembly. All ex-deputies are going to be invited to meet in counsel and discuss the electoral basis and the method of election. It is, I think, rather a brilliant idea—we owe it to Mr. Forbes, the judge. . . .

I dined last night with the Bowmans—they had an Arab dinner party, very pleasant. . . .

I went to tea at the Civil Hospital with the French nuns in order to make arrangements with Capt. Braham for the opening of a small private hospital for better-class women. I have collected something over Rs. 20,000 towards it and though that isn't enough to build with it will suffice to put into order and furnish a little detached building which already exists. We shall have 4 rooms each with one bed and that will make a beginning. . . .

To H.B.
BAGDAD, July 20th, 1920.

Aurelia dined with me . . . . Still not very well. My household has been enlarged by the gift (from the Mayor's son) of a very young mongoose. It's a most attractive little beast. It sat in my hand this morning and ate fried eggs like a Christian.

The weather is fortunately mild, only about 106.

To H.B.
BAGDAD, July 26th, 1920.

. . . . Soon after I got to the office to-day I was visited by two distinguished Sunni magnates, fathers of turbans, one of them an advanced nationalist. I made them welcome and said it was long since I had had the pleasure of seeing them.

"Yes," they said, " we've come to you because you're beloved. Everyone in Bagdad praises you." This prelude indicated that there was something in the wind so I put a few tactful questions and discovered that they had come to find out if anything would be done to pacify the tribes. The upshot of it was that we sketched out a scheme for a joint Sunni and Shiah commission to go to Karbala and Najaf, and I took it to A.T.. . . The two are coming to-morrow to give a final decision, but I'm rather afraid they'll say they can't take it on. . . .

Well, if the British evacuate Mesopotamia, I shall stay peacefully here and see what happens. . . .

Darling Father, I do hope you enjoy my letters as much as I enjoy writing them! If they seem to you rather mad, I can only offer as excuse that I'm living in a perfectly mad world. Added to which the heat makes one a little light-headed. One just accepts what happens, from day to day, without any amazement. . . .

To H.B.
BAGDAD, August 2nd, 1920.

MY world hasn't grown any saner since I last wrote. . . . My view of the matter is in a nutshell this: whatever our future policy is to be we cannot now leave the country in the state of chaos which we have created, no one can master it if we can't. If we decided to withdraw at once we should have to send at least two divisions from India to extricate the troops and personnel we have here. Those 2 divisions or less might just as well be employed in bringing the country back to order. When that is done we can begin talking. . . .

I would give the Arabs a very long rope, as I've often said before, in the assurance that it is only if they want our help that we can help them, and in the certainty that if they are assured of the honesty of our intentions they will want our help. . . .

Capt. Clayton, Major Bullard and I, Major Bowman and others went to a patriotic play which was got up by ardent young nationalists. . . . Whenever the word independence occurred—which it did often—they clapped to the echo. I met on the most friendly terms everyone who had been doing his damnedest against us and we all shook hands in the greatest amity. While one of those who sit studiously on the fence whispered to me in anxiety "When in God's name are you going to release us from the terror of the tribes?" . . . . . .

It is touch and go—I'm quite unable to predict what will happen. Another episode like that of the Manchesters would bring the Tigris tribes out immediately below Bagdad. We are living from hand to mouth—I know it—and the situation is serious and might become very grave with any little swing in the scale.

Meantime I shall not go to India. . . .

The waste it all means and the inevitable bitterness it must engender, the difficulty in pulling anything straight after this terrific upheaval—well, it's no good thinking of it.

At least it's more profitable to think of how to find immediate palliatives.

Goodbye, dearest family.

To H.B.
August 8th, 1920.

The political situation is improving. The military position is growing more stable with the arrival of fresh troops from India. The Euphrates tribes are still in full rebellion but they have had one or two nasty knocks and they are said to be getting a little tired of jihad. If only they would throw their hands in before we are in a position to take extreme measures it would be an immense relief. Order must be restored but it's a very doubtful triumph to restore it at the expense of many Arab lives. . . .

To H.B.
BAGDAD, August 16th, 1920.

It's dawn of Monday morning. I've got to go to a prize giving at the native Church at 7:30 and I'll put in the time before I need dress in writing to you. Sunday is generally letter day but I was very busy yesterday getting ahead with a précis of the revolutionary movement which A.T. has asked me to write. It is a very difficult business to write history at such close quarters and it's complicated by the fact that one is so often interrupted in the morning at the office that there's seldom a good clear hour. . . .

The Bowmans left for Egypt yesterday—as much regretted by their Arab as by their English colleagues. Personally I shall miss them dreadfully.

And now I'll tell you about the revolution. The committee of ex-deputies co-opted at the beginning of the week a number of people among whom were 4 of the leading extremists. On Wed. these 4 all refused the invitation and at the same time the police gave warning that there was to be a monster meeting in the big mosque next day, after which a procession through the town was to be organized. It would undoubtedly have led to disturbances and that was the object desired. For the extremists have seen the ground cut under their feet by the formation of a moderate constitutional party round the committee of ex-deputies and they have no card left but an appeal to the mob. The police were therefore ordered to arrest the 4 leaders. I think they must have bungled the matter for they only got one, the others got away to Kadhimain and are now, I hear, in Najaf. Orders were then issued forbidding the holding of meetings in Mosques, together with a curfew—no one to be out in the streets after 10 p.m. The combined effect has been excellent as far as Bagdad is concerned. The town has returned to its normal life and I think there is scarcely anyone who doesn't breathe a sigh of relief. Most of them asked why it wasn't done sooner but I think that A.T. has behaved with great wisdom in the matter. He has waited until it was clear that if the agitation was allowed to continue the town would be given over to rioters—most of those who attended the mosque meetings were riffraff of the worst sort—and there he has struck for the protection of public security. And everyone knows that it isn't an attempt on his part to suppress Arab nationalist sentiment.

The worst news is that Col. Leachman has been ambushed and killed on his way from Bagdad to Ramadi. He was holding the whole Euphrates up to Anak single handed by means of the tribes, troops having all been withdrawn, and we don't know what will happen in those regions. . . .

[Mr. Humphrey Bowman was Director of Education in Iraq. He sends me the following striking account of Gertrude as seen in the midst of an Arab circle, not in the desert, but in Bagdad:

"Sir Edgar Bonham Carter was giving an At Home to a number of Arab notables in Bagdad in 1919. Only one or two British were there, Cooke and myself, possibly another. We were all sitting on chairs round the room as we do in the East, getting up whenever some special guest entered. At last the door opened and Gertrude came in. She was beautifully dressed, as always, and looked very queenly. Everyone rose, and then she walked round the room, shaking hands with each Arab in turn and then saying a few appropriate words to each. Not only did she know them all by name—there must have been 40 or 50 in the room—but she knew what to say to each . . . . . ."]

To H.B.
August 23rd, 1920.

We have also had the staunchest adherence from Fahad Bey of the Anazeh— the donor of my dogs. He wrote to A.T. and me last week saying that nothing would make him budge from his firm allegiance. From first to last he has never wavered and has given us all the help he can.

It has been rather cooler this week—enough cooler to make me catch cold, which doesn't however mean much as I do it easily. It's very difficult not to, for you go to bed in a temp. which makes a sheet too heavy a covering and wake at dawn chilled to the bone by a sudden drop of many degrees. We are sending away the wives of P.O.'s in the Provinces. I think it is the only thing to do. They have nearly all come in to Bagdad, where we haven't room for them, and the future is so uncertain that it's doubtful whether they will ever be able to go back— or their husbands either in many cases. I don't anticipate that we shall reinstall the political service in the Euphrates area, though what will take its place we don't foresee. It's a sad business to see the whole organisation crumble.

To H.B.
BAGDAD, August 30th, 1920.
[Gertrude visits the Naqib.]

While I was sitting with him this morning listening to his explanation of his neutral attitude throughout Ramadhan I was overcome—as I not infrequently am—with the sense of being as much an Asiatic as a European. For if I'm not too Asiatic to form a clear opinion, he made a pretty good case. . . .

To be able to exchange the frankest views with the Ancient East, as I do with the Naqib, is both amazing and delightful.

To F.B.
BAGDAD, September 5, 1920.

The truth is I'm very tired of being so hot. One always feels in September as if one could not bear it any longer. We had some bad days this week with a blazing wind, but really it's beginning to cool off a little. One doesn't need a fan till about 10 a.m., but fan or not my office nears 100 every afternoon. . . .

The problem is the future. The tribes don't want to form part of a unified state; the towns can't do without it. How are we going to support and protect the elements of stability and at the same time conform to the just demand for economy from home? For you can't have a central government if no one will pay taxes and the bulk of the population won't pay taxes unless they are constrained to do so. Nor will they preserve a sufficient amount of order to permit of trade. . . .

We are now in the middle of a full-blown jihad, that is to say we have against us the fiercest prejudices of a people in a primeval state of civilisation. Which means that it's no longer a question of reason. And it has on its side the tendency to anarchy which is all over the world, I think, the salient result of the war. When one considers it, it's very comprehensible that the thinking people should revolt at an organisation of the universe which could produce anything so destructive to civilization as the war. The unthinking people, who form the great mass of the world, follow suit in a blind revolt against the accepted order. They don't know how to substitute anything better, but it's clear that few things can be worse. We're near to a complete collapse of society— the end of the Roman empire is a very close historical parallel. We've practically come to the collapse of society here and there's little on which you can depend for its reconstruction. The credit of European civilisation is gone. Over and over again people have said to me that it has been a shock and a surprise to them to see Europe relapse into barbarism. I had no reply—what else can you call the war? How can we, who have managed our own affairs so badly, claim to teach others to manage theirs better? It may be that the world has need to sink back into the dark ages of chaos, out of which it will evolve something, perhaps no better than what it had.

To H.B.
BAGDAD, September 12th, 1920.

It's getting a little cooler, thank Heaven; but Sep. is a disagreeable month. The air is very still and rather sticky—where it gets its stickiness from I can't think—and the dust hangs in long low lines over the world. This morning I was out riding just after sunrise—it was difficult to decide whether the earth or the air was the more solid. The dust bars hanging over the horizon were like slabs of desert in the sky, and in the uncertain light of sunrays dust and damp, when I turned round to look for my dogs I couldn't see anything tangible, but I marked each one by the little golden dust cloud that it made as it ran. My dogs are very well. So's the parrot. But the mongoose has run away.

To H.B.
BAGDAD, September 19th, 1920.

. . . . Sir Percy knows what complete confidence there is between us and that I should always tell you exactly what I think or do. That I should be able to do so is to me the foundation of existence and it is entirely owing to you that you are to me not only a father but also the closest and most intimate friend. You have been the only person to whom I have related fully the ups and downs of these extremely difficult months and as far as anyone can relate without prejudice circumstances in which they have played a part, I have done so to you. You will therefore believe me when I tell you that it is only quite recently that I have realized how prominent a place I have occupied in the public mind here as the pro-Arab member of the administration. Over and over again lately I have heard from the frequenters of the coffee shops, my own servants and casual people up and down the bazaars, that I am always quoted in the coffee shop talk as the upholder of the rights of the Arabs. I have invariably replied that the talk is incorrect; it is H.M.G. which upholds the rights of the Arabs and we are all of us the servants of H.M.G.

To H.B.
BAGDAD, September 27th, 1920.

The most remarkable feature this week has been the weather. On the 21st, it rained quite hard enough to lay all the dust. There hasn't been anything like it since 1907, they say, and then not quite so early. Then we had two days of South wind and cloud, very hot and stuffy and finally the most terrific dust storm lasting many hours and followed by violent thunder storms. . . .

A. T. is going to India, Egypt and C'ple on his way home—that's his scheme. He wants to get a comprehensive view of the Eastern question. I told him you would be very glad to see him in London. . . .

What I hope Sir Percy will do is to give a very wide responsibility to natives of this country. It is the only way of teaching them how hard the task of government is. I think we must now wade through a long period of uncertainty and mistakes which, if they are wise enough and we patient enough may result in a more equable division of our respective spheres of activity. Up to now we've done it all. I should stand by and let them do it all for a bit and then see if a better adjustment is not possible. . . .

To H.B.
October 3rd, 1920.

This morning being Sunday I rode out before breakfast to see Haji Naji. He had a party of guests sitting in his arbour and he was showing off the 'sécateur' you sent him. "The first," he said, "that has been seen in the Iraq," and he proudly snipped off the branches of an adjacent mulberry tree to show how well it worked. I wished you had been there to see. I've been very agricultural this week. I attended a demonstration at the cotton farm where experiments are being made in various kinds of cotton and various treatments. About a dozen Bagdad landowners were present and were deeply interested. So was I. On an average of 3 years, a certain long-stapled American variety seems to be the most promising. There seems every reason to believe that we shall produce as good cotton as is grown anywhere in the world, and their yield is very large. . . .

There is one other party I didn't tell you about. Capt. Clayton and I went to tea with one of the leading Agail of Bagdad. The Agail are nearly all central Arabians; they invariably speak of themselves as subjects of Ibn Saud. They are the merchants and caravan leaders of the desert. I had an Agaili with me when I went to Hayil. They live in the right bank part of Bagdad—Karkh is its name— and they have a famous coffee shop of their own. I'm in intimate relations with them for they are the people from whom I get news. I do them a good turn whenever I can and they respond by coming in to see me whenever they return from Syria or Arabia and telling me what they've heard and seen. . . . The tea party was delightful. The walls of the divan are mellow with decades of tobacco smoke, the only furniture, benches round the room and one table for us at the upper end. In order to do us honour he had provided a tinned plum pudding for our special benefit. We scooped it out of the tin and eat it cold. A large and distinguished party of Agaili had been invited to meet us—all frequenters of my office—and we talked Arabian politics with great gusto for an hour and a half. During all that time Suliman stood in front of us and talked. It was a miracle of grace and poise. Incidentally, he has, like all Najdis, the most slender hands with long fingers and nails an American beauty might envy. Their hands are their most characteristic feature. They are seldom shaved but as a rule their beards are scanty—it is rare to see a full thick beard. Some are Wahabis, i.e., they do not smoke, but most of the frequenters of cities abandon the stricter rules of the desert creed. I do like them so much. They are to me an endless romance. They come and go through the wilderness as if it were a high road, and they all, most politely, treat me as a colleague, because I too have been in Arcadia. When they talk of tribes or sheikhs or watering places I don't need to ask who and where they are. I know; and as they talk I see again the wide Arabian horizon. . . .

To H.B. and F.B.
BAGDAD, October 10th, 1920.

I don't know what I should do without your weekly letters, they are the only link I have with the outer world. I do sometimes feel dreadfully isolated.

The Coxes were to have arrived yesterday but they've stayed an extra day in Amarah and Kut and don't get here until to-morrow. The delay was a godsend as far as I was concerned for I was prostrated with a violent cold yesterday and did not go out of the house. I'm better to-day and I hope I may be all right, to-morrow. . . .

I had a long talk with Sasun Eff the other day—I went to call on his sister-in-law and found all the men there eager to embark on talk. Sasun Eff said he felt sure that no local man would be acceptable as head of the state because every other local man would be jealous of him. He went on to throw out feelers in different directions—one might think of a son of the Sharif, or a member of the family of the Sultan of Egypt, if there was a suitable individual, or of the family of the Sultan of Turkey? I said that I for my part felt sure that Sir Percy didn't and couldn't mind whom they selected except that I thought the Turkish family was ruled out—it ought to be an Arab Prince. . . . Any one they think we are backing they will agree to, and then intrigue against him without intermission. It is not an easy furrow to plough! These reflections will throw an illumination on what is being said in the English papers, from which it would appear that Sir Percy has only to say "Hey Presto" for an Arab Government to leap on to the stage, with another Athene springing from the forehead of Zeus. You may say if you like that Sir Percy will play the role of Zeus but his Athene will find the stage encumbered by such trifles as the Shiah problem, the tribal problem and other matters, over which even a goddess might easily stumble. But if he's not a Zeus he is a very skilful physician and one in whom his patient has implicit confidence. That last item is our chief asset and it's clear to me that whatever line he may decide to pursue, it's up to us to follow him with all the strength and ability we may individually possess. The underlying truth of all criticism is however— and its what makes the critics so difficult to answer—that we had promised self-governing institutions, and not only made no step towards them but were busily setting up something entirely different. One of the papers says, quite rightly, that we had promised an Arab Government with British Advisers, and had set up a British Government with Arab Advisers. That's a perfectly fair statement. . . .

As to expenses, you realize that my living expenses here don't include what I get from England, clothes, books, etc. The price of everything is really appalling but the best way to remedy that is to get nothing more. Meantime as far as I'm concerned that's the course which providence has marked out for nothing has come though I've got bills for tricotine and things which Elsa kindly bought for me. I shan't pay them till the things arrive.

Tuesday, 12th October. A word to say that Sir Percy arrived yesterday, thank Heaven. The office is in rather a turmoil with no one knowing exactly what they ought to do next, so I can't write at length about his reception—I will next week. I'm taking on a sort of temporary Oriental Secretary job till people find their feet.

[I include here two historical summaries, written by Sir Percy Cox and Sir Henry Dobbs, respectively, of the years during which Gertrude worked under them in the East. I am most grateful to them for this very valuable help.]

By Major-GENERAL SIR PERCY COX, G.C.M.G. ETC.

Lady Bell, having decided to publish a series of letters written from the Middle East by her distinguished and lamented daughter, has requested me and my successor as High Commissioner, Sir Henry Dobbs, to write, each of us, a background to those letters, a sketch of events for the period during which her daughter was associated with us in the responsible and absorbing task of establishing national Government in Iraq under the guidance of Great Britain.

I cordially welcome the opportunity thus afforded me of paying a small tribute to the memory of a dear friend and most loyal and devoted comrade through eight years of strenuous service.

I first met Gertrude Bell at the house of mutual friends, the late Sir Richmond and Lady Ritchie, during the winter of 1909, which found me at home for a few weeks on duty from the Persian Gulf Residency. Sir Richmond had arranged for us to meet in order that Miss Bell might have an opportunity of discussing with me the possibility of carrying out during the coming year her long cherished ambition to penetrate into Central Arabia. Her particular objective at the time was Northern Nejd, the principality of Ibn Rashid, whose forbears, with their capital at Hayil, figured so prominently in the immortal pages of Charles Doughty. She was anxious to enter from one of the ports of the Arab coast of the Persian Gulf, lying within my sphere as British Resident. Unfortunately at that particular juncture inter-tribal relations between the principalities of Eastern Arabia were so disturbed that an expedition from that side would have been fore-doomed to failure and I was obliged to advise her to wait for a more favourable opportunity. She accordingly turned her attention once more to the western borderlands and the early spring of 1910 found her back again in Syria embarking on a five months expedition from Aleppo to Bagdad and thence onwards through northern Mesopotamia to Konia, a journey which she described on her return in a second book of travels, "Amurath to Amurath," published in 1911.

It was not until four years after our meeting, that she found herself, in

December 1913, once more in camp near Damascus, and this time she succeeded in giving the slip to tiresome Turkish officialdom and made a bid for northern Nejd. After an eventful and venturesome journey she returned safely from her wanderings in March 1914, with her object accomplished, but tired out with the trying conditions of desert travel and badly in need of repose; and hardly had she time to recover normal health, much less to devote herself to any account of her experiences, when the Great War broke out and claimed her for other service. There is little doubt that if she had been spared to return once again from Bagdad for a spell of leisure at home, her first task would have been to work up her notes for publication; but as, alas, this was not to be, it is some consolation to know that her old friend Dr. David Hogarth, our great authority on Arabia has prepared from her notes a paper which he will have read before the Royal Geographical Society ere this volume is in print; so that, at any rate, the results of the expedition have not been lost to geography.

After the brief intercourse of 1909-1910 above referred to, I did not meet Gertrude Bell again until the spring of 1916, when after a period of some months spent in our Arab Intelligence Bureau at Cairo, working up Arab questions and more particularly inter-tribal relations, she was sent on deputation to G.H.Q. Intelligence in Mesopotamia and reported herself at General Sir Percy Lake's Headquarters at Basrah. The intention was that having thoroughly mastered on the record the intricacies of Arab politics in the Hejaz she should now work up tribal questions from the Iraq side and maintain liaison in regard to these matters with her late comrades of the Arab Bureau at Cairo. After she had spent some weeks at her task, the military authorities decided that the particular service for which she had been deputed to Basrah had been completed as far as it could be for the time being, and finding a member of her sex a little difficult to place as a permanency in a military G.H.Q. in the field, they offered her services to me in my capacity of Chief Political Officer,—services which were gladly accepted. Thus began the 10 years of devoted service to myself and my successors, which were only terminated by her untimely death in harness on 11th of July 1926.

My duties as Chief Political Officer to the G.O.C.-in-Chief at the period when she joined me were partly military and partly civil. In the first place I was the medium of communication between the Military Commander and the civil population, and his adviser in his political dealings with them. For this purpose I worked as a member of his G.H.Q. Intelligence and was always in close touch with that branch, assisting in the examination of prisoners and spies, the sifting of infornation, the provision of informers and interpreters and so on. On the purely civil side it devolved on me, under the G.O. C.'s supreme control, to implement as far as the fluctuating tide of war allowed, the assurances which we had given to the Arabs at the beginning of the campaign, both in the Persian Gulf and in lower Mesopotamia,—assurances which it may be well to emphasise here.

As regards the Persian Gulf, our self-imposed task of maintaining Pax Britannica, had inevitably created for us in the course of several generations a series of treaties and obligations of responsibility towards the Arab rulers on its shores which there could now be no question of our disregarding. We had treaties of old standing with the Sultan of Muscat; with the Sheikhs of the Pirate (now the Trucial) Coast of Oman, with Bahrein, and with the Sheikh of Qatar. We were on intimate terms with Ibn Saud, the Wahabi chieftain of southern Nejd, who in 1913 had succeeded in extending his independent authority to the Coast of the Persian Gulf, and whose future prosperity and success depended mainly on our recognition and sympathetic co-operation in his plans of progress and reform. At the head of the Gulf the Sheikh of Koweit had been assured of our support against any Turkish encroachment on his independence; and finally, on the banks of the Shatt-el-Arab was the Sheikh of Moharnmerah, Arab by race though subject to Persia, who looked to us in view of the commercial stake we enjoyed in his territory to secure fair play for him in his relations alike with Persia and with Turkey.

These close connections of treaty and friendship were an invaluable asset to us when the time came to contemplate the lively probability of Turkey's entry into the war against us; but if an advantage was to be taken of them, it was clearly of primary importance that we should demonstrate to our friends at the outset the circumstances in which war had been forced upon us and should take such prompt action as would convince them that we were alive to the danger in which they would be placed, as friends of ours, and intended to take adequate steps to safeguard their interests as well as our own. Accordingly, the moment news of the outbreak of war with Turkey was received I was instructed to issue a proclamation in the above sense, assuring our Arab friends at the same time that their liberty and religion would be scrupulously respected, and that all we asked of them was that they should preserve order in their own territories and ensure that their subjects indulged in no action calculated to injure British interests. This was followed by a further proclamation guaranteeing to them and to Islam in general that so far as we were concerned, the Holy Places in the area of war should have complete immunity from molestation. With these assurances the Arab potentates were fully satisfied and thus it was that the benevolent policy pursued by us for many years past in our dealings with them now found its reward in an unwavering friendship, which was of incalculable value to us throughout the campaign.

It 'was in the same spirit that a few days later when the British Expeditionary Force first set foot on Turkish soil at Fao, I issued a similar announcement to the riverain Arabs, assuring them that it was with the Turks only that we were at war and not with the inhabitants of the country and that so long as the Arabs showed themselves friendly and refrained from going about armed or harbouring Turkish troops, they had nothing to fear from us.

In furtherance of this policy it was our duty as far as military exigencies permitted, to enable the peaceable inhabitants of the territory gradually falling under our occupation, to carry on their normal vocations; but the initial difficulties involved in setting up a civil administration with war in lively progress were naturally considerable and were greatly enhanced in this case by the fact that the Turkish régime having been almost entirely alien, all Turkish officials and those non-Turks who had been employed in the administration, fled with the retreating armies as each centre was evacuated, and we found no local material whatever with which to replace them. Consequently for the time being, and indeed for the whole duration of the war, personnel for the administration had either to be recruited from the British and the British Indian material serving with the Army, or to be borrowed from India. Nevertheless, as soon as we had settled down in Basrah a beginning was made towards the establishment of a system of government which would be consonant with the spirit of our announcements. For this branch of my duties I had separate Offices and Staff and divided my working hours between the Army G.H.Q., whether at the Base or in the Field, and my Civil Headquarters at Basrah. It was here that Gertrude Bell joined me in the circumstances above described, as also did Captain Arnold Wilson, (now Lieut. Colonel Sir Arnold Wilson, K.C.I.E., etc.). The latter had been serving with me for some years before the War, first in the Persian Gulf Residency and later at Mohammerah, but for the past year he had been on deputation as one of the British representatives on the TurkoPersian Boundary Commission, a body which had been surprisingly successful in its labours and had fortunately completed them just in time for its members to disperse before hostilities commenced. About the same time too I received a valuable reinforcement of officers from the Government of India, including Mr. Henry Dobbs, who later on, as Sir Henry Dobbs, was to succeed me as High Commissioner in Mesopotamia—a senior official of the Indian Civil Service, with mature experience in revenue and fiscal matters, who at once set himself to get the revenue administration on to an effective working basis. Other senior members of the Political Department of the Government of India placed at my disposal about the same time were Colonel S. G. Knox, afterwards judicial Commissioner and Colonel R. E. A. Hamilton, now Lord Belhaven and Stenton, who became Political Agent at Koweit, in succession to Major W. H. L. Shakespear. The latter had been deputed to the court of His Highness Ibn Saud on the outbreak of war and his tragic death in a desert battle between Ibn Saud and his rival Ibn Rashid deprived his country of a most gallant and capable officer whose services could ill be spared at the time. Another newcomer was Mr. H. St. J. Philby of the Indian Civil Service, afterwards to earn distinction as a traveller in Central Arabia. Other good men and true came and went according to the needs of my working staff which had to be augmented or modified as the tide mark of war advanced in our favour and left a continually expanding tract of country under our administration.

In this brief sketch it is not possible or necessary for me to deal with the military aspects of the campaign and I must pass over the eventful winter of 1915 and the spring of 1916, which witnessed Townshend's victorious advance up the Tigris, culminating in the battle of Ctesiphon; his retirement to Kut, with its siege and final surrender; and the terrible trials of our troops in their gallant attempts to relieve the beleaguered garrison, the moving story of which has been told so graphically by the official "Eye-witness," the late Umund Candler, in his

"Long Road to Bagdad."

During this period steady progress continued to be made with the creation of administrative machinery in all its branches throughout the Basrah Vilayet, and Gertrude Bell worked devotedly as Oriental Secretary to myself or my deputy, Captain Wilson, in the Bastah Secretariat. During the late summer of 1915, I had arranged to rendezvous at Ojair with the Sultan of Nejd for the purpose of concluding the Treaty negotiations, which had been interrupted by His Highness' abortive campaign above referred to, and a year later after the final signing of the documents, His Highness was invited first to a durbar at Koweit to meet the Sheikhs of Koweit and Mohammerah and other important tribal Sheikhs with whom we were now in touch; and afterwards to Basrah for a short visit, in the belief that it would be of interest and value to him to see the working, and the immense proportions, of a great military base and port such as Basrah had now become, and would also be a useful means of demonstrating to the inhabitants of the Basrah Vilayet the very close relations existing between us and the great Arab Chiefs of the principalities on their borders. I remember well with what delight and enthusiasm Gertrude Bell entered at this time into all the arrangements for Sultan Ibn Saud's visit, looking forward keenly as she did to making the acquaintance of this great and attractive actor on the Arabian stage; alike for the immediate interest of the prospect and also, I cannot help thinking, in the latent hope that it might lead to an expedition to his capital when the clouds of war had dispersed. Ibn Saud, who had heard me speak of Gertrude Bell and of her pre-war expedition to Hayil, had never before come in contact with any European woman and the phenomenon of one of the gentler sex occupying an official position with a British Expeditionary Force was one quite outside his Bedouin comprehension; nevertheless when the time came he met Miss Bell with complete frankness and sangfroid as if he had been associated with European ladies all his life.

Except for the interruption of this "royal visit" " and an occasional week end trip to Basrah to enable me to keep in touch with passing events in the sphere of the civil administration and to see to the welfare of my wife, who at this time was engaged in good works among the troops in Basrah, I was able to remain with Sir Stanley Maude's Headquarters on the Tigris front throughout the winter campaign, which saw the recovery of Kut, the sudden crossing of the Tigris at Shimran and the subsequent advance on Bagdad, ending in its occupation on the 11th of March 1917.

The fall of Bagdad was an event full of significance and pregnant with possibilities both for ourselves and for the enemy. Throughout the Empire and among our allies the brilliant success of General Maude's campaign aroused the utmost enthusiasm, so that the tragedy of Kut seemed almost effaced in the public mind; while for the Turks the loss of Bagdad not only deprived them of their base of operations in Mesopotamia but laid them open to an Anglo-Russian offensive in the Mosul Vilayet. The prospect of joining up with our Russian allies as a prelude to concerted operations in northern Mesopotamia had always been one to conjure with in Force "D." A year previous a Russian

Cossack patrol from General Baratoff's force, then at Kermanshah, had reached our lines at Ali Gharbi on the Tigris after a daring ride of 200 miles through the mountains of Pusht-i-kuh. They were naturally welcomed by us with great cordiality, and during the few days that they remained in our Camp to rest their horses before starting back, their Officers were decorated by the G.O.C.-in-Chief with the British Military Cross " in recognition of this exploit and on this, the first meeting of British and Russian troops, as allies in the field, for 100 years." The meeting of the two armies later on was consequently looked forward to with great expectations, destined unfortunately to be grievously disappointed. Though we knew it not at the time, the date of our victorious entry into Bagdad coincided almost exactly with the abdication of the Tzar and the Bolshevik upheaval, and the Russian Troops on the Persian line had already been impregnated with the virus of bolshevism and were getting out of control. It was consequently the more unfortunate that military exigencies not only precluded our extending our occupation up to the frontier of Iraq near Khanikin, but obliged us to acquiesce in the occupation of that town by General Batatoff's troops. Whatever its Military aspect might be this phenomenon greatly upset the political situation at the time. The inhabitants of Khanikin Had had bitter experience of a hostile Russian occupation in 1916, but now decided to refrain from all opposition, because on this occasion the Russians came as our allies and with our consent, if not at our request. A great revulsion of feeling, however, was caused by their behaviour and in the process we ourselves rapidly lost prestige and sympathy among a race which had always been friendly to us. Military considerations were of course paramount but this Russian occupation left us a legacy which gave trouble for a long time to come. After a couple of months the Russian force withdrew and their ravages in the district were completed by the Turks who forthwith reoccupied it and it was not until December 1918 that we were in a position to assume control ourselves. When we did so we found the town in a state of acute misery, for the Turks when they retired had left it in the joint clutches of starvation and disease and it was with these formidable adversaries that the work of administration was confronted. Major E. B. Soane, the remarkable character to whom the charge was entrusted and who in addition to a very strong personality possessed the then rare accomplishment of a fluent knowledge of the Kurdish language, laboured devotedly for months at his task, which grew in direct ratio to the success achieved, for no sooner did the Kurds on either side of the frontier hear that help was to be had from the British Authorities at Suleimaniyeh than they poured down from the mountains starving and typhus stricken, to be brought slowly back to health or else to die in our camps and hospitals. Nevertheless by the early summer of 1918 when Major Soane, worn out by incessant toil, was compelled to take a year's rest, the battle was won and his successor Major Goldsmith, found the crops springing up and repeopled villages arising from the ruins which had been wrought.

But I am straying too wide from the track and will return for a few moments to the days of our entry into Bagdad. We found the pre-war British Residency in use as a Hospital, in which the Turks had left us an unwelcome legacy in the shape of their worst cases of wounds and disease. Its sanitary condition was indescribable, but other hospitable accommodation was gradually found for the inmates and the Residency after a thorough cleansing and overhaul was fitted up as Army Headquarters, a function which it still fills for the Royal Air Force today: but whereas the military staff was already in being, my civil staff for the Bagdad Vilayet was nonexistent and had to be created. I was allotted a house on the river bank below the Residency which had before our entry been the Austrian Consulate and there I began to form a Secretariat. My first act on arrival had been to seek out any of the old local employees of the pre-war Residency Staff, both because I was anxious to learn what might have happened to them at the hands of the enemy and also because, if forthcoming, I knew they could be very useful to me at this period, with their knowledge of the communities and individual inhabitants of Bagdad. To my great regret I found the family of Narcessian, the faithful Armenian Dragoman of the Residency, in the depth of despair; their father had been sent for by the Turkish Police shortly before our arrival and had not returned. He was never heard of again nor was I able to obtain any evidence as to the precise fate which had befallen him, but he was a man who had doubtless made enemies in the course of his duties as British Dragoman, quite apart from any grudge the Turkish Police might have had against him, and there seemed little doubt that he had met with a violent death during the period of uproar which intervened between the Turkish retreat and our arrival. My next act was to visit His Reverence Saiyid Abdurrahman Effendi, the Naqib, or Chief Noble, of Bagdad; head of the Sunni community and custodian of the shrine of Abdul Qadir Gilani, upon whose attitude towards us and influence with the people of Bagdad a good deal depended. Under the old régime of Sultan Abdul Hamid the Naqib had enjoyed a position of great dignity and stood high in public esteem and no doubt owed a considerable debt of obligation to the former Government; but under the Young Turk régime he had become of less account and indeed had little to thank them for. At this time his position was obviously a delicate one and his attitude had naturally to be one of reserve, yet I enjoyed his frank and wise co-operation in all measures affecting the welfare of his countrymen and likely to mitigate as far as might be the rigours and inconveniences of a military occupation. I saw a great deal of him in the course of my duties and the feelings of mutual confidence which were established between us at this time were to stand me in good stead later on, and are now a grateful memory.

Directly the news of our occupation of Bagdad got abroad I was perforce overwhelmed with visitors; first the notables of Bagdad and then the tribal Sheikhs from near and far, many of whom had never submitted to the authority of the Turkish Government and were complete strangers to Bagdad. Some attempt had to be made to determine and record from whence these visitors came, what their relations were to one another and what was their relative importance among themselves, matters not at all easy for new comers to diagnose. It was in connection with this task that I began to feel the want of

Gertrude Bell's indefatigable assistance and decided to bring her and one or two others up from the Basrah Office to form a nucleus for my Secretariat at Bagdad. All sheikhly visitors from the countryside had to be interviewed, entertained, given small presents and sent back to their homes with injunctions to keep the peace and get busy with their agriculture; so that a great proportion of my time during daylight was spent in these interviews and Miss Bell acted as the strainer through which the individuals filtered through to me, accompanied by a brief note as to what their tribe was, where they came from and what they wanted. I was thus saved endless time in getting to the point. I remember that when I told him that some of my office staff were coming up from Basrah, including Miss Bell, the G.O.C.-in-Chief expressed considerable misgiving at the news, as he feared her arrival might form an inconvenient precedent for appeals from other ladies, but I reminded him that her services had been specifically offered to me by his predecessor as an ordinary member of my Secretariat; that I regarded and treated her no differently from any male officer of my Staff, and that her particular abilities could be very useful to me at the present moment. In due course she arrived and was not long in establishing happy personal relations with Sir Stanley Maude and it is a sad memory to me now that she and I were both members of his party at the entertainment in Bagdad City a few months later which proved to be his last appearance in public, before his tragic death from cholera a few days later, at the height of his success.

These first six months of our occupation of Bagdad were indeed no easy period for the Civil Administration. The Army was fully occupied consolidating its position round Bagdad and needed to husband its strength to the utmost for the coming winter campaign and so detachments for outlying places could not be spared; nor, for fear of inconvenient incidents, could civil officers be allowed to go far afield. In these circumstances it was naturally difficult for tribesmen to believe, especially in the face of the violent Turko-German propaganda which was rife at the time, that the existing régime at Bagdad was at all secure or that the Turks would not eventually return. Even in Bagdad itself great uncertainty prevailed as to the intentions of the Allies, even if they did win the war; in fact up to the time of our successful offensive in the Autumn of 1918 it was the general impression that the Central Powers would be victorious or at any rate that nothing more than a stalemate would result.

Those who prided themselves on their intimate acquaintance with world politics declared that Iraq would undoubtedly be handed back to Turkey in exchange for the liberation of Belgium. Such rumours found their echo among the Sheikhs in general, causing many of our firmest friends to waver, or at least to wait on events. Altogether, in view of the actual political situation and the fact that with our Occupation of the Bagdad Vilayet the military régime found itself confronted with many difficult problems of a non-military aspect, H.M's Government came to the conclusion that some development of my status as Chief Political Officer to the G.O.C.-in-Chief was now called for. Accordingly, from the beginning of July 1917, my designation was altered to that of " Civil Commissioner," and while I still, of course, remained subject to the supreme authority of the Army Commander I was given the right henceforth of direct communication with the Secretary of State for India, in whose name the instructions of H.M's Government, in other than military matters, were thereafter issued; and sound advice and judicious support from that Department of State never failed the head of the Civil administration during the three difficult years which were to pass until 1921, when in connection with a new and significant development of policy the direction of affairs in Iraq was transferred to the Colonial Office. But of this more anon.

During the period of which I am speaking, the summer of 1917, the limits of our occupation beyond Bagdad were roughly; on the right flank, Baquba, on the river Diyala; in the centre, Samarra, on the Tigris line; and on the Euphrates west of Bagdad, Falluja; and thence back to the Hindiyeh barrage on the same river.

On the Diyala the process of consolidation was necessarily slow, for not only had the country suffered greatly from long devastation by Turkish troops, but until the autumn of 1917 the canal-heads were still in the enemy's control.

The Tigris gave us no further trouble; those tribal leaders who had joined the Turks again on our retirement from Ctesiphon had thought it safest to remain with them when they in turn retreated towards Mosul; meanwhile their sons, or other suitable kinsmen, had been installed for the time being in their holdings along the river and were now occupied in the cultivation of their lands, much as in time of peace. A most favourable impression was created at this time in the Tigris area by our decision to rebuild Kut-al-Amara, a task which was undertaken partly from expediency and partly in the way of a memorial to those among the beleaguered garrison and friendly Arab inhabitants who had given their lives in the defence of the town. Kut, since the Turks evacuated it in their hurried flight before General Maude had been left completely deserted; a tottering ruin among the palm groves; its streets choked with mud or blocked with barricades; its houses riddled with shells or undermined with dug-outs. The work of reconstruction was supervised with much skill and judgment by the District Political Officer and the country-side saw in the regeneration of the town not only profit and advantage to themselves but also some pledge that a new order of things so solidly established must have come to stay.

On the Euphrates west of Bagdad there was little to be done for the moment and it was not until Sir Harry Brooking's successful push in November 1917 had brought about the capture of Ramadi that the tribal Sheikhs of that area began to come in.

On the middle Euphrates, from the Hindiyeh barrage to Samawa, the position was a curious one. Not a single British soldier was located south of the barrage until December 1917; nevertheless that area being the centre of an important grain growing district, irrigated by the Euphrates canals, could not in the interests of the Army be altogether neglected and a Political Officer had accordingly been sent to Hillah in May 1917. His authority however did not extend to Diwaniyeh and southward thereof, where the local Sheikhs, after their visit to me on our first entry into Bagdad, had to be left pretty much to their own devices. It was typical of our slender hold on the middle Euphrates during this first summer that a small Turkish detachment which on our occupation at Bagdad had found itself isolated at Diwaniyeh and unable to get away with the retreating army, held out there until the end of August. It was commanded by a fire-eating Circassian, who, having shot his superior officers when they showed a disposition to surrender, had barricaded himself and his party in a caravan-serai on the river bank and completely terrorised the inhabitants, who regarded their unwelcome guest and his bomb-throwing men with no little dismay and made several attempts to oust them lest their presence should involve the town in hostilities with us. It was only when a visitation from some air-craft convinced him that the game was up that he surrendered with the 30 odd men who had stood by him to the end. On his arrival at Bagdad I had occasion to interview this gentleman and learnt that he considered that the Turks having forgotten him and left him completely in the lurch., he was now free to offer himself for service either with us or with the Arab Army in Hejaz. His artless overture could not however be accepted and as an officer-prisoner he spent the remainder of the war in the less exciting atmosphere of a prisoner's camp in India. He was a stout-hearted, attractive fellow; I trust fortune has since smiled on him.

But the most thorny problem on the Euphrates at that time was not so much the tribes as the Holy Cities of Islam, Karbala and Najaf. As in other cases on the lower Euphrates the Sheikhs of these towns, after their visit to me at Bagdad, had been sent back to their homes with pious instructions from me to maintain law and order themselves; and in order to strengthen their hands and give them some official recognition, small monthly allowances were provided for them; but before many weeks had passed it became evident that the arrangement was working unsatisfactorily both for the towns and for us. On the one hand the Sheikhs were found to be abusing their positions and making hay while the sun shone; while, worse still, the existence of a brisk trade in supplies to the enemy, both on the Iraq front and in Syria, was brought to light. If further trouble was to be avoided closer control had clearly become essential, and British Political Officers were accordingly posted at Karbala, and at Kufa in the Shamiyeh district on the border of which lies Najaf. These officers for the time being had to rely entirely on their own judgment and force of character and were often placed in positions of great difficulty and no little personal risk. Karbala it is true gave no serious trouble, but Najaf, where the town was in the hands of a lawless crew of local Sheikhs, remained a thorn in our side for some time to come. Fortunately, while the urgent need of food supplies for the population no less than for the army endowed the Euphrates basin with an ever increasing importance, military stringency had been somewhat eased as the danger of any serious attempt on the part of the enemy to move against Bagdad was diminishing, and so it was considered that troops could now be spared to complete the effective occupation of the area behind our fighting line. I accordingly made a tour of the district in December 1917 in order to be in a position to advise the G.O.C.-in-Chief as to the various points where, from the administrative point of view, detachments could advisably be placed. It was of course undesirable, and indeed incompatible with our previous announcements, to place troops in the Holy places themselves, and this made it especially difficult to exercise full control at Najaf, where the lawless elements in the town were being excited by persistent Turko-German propaganda, clear evidence of which was found a little later among enemy papers captured by our troops at Ramadi and Hit. Unfortunately affairs here culminated in the murder of a most promising young officer, Captain W. L. Marshall, who after serving with much credit in a similar post in the Holy City of Kadhimain was selected for the difficult charge at Najaf on account of his special qualifications and experience.

At the time of this tragedy I myself was on my way to Cairo to attend a conference regarding Arab affairs, but thanks to effective handling of the matter by the Commander-in-Chief and my deputy Colonel Arnold Wilson, heavy retribution was meted out to those concerned, 12 persons suffering the death penalty, while five were transported for life and two for a shorter period.

At Cairo under the hospitable roof and wise direction of the High Commissioner, Sir Reginald Wingate, I found a gathering of distinguished officers immediately concerned with the Arab problems of the moment; David Hogarth, once "A Wandering Scholar in the Levant" now, as I write, President of the Royal Geographical Society, at that time (as Commander Hogarth, R.N.V.R.) Director of the Arab Bureau: Ronald Storrs, Oriental Secretary at the Residency, the "Perfect Storrs" of King Hussein's despatches, since knighted and now Governor of Cyprus : Gilbert Clayton, Director of Intelligence at Cairo, now Sir Gilbert Clayton and (1927) on an important mission to King Ibn Saud: George Lloyd, now Lord Lloyd, our High Commissioner in Egypt: and last but not least T. E. Lawrence, soon to win lasting fame for his exploits with the Arab contingent and later for his wonderful story of "The Revolt in the Desert." A truly brilliant constellation!

Our deliberations ranged over all the problems in which we in Mesopotamia and they in the Hejaz were mutually interested. I was chiefly concerned with the difficult one with which both alike were confronted in the bitter personal relations existing between our two Arab allies King Hussein and the Sultan of Nejd; relations which made it hard to decide how most advantage could be derived from their co-operation, either in combination or independently. I should mention that during the preceding winter an important Mission, consisting of Mr. H. St. J. Philby, on my behalf, Colonel R. E. A. Hamilton, Political Agent at Koweit, representing Koweit interests, and Colonel F. Cunliffe-Owen, on behalf of the military authorities at Bagdad, had proceeded to the capital of the latter potentate at Riyadh, to report on the situation in Central Arabia generally and in particular on the possibilities of a renewed campaign against Hayil, where Ibn Rashid was still active in Turkish interests and a difficult factor in the situation. Their report had been received shortly before I left for Cairo.

While there I received a summons to proceed on to London for the discussion of various current questions connected with Mesopotamia, and again, while en route back to Bagdad, I was directed to make a further diversion to

Simla to confer with the Government of India. On arrival there I learnt that His Majesty's Minister at Teheran, Sir Charles Marling, who for months past had been having an extremely harassing time in the endeavour to combat Turko-German activities in Persia and the lively pressure which they were exercising upon the Persian Government, had been ordered home on sick leave and that it was desired that I should relieve him. I ventured to urge that having been with the Army in Mesopotamia from the commencement of the War I would much prefer to see the campaign through in my present post, but as it was considered that with British troops on the Bagdad-Enzeli line and questions for discussion continually arising between His Majesty's Minister and the G.O.C. in Mesopotamia, it was of great importance that the incumbent of the British Legation for the time being should be an officer with war-time experience of events and conditions in Mesopotamia and Persia, I did not feel justified in pressing my objections and left forthwith for Bagdad and Teheran. I halted at Bagdad only long enough to collect a convoy of cars for the conveyance of my wife and myself and our meagre war-scale belongings and we proceeded with all despatch to Teheran. At the moment of our passage the question of Persia's entry into the war against us was hanging by the slenderest of threads, her idea apparently being that as the Central Powers were evidently going to win, it would be profitable for Persia to be in with them at the finish. I even received a telegram at Hamadan, en route, suggesting that I was too late for the fair and had better not come further, but we pushed on without incident and I relieved Sir Charles Marling on the 15th September 1918, he returning by the same convoy next day.

During the 20-odd months that I spent as British representative at Teheran events had continued to move apace in Mesopotamia. In fact at the time I left Bagdad both General Allenby and General Marshall were on the point of launching their respective autumn campaigns. In Palestine the former's forces were concentrating in the coastal plain and on September 19th commenced those brilliant operations which resulted in the destruction of the Turkish army, and the occupation of Damascus and Aleppo. On October 1st the desert mounted corps and the Arab army entered Damascus amidst scenes of great enthusiasm.

In Iraq, Sir William Marshall opened his campaign on the 23rd October, determining to combine a frontal attack on the Turkish position across the Tigris at the Fatha Gorge, with the advance of a column simultaneously from Kifri, with the object of threatening the Turkish communications. With such success were his plans crowned that by the 30th October the greater part of the opposing force had surrendered and the pursuit of the remainder was in active progress; we were within 12 miles of Mosul the following day when news of the Armistice reached the Commander-in-Chief. Two days later Mosul itself was occupied.

As I have explained in an earlier paragraph, the Turkish Administration in Mesopotamia having been almost entirely an exotic one and the personnel having disappeared with the retreating troops as we advanced, we had no alternative, if we were to fulfil our promises to the inhabitants, but to create a provisional administration from the only sources available to us during the war, namely British and British Indian personnel drawn from the Army or borrowed from India. No other course was possible either for myself, in so far as there was any personal element in the matter, or for my locum tenens, when I proceeded on deputation to Persia. There has been a disposition in some quarters to suggest that having regard to the pronouncement made to the inhabitants by Sir Stanley Maude on our entry into Bagdad, under instructions from home, and to the Anglo-French declaration promulgated by his successor Sir William Marshall in November 1918, alluding respectively to the realization of the "natural aspirations of the noble Arabs" and "the establishment of national government" that, on the conclusion of the Armistice some prompt nationalization of the administration should have been attempted. This argument is plausible in theory and had the settlement of the peace terms followed closely on the heels of the Armistice it might have been feasible in practice; but the actual course of events was far otherwise.

The work of peace proceeded very slowly; six months had already elapsed before the terms to be imposed on Turkey were even discussed. It was not until May 1920 that, as the result of the San Remo Conference, the allocation of the Mandate for Mesopotamia to Great Britain was made known and even this announcement remained inoperative until confirmed in August 1920 by the Treaty of Sèvres, destined in turn never to be ratified. Meanwhile the spirit of President Wilson's 14 points, with their potent element of " self determination," was gradually permeating the East—not only Mesopotamia but Islam in general—while at the same time our military position in the conquered territory was rapidly being weakened by the reduction of the army in Iraq to the irreducible minimum. A vast tract of country from Mosul to the Persian Gulf now lay under our civil administration and it would have been nothing short of dangerous, apart from the mere loss of efficiency involved, to embark upon any drastic change in the structure of that administration while the situation was so fluid. I emphasise this aspect of the question because when disturbances arose later, there was a disposition, as is so often the case when arrangements do not work quite according to plan, to confuse incidental phases of the unrest with its fundamental causes.

By the end of the war the people of Mesopotamia had come to accept the fact of our occupation and were resigned to the prospect of a permanent British administration; some, especially in Basrah and the neighbourhood, even looked forward with satisfaction to a future in which they would be able to pursue their commerce and agriculture with a strong central authority to preserve peace and order. Throughout the country there was a conviction, which frequently found open expression, that the British meant well by the Arabs, and this was accompanied by a frank appreciation of the increased prosperity which had followed in the track of our armies and, no doubt, by a lively sense of favours to come, in the way of progress and reform. But with the Armistice, and the Anglo French declaration by which it was immediately followed, a new turn was given to the native mind. In Bagdad, where political ambitions are more highly developed than elsewhere in Iraq, within a week of the publication of the Declaration the idea of an Arab Amir for Iraq was everywhere being discussed and in Mohammedan circles met with universal approval, though there was no consensus of opinion as to who should fill the rôle. At first the choice hovered between a son of Hussein, Sherif of Mecca, (later become King of the Hejaz); a member of the family of the Sultan of Egypt; and a magnate of Mosul. The venerable Naqib of Bagdad was also mentioned, and in some quarters a preference for a republic was expressed; but the latter idea was repugnant to most Moslems, while the Naqib showed no disposition to abandon his dignified religious seclusion in exchange for High Office of State.

Meanwhile Colonel Wilson, Acting Civil Commissioner, received instructions from H.M's Government to endeavour to elicit the views of the population of the occupied territories on the following points:-

(1) Were they in favour of a single Arab State under British guidance extending from the northern boundary of the Mosul Vilayet to the Persian Gulf?

(2) If so, did they consider that the new State should be placed under an Arab Amir?

(3) In that case, whom they would suggest?

On the first point there proved to be unanimous agreement. On the other two points the replies forthcoming were so divergent that they afforded little indication to H.M's Government as to the general feeling of the country and for the moment the solution of the problem remained in abeyance; I am speaking of the winter of 1918-19. During the ensuing year considerable progress was made with the introduction of natives of the country into the administration in subordinate positions, but not always with happy results. Meanwhile uncertainty as to the policy and precise intentions of H.M's Government still prevailed and the local situation was much complicated by the course of events in Syria. There an Arab Government assisted by several British advisers had been set up, from Aleppo to Damascus, immediately after General Allenby's entry in October 1918. At its head was the Amir Faisal, and it was practically independent as far as administration was concerned, though under the supreme control of the British Commander-in-Chief and upheld by the presence of his troops. During the campaign of the previous year the leading officers of Faisal's army had been nearly all of Iraqi origin, many of them Bagdadis, and they avowedly aimed at a federated Arab state of Syria and Iraq under an Arab prince; accordingly when in March 1920 Faisal was proclaimed King of Syria the Iraqis responded by proclaiming his brother the Amir Abdullah, King of Iraq. Hardly had this incident occurred when on the 5th May the assignment of the Iraq mandate to Great Britain was publicly announced, and of course set all tongues a wagging.

Meanwhile, as acting Minister in Persia, I was naturally absorbed in the heavy duties of my own sphere and had not fully realised the turn which matters were taking in Iraq. I was the more surprised therefore to receive a telegram one morning from H.M's Foreign Office, informing me that it was desired that I should return to my post in Mesopotamia; but that on handing over to my successor in H.M's Legation I was to come first to London. The particular juncture from the point of view of our Persian interests seemed to me the worst possible one for a change of horses, but there were obvious limits to which I could press that point of view without danger of being misunderstood and having with due deference submitted my own opinion I resigned myself to the final instructions of H.M's Government and began to prepare for early departure. In due course my relief arrived and on 10th June my wife and I left Teheran, reaching Bagdad 4 days later. There we stayed with Colonel Wilson for 2 days while arrangements were being made for our onward journey, and I was able to learn from him and from Gertrude Bell the latest developments of the situation. A few days previously, on the 2nd June, Colonel Wilson had interviewed a self appointed Committee of 15 Bagdadis, which had been formed to voice opposition to the Mandate and had asked to be allowed to lay their views before the Civil Commissioner. After hearing what they had to say Colonel Wilson had undertaken to urge H.M's Government to expedite to the utmost a definite pronouncement of policy and in communicating the purport of the interview to London, he suggested abandonment of the idea of a provisional Government, recommending in the alternative that as soon as the terms of the Mandate had been settled a Constituent Assembly should at once be convened to deliberate upon the future form of Government. An announcement was accordingly drafted in the terms of which, just before leaving Bagdad, I concurred so far as concerned myself, and with the approval of H.M's Government this was sent to the leading delegates a few days later, on the 20th June. It stated that Mesopotamia was to be constituted an independent state under the guarantee of the League of Nations and subject to the Mandate of Great Britain, and that Sir Percy Cox was to return in the autumn to establish a provisional Arab government, pending preparation of a permanent organic law, to be framed with due regard to the rights, wishes, and interests of all communities of the country. But, alas, by now the fuse of disaffection had burnt too close to the powder, and probably nothing could have prevented the explosion. On 2nd July the tribesmen at Rumaithah, in the Lower Euphrates area, broke into open revolt.

By the time I reached London a few days later, the public at home were thoroughly disturbed at the turn things were taking in Iraq and a strong agitation was at work in a certain section of the Press which demanded that we should cut our losses and evacuate the country.

H.M's Government too were greatly exercised by the disquieting telegrams now coming in from Bagdad and there was considerable divergence of view as to what was the wisest course to pursue. But in any case it was clear that the rising must be suppressed before any other course of action was possible and the question at issue really was as to whether, after the restoration of law and order, we should cut our losses, abandon the Mandate and evacuate the country, or immediately set up a national Government, if that was really a practical alternative with reasonable chances of success. Asked for my opinion as the officer on the spot, I replied that to my mind evacuation was unthinkable; it would mean the abandonment of the Mandate and of the seven or eight millions worth of capital assets which we had in the country; the complete violation of all the promises we had made to the Arabs during the war, and their inevitable re-subjection to chaos and the hated yoke of the Turk as soon as we left; and lastly that an evacuation, which would arouse the active resentment of the betrayed inhabitants, could only be carried out without bloodshed if at least another division were sent to see it safely through. As to whether the alternative policy of establishing forthwith a national Government had a reasonable chance of success, I replied that without being too confident, I thought it had, and that the risk was at any rate worth taking if regarded as the only alternative to evacuation. Considerable discussion followed but ultimately I was asked whether if this course was decided upon I was prepared to undertake the task. I replied in the affirmative and left for Bagdad with my instructions by the next mail. It is no little satisfaction to me, six years later, to know that the ship thus launched on a somewhat tempestuous sea has safely reached port, and that so far as we are concerned the venture may be regarded on the whole as an imperial success. The Kingdom of Iraq has been placed on its feet, and its frontiers defined its future prosperity and progress rest with the Iraqis themselves.

But come what may, I can imagine no case in which H.M's Government have implemented their promises and obligations and pursued their settled policy with more complete good faith and resolution; dismayed neither by persistent and organised newspaper campaigns, nor by the interminable delays and difficulties which marked our peace negotiations with Turkey.

While these deliberations were going on in London, the rising in the Bagdad Vilayet was gathering force and reinforcements had to be drafted in from India for its suppression, so that by the time I reached Basrah on 1st October 1920, though active disaffection still smouldered in some places, the main centres of disturbances were under control, and the general situation no longer gave much cause for alarm.

I reached Bagdad on 5th October and a day or so later took over charge from Sir Arnold Wilson, who proceeded on leave. The task before me was by no means an easy or attractive one. The new line of policy which I had come to inaugurate involved a complete and necessarily rapid transformation of the facade of the existing administration from British to Arab and, in the process, a wholesale reduction in the numbers of British and British-Indian personnel employed. Many of the individuals affected had served with the utmost devotion during most difficult times and some had even abandoned all idea of returning to their pre-war posts in the hope of making a career in Iraq., Added to that not a few of the British element were sceptical—and one could not blame them for their misgivings—as to the likelihood of the new enterprise succeeding, and did not disguise their feelings. But fortifying myself with the conviction that the project had at least an even chance of success, and was at any rate the only alternative to evacuation, I took heart of grace. My position however, was a very solitary one to begin with and the presence of Gertrude Bell and of Mr. Philby and Mr. C. C. Garbett both of the I.C.S. whom I had brought out with me from home was a great asset to me at this time. Except for a short spell of leave in England and a sojourn in Paris in the summer of 1919, the former had been in Bagdad with Sir Arnold Wilson throughout the two years of my absence at Teheran and had all the personnel and politics of the local communities at her fingers end, while I knew that her own ideas and those of the two Indian Civilians on the subject of Arab aspirations were such that I could be sure that at any rate in principle they were heart and soul in sympathy with the present policy of government. A year later I had to part company with Mr. Philby because at the stage of development at which we had then arrived his conception of the policy of H.M's Government began to diverge too much from mine, but I none the less readily recognise the great value he was to me in the early days. As regards the others, many of whom were strangers to me, it necessarily needed a little time for me to get my bearings; but whatever the primary feelings of many of my comrades may have, indeed must have been, most of them gradually came round to the view that as an alternative to the bag and baggage policy the new experiment was worth trying and was not necessarily doomed to failure. At any rate they rendered devoted service notwithstanding that for a long time to come the question of their future careers continued to hang in the balance, pending conclusion of peace with Turkey.

Though, as I have said above, the back of the rebellion was practically broken by the time I reached Basrah, a good many sections of the tribes in the Bagdad Vilayet were still "out," and it was not until February that the rising could be said to have been finally cleared up. Meanwhile, it did not take me long after my arrival at Bagdad to realise that I was being confronted at every turn with questions of policy affecting the future of Iraq which I did not feel justified in disposing of myself without consultation with the representatives of the people. As an immediate expedient therefore, I determined to institute at once a Provisional Government which, under my control and supervision, should be responsible for the administration and political guidance of the country until the general situation had returned to normal and a start could be made with the creation of national institutions. It was here that I felt that my venerable friend the Naqib, who had given me such friendly co-operation on our first occupation of Bagdad, could now—if he would—render great and patriotic service, and I decided to appeal to him to preside over the proposed Council of State. Age and failing health might well have excused him from emerging from the studious seclusion of a Darwish in which he had preferred to spend the latter years of his life, but on October 23rd when I appealed to him, in the interests of his country, to shoulder the task, he courageously rose to the occasion, though with no little hesitation, and agreed to undertake the formation of a Cabinet. The high religious and social position of the Naqib and the universal respect he inspired placed his motives above all suspicion and endowed the Council of State with the necessary dignity and I shudder to think how my early efforts would have fared had he failed me at this time. For one of his venerable age and retired habits, it was a signal act of patriotism for which I could not be too grateful. The Council comprised 8 portfolios, Interior, Finance, Justice, Defence, Public

Works, Education and Health, Commerce, and Religious Bequests, and included, Saiyad Talib Pasha, eldest son of the Naqib of Basrah; Sassun Effendi Heskail who commanded universal respect and confidence as a leading representative of the Jewish Community in Baghdad; General Jaafar Pasha el Askeri who had served with much distinction both during the war and afterwards in King Faisal's regime in Syria; and Abdul Latif Pasha Mandil a native of Nejd and one of the leading notables and merchants of Basrah.

The principal questions to which the Council had to give attention were the return from internment on Henjam Island of a number of the leaders of the late revolt; the repatriation, at the expense of the Government, of Iraqi Officers who had been serving in the Hejaz Army or in the Arab régime at Damascus, and who were left stranded on its collapse; the organization of a Civil Administration under Iraqi officials; the drafting of the electoral law; and a scheme for the formation of an Iraq Army. Under the Naqib's wise direction the Council carried on their work with surprising efficiency and absence of friction; and in the meanwhile many other Iraqis of experience and education who had held civil or military appointments under the Turks, as well as private individuals, were streaming back to their country and becoming available for employment under the new régime. It was in fact the advent of this contingent from Syria, who had mostly been enthusiastic adherents of Amir Faisal's cause, which started, or revived, the demand for him in Iraq, and of course at this time the question of the new ruler and the character of the permanent government which was to succeed the present provisional régime was being discussed in every coffee-shop.

In the meanwhile, in connection with the new departure of policy in Iraq the control of its destinies had been transferred from the India Office to the Colonial Office, of which Mr. Winston Churchill had now assumed the portfolio on transfer from the War Office. In order speedily to acquaint himself with the strings of his sphere and to consider the various aspects of the future of the Middle East, he determined to summon a conference at Cairo early in March, which I, among other British representatives in this region, was bidden to attend. Thanks to the satisfactory working of the provisional Government, I was able to leave Bagdad at the end of February in H.I.M.S. "Hardinge" in company with Sir Aylmer Haldane, G.O.C. in Mesopotamia, taking with me Sasun Effendi, Minister of Finance, and Jaafar Pasha, Minister of Defence in the Provisional Iraq Government; and among the British Staff, Major General E. H. Atkinson, Adviser to the Ministry of Works; Lieut. Col. S. Slater, I.C.S., Financial Adviser; and Miss Gertrude Bell, Oriental Secretary. Major General Sir Edmund Ironside, Commanding the troops in Persia was also a member of the party, while Sir Edgar Bonham Carter, Judicial Adviser, held charge during my absence.

Apart from the incidental advantage of achieving personal touch with our new Ministerial Chief, who had been Secretary of State for War when I had last met him in the council chamber, and of being able to discuss with him Mesopotamian problems in general, it was clear that the main questions which would have to be threshed out at the Conference would be, the reduction of the present heavy expenditure; the qualifications of the various possible candidates for the throne of Iraq; the treatment of the Kurdish provinces; and the nature and composition of the force to be created for the defence of the new State in the future.

As regards the question of expenditure, if my memory serves me right the figure for the past year had been 37 millions sterling, whereas the Commander-in-Chief and I had come prepared with a draft scheme providing for reduction forthwith to 20 millions, with a progressive annual reduction thereafter, until the irreducible minimum should be reached.

The Secretary of State seemed no little relieved at the receipt of this preliminary news on our arrival.

As to the second question, it was easiest to arrive at a result by the process of elimination. My experience of public feeling on the question in Iraq had convinced me that among the several local candidates whose names had been suggested from time to time there was no individual who would be accepted or even tolerated by all parties in Iraq, while among the non-Iraqi possibilities there was no doubt whatever that one of the family of the Sherif of Mecca (King Hussein of the Hejaz) would command the most general if not the universal support of the inhabitants. I myself knew none of the family except from hearsay, but in the absence of any fresh candidate who might be suggested at the Conference, I went to Cairo prepared to recommend that that one of King Hussein's 4 sons whom a consensus of opinion should decide to be the most likely to fit the part, should be allowed to take his chance with the people of Iraq. It is common knowledge that the Amir Faisal won the ballot.

The other important question discussed was the treatment to be accorded to the Kurdish districts in the mandated territory and in this connection it was decided to make an attempt to ascertain the wishes of the Kurdish communities as to the degree of their prospective inclusion in, or separation from, the Iraq State.

But before the results could be made public it was incumbent on the Secretary of State on his return home to lay before the Cabinet the conclusions reached at the Conference, and unfortunately owing to the pre-occupation of H.M's Government with matters of grave importance at home, the much needed announcement on the subject by the Secretary of State was delayed until June.

On the 13th June, on the strength of telegrams received by Iraqis from the Hejaz, news was published in Bagdad that the Amir Faisal was leaving for Iraq. Friendly telegrams passed a day or two later between King Hussein and His Highness the Naqib and on 22nd Amir Faisal sent a personal wireless greeting to the Naqib announcing his early arrival at Basrah. Meanwhile the publication of the Secretary of State's pronouncement of policy had given to the bulk of the population that for which they had been asking, namely guidance from the Government whose obligation it was to offer advice. The express exclusion of a republican form of Government was recognised to be in accord with the traditions of Islam while the assurance of H.M's Government that they would regard the Amir Faisal as a suitable ruler should he be chosen by the people of Iraq dissipated apprehensions born of previous misunderstandings. But the Amir himself was his own best advocate. It was as the result of the popular tributes that he received during the first fortnight of his presence in Iraq that His Highness the Naqib, without any consultation with me, proposed to the Council on July 11th a resolution, which was unanimously approved, that the Amir Faisal should be declared King, on condition that his government should be a constitutional, representative and democratic one. On receiving a copy of the resolution according to the usual routine, I replied that before concurring in or confirming it I felt it necessary to fortify myself with direct evidence of the choice of the people by means of a referendum and the task of carrying out the measure was at once put in hand. The people of the Sulaimaniyeh District of Southern Kurdistan decided to abstain, as they were at liberty to do, from taking any part in the election of a King for the Iraq; with this exception the referendum was applied throughout the country and the results showed 96 per cent. of the votes to be in favour of the Amir Faisal's election, the remaining 4 per cent. coming mainly from the Turcoman and Kurdish communities of Kirkuk. On 18th August the Ministry of the Interior informed His Highness the Naqib, as President of the Council, that an overwhelming majority of the people supported the Amir Faisal's election and accordingly on 23rd August in the presence of representatives of all local communities and deputations from every Liwa and Iraq, except Sulaimaniyeh and Kirkuk, I proclaimed His Highness the Amir Faisal to have been duly elected King of Iraq and at the same time announced his recognition as King by His Britannic Majesty's Government.

Careful to tread with dignity and in conformity with the constitutional practice usual on the accession of a Sovereign, His Highness The Naqib and the Provisional Government formally tendered their resignation to the King, who while thanking them for their services requested them to continue in Office until a new Cabinet should be formed. It was then my grateful duty to intimate to the Naqib that His Majesty George in recognition of his services to his country had pleased to confer on him the high distinction of Knight Grand Commander of the Order of the British Empire. King Faisal followed with a speech in which he stated the principle by which his Government would be guided, insisting on the maintenance of the alliance between Great Britain and Iraq which he said should be embodied in an instrument to be confirmed by the National Congress as soon as convened.

But it was an insecure and troubled heritage on which the new King of Iraq had entered. On the North the Turks, though theoretically the position was one of prolonged armistice, pending conclusion of peace, were in fact clearly hostile. Turkish garrisons and posts along the frontier were increased and the Kurds incited to rise. In June 1921 a Turkish Official reached Rowanduz within the Iraq frontier, with a small party of irregulars, stirred up all the tribes in the neighbourhood and intermittently kept the whole of Kurdistan in a ferment until finally expelled in the spring of 1923. In June 1922 an able Commander of

Turkish Irregulars, bearing the sobriquet of " Yuzdemir," arrived in Kurdistan and embarked on an intensive campaign among the tribes, some of their contingents advancing as far as Rania. Disaffection soon spread to the tribes of Sulaimaniyeh; the Harnavand revolted and a general cry arose from Sulaimaniyeh that the only way to compose the situation was to allow back Sheikh Mahmud who had been deported by us in 1919. As we were not disposed to reoccupy the district for the present nothing was to be lost by giving Sheikh Mahmud another trial and he was installed after giving the most binding assurances. Similarly, on the desert frontier of Iraq to the south-west, the Bedouin tribes had since the early part of 1921 been in a continual state of unrest as the result of the operations of the Sultan of Nejd against his enemy Ibn Rashid and the Shammar tribes of Hayil. In consequence a large influx into Iraq of fugitive Shammar went on throughout the year 1921 and naturally had a deplorable effect on the relations between Iraq and Nejd, which was aggravated, when, exalted by his capture of Hayil in November, Ibn Saud claimed allegiance from the eastern Anizah tribe which had always been attached to Iraq. In the following March a serious attack took place by a strong raiding party of Ibn Saud's "Akhwan," as the Wahabis now style themselves, upon a harmless encampment of pastoral nomads guarded by a detachment of the Iraq Camel Corps, some 30 miles south of the railway line and near the provisional frontier. It could be taken for granted that the Sultan, at his distant capital, would repudiate the hostile action of his hot-headed tribesmen, and for us to have taken measures of retaliation without first communicating with the responsible Ruler, might have resulted in a state of war between the Sultan of Nejd and Iraq, which would have been a calamity from all points of view; nevertheless some aeroplanes which were sent to obtain news, having been fired on, were obliged to reply and a grave warning was immediately addressed by me to Ibn Saud remonstrating with him for this unprovoked raid by his tribesmen; reminding him of the provisional frontier which had been agreed upon and urging him to concert with me arrangements for its formal settlement.

Ever since King Faisal's advent to Iraq I had left no stone unturned in the difficult endeavour to promote cordial relations between the two potentates, both allies of H.M's Government and regarded with affection by myself, and it would have been a bitter personal as well as official disappointment to me, had a serious breach occurred. But the position of H.M's High Commissioner was a most delicate one at this time. The news of the raid had created profound indignation in certain quarters in Bagdad and immediate reprisals were demanded without any reflection as to whether means existed for carrying them out. It was even suggested quite seriously that the raid had been instigated by the British authorities as a means of making Iraq realise the extent of her dependence upon us! Unfortunately the episode took place at a moment when a serious divergence of view already existed between the British and the Iraq Governments as to the precise nature of their relations with one another. It was extraordinary with what aversion the mandatory idea had always been regarded in Iraq. The mere terms "Mandatory" and "Mandate" were anathema to them from the first, for the simple reason, I am convinced, that the words translate badly into Arabic, or rather were wrongly rendered in the Arabic press when they first emerged from the Peace Conference. I assume the term mandatory to have been introduced by its sponsor, President Wilson, in the particular and recognised sense of "one who undertakes to do service for another with regard to property placed in his hands by the other"; "the other" in this case being the League of Nations, while the "mandate" is the contract under which service is performed. But it was taken in Iraq in its other sense, "of an authoritative requirement, as by a sovereign"; and the "mandatory" as one who exercised the authority. Two widely different conceptions. Misunderstanding their meaning, as they did, there was always intense eagerness on the part of those in authority in Iraq, to get rid of the hated expressions, as defining their relations with us, and much needless controversy was the result.

H.M's Government had indeed agreed on my recommendation, that the terms of our mandatory relations with Iraq should be set out in the form of a treaty, instead of as first drafted, but King Faisal and his Ministers now went further and pressed for the complete abrogation of the mandatory relation, as being incompatible with the country's independence, and its replacement by a simple treaty of alliance; whereas the British Government had in mind a treaty within the scope of the mandate. It was as I have said unfortunate that this acute difference should have been synchronous with the incident of the desert raid. The anti-mandate agitation gained impetus and continued throughout the summer. In June, a vigorous campaign started in the Arab Press; symptoms of disorder again began to appear on the Euphrates, while the collection of revenue dropped to vanishing point, and though at the end of June the Council of Ministers accepted the treaty, it was with the characteristic reservation that it should not be ratified until agreed to by the forthcoming Constituent Assembly. The month of August was marked by the formation of two extremist political parties, and on the 16th of that month the whole of the existing moderate Cabinet, unable to keep the extremist elements within bounds, resigned, with the exception of the Naqib, who retained his post as Prime Minister in the hope of preventing a land-slide.

Meanwhile the extremist elements proclaimed that a new Cabinet was to be formed out of their number, under the presidency of a certain religious firebrand and a joint manifesto was published in the vernacular papers demanding that the British element in the administration should be entirely eliminated.

It was in such a highly charged atmosphere that on a stifling day in August, the 23rd to be precise, I proceeded officially to the Palace to offer my congratulations to His Majesty on this the first anniversary of his accession, and just before entering the building was treated to an anti-mandate demonstration by what proved to be a small packed crowd. I took immediate steps to demand an apology, which was accorded, but at the same moment it was announced that King Faisal had been struck down by a sudden and dangerous attack of appendicitis, necessitating an immediate operation and involving his complete insulation from the affairs of state for some time to come. I was thus faced with a unique if critical situation. The cabinet had resigned; the King was incapacitated; the Bagdad Vilayet and the Euphrates tribes were on the verge of rebellion to all appearances likely to be not less serious than that of 1926 and organised by the same elements. The Turks at the same moment, with their prestige greatly increased by their defeat of the Greeks, were in Rowanduz and Rania and were threatening Sulaimaniyeh. No authority was in fact left in the country except my own as High Commissioner and I felt bound to use it to the full. Accordingly a proclamation was at once issued explaining the situation and stating that the emergent measures which were being taken did not portend any change in the settled policy of H.M's Government. At the same time all friendly and moderate persons who had the welfare of their country at heart were called upon to rally to the side of the High Commissioner and resist irresponsible agitators. The ringleaders were forthwith arrested; the two new extremist parties closed down and certain mischievous papers suppressed. At the same time the two Persian divines who had been responsible for the anti-Foreign manifestoes were advised to repair to their own homeland for the benefit of their health, while some of the Arab officials on the Lower Euphrates who by their intrigues had fostered the disaffection, were dismissed or transferred.

The effect of these measures was instantaneous; and except for a few isolated acts of defiance, and the chronic unrest in the Kurdish districts which continued for some time to respond to Turkish propaganda and incitement, the whole of Iraq proper was quiet by September 10th. On that date King Faisal was reported strong enough to give me an interview, whereat he thanked me cordially for the action taken during the interregnum.

But the north-eastern frontier continued to give cause for anxiety. A Levy force from Sulaimaniyeh, pursuing a band of Kurdish rebels having become involved too far from their base, an Indian regiment was sent to reinforce them; the combined force getting into difficult country suffered a reverse near Rania on 1st September 1922 and was with difficulty extricated; in consequence it was decided to withdraw all British personnel from Sulaimaniyeh and the withdrawal was carried out by air in the course of a day without the slightest hitch—a remarkable example of the utility and efficiency of the air-method in such circumstances. It was undoubtedly a disappointing setback, but with Sheikh Mahmud in control of the town effective administration from Bagdad east of Erbil, Kifri and Kirkuk had become impossible.

Fortunately at this stage the face of the picture was transformed by the execution of a measure decided upon in principle at the Cairo Conference eighteen months before, namely the placing of all the Imperial Forces in Iraq, Ground Troops, Levies and Royal Air Force, under the Command of the Air Officer Commanding. It had not been intended to bring the change into force until a settlement had been reached with Turkey and the northern boundary determined, but Air Marshal Sir John Salmond assumed charge from 1st October 1922, and the vigorous air action taken from that date against the Turks and their adherents whenever they showed their heads had the effect 4 months later of forcing them to withdraw entirely from the Rania district and to concentrate in Rowanduz, whence they were finally ejected in April 1923. With the restoration of the King's health the moment had come for the instalment of a new Cabinet, which the Naqib had succeeded in forming by the end of September 1922. Difficulties with regard to the Treaty and the Mandate had by now been cleared away in correspondence with the Secretary of State and on October 10th His Highness the Naqib and I signed the Treaty of Alliance between Great Britain and Iraq, which was published on 13th October, together with a Proclamation by His Majesty King Faisal to his people expressing his profound satisfaction with the event. The period for which this, the original Treaty, was to run was 20 years, and during the long negotiations which led up to it nothing less than 15 years was ever discussed, but, as the sequel shows, the period was destined to be considerably curtailed.

With the near approach of the first Lausanne Conference Turkish propaganda, suggesting the intended restoration of Iraq to Turkey, grew stronger and stronger and had considerable effect both on the Sheikhs of the Euphrates and the inhabitants of northern Iraq. The King's Irade on 21st October ordering elections for the Constituent Assembly, which was to accept the Treaty and pass an Organic Law laying down the Constitution was countered by a "fatwah" or religious decree countersigned by some disaffected divines of Karbala and Kadhimain, forbidding participation in the elections.

It was now realised that a more vigorous line of action on the part of the Iraq Government was needed to cope with these adverse forces, and the venerable Naqib who had remained at the helm of affairs so gallantly through so many changes of weather felt that the time had come when he could resign the ship of state to the command of a younger man, and he was succeeded by Abdul Muhsin Bey, who reconstructed the Cabinet.

At this juncture a change of Government took place in England which profoundly affected the future in Iraq. The Coalition Government under which the Iraq Treaty had been framed and signed had resigned on 23rd October, 10 days after its signature, and the question of Iraq became a prominent plank in the course of the general election which followed; a fierce newspaper campaign being conducted against the expenditure of British money in the country and several members of the new House of Commons pledging themselves to work for its evacuation by the British at the earliest moment. As a consequence, a Cabinet Committee was set up in London in December 1922 to decide upon the future of Iraq. Meanwhile the Treaty lately signed, with its 20 years duration clause, had not been ratified, while at the first Lausanne Conference the Turkish delegates had resolutely refused to entertain any idea of the Mosul Vilayet remaining with Iraq, or to refer the Turco-Iraq frontier question to the League.

It was of course open to Great Britain to refuse to ratify the Treaty and thus for 4 months Iraq remained in dire suspense (flooded all the time with Turkish propaganda) as to whether she would not after all be handed back to Turkey. I was called home to attend the deliberations of this Conference and Sir Henry Dobbs having in the meanwhile arrived, on appointment as Counsellor to the High Commission, with the prospect of succeeding me at the end of my term, I left for London on 19th January 1923, leaving him in charge, and though he was no stranger to the country, having served with me for 2 years, early in the war, the situation which he had to take over was full of awkward possibilities.

I returned from my mission on 31st March bringing with me the results of the deliberations of H.M's new Government. They were in the shape of a draft Protocol to the Treaty of Alliance, reducing the duration of the treaty from 20 years to 4 (the period to commence on the date of the ratification of the Treaty of Peace by Turkey) but concluding with a consoling provision that "Nothing in this Protocol shall prevent a fresh agreement from being concluded, with a view to regulate the subsequent relations between the High Contracting Parties; and negotiations shall be entered into between them before the expiration of the above period." This document was signed by the Prime Minister of Iraq and myself on the 20th April 1923, and may be said to have been my last official act as High Commissioner; for being due for leave before the advent of the hot-weather pending retirement from the service and having many things to see to before my departure, I was content to leave the direction of current affairs in the experienced hands of my Counsellor and successor, Sir Henry Dobbs.

In compiling this condensed narrative of the period of our association, it has not been possible for me to allude repeatedly to the great degree to which Gertrude Bell enjoyed my confidence and I her devoted co-operation, a co-operation which I know from my successor she rendered with the same singleness of purpose to him. Her letters will tell their own story.

P. Z. C.

By H.E. SIR HENRY DOBBS, K.C.S.I., ETC.
High Commissioner for the Iraq

On 22nd December, 1922, I arrived in Bagdad to take up the newly created post of Counsellor to the High Commissioner, with the prospect of succeeding Sir Percy Cox when, as was understood, he retired in the ensuing year. The prospect was not a firm one, since it was possible that, as a result of the deliberations of the British Cabinet, there might shortly be no High Commissioner to succeed. Almost immediately on my arrival, Sir Percy Cox was summoned to London to assist in those deliberations, and he left Bagdad by air on 19th January, 1923. He did not again take an active part in the general work of the High Commissioner, returning only to announce the new policy of the British Government, to sign the Protocol of the Treaty necessitated by the change, and to prepare for his final departure on leave, which took place on 3rd May, 1923.

On taking up the work of High Commissioner in January, 1923, I found that all hope of holding an early election for the Constituent Assembly had vanished, while the Turkish threat on the north was growing more insistent. The first Lausanne Conference was on the verge of collapse. In Sulaimaniya the newly restored Sheikh Mahmud was already showing signs of revolt. The mass of the people of Iraq were silent, showing that strange and admirable restraint with which Oriental peoples await the fulfilment of the purposes of God; but unshakeable through all had been their belief (dimmed only for a time in the murk of the years succeeding the war) in the generosity and high purpose of Great Britain towards weaker peoples.

Sir Percy Cox returned on the 31st March, 1923, bringing with him the result of the deliberations of the British Government in the shape of a draft Protocol to the Treaty of Alliance. The Protocol cut down the period of the Treaty from twenty years to a maximum of four years from the date of ratification of peace with Turkey, and provided that, if before the lapse of that maximum period, Iraq became a member of the League of Nations, the Treaty should terminate immediately. The Protocol was signed on 30th April 1923. The more farseeing people feared that the reduced period was too short to enable Iraq to stand upon her own feet, and the so-called pro-British sections of the populations, especially some of the Euphrates tribes, the inhabitants of Basra and the Assyrians of Mosul, professed to regard this reduction as a betrayal of their interests. But the politicians of Bagdad and Mosul welcomed it with enthusiasm, and even King Faisal and his Ministers, while expressing constant gratitude for the support and favours received in the past, were undisguisedly delighted that a near term had been put to authoritative control by Great Britain of their affairs.

Sir Percy Cox left Iraq at the beginning of May, 1923, amid spontaneous demonstrations of affection and regret from all classes of the population. During his absence in London I had in January, 1923, taken steps to restore general confidence in the face of the Turkish threats. For this purpose a force, composed partly of British and partly of Iraq troops, moved up to Mosul, and His Highness the Amir Zaid, the brother of King Faisal, who had arrived in Iraq in November, 1922, took up his residence at Mosul to initiate political measures for winning over Kurdish sentiment to the Iraq side. He also superintended the formation of a force of Arab tribal irregulars to operate, if need be, against invaders of the plains to the west of Mosul. This demonstration, combined with the firm stand of the British representatives at Lausanne, had an immediate effect on the whole country. But Turkish irregulars remained at Ruwanduz, and plans for a Kurdish rising with the co-operation of Sheikh Mahmud of Sulaimaniya came to light. To forestall such a combination, Sheikh Mahmud's headquarters were bombed from the air and he took to the mountains. It was now time to complete the pacification of the frontier by the reoccupation of Ruwanduz. Two columns of troops advanced on the town, which the Turkish irregulars and their leader, Euz Demir, evacuated without fighting on 22nd April, 1923, two days before the second conference of Lausanne began its sittings.

The district of Ruwanduz was placed under the Arbil Division and the Kurdish leader, Saiyad Taha, the hereditary chieftain of Neri, who was at that time a refugee in Iraq, was appointed Qaimmaqam. He was a man of strong character and of great reputation among the Kurds, and his appointment was an earnest of the wish of the British and Iraq Governments to administer the Kurdish districts through Kurdish officials. Helped by the presence of a battalion of Assyrian Levies, he succeeded in excluding Turkish influence from the important strategic centre of Ruwanduz.

A few weeks after the reoccupation of Ruwanduz, Sulaimaniya was temporarily occupied and Sheikh Mahmud fled across the Persian border. it had been hoped to set up some form of autonomous administration there with the help of friendly Kurdish leaders, but it proved impossible to lock up a large number of troops which might still be needed on the northern frontier, and no Kurdish chief could be found strong enough to resist the influence of Sheikh Mahmud without such backing. Sulaimaniya was accordingly evacuated on 20th June, 1923, and Sheikh Mahmud allowed to return there for a time and to resume his domination of the centre of the division, while the outlying parts were detached and placed under the Iraq administration.

The frontiers having thus been strengthened and the Turkish menace for the time staved off, the field was free to deal with the agitation of the reactionary Shiah divines against the elections for the Constituent Assembly. By July, 1923, their demeanour towards King Faisal and towards the Iraq Government had become intolerably arrogant, and King Faisal saw no other way than to authorise the deportation of their leader, Sheikh Mahdi al Khalisi. The deportation was arranged and carried out exclusively by Arab agency, and was followed by the voluntary exodus to Persia of several other prominent Persian divines as a public protest. The Iraq Government decided that it would be unsafe to permit any of these personages to return before the conclusion of the elections and the ratification by the Constituent Assembly of the Treaty of Alliance with Great Britain. This decision, although it caused agitation in Persia, was accepted as wise throughout Iraq. King Faisal had during this period made a progress throughout the whole country for the purpose of explaining his policy and exhorting the people to take part in the elections, and I followed shortly afterwards in his steps, so that the people were left in no doubt as to the identity of purpose of the British and Iraq Governments. Having thus prepared the ground, the Iraq Government ordered that the elections should begin again, and the completion of the registration of primary electors, which had before been found impracticable, was everywhere carried through with success, the most distant tribesmen of the Euphrates and of the Kurdish hills enrolling themselves with astonishing alacrity. The political atmosphere had, in fact, cleared as if by magic and the progress of the elections, notwithstanding the complications of the Electoral Law, threatened to be so swift that it was necessary to delay it, for fear that the Constituent Assembly should sit before the various agreements subsidiary to the Treaty of Alliance with Great Britain were ready for its consideration. The registration of primary electors was finally completed by 16th December, 1923, secondary elections began on 25th February, 1924, and all results were declared by the middle of March, 1924.

Apart from the labours of the Iraq Government and myself over the provisions of the "subsidiary agreements," the late summer and autumn of 1923 were marked only by the growing tension between Iraq and Ibn Saud consequent partly on raids carried out upon Nejd territory by the Shammar who had taken refuge in Iraq when Ibn Saud took Hail in 1921. Finally a conference was arranged at Kuwait under the presidency of Colonel Knox, lately Acting Resident in the Persian Gulf, to decide outstanding questions not only between Nejd and Iraq but also between Nejd and Hejaz and Trans Jordan. It met on 17th December, 1923, and was in a fair way to achieve some settlement, at all events between Iraq and Nejd, when on 14th March, 1924, a very serious raid by Akhwan, not less than 2,000 strong, was carried out upon the Iraq frontier nomads, 186 persons, men, women and children being killed, and 26,000 sheep and 3,700 donkeys captured. This aroused such indignation in Iraq that the conference had to be abandoned.

In the meantime the Cabinet of Abdul Muhsin Beg had resigned on 16th November, 1923, as a consequence of differences of opinion with His Majesty King Faisal, leaving the subsidiary agreements incomplete. Jafar Pasha succeeded him as Prime Minister and concluded the discussion of the Agreements subsidiary to the Treaty. They were signed on the 25th March, 1924. The whole Instrument of Alliance was thus ready for submission to the Constituent Assembly, which was opened by His Majesty King Faisal on 27th March, 1924. The month had already been made eventful by the declaration of King Husain as Khalifa, which enhanced the prestige of the Hashimite house.

The debates on the Treaty and Agreements in the Constituent Assembly lasted until 10th June, 1924, the issue growing more and more doubtful as the country deputies fell under the influence of certain extremist lawyers and coffee-house politicians of Bagdad. There was much misrepresentation and some solid ground for dissatisfaction in the heavy burdens imposed on Iraq by the obligation simultaneously to expand the Army, redeem the capital cost of the railway and shoulder a large share of the Ottoman Debt. This difficult position had been brought about mainly by the cutting down of the Treaty period from twenty to four years. For whereas, under the arrangements contemplated in the original Treaty, Iraq would have been able to expand her army very gradually, she was now forced into a feverish and most expensive programme, with little real hope of being able in so short a time to produce an army fit for external defence. Moreover, at the Cairo Conference of 1921, which laid down the original policy, the future revenues of Iraq had been gravely overestimated on the basis of the momentary prosperity succeeding the war. With shrunken revenues and increased obligations, it was feared that the conditions of the Financial Agreement must, if Iraq attempted to fulfil them, drive her to bankruptcy. Another great objection felt to the Treaty was that it contained no definite undertaking that the economic and judicial capitulations, formerly enjoyed in the old Turkish Empire by certain European Powers and by the United States of America, should be abrogated. There was merely a clause laying down that in consequence of the "non-application" of these immunities, effect would be given to reasonable provisions to safeguard the interests of foreigners in judicial matters.

On 20th April, 1924, the Committee of the Assembly, appointed to study the Treaty and Agreements, presented a report containing some able criticism, the work of Yasin Pasha, President of the Committee. Agitation against the Treaty, which had already led to the attempted assassination of two pro-Treaty deputies, increased and it became clear that, without some assurance regarding future financial treatment, there was little hope of passing the Treaty. On the other hand it was not feasible to accept any amendments in the Treaty and Agreements before ratification, as this would have thrown all the relations between Great Britain and Iraq back into the melting-pot and have created difficulties both in England and in Iraq. Finally, His Britannic Majesty's Government gave an undertaking that, after ratification, they would reconsider the financial obligations of Iraq. This somewhat eased the situation, but also in some quarters increased the expectation of further British concessions and the anti-Treaty agitation continued. His Britannic Majesty's Government therefore resolved to put an end to a tension which was becoming dangerous, by bringing the Iraq Mandate before the League of Nations at the session of June, 1924, and announced that, if the Iraq Assembly had reached no decision by 10th June, this would be taken as a rejection of the Treaty. As a result, the Constituent Assembly accepted the Treaty and Agreements shortly before midnight on 10th June, stating in a rider to their resolution that they did so in reliance on the assurance that, after ratification, the British Government would "amend with all possible speed the Financial Agreement in the spirit of generosity and sympathy for which the British people are famous."

The acceptance of the Treaty was a notable landmark, for it has been the only instance since the close of the war of a complete and voluntary agreement to define future relations between Great Britain and an Arabic speaking community, made under freely elected representative institutions on both sides. That the nation on the whole was satisfied with the decision was testified by the number of congratulations which I received from all parts of the country.

The Treaty and agreements were placed before the Council of the League of Nations on 20th September, 1924. The League took note of these documents and, on 27th September, 1924, accepted them as giving effect to the provisions of Article 22 of the Covenant of the League for the regulation of the relations between Iraq and the Mandatory Power. The Treaty and Agreements were ratified by His Britannic Majesty King George V on 10th November, 1924, and by His Majesty King Faisal on 12th December, 1924.

After disposing of the Treaty the Constituent Assembly proceeded to the consideration of the Organic Law and the Electoral Law, which were passed, the first on 10th July and the second on 2nd August, 1924. The programme laid down for Iraq in Mr. Winston Churchill's announcement of 12th October, 1922, as a necessary preliminary to the admission of Iraq to the League of Nations and the termination of mandatory relations, had been the ratification of the Treaty and subsidiary Agreements, the bringing into effect of the Organic Law and the delimitation of the frontiers. Iraq had now fulfilled her part of the programme. The delimitation of the frontiers depended on Great Britain and Turkey. Jafar Pasha and his Cabinet, exhausted with their efforts, resigned office, the Constituent Assembly was dissolved, and Yasin Pasha al Hashimi was made

Prime Minister.

The northern frontier and the Kurdish mountains had been fairly peaceful during the latter part of 1923, and the first half of 1924. In Sulaimaniya, however, Sheikh Mahmud had persisted in overstepping the boundaries laid down for him when allowed to return after the withdrawal of the troops in July, 1923, and he had to be continually threatened from the air, his headquarters being occasionally bombed. In the middle of May, 1924, exaggerated reports of the agitation in Bagdad against the Treaty had encouraged him to more active rebellion. The adjoining division of Kirkuk became affected and intensive air action was taken against Sheikh Mahmud, with the result that he abandoned Sulaimaniya, which was occupied in July, 1924, by a column of Iraq Army Cavalry, supported by Assyrian Levies. Sheikh Mahmud again fled over the Persian frontier and the remaining portions of the Sulaimaniya Division were placed under a very loose form of civil administration on behalf of the Iraq Government. This has not secured complete tranquillity from the local depredations of outlaws, but the town of Sulaimaniya is now again flourishing and the prosperity of the district is gradually returning. The zone of disorder has, at all events, been pushed far back from the borders of the settled districts of Kirkuk and Arbil. Sulaimaniya itself, like the Indo-Afghan border, has never from the remotest times been completely pacified, and it is too much to expect that this will now be accomplished in the twinkling of an eye.

In Article 3 of the Treaty of Lausanne it had been provided that the frontier between Turkey and Iraq should be laid down in friendly arrangement to be concluded between Turkey and Great Britain within nine months, and that, in the event of no agreement being reached, the dispute should be referred to the Council of the League of Nations. Pending the decision, the two Governments had undertaken that no military or other movement should take place which might modify in any way the present state of the territories in question. During May and the first week of June, 1924, Sir Percy Cox had carried on in Constantinople fruitless negotiations with the Turkish Government on the frontier question. The Turks had been adamant in their demand for the whole Mosul Vilayat, and their intransigence had probably been encouraged by the reports from Bagdad that the Iraq Constituent Assembly was about to reject the Treaty with Great Britain. On 9th June, 1924, the day before the Iraq Assembly accepted the Anglo-Iraq Treaty, the Constantinople negotiations had broken down. There was now nothing left but a reference of the frontier dispute to the League of Nations, and, in the meanwhile the Turks became active on the frontiers. They sent the Wali of Julamerk with a small escort to visit Chal, which they had been informed in October, 1923, was claimed by the British Government to lie within the sphere of the Iraq Administration, and in the course of his progress he was ambushed by some Assyrian Christians and taken captive, but released. At the beginning of September, 1924, the Turks concentrated troops for the invasion of the Assyrian area, and on the 14th they crossed the River Haizil into what was undoubtedly Iraq territory. They were met by an attack from the air and driven back and thereafter diverted their march to the north through the territory of the Sindi Guli Kurds (still Iraq territory), through which they moved and laid waste the Assyrian country, driving the Assyrians, some 8,000 in number, down into the valley of Amadia, where they had to be supported by the Iraq Government. It was a remarkable testimony to the success of the Iraq Administration and to the good relations maintained with the Kurds that this incursion by the Turks did not lead to a general rising on the Mosul frontier against Iraq, which would have been unfortunate, as the League of Nations was at that moment sitting at Geneva to determine the delimitation of the Turco-Iraq frontier. Ultimately, the Turks agreed before the League to preserve the status quo until the frontier was decided. A preliminary dispute as to the line of the status quo was settled by a special meeting of the League at Brussels in October, 1924, and this provisional line has since been known as the "Brussels Line."

The Frontier Commission, consisting of three Commissioners, eminent subjects of Sweden, Belgium and Hungary, reached Bagdad in January, 1925, and spent three months in examining the frontier. They were accompanied by General Jawad Pasha, who had recently commanded the Turkish forces on the Iraq frontier, as Turkish assessor, and Mr. Jardine, a British Administrative Inspector in the service of Iraq, as British assessor. The Turks had, in the preceding negotiations, demanded a plebiscite of the inhabitants of the Mosul Vilayat, but this had been resisted by the British on the grounds that the circumstances of the population made a plebiscite impracticable. The League of Nations had left the methods of enquiry entirely to the discretion of the Commissioners, who went a long way towards satisfying the Turkish demand and besides undertaking a detailed study of the racial, geographical and economic factors of the problem, made secret enquiries from representatives of all sections of the inhabitants in the territories under dispute, as to which government they would prefer, that of Turkey or Iraq.

QUESTION OF THE CHRISTIANS OF MOSUL AND OF THE NESTORIAN OR ASSYRIAN MOUNTAINEERS.

One of the chief matters of concern to the Frontier Commission appeared to be the future of the Christians of Mosul, and especially of the Nestorians or Assyrians, who, as narrated above, were at the time of the visit of the Commission refugees in Iraq territory. They numbered altogether about 20,000 souls, some from regions lying considerably beyond the northernmost frontier claimed by Iraq and some from the Hakkiari mountains north of Amadia, which were included in the Iraq claim. They had revolted against Turkey in 1916 at the instigation of Russia, and then, being deserted by the Russians after the revolution, had fought their way through Persian territory to a junction with the British troops, losing two-thirds of their number in the process. The British had brought them into Iraq and maintained them there for three years, after which some were temporarily settled on vacant Iraq lands near Amadia and some encouraged to filter back to their deserted homes to the north. There they had stayed, repairing the damage as best they might, until once more expelled by the

Turkish incursion of September, 1924. Numbers of them had, from 1921 onwards, entered the British service as Levies and had displayed magnificent fighting qualities, helping in the suppression of sporadic Kurdish insurrections and in the expulsion from Ruwanduz in 1923 of the Turkish irregulars. They were united in a determination never again to submit themselves to Turkish rule. In order to reassure them as to their future, two successive Iraq Cabinets, those of Jafar Pasha and of Yasin Pasha, officially pledged the Government of Iraq to provide lands in Iraq for those Assyrians who might be dispossessed of their original homes by the decision of the League of Nations and to devise a system of administration for them which should ensure to them the utmost possible freedom from interference. It can hardly be doubted that this liberal attitude on the part of the Government of Iraq had its influence on the deliberations of the Frontier Commission. The Commission terminated its labours in the third week of March, 1925. Its report could not be prepared in time for the June session of the League, and was held over till September..

POLITICAL EVENTS AFTER THE DEPARTURE OF THE FRONTIER COMMISSION.

It had not been thought advisable to proceed with elections for the first regular Iraq Parliament until the Frontier Commission had completed its labours. The promulgation of the Organic Law passed by the Constituent Assembly in July, 1924, had consequently been delayed, so as to avoid an interregnum between the close of arbitrary Cabinet Government and the introduction of a Parliamentary régime.

On 21st March, 1925, on the eve of the departure of the Commission, the Organic Law was officially promulgated amid widespread rejoicings, and orders were given for the completion of the new lists of primary electors and for the commencement of the parliamentary elections. The Cabinet of Yasin Pasha had, shortly before taking these steps, passed four notable measures vital for the future prosperity and stability of Iraq. The first was the signature of an agreement with the Anglo-Persian Oil Company for the dredging of the bar at the mouth of the Shatt al Arab, so as to allow vessels of heavy draught to enter the Port of Basra. The second was the signature of a trade transit convention with Syria. The third was the grant to the Turkish Petroleum Company of a concession for the development of oil throughout the Bagdad and Mosul Wilayats, and the fourth was the signature of long term contracts with some hundred British advisers and officials, whose experience and devoted industry were thus secured for Iraq throughout the first and most difficult stage of her career as an independent State.

While the elections were in progress the Secretary of State for the Colonies despatched to Iraq a Financial Mission to enquire into the financial position and prospects of Iraq, so that the British Government might be able to carry out their promise to reconsider the provisions of the Financial Agreement after its ratification. The report of the Mission, which was completed by 25th April, 1925, partially justified many of the criticisms of the Financial Agreement made in the Constituent Assembly of 1924, as throwing upon Iraq burdens greater than she could bear. Its recommendations for the alleviation of these burdens were, when published, the cause of much public satisfaction in Iraq, and contributed to the election to the first Iraq Parliament of a majority of deputies actuated by the friendliest sentiments towards the British Alliance.

Another factor in this favourable situation was the visit to Iraq in the first half of April, 1925, of the Right Honourable L. S. Amery, Secretary of State for the Colonies, and of the Right Honourable Sir Samuel Hoare, Secretary of State for Air. The visit cheered and encouraged those whose minds had been upset by the inquisitions of the Frontier Commission and convinced the Government and people of Iraq of the steadfastness of the interest of Great Britain in their affairs. It gave an unique opportunity to His Majesty King Faisal and the leading personages in Iraq to bring their various difficulties and anxieties fully and frankly before the British Government, and the substitution of personal discussion for paper impersonalities had the happiest effect. Particularly valuable were the discussions which took place between Mr. Amery and King Faisal and his Prime Minister as to the prerogatives and duties of the King under the newly promulgated Constitution, a question which urgently needed discussion, since His Majesty King Faisal had been inclined to withdraw more than was desirable from influencing the conduct of affairs of State after the coming into force of the Organic Law. The main preoccupation of the two Secretaries of State was, however, the more rapid improvement and training of the Iraq Army. Many conferences were held on this subject, and, before the Secretaries of State left, a scheme had been accepted which should enable the Iraq Army in a short time to take the principal part in the maintenance of internal security and the control of the Iraq frontiers, and should relieve the British Exchequer of its burden on this account.

After the departure of the Secretaries of State, the elections were pushed on and were completed by 23rd June, 1925. There was no sign of any definite party activity, the various political parties which had been constituted in former years having died of inanition. On completion of the elections, the Cabinet of Yasin Pasha resigned as, owing to differences of opinion between the Prime Minister and the Minister of the Interior (Abdul Muhsin Beg), they felt they could not face the Parliament as a united Cabinet. The King invited Yasin Pasha to form a new Cabinet, and on his failing, invited Abdul Muhsin Beg to do so. The Cabinet of the latter took office on 26th June, 1925.

The first Iraq Parliament met on 16th July, 1925, and was opened by King Faisal. Its first session has been devoted to the discussion of its own rules of procedure, to certain necessary amendments to the Organic Law, and to the consideration of the Budget for 1925-26 in the light of the recommendations of the Finance Commission. Its debates have, so far, been characterised by earnestness and good sense.

Thus Iraq had in July, 1925, attained the first stage of her development. She had accepted, through her representatives, a Treaty of Alliance with Great Britain; she had passed an Organic Law and set up a stable and constitutional government under it. It only remained for her frontiers to be fixed according to the decision of the League of Nations, before she could apply for admission to the League of Nations and take on the full status of an independent State.

In August, 1925, King Faisal's state of health necessitated his departure for England to undergo medical treatment. His Majesty appointed his younger brother, the Amir Zaid, as Regent, left Bagdad on the 5th August, returning on the 15th November.

Meantime, in August, 1925, the report of the Frontier Commission had been published. Before it could be translated in extenso the Prime Minister explained to the Chamber that it was proposed, if all the Mosul Wilayat were to be retained, that the relation of Iraq to Great Britain should be prolonged for a period of about twenty-five years. He added that there was no one who did not recognise the value of the existing relations with Great Britain and the advantages to the country which had accrued there from. There was a striking unanimity in both Houses in favour of prolonging these relations and when the Council of the League met in September and Mr. Amery accepted on the part of the British Government the terms proposed by the Commission, both Chambers telegraphed to thank him for his defence of the rights of Iraq. It had indeed alarmed the ultra-nationalist party to find a section of the British press averse from the extension of the alliance. It was even suggested as a possible explanation that these British papers were in the pay of the Turkish Government. Though the settlement which had been hoped for was not reached at the September meeting, owing to the reference of certain legal points to the Permanent Court of International Justice at the Hague, the speeches of Mr. Amery and Mr. Baldwin had a most reassuring effect on public opinion and it was never doubted by the large majority of Iraqis that Great Britain would support their rights.

In January, 1925, a protest had been lodged with the Turkish Government, through His Britannic Majesty's Representative in Constantinople, against violation of the status quo boundary. In May, a police patrol was ambushed south of the "Brussels" line by a band under Turkish instigation and, in June, enquiries were addressed by His Majesty's Government to the Turkish Government as to the reason for the large concentration of troops in the area north of the Iraq frontier, since it had been officially declared that the Kurdish rebellion had been suppressed. At the same time reports began to come in that the Turks were taking vengeance on the Christians and Kurds of Goyan, who had testified to the Frontier Commission their desire to be included in Iraq, and some 500 refugees arrived at Zakho. Early in September, reports began to be received of atrocities committed on Chaldean villages north and also south of the provisional frontier. The villagers, though they had never taken part against Turkey during the war, were being systematically removed from the neighbourhood of the frontier and transported into the interior, but many escaped, in a pitiable state of destitution, and reached Zakho with tales of massacre and violence. The Iraq Ministry of Interior placed a sum of money at the disposal of the Mutasarrif of Mosul for the relief of these unfortunate people. Mr. Amery brought the matter in strong terms before the Council of the League at the meeting in September, 1925, the Turkish delegate equally hotly denied the accusations: and the Secretary of State requested the Council to send an impartial commission to report on the matter and also on charges and counter-charges as to the violation of the provisional frontier. The Council entrusted the task to a distinguished Esthonian, General Laidoner, and the Commission arrived on 26th October. The Turkish Government refused to allow General Laidoner to pursue enquiries north of the "Brussels" line, so that the Commission had access to such evidence only as could be gathered within Iraq territory. Immediately before its arrival the refugee camps were visited by the General Secretary of the Friends of Armenia Society, who satisfied himself that the Iraq authorities were diligent in their efforts to succour the refugees, but that owing to their number and their desperate plight, help from outside was required.. He sent telegrams to various Christian societies and communities, and a committee was formed in London to collect funds which were despatched to the High Commission and distributed through a committee of three British officers well acquainted with conditions on the frontier. In December, Colonel Fergusson, a member of the King's Bodyguard, was sent out by the British committee to administer all monies collected.

General Laidoner and his colleagues made a careful examination of the frontier and the relief camps, at the close of which the General telegraphed to the League, stating that the Turks had undoubtedly deported Christians from south of the "Brussels" line, that the deportees deposed that they had been removed by force and violence, and that the Turks had committed crimes, atrocities and massacres. He added that without means of enquiry on the Turkish side of the frontier, it was impossible to define the true reasons for the deportations of Christians, but that these deportations might well have results deserving the attention of the Council.

General Laidoner and part of the Commission left Iraq on 23rd November, but two members remained at Mosul to examine any further complaints which might arise. The full reports of the mission were presented to the Council of the League during the meeting in December, 1925.

The opinion of the Hague Court was received on 25th November, 1925. It was to the effect that the "decision to be taken" by the League Council would be in the nature of an arbitral award binding on both parties, that this decision must be unanimous, and that though both Great Britain and Turkey had the right to be represented and to vote, such votes, if adverse to the otherwise unanimous opinion of the Council of the League, would not be taken into count. This opinion was formally adopted by the League Council on 8th December. In this decision, which was published in Bagdad on 17th December, the Council unanimously held that the Turco-Iraq frontier should be the Brussels line on condition that Great Britain undertook by means of a new treaty with Iraq to continue her present relations with Iraq for a period of 25 years, unless before the expiry of that period Iraq were admitted to membership of the League. The Turkish delegate refused to recognize the arbitral authority of the League

Council and was not present at the meeting. At its close, Sir Austen Chamberlain expressed the hope that the situation between Great Britain and Turkey would be regulated by friendly agreement between the two governments.

King Faisal telegraphed to King George his sincere thanks and gratitude. The Prime Minister telegraphed to Mr. Baldwin and to the Secretary-General of the League, and Mr. Amery was the recipient of many grateful messages. All through Iraq there was a general sense of deep relief, and of hope that the stability thus attained would be reflected in the prosperity which the country would now be able to achieve.

Conversations with regard to the new treaty were begun before the end of the year. The King and the Cabinet showed the utmost willingness to comply with the request of Mr. Amery that the terms of the alliance should be accepted by Iraq before the re-assembling of the British Parliament in the beginning of February, 1926. On the part of the Opposition, now definitely constituted under the name of the People's Party, with Yasin Pasha as leader, doubts were expressed as to the advantage to Iraq of the extension of the 1922 Treaty for 25 years, and more particularly of the similar extension of the subsidiary Agreements; but it was clear from the first that the majority, both inside the Iraq Parliament and outside, agreed that the permanent welfare of Iraq was bound up with her connection with her ally. To this was added the consideration that the period of the new instrument of alliance might, and most probably would, as Mr. Amery had stated, be reduced by the entrance of Iraq into the League of Nations, a step which the British Government would be as anxious as that of Iraq to bring about, since it would relieve Great Britain of the responsibilities imposed by the treaty.

After considerable discussion the text of the new Treaty as approved by the British Government reached Bagdad on 27th December, 1925. The Cabinet was anxious that some specific allusion should be made to the early amendment of the Military and Financial Agreements and that provision should be made for the periodic review of the situation in order to determine whether Iraq were fit to enter into the League and whether the change in the general situation admitted of further alteration in the Agreements. The Secretary of State saw no objection to these requests and the treaty was accepted by the Cabinet on 10th January and signed on 13th January. It was laid before Parliament on 18th January. Yasin Pasha, heading the Opposition, asked that it should be referred to a Committee. The Prime Minister replied that 42 members of the Hizb al Taqaddam, the Government party, had signed a petition that discussion should take place at once in the House; he asked that the public should be excluded and the debate continued in secret. The Opposition headed by Yasin Pasha, numbering 19 members, then walked out. The public was excluded and, after a debate lasting one and a half hours, re-admitted. The President took the vote by calling on each member by name to express agreement or disagreement. Agreement was unanimous.

The House is composed of 88 Deputies. Of these 58 voted for the Treaty. 9 were absent (including 3 of the Opposition). 19 walked out in protest. 1 seat is vacant. 1 is held by the President.

The Senate passed the Treaty on 19th January, 17 members voted in favour, 1 against, 2 were absent.

The most notable events following the passage of the new Treaty were the formation of a new Kurdish independence Movement which spread rapidly along the eastern borders, and the influx into Iraq of large numbers of Kurdish refugees as a result of Turkish operations against the Kurdish tribes.

In May, 1926, Sir Ronald Lindsay, His Britannic Majesty's Ambassador at Constantinople, entered on negotiations with the Turkish Government necessitated by its refusal to recognise the arbitral authority of the Council of the League of Nations regarding the Iraq frontier. Turkey showed a most welcome readiness for friendly discussion, and negotiations advanced so rapidly that a tripartite Treaty was signed at Angora on the 5th June, 1926, between Great Britain, Iraq and Turkey, and Nuri Pasha, the representative of the Iraq Government in the negotiations, reached Bagdad with the Treaty on the 13th June. By this Treaty Turkey recognised the existing frontier or "Brussels" line, subject to one very slight variation, and Turkey and Iraq entered into mutual obligations of "bon voisinage." On the 14th June the two Chambers of the Iraq Parliament accepted the Treaty, and King Faisal immediately ratified it. On the 25th June the King gave a State banquet to celebrate the signing of the Treaty at which His Majesty expressed his profound thanks to the British Government and its representatives for all that they had done for Iraq. Miss Gertrude Bell was one of the most prominent of the guests at this banquet and shared conspicuously in the general atmosphere of congratulation which marked the close of the first stage in the existence of Iraq. It was the last State function which she attended.

CHAPTER XIX
1920

BAGDAD

To H.B.
Sunday, 17th Oct., 1920.

I must try and give you an account of this remarkable week. Sir Percy arrived on Monday, 11th, at Bagdad West. When we got to the station, about 4:30, his train being due at 5:30, we found a sort of reception room, flagged and carpeted, with the railed off approach to the line . . . I was told to go into the reception room, where gradually there collected some 20 or 30 Magnates of Bagdad . . . the C. in C. with his staff, the heads of the departments and officers of Sir Percy's H.Q. here. The salute of 17 guns was fired outside the town, and the wind being contrary we didn't hear it, so that quite suddenly we were told the train was in sight, and we hurriedly took up our positions in the railed off space; on the right Sir Edgar with the heads of departments and me, next to us the consuls, then the religious heads, on the left the C. in C. with his staff, Saiyid Tahb and the deputies, the mayor and one or two magnates, such as the eldest son of the Naqib. Outside the enclosure was a crowd of people, British officers and their wives and a lot of others whom I couldn't distinguish—more of these later. It was near sunset when the train drew up and the C. in C. went forward to greet Sir Percy. He came out dressed in white uniform, and after shaking hands with the C. in C. stood at the salute while the band played "God save the King." I thought as he stood there in his white and gold lace, with his air of fine and simple dignity that there had never been an arrival more momentous—never anyone on whom more conflicting emotions were centred, hopes and doubts and fears, but above all confidence in his personal integrity and wisdom . . . When he came into the enclosure Sir Edgar presented me, while I made my curtsey, it was all I could do not to cry.

As soon as the presentations were over Jamil Zahawi the famous Bagdad orator read him an address of welcome, to which Sir Percy replied in Arabic that he had come by order of H.M.G. to enter into counsel with the people of the Iraq for the purpose of setting up an Arab Govt. under the guidance—the word he used was " nidharah," which means exactly "supervision"—of Great Britain, and he asked the people to co-operate with him in the establishment of settled conditions so that he might proceed at once with his task. His words were interrupted by expressions of assent and agreement on the part of his audience.

Lady Cox, Mr. Philby and Captain Cheesman (the latter is Sir Percy's private secretary) had got out of the train by this time, and we had all exchanged warm greetings. Lady Cox stepped out after ten hours of dusty journey, looking as if she had emerged from the finest bandbox—a miracle, as we told her. Then we all drove to Sir Percy's house . . . Lady Cox, after giving us tea, disappeared with Capt. Cheesman to look at their new house above the bridge which isn't ready yet for them, while Sir Percy, Mr. Philby and I sat down to talk. From the first moment I saw that all was well. He said he intended to set up an Arab Ministry at once as a temporary expedient without waiting for the complete pacification of the country. His scheme was to call on someone to form a cabinet and he himself would appoint British Advisors to the Ministers. We all agreed that the difficulty was to hit on the right person to summon in the capacity of Prime Minister. His first idea had been Saiyid Talib but it was a matter which needed consideration. I said I thought he had better see people here and form his opinion; whatever he decided upon we would do our utmost to further; the main thing being to decide on something and get it done.

It is quite impossible to tell you the relief and comfort it is to serve under somebody in whose judgment one has complete confidence. To the extraordinarily difficult task which lies before him he brings a single-eyed desire to act in the interests of the people of the country. . . .

With that we all dined with the C. in C. I sat by Sir Percy and had a most enjoyable dinner in spite of the fact that I was sitting in a raging draught. I forget if I told you that I've got bronchitis. Well, I have, and I don't see much chance of curing it. However, that's a minor consideration.

Next morning I went early to the office. Sir Percy called me up at once and we talked over some telegrams—I trying to conceal the fact that it was a wholly novel experience to be taken into confidence on matters of importance! No sooner had I got to my office than I began to receive letters and visitors., each more indignant than the last, saying that the whole town was in an uproar over the reception ceremony because the notables who had been invited were herded together, all but a very small number, in the dust outside the enclosure and hadn't not even had the opportunity of shaking Sir Percy by the hand. "We came in love and obedience," said a really furious old sheikh of distinction, "and when we tried to get near His Excellency we were pushed away." Even the brothers of the Naqib had been treated with this same lack of ceremony. . . .

So I decided at once to invest myself with the duties of Oriental secretary, there being no one else in the office who knows Bagdad, and calling in Mr. Philby for help we drafted a form of invitation to all the notables of Bagdad for the following morning. It was almost lunch time before we got hold of Sir Percy, but meantime I had prepared the list of names—over 100—and drawn up also a small list of people to whom he ought to give private interviews. He approved everything and gave me a free hand . . . and we had the invitations out that evening. It still makes me hot and cold to think what would have happened if we hadn't tackled the situation promptly, for there wasn't a single person in authority who was thinking of the Arab side of the matter and of how supremely important it was that Sir Percy should be put into immediate personal touch with the town. That night Mr. Philby dined with me and we had a long and profitable talk. He had been to tea with me also and I had Sasun Eff. to meet him, which was most valuable, for Sasun is one of the sanest people here and he reviewed the whole situation with his usual wisdom and moderation.

Next morning we had our reception—a huge success. The space in Sir Percy's room being rather limited I had sent out the invitations in 3 batches, leaving half an hour between each batch. We seated about 30 people at a time in Sir Percy's room and had them in 4 relays; those who were waiting were entertained by Mr. Philby and me in the waiting room next door to Sir Percy. But I went in with one of the batches and saw how well it was going with all the people sitting round and being properly served with coffee and cigarettes, while Sir Percy explained his programme and asked their opinions. It is the kind of thing Sir Percy is extremely good at, and everyone went away delighted. I got Abdul Majid Shawi, the mayor, for a private interview in the afternoon; next morning Sasun Eff. and others, and another batch on Friday morning. What with getting the right people to come and keeping the small fry of unworthy place-hunters off, I've had my hands full. Capt. Cheesman and I keep Sir Percy's list of engagements between us, for the moment. I, the Arabs and he the English, and the scheme works beautifully.

On Thursday afternoon Sir Percy called me in to discuss some advice Sasun Eff. had given him about the pacification of the Baqubah area to the effect that the big people of Bagdad who own estates there should be asked to send for some of their tribal tenants, explain Sir Percy's intentions and ask them what in the name of wonder they are now fighting for. Sir Percy at once saw this was a step in the right direction, because it calls on the Bagdadis to take a hand in what is after all their own game . . . I told Sir Percy who were the people to ask and undertook to write the letters. He then dictated to me a Proclamation in the same sense and told me to get it out at once in Arabic, consulting with Mr. Philby. I must tell you in the morning important news had come in from the Euphrates saying that we had occupied Tuwairij and that Karbala was ready to make submission. On this Sir Percy held a Council consisting of Evelyn [Howell], Mr. Philby and me in which it was decided that the provisional govt. at Karbala set up by the insurgents should be told that they must make unconditional surrender and come in under guarantee to see Sir Percy. The Euphrates news has made a deep impression in the town.

To finish the Diala story, all the landlords have acquiesced with satisfaction in Sir Percy's suggestion. The Naqib is sending out his son Saiyid Safa-al-Din who came to see me this morning and told me all he was going to do. Close on his heels came Fakhri bringing telegrams to his tenants. So that's a success.

On Thursday evening after Sir Percy had laid his definite selection of A&B Ministers before Mr. Philby and me, I got him to meet the rest of our group— Major Murray, Major Yetts and Capt. Clayton, and we had a most satisfactory talk. I wanted him to realise that these were the men who would work heart and soul with him, and it didn't take him long to find it out. At the end he told Mr. Philby to submit to him a scheme for his own secretariat. This is the most thorny of all questions, because it is the personal one. We think he ought to have a complete secretariat at the Residency, Civil Secretary, Political Secretary, Military Secretary and Private Secretary . . .

I have kept religiously out of the controversy, the more readily because I feel perfectly certain that Sir Percy will go his own way. They were as bitterly opposed to an Arab Cabinet, but Sir Percy had gone straight through. He knows there is no alternative, and having made up his mind, nothing moves him. His direct simplicity is beyond all wonder . . . it's still like a dream to find all things one has thought ought to be done, being done without question. I feel equally sure that when it comes to the difficult point of dealing with the tribal insurgents on the Euphrates he will drop all the silly ideas of revenge and punishment which have been current . . . and be guided only by consideration for the future peace of the country under an Arab Govt. The first question is whom to call on to form a Cabinet? Most of the people he has seen have suggested the Naqib, and I think he will make an attempt in that direction to-morrow. I am convinced not only that the Naqib will refuse for himself, but that he will also refuse to recommend anyone. . . .

If the Naqib refuses to step into the breach the only alternative that I see is for Sir Percy himself to summon and appoint the members of the provisional cabinet. The moderates are themselves taking up the idea; Fakhri Jamil suggested it to me this morning. I need not say that I greeted it with the greatest show of surprise and interest, because I want everything to come from them and not from us. But if they do urge this scheme upon Sir Percy, what a striking proof it will be of my favourite maxim that if you thrust responsibility on them they are bound to turn to you for help.

The object of the provisional cabinet is merely that it should prepare for and hold the first general election. As soon as you get an elective body, that body chooses its own official representatives and the provisional govt. vanishes. While a good third of the country is still in open rebellion, it's obvious that you can't hold a general election, yet it's equally obvious, as Sir Percy sees, that you can't delay in setting up some form of native institutions. They all expect that he will do something at once, and if he doesn't the golden opportunity will be lost and confidence shaken.

I stayed at home all to-day except for half an hour with Sir Percy in the office this afternoon. He asked me if I would come on to his personal staff as Oriental Secretary or anything he decided, and I said I would love to serve with him in any capacity he chose . . . I found him in talk with the editor of the Nationalist paper here, an ardent Nationalist, on whom he was making the most favourable impression. . . .

I'm now going to be very sensible and perhaps stay at home to-morrow so as to get quite well.

To H.B.
BAGDAD, Oct. 24th, 1920.

I mentioned bronchitis last week—well, it's won and I've spent the last six days in my house and partly in bed. As a result of which I'm now very nearly all right. In a way I'm not sorry, tiresome as it was to be laid up, to have been removed from the fierce personal controversies of which the echoes have reached me, and the inhabitants of Bagdad have seen to it that I've not been removed from the political crisis. For they have been at all hours by my side . . . On the plea of enquiring after my health they have sat on my sofa—the big

Persian sofa in my dining-room which has arrived since you left—and poured out their hopes and fears. I made an attempt to close my doors up to 11 a.m. but it wasn't very successful. When the Mayor of Bagdad rolled up at 9 or the Naqib sent his son Saiyid Mahmud I was obliged to 'endosser' dressing gown and go out to see them. The worrying thing was that we were not getting a move on. Sir Percy was being submerged in details which left him no leisure to consider the big issues, and there seemed to be no one in the office who had sufficient presence of mind to stand in his doorway and block their passage. So all I could do was to send in a daily report of the gossip, the rumour and the impatience with which the town was seething and point that nothing but a quick decision could end them. He had already come to the decision that his first step would be to invite the Naqib to form a provisional Council but day after day passed and could not get time to take it.

On Wednesday I had the Euphrates Sheikhs fresh from the interviews with Sir Percy, first Fahad Bey of the Anazeh, looking younger than ever (he's not far short of eighty) and proudly informing me that he has recently married two new wives. After which he expounded to me his simple scheme for the future, which was that in all Tribal matters Sir Percy should rely upon the advice of Fahad and as for the rest he should seek counsel with the Naqib and two other old turbaned worthies. Then came Ali Sulaiman the head Sheikh of the Dulaim, a very able man with plans better suited to modern conditions than those of Fahad—and after him various smaller fry, none of them fools.

On Thursday Sir Percy sent round a message to say that he had called a council of state for that afternoon in my house, since I couldn't come to the office. They assembled at three o'clock, Sir Percy, Evelyn Howell, Mr. Philby, Mr. Bullard, Sir Edgar and Col. Slater. Then followed three hours of poignantly interesting discussion for Sir Percy produced his scheme for a provisional cabinet, Arab Ministers and British Advisors . . . Finally he carried his scheme through with unimportant alterations, and announced that he was now going to lay it before the Naqib.

On Friday nothing further happened. I had innumerable visitors and all the restlessness of Bagdad seemed to eddy round my garden. In the evening came the Tods with the same story. "Make haste, make haste." And on this note I sent my daily report to Sir Percy.

Saturday began with a notable visit from Jafar Pasha. He is the Major General of distinguished service first with the Turks and then with Faisal. I saw him in Damascus last year, and he had repeatedly written to me. During the winter he came to me hot-foot from an interview with Sir Percy . . . I told him it was his duty as an individual and a Nationalist to assist in establishing Arab institutions of whatever form and that if he and others went boldly forward relying on our support, they would silence criticism. Whether he believed me or not I don't know . . . Jafar is the first of the Mesopotamians to return from Syria, and on his attitude much will depend. . . .

Saiyid Hussain Afhan came in. I had just embarked on a heart to heart talk with Saiyid Hussain about some leading articles which he proposed to publish in his paper, when in came Mr. Philby and others, and on top of them Sir Percy. Everyone but Mr. Philby melted away, and we two turned to Sir Percy, breathless with excitement. "Well," he said, "he has accepted." He had come straight from the Naqib who had agreed to undertake the formation of the provisional govt. So the first success is scored and no one but Sir Percy could have done it. Indeed, that even he should have induced the Naqib to take a hand in public affairs is nothing short of a miracle. Sir Percy's delight and satisfaction was only equal to ours and we all sat for half an hour bubbling over with joy and alternatively glorifying the Naqib and the High Commissioner.

I woke this Sunday morning with an infinite sense of relief., and sent a note to Sir Percy begging him to follow historic precedent with regard to the Seventh Day . . . The Naqib's invitations to the members of the future Cabinet will be out to-morrow . . . I believe the thing will go through. And this first and most difficult beginning will have been made.

I've just had my carpets all put down after having them up all summer. They do look nice.

To H.B.
BAGDAD, November 1st, 1920.

We have had a very critical week, but on the whole things are going as well as could be hoped. On Monday night the Naqib's letters and telegrams to the 18 people whom he invited to form the Council of State were prepared. That night I dined with Capt. Clayton and Major Murray to meet Jafar Pasha. It was an amazing evening . . . I said complete independence was what we ultimately wished to give. "My Lady," he answered—we were speaking Arabic—"complete independence is never given; it is always taken"—a profound saying . . .

The man is an idealist with a high purpose, animated by fervour for his race and country . . . When we parted that evening I did not think he would refuse the Naqib's invitation to join the Cabinet as Minister of Defence. Nor did he. . . . That day a number of acceptances came in. In the afternoon I gave a great tea-party in my garden to Fahad Bey and the Agail . . . It was really splendid. Fahad Bey sat and told tales of the desert and ended by opening his robes and showing me a huge hole in his breast formed by a lance thrust into his back in a youthful raid. "And I looked down and saw the head of the lance sticking out here." No one but an Arab of the desert could have recovered . . . On Wednesday morning all seemed to be going well. In the afternoon Major Yetts dropped in to tea with the Tods. Mr. Tod sprang upon us that he had called on Sasun Eff. to congratulate his becoming Minister of Finance, and found him with Ramdi Pasha Baban (who had been offered a seat in the Cabinet without portfolio) both in the act of refusing . . . I left my cup of tea undrunk and rushed back to the office to tell Mr. Philby. He wasn't there, but there was a light in Sir Percy's room. I went in and told him. He bade me go at once to Sasun Eff. and charged me to make him change his mind. I set off, feeling as if I carried the future of all Iraq in my hands, but when I got to Sasun's house, to my immense relief, I found Mr. Philby and Capt. Clayton already there. The Naqib had got Sasun's letter and had sent Mr. Philby off post haste. I arrived, however, in the nick of time. They had exhausted all their arguments, and Sasun still adhered to his decision. I think my immense anxiety must have inspired me, for after an hour of concentrated argument he was visibly shaken, in spite of the fact that his brother Shaul (whom also I admire and respect) came in and did his best against us . . . We got Sasun Eff. to consent to think it over and see Sir Percy next day. I had an inner conviction that the game was won—partly, thank heaven, to the relations of trust and confidence which I had personally already established with Sasun—but we none of us could feel sure. I didn't sleep much that night. I turned and turned in my mind the arguments that I had used and wondered if I could not have done better.

Next morning, Thursday, Sasun Eff. came in at ten; I took him straight to Sir Percy and left them. Half an hour later he returned and told me that he had accepted. He asked me what he could now do to help and I sent him straight to the Naqib. The leading Sheikh of Bagdad had also refused to join the Council, and it was essential to get him to. In the midst of this talk Sir Percy sent for me. I left Sasun to Mr. Philby and went to consult with Sir Percy. We agreed that I should send at once for Jafar, tell him what had happened and bid him bestir himself. It was past one o'clock before I caught Jafar. We had the most interesting conversation. He told me the misgivings and motives with which he had accepted the invitation to come into the Cabinet. . . .

We then discussed how to win over the extremists, assured him that that was Sir Percy's chief desire, and, taking heart, he asked if he might talk to Sir Percy. I took him at once to Sir Percy and left them together, with the assured conviction that Sir Percy was the best exponent of his own policy.

On Saturday morning Mr. Philby and I went to the Naqib . . . Mr. Philby has been Sir Percy's go-between with him, and most excellently he has done it. We found the Naqib radiant, not only full of good sense but also full of the determination to run the show himself. His one wish is to work hand in hand with Sir Percy, but he doesn't intend to let any other member of the cabinet be Prime Minister, and I'm heartily glad of it. He sent a message to Sir Percy to say that whenever Mr. Philby couldn't come he would like me to be Sir Percy's agent.

Long Life to the Arab Government. Give them responsibility and make them settle their own affairs and they'll do it every time a thousand times better than we can.

I ended the day by giving a dinner party to Sasun Eff., Jafar Pasha and Abdul Maji Shawi with Mr. Philby, Capt. Clayton and Major Murray to help. For I wanted to bring the first named three into touch with one another. It was immensely interesting; Abdul Majid told Jafar the whole story of the origins of tribal rebellion. Jafar with great eloquence, pleaded the need of an immediate settlement with the insurgents. "The peasant must return to his plough, the shepherd to his flock. The blood of our people must cease to flow and the land must once more be rich with crops. Shall our tribes be wasted in battle and our towns die of starvation?"

Jafir is right and the first great work of the Council must be to bring about pacification. To this end, as Sasun justly observed, it would be well for the Naqib to summon to the Council a leading man from Karbela and Najaf. One of the difficulties is that all or nearly all the leading men of the Shiah towns are Persian subjects and must be made to adopt Mesopotamian nationality before they can take official positions in the Mesopotamian State.

In the evening we talked of the Arab Army. Under the terms of the Mandate conscription may not be applied, and Jafar is beginning to wonder how he will get recruits—a difficult problem. Jafar also described his efforts to get into touch with the holy element in Kadhimain. He had been to the great people and tried to prove to them that the sole object of the Provisional Council summoned by the Naqib was to lay the foundations of National Institutions. But they would reply only that they wanted a govt. elected by the people, and that nothing else was of any use. "But you can't hold a general election in a day," said Jafar, "and we want to get to work at once." They offered no suggestion and remained obdurately hostile. "What did you say next," I asked. "I was silent," he answered. That's the Shiah attitude, and it's only countrymen—so far as Arabs can be called the countrymen of Persian divines—who will be able very gradually to bring them into line. Finally I hope a section will become definitely Arab and take a hand in the State. . . .

Mr. Philby, Capt. Clayton and I went to tea with Shukri Alusi who is the most learned of the learned and a great recluse. It's an immense source of pride to me that I may go to his house whenever I like.

Oh, if we can pull this thing off; rope together the young hotheads and the Shiah obscurantists, and enthusiasts like Jafar, polished old statesmen like Sasun, and scholars like Shukri—if we can make them work together and find their own salvation for themselves, what a fine thing it would be. I see visions and dream dreams. I omitted to mention that the Council of State of the first Arab Govt. in Mesopotamia since the Abbassids meets to-morrow.

To H.B.
BAGDAD, November 7th, 1920.

This week has been comparatively uneventful. The Cabinet met for the first time on Tuesday, but it doesn't seem to have done much except discuss what would be the relations between the Ministers and their advisors, and finally to resolve to ask Sir Percy to explain. He has gone into the whole matter very carefully with the Naqib, on the basis of an excellent memorandum drawn up by Mr. Philby, and I believe he meets the Cabinet to-morrow.

After the Cabinet Meeting the Naqib sent for Fahad Bey and asked whether he would be prepared to take a message from the Cabinet to the Insurgent Tribes. Fahad came hotfoot in to me. "Khatun," he said, "you I know and Kokus I know, but of Arab Governments I have no knowledge. Never will I give any answer to the Naqib till I'm assured that Kokus would approve." I brought in Mr. Philby and together we assured him. "Oh, Khatun," said he, " Oh, Veelbi, on your heads you tell me that Kokus would approve."

And he was so much perturbed that he came in the following day and said he hadn't been able to sleep for fear of doing anything contrary to the policy of Kokus. I couldn't help feeling that with such staunch allies as Fahad there was little fear that the influence of Kokus would not avail!

But if we had been setting up native institutions in the midst of order instead of disorder the task would have been incomparably easier. . . .

Apart from the Pro-Turks, the Naqib's Council has against it almost the whole body of Shiahs, first because it's looked upon as of British parentage, but also because it contains considerably less Shiahs than Sunnis. The Shiahs, as I've often observed, are one of the greatest problems . . . and their leading people the learned divines and their families are all Persian subjects. I find that the best argument when people Come to me and complain that So-and-So has not been included in the Cabinet, "Effendim, may I ask whether he is a subject of the Mesopotamian State?" "Effendim, No; he is a subject of Persia." Then I point out that in that case he can't hold office in a Mesopotamian Government. And none of my interlocutors have found an answer.

I attempt to give you the picture so that you may realise the problem; it's true that few are pleased, but they wouldn't have been pleased with any line whatever. I honestly believe that Sir Percy has chosen the best possible path. But it won't lead to immediate peace and contentment. That's not possible.

As soon as we can we must proceed to the election of an Assembly. And I shall be very much mistaken (but then I often am) if they don't ask for the son of the Sharif as an Amir. I regard that as the only solution. . . .

To H.B.
November 14th, 1920.

Things are getting on. The Cabinet have accepted practically without alteration Sir Percy's scheme for the working of Ministers and their advisors. It was admirably drafted by Mr. Philby, and I think it is a real feather in his cap. Tomorrow the Ministry of the Interior gets into its new quarters in the Sarai— the old Turkish offices. They were turned, last year, into billets for officers and their wives, and it is a real dispensation that the W.O. ordered all the wives home otherwise we should have had great difficulty in recovering them . . . There was no other possible place to put the Arab Govt. and people made a great point of having the old offices to which they were accustomed. To get the Ministries installed there is the only way of demonstrating that the Arab Govt. is a real thing. The Shiahs remain hostile, their chief grievance being that there is not a Shiah with a portfolio, I think there's going to be a shuffle in the Cabinet so as to admit one of them. There is also a pretty definite pro-Turkish party, consisting mainly of ex-Turkish officials, civil and military. They don't want an Arab Govt. and declare that they won't come in to it because the Turks must certainly and inevitably return.

Sir Percy preserves a calm and equitable judgment which is the most encouraging part of the whole business. Meantime, without waiting for further developments, I'm beginning to shape my branch of the Secretariat on the principle that the main thing is to get going. This week I shall bring out my first fortnightly intelligence Report—which is to be our official (and very confidential) contribution to the news of the world . . . It's great fun, I need not tell you, to be creating a new office with Sir Percy's unfailing help and approval. This last week it has made a good step forward out of chaos.

To H.B. and F.B.
BAGDAD, November 22nd, 1920.
Man for man we may say without fear that the. British adviser is better than the Turkish and we want to give this country the best chance we can. The thing is to induce the Arabs to accept the chance. I believe we can if events beyond our control don't unseat us. If we had done 18 months ago what we are doing now the problem would have been infinitely more simple.

My garden is a mass of chrysanthemums—brown and yellow and white and pink. It's very cold—the cold has come early—and the dogs have been obliged to wear last year's coats till Marie has time to make new ones., that will be after she has made a gown for me. They are disgracefully ragged and look like beggar dogs. . . .

To H.B.
BAGDAD, November 29th, 1920.
We are greatly hampered by the tribal rising which has delayed the work of handing over to the Arab Govt. Sir Percy, I think rightly, decided that the tribes must be made to submit to force. In no other way was it possible to make them surrender their arms or teach them that you mustn't lightly engage in revolution, even when your holy men tell you to do so . . . Without the lesson and without drawing their teeth by fines of arms (impossible to obtain except by force) we should have left an impossible task to the Arab Govt. Nevertheless, it's difficult to be burning villages at one end of the country by means of a British Army, and assuring people at the other end that we really have handed over responsibility to native Ministers. . . Meantime, Sir Percy has held strictly to his doctrine that a general amnesty must wait on submission. The Ulama have done their best to make him accept them as intermediaries; the tribes have repeatedly asked that negotiations should be conducted through the premier Mujtahid, at whose orders they would lay down arms. Sir Percy has stoutly refused—more power to him! The claim of the Ulama to loose and bind is one of the most formidable problems of the Arab State; the refusal to recognise their political authority is unmitigatedly to the good . . . And it's done with such skill, with such courtesy, the letters to the Ulama are such as Sir Percy alone knows how to write.

Finally I'm summing up our difficulties—there is the fact that Govt. can't be passed from one hand to another in the twinkle of an eye. . . .

A momentous Cabinet meeting took place this afternoon but I've not heard yet what happened . . . The number of heart to heart talks which take place in my office would surprise you! All the busybodies come in to say what they're busy bodying and have to be listened to with sympathetic interest and given advice which it's little likely they'll follow. I sometimes wonder whether 'au fond' I'm not a busybody myself.

Sir Percy generally sends for me towards the end of the morning and we exchange experiences. I then lunch with him and Lady Cox and Capt. Cheesman, and though we don't as a rule talk of Mesopotamia, we tell each other stories, relate comic episodes and generally keep in touch. Therefore though an hour in the middle of the day is very difficult to spare, I feel that the constant unofficial intercourse is very valuable. Also we often have a Sunday outing. Yesterday Sir P. and I and Capt. Cheesman and Capt. Pedder (my host of last Sunday) went out shooting on the river bank opposite Ctesiphon . . . We had about 20 Arab beaters. There were little encampments in the heart of what we call here the forest and the people were cutting liquorice and poplar for fuel to send to Bagdad and digging up the liquorice roots.

I love walking with the beaters and hearing what they say to each other in the broadest Iraq dialect which I'm proud to understand. Their clothes are amazingly unfitted for any job they're likely to undertake, especially struggling through thorns. They treat me with constant solicitous politeness, beat down the thorns with their bare feet so as to let me pass and bustle out of the way to give me the easiest place. You're not an Oriental for nothing. . . .

To H.B.
BAGDAD, December 4th, 1920.
I wish I kept a diary. My only record of this time is my letters to you. . . . .

Yesterday afternoon I rode out to Kadhimain to see an old Persian Princess. Banu Ozma is her title, and she is a daughter of Nasr al Din Shah. . . .

She has come to Kadhimain on a visit and has hired a small house. There I found her in a little room opening on to the Courtyard, carpeted cushioned and curtained to keep out the cold. A charcoal brazier and a parrot in a cage completed the furniture. She was lying on a mattress on the floor, leaning against cushions and covered with a padded quilt. What you could see of her was swathed in black, down to her eyebrows and up to her chin. All that was visible were voluble hands and finely cut face with enormous eyes behind spectacles. She must at one time have been very beautiful; the Kajar women are famous for their looks. She lay there and talked the most exquisite Persian, quick and sweet and faint like the shadow of a wonderful voice. These Kajar Princesses who turn up from time to time, mostly on pilgrimages, are extraordinarily interesting— they are such great ladies—but Banu Ozma is the one we liked far the best. I never saw greater native distinction than in that little old Persian lady lying on the floor.

To H.B.
BAGDAD, December 11th, 1920.
It is exactly three weeks since the last Mail came in. Do my letters arrive with any regularity? I write as you do every week. But this week there's not much to write about for I've been rather a poor thing with a chill. I stayed at home two

days and then couldn't bear it any longer so I went back to the office.

The idea is to have 30 tribal members in the election assembly, 20 being representatives of the 20 biggest tribes and the other ten one apiece for the small tribes grouped together in each of the new ten divisions. I have supplied the data to the Electoral Law Committee and selected the 20 Tribes. I don't think the Council will quarrel with my selection.

All the big landowners on the Council will try to keep the tribes out, I expect the tribes will vote through a committee of their chief Sheikhs who will select one of themselves . . . . As I write a mail at last with delightful long letters. As for what you and Mother say about my letters, I can't tell you what it is to me to be able to write to you so fully and to know that you're both interested. Of course it makes it infinitely easier to write in such detail that you, Father, should have been actually here and seen the people and conditions . . . I should not keep a record of all this time if it wasn't that I wanted to send it to you, and very often I feel that in writing to you I'm clearing my own mind. . . . It helps me enormously.

To H.B.
BAGDAD, December 18th, 1920.

The Council is aware and Sir Percy has constantly impressed upon them, the vital need of getting down to the formation of a native army to relieve ours. Incidentally, Jafar Pasha doesn't think that without conscription in some form they can raise an army which won't be prohibitively expensive. If they have to compete in the labour market they must reckon on paying their men at least Rs 60 a month . . . However, that's a question which could only be settled by an elective assembly. Meantime Jafar has a committee of experts from G.H.Q. (at his request) and they're considering what steps should be taken. Roughly speaking, they think we might have a brigade by the autumn of 1921, and an Arab Division by the Autumn of 1922, which means that by that date we can reduce our force here to 1 Division, keeping it up to 2 Divisions till then. . . . No Govt. in this country whether ours or an Arab administration, can carry on without force behind it. The Arab Government has no force till its army is organised, therefore it can't exist unless we lend it troops . . . The bedrock on which this argument rests is that no administration can exist without force behind it. I think you have seen enough of the country to know that it's correct. Mesopotamia is not a civilised state, it is largely composed of wild tribes who do not wish to shoulder the burden and expense of citizenship. In setting up an Arab state we are acting in the interests of the urban and village population which expects and rightly expects that it will ultimately leaven the mass. Till the leavening has gone a good bit further than it has at present, this citizen population must control the mass, constrain it. That is why it needs force for the maintenance of internal order.

Meantime we've been busy with other matters. The early part of the week was devoted to the electoral law about which I wrote you last week. It was presented to the Council on Monday and with 5 exceptions they were all dead against making any special arrangement for tribal representation, and in favour of letting the tribes register and vote like the rest of the population. That would have meant that the tribes would have taken no part, for as Abdul Majid Shawi rightly pointed out, whereas the population of Iraq is mainly tribal and Shiah, in the course of four general elections held under the Turks no tribesman or Shiah has been returned. Next morning Sasun Eff. and Daud Yusafani (of Mosul) came into my office to talk the matter over. We were all agreed that it would be disastrous if the tribesman were to swamp the townsmen, but I pressed upon them the consideration that whatever may have happened in Turkish times, an Arab National Govt. could not hope to succeed unless it ultimately contrived to associate the tribesmen with its endeavours. They raised good objections against providing for representatives from selected big tribes, but we also agreed that that might be got over by providing for a fixed number of tribal representatives for each division to be selected by all the tribes of that Division, i.e., by the Sheikhs. The ordinary tribesmen won't take part. It was clear that there was a good deal of misunderstanding as to what Sir Percy's views were and why he looked on adequate representation of the tribes as essential and I reported the whole conversation to him, with the result that he sent an admirable letter to the Council saying that in the election assembly which was to decide on the future of the Iraq, every section of the community must be represented and that he must be able to assure his Govt. that this was the case. Jafar Pasha propounded the possible alternative of securing representation by divisions not by specified tribes. I said I thought that would meet the case excellently. Next morning, he and Sasun returned with a revised scheme—2 tribal representatives for each Division, but any tribesman who liked to register could vote in the ordinary way—first-rate proposal, for while it secures a minimum of ten tribal members in the assembly, it does not preclude tribesmen from taking part in elections like other registered electors—if they like.

This was finally carried in the afternoon's sitting, no doubt Sir Percy's letter helping to the desired result. . . .

In the course of the week I had long visits from the two tribal chiefs on the Council. Both are satisfied with the turn the Electoral law has taken . . . I said the matter was entirely in their hands, we didn't care whom they put up as Amir or what kind of Govt. they selected to have, provided we felt sure the choice was freely and fairly made without pressure or intimidation. . . .

To sum my impression of the week, I feel more and more how anxious the people are here with whom we're dealing to work in with us and follow our advice. On big matters and on little matters they are always dropping in to my office to consult me as to Sir Percy's views. So and So is suggested as Mutasarrif of Hillah—will that be all right? Yes, I say firmly, that's all right. My interlocutor breathes a sigh of relief and goes off to vote for him. . . . So with the electoral law—from Sasun downwards they all want to know how they had best meet our views. I never lose an opportunity of saying that our view is guided only by a desire to do the best by them and the country—they know the country best, how do they think this end is to be attained? and on that basis we discuss the matter, whether it's a law or an invitation to dinner! and unless I'm very much mistaken we have got the confidence of the people we're working with. . . .

Oh dear ! I wonder what they'll decide on, and what we'll decide on, and all! What an interminable letter this is—do you mind? . . . .

To H.B.
BAGDAD, December 25th, 1920.

I must tell you a silly story, to understand which you must learn a little Turkish. There's an amusing idiom in Turkish by which you say "such like" by repeating the original word, only changing its initial letter to "M". . . We got recently an account of the conversation between the Sharif and an Arab of these parts—the latter told us the story. The Sharif was fuming against all and sundry: "Who" he cried "is this Kokus Mokus and this Philby Milby Sir Percy was delighted. . . .

I've been feeling a good deal lately how much the Arabs who are our friends, want us to give them lead. They constantly come to me, not only for advice on immediate conduct but in order to ask about the future: "But what do you think, Khatun?. . . . I feel quite clear in my own mind that there is only one workable solution, a son of the Sharif and for choice Faisal: very very much the first choice . . . .

CHAPTER XX
1921

BAGDAD

To H.B.
BAGDAD, January 3rd, 1921.

The big Dulaim Chiefs who live in tents all the winter (only Ali Sulaiman lives in a house outside Ramadi) inhabit during the summer dwellings which are unknown elsewhere. They are called Mahrab and they are, as you might say, the mud counterpart of a tent—a long narrow room with very thin mud walls, windowless, but low down in the North wall just where your head comes when you are sitting on the floor a line of little openings made in patterns by the omission of mud bricks at regular intervals, so that the north wind blows in to cool you. Some square openings at the top of the wall takes off the hot air and they say the room keeps wonderfully fresh. In the men's room the East end is left open and terminates in an open-air divan, a mud floor with a low wall round it, where they sit at night; but by day it can't be as cool as the women's room which is closed on all sides. No one builds these Mahrab but the Dulaim.

Hit on its ancient mound with the pitch wells bubbling up around it, is like nothing else in Mesopotamia, but to me its too full of the memories of rollicking journeys, of ghosts, riding about on camels before the world which was my world cracked together and foundered. I don't think I'll go there again, I don't like the look of those ghosts—they are too happy and confident. It's I who feel a ghost beside them.

We walked round the town in the afternoon and amused ourselves by getting one of the pitch wells alight. The gas laden water came bubbling up, carrying with it writhing black snakes of pitch which form a crust on the pool. We threw in a lighted newspaper and the gas flamed and flickered over the bubbling pool, as if the water burned; then suddenly, after we had watched this devil's miracle for a long time, a thick pitch snake struggled up, and choked for a moment the bubbling water and gas, and the flame went out. Two boys were drawing off the pitch crust, twisting and breaking it off like toffee (a very difficult trick though it looks easy enough in their skilled hands—from father to son they've been at the job some 5,000 years) and throwing it up to where a donkey stood waiting for his load. . . .

North of Hit is No Man's Land. Since we withdrew, the tribes rob and loot all passers by and each man's hand is against his neighbour. Emissaries of Mustafa Kemal drift down through this chaos and Hit has the whole unrest of Asia at its doors. . . .

Upon my soul I'm glad I don't know what this year is going to bring, I don't think I ever woke on a first of January with such feelings of apprehension. You can struggle through misfortune and failure, when they approach you slowly—you see them coming and gradually make up your mind to the inevitable. But if the future opened suddenly and you knew when you woke on the first of

January all that lay before you it would be overwhelming. For the truth is there's little that promises well. . . .

Perceive that I'm not your daughter for nothing for the only fitting end to this tirade is a "God bless my soul—how any sane," etc.! I do write long letters don't I father . . . aren't fools damnable.

To H.B.
BAGDAD, January 22nd, 1921.

I've just got Mother's letter of December 15th saying there's a fandango about my report. The general line taken by the Press seems to be that its most remarkable that a dog should be able to stand up on it's hind legs at all—i.e., a female write a white paper. I hope they'll drop that source of wonder and pay attention to the report itself, if it will help them to understand what Mesopotamia is like. . . .

Talib seems to me to be doing very well. He put up to the Council the other day a long list of proposals for administration appointments in the provinces, Mutasarrifs and Kaimakams. It is very essential to get these appointments made so that people in the provinces may see Arab officials stepping in and realise that there is an Arab Government. . . .

I've a feeling that we're making good progress. There's a greater sense of stability, the Arab Government is gaining ground and people begin to see that we really intend to do by it all we say. Poor human kind that has to spend so much of its time in trying to convince its fellows of the loyalty of its motives! . . . Our task has been complicated by the fact that there was so much suspicion to get over. I know most of the people we are now working with trust us and that's a beginning. . . .

We had to go to the funeral of the woman who was Matron in chief during the war and had come back here to help up with the organisation of our civil hospital. . . . But as Matron in chief she was a tower of strength and I personally loved her for all her kindness to me, beginning from the time when I had jaundice in Basrah and not a soul to look after me. She was an angel of goodness, poor Miss Jones . . . and they gave her a military funeral with the bugle call of the last Post and the salute of rifles into the empty air. And I hoped as I walked behind the Union Jack that covered her coffin that when people walked behind my coffin it would be with thoughts even dimly resembling those that I gave to her. . . .

To H.B.
BAGDAD, Jan. 22nd, 1921.

We have had a distracted week on account of the races. I didn't intend to go more than one day, but the first day Thursday, Aurelia telephoned and said I must come, so I went with them. There was a pretty good sprinkling of Bagdad Magnates and I thought it fairly amusing, so I went again to-day and was very much amused . . . It was Cup Day, I must tell you; we didn't go till after lunch but the Coxes went in state at 11 a.m. and stayed the whole day. Sir Percy wore a frock coat and a grey top hat to the admiration of all beholders. I may mention that I was also very smart in a Paris hat and gown—it's really quite nice to dress up for once, a thing I haven't done for months. . . .

I hear rumours that the Sunnis of Bagdad are considering whether it wouldn't suit their book best to have a Turkish prince as King. They are afraid of being swamped by the Shiahs, against whom a Turk might be a better bulwark than a son of the Sharif. The present Government which is predominantly Sunni isn't doing anything to conciliate the Shiahs. They are now considering a number of administrative appointments for the provinces; almost all the names they put up are Sunnis, even for the wholly Shiah province on the Euphrates, with the exception of Karbala and Nejd where even they haven't the face to propose Sunnis. . . .

Sir Percy will have to intervene when the names come up to him for sanction, for if anything is certain it is that the Euphrates won't put up with Sunni officials. They must make up their minds that they can't have it both ways. If they want popular native institutions, the Shiahs, who are in a large majority, must take their share. There are a number of leading Shiahs on the Euphrates who would prefer British administration (which they can't have) to an Arab Sunni administration or a Turkish Sunni. But when it comes to the point the Moslem never dares to raise his voice against the Moslem, even if it's a kind of Moslem he hates. I believe if we could put up a son of the Sharif at once, he might yet sweep the board; if we hesitate, the tide of public opinion may turn overwhelmingly to the Turks. . . .

To H.B.
BAGDAD, Jan. 30th, 1921.

Do you know this is the eighth Xmas I've been away—1913 Arabia, 1914 Boulogne, 1915 Egypt, 1916 Basrah and the rest Bagdad. Extraordinary isn't it. . . .

To H.B.
BAGDAD, Feb. 7th, 1921.

We've had a rather stormy week owing to heated disagreement between two of the Advisors . . . over the question of how to dispose of the Arab Levies (sort of Gendarmerie). They excited their respective ministers . . . to such a pitch that it was a question whether Sasun wouldn't resign when the decision of the Council went against his voice and the Levies were placed under the Interior instead of under Defence. The decision was a wrong one, I think, but it didn't very much matter, so long as they were placed under some Arab Ministry at once for we want them to take over in the middle Euphrates when British troops are withdrawn from there, as they will be in a fortnight or so. . . .

The Council has made a number of appointments to administrative posts in the provinces—Mutasarrifs and Kaimmakams. Most of them are pretty good, some of them pretty bad. Sir Percy gives way when the Naqib insists. I think he is quite right. We have got to sit by and see them make mistakes. The appointments all originate in the Interior.

To H.B.
BAGDAD, Feb. 13th, 1921.

I write you such long letters because its the only form of diary I keep. . . .

It has been an interesting week marked first by the return of some twenty or more of the deportees whom A.T. sent to the Henjam including one of the ringleaders from Bagdad. And the very next day his son was arrested with a batch of other agitators who owned, wrote or inspired the Istiqlal—of which I sent you extracts last week. The suppression of the paper had been for some time under discussion but Sir Percy said rightly that it was for the Ministry of Interior to take action. It seems to have been entirely successful. . . .

The present Government has got no hold in the Provinces but I think it is gaining ground here. . . .

I don't know what hanky panky the Allies are up to about the mandates, but I'm all on the side of the League of Nations in protesting that they must be made public. That's the essence of them, publicity. . . .

I'm often wrong in prophecy but I believe if we were to refuse the mandate we should have a clamour through the country begging us to accept it. . . .

Meantime the Shiah question is a very burning one. Everyone from the Euphrates provinces says the people there won't accept Sunni officials and the Council goes on blandly appointing them. . . A Shiah of Karbala has at last accepted the ministry of Education which the Naqib was induced to offer him. . . .

Another burning question is that of general amnesty. I feel sure the time has come, or is very near, when we must proceed to this. It will be bitterly opposed by the Military authorities.

. . . . I want to have the kudos of taking the steps ourselves and not to look like one who gives way to pressure from the Arabs. We never do things in time. Sir Percy is very stiffly determined to do what he thinks right, no matter how many soldiers protest, more power to him. For as he rightly says its he who is responsible. . . .

Anyway Sir Percy is standing out firmly about the Shiah appointments. . . . .

The other event of the week besides the suppressing of the Istiqlal, is the arrival of an emissary from Ibn Saud. Ahmad Thanayan is a relation of the Imam and was with his son Faisal in England in 1919. He was brought up in Constantinople and even knows a little French. A very delicate ailing man of about 30, with the fine drawn Najd face, full of intelligence and drawn yet finer by ill health. He has with him Ibn Saud's doctor, Abdullah Ibn Said, a Mosuli by origin, educated in Constantinople. They have come to discuss the interminable question of Ibn Saud's quarrel with the Sharif—for which I think there's no solution; we can only hold it in suspense. . . . and I had them to dinner to-night. It was the most interesting and curious dinner party I ever gave. Besides the two Najdis I had Major Eadie, Saiyid Muhi ud Din and Shakri Eff. al Arusi. The latter is one of the finest figures in Bagdad. An old scholar who comprises in himself all knowledge as such is understood by Islam—he teaches mechanics, using the Hadith (traditions of the prophet) as text book and other sciences by like methods—a true Wahhabi, he neither drinks nor smokes, and he is the only known Mohammadan who has never married. . . . He found in Wahhabi, Central Arabia the land of his dreams and looks upon it as the true source of all inspiration and learning. When he came in he fell on Ahmad Thanayan's neck while the latter fished among his beautiful embroidered cashmiri robes and produced from them a letter from Ibn Saud to Shukri. And to crown the cordiality of the gathering, Muhi ud Din discovered in the Doctor a former Constantinople acquaintance, and the embracing began afresh on their part. So we sat down to table—as queer a gathering as you could well see; Shukri, the unworldly old scholar, hanging on Ahmad Thanayan's words while the latter described the immense progress of the extreme Wahhabi sect, the Akhwan, (brotherhood) in Najd; Muhi ud Din, the smooth politician and divine,. . . . and Abmad with his long sunken face lighted up by the purest spirit of fanatical Islam. "The Imam, God preserve him, under God has guided the tribes in the right way." "Praise be to God," ejaculated Shukri—"They are learning wisdom and religion under the rules of the Brotherhood,"—Shukri Eff: "God is great . . . .. Not that they show violence,"—Ahmad Effend. "God forbid,"—"No such things happen among us as happened in Europe with the Inquisition and with Calvins"—(I must tell you incidentally that the Akhwan when they do battle kill all wounded and then put the women and children of their enemies, who are also infidels else they wouldn't fight the Ahkwan, to death . . . .) After dinner my four Arab guests carried on a brisk conversation among themselves. They discussed medicines and the properties of herbs, the doctor, incidentally, stating that incense was a capital disinfectant, they discussed the climate and customs of Najd and other matters of importance. Major Eadie and I sat listening and I felt as if we were disembodied spirits playing audience to an Oriental symposium, so entirely did our presence fail to impede the flow of talk which the learned men of the East are accustomed to hold with one another. Muhi ud Din played the game with the perfection of courtesy, but when they all went away, he last, I whispered in his ear "For all that I shall not join the brotherhood," "Nor I," he whispered back fervently. It's an interesting world I'm living in isn't it? . . . .

To H.B.
On the way to Cairo, February 24th, 1921.
On the Tigris boat and continued on the Hardinge

We're off and I've put off writing this week till I got on to the ship as any way I shall carry a letter myself quicker than the post would carry it. . . .

The last week has seen the first arrival of a new element, the Mesopotamian officers who were in Syria are beginning to return, the first to come being Nuri Pasha Said, Jafar's brother-in-law. He came last week. . . The day after his arrival Jafar telephoned to me and asked when Nuri could see Sir Percy. Sir Percy asked them to come at once and stay to lunch. They came at 12 and sat for an hour with me. I called up Capt. Clayton, who knew and liked Nuri in Syria; Major Murray dropped in and we had a momentous talk. The moment I saw him I realised that we had before us a strong and supple force with which we must either use or engage in difficult combat. We began very gently feeling the ground as we went; my first questions he answered very warily; then as I persisted, he took his line and in a few sentences developed his programme—the summoning of the constituent assembly which was to perform four tasks: (1) to appoint a Cabinet, (2) to select a ruler, (3) to pass a law authorising some form of conscription for the Arab Army, (4) to design a flag. "That's all right," said we, and proceeded to discuss the points in detail. . . .

[There are no letters from Gertrude during the Conference—Her father joined her in Cairo for a while.]

To H.B.
BAGDAD, April 12th, 1921.

I spent the whole of next day, Sunday, getting through papers in the office and came back to tea, and a number of visitors, mostly European. Yesterday and to-day have been very busy days with a great deal of work and a great many callers. Faisal arrives at Suez to-morrow so that in a week or ten days we ought to be receiving the telegrams he is to address to his supporters announcing his candidature. By that time Sir Percy ought to be able to make a fuller pronouncement for he will have received permission from Mr. Churchill who will have consulted the Cabinet at home. Things should therefore begin to move pretty quickly. . . . .

To F.B.
BAGDAD, April 16th, 1921.

Will you send me some thick woollen tricotine of a blue as near as may be to the enclosed colour, enough for Marie to make me a winter everyday gown, jumper and skirt. Also some soft blue silk on which to mount the skirt, the same colour. Further will you give a pattern of the blue to my hat maker, Anne Marie in Sloane Street, and tell her to send me by parcel post a blue felt hat—she knows the kind of shape like the green felt she made for me last year trimmed with reddish brown wings, pheasant would do or a red brown feather trimming of some kind. Not ostrich feathers, that's too dear.

To H.B.
BAGDAD, April 17th, 1921.

. . .There was a rumour—that on the way down to Basrah when we went away, I had said to persons not named that the object of the conference was to declare Faisal King . . . it was entirely untrue, but no doubt he knows that formerly when people pressed me to give my own opinion I have always said that Faisal would I thought be the best choice. I am therefore identified as a Sharifian, which I don't mind at all, but I have always been careful to say that the choice must rest with the people, and I am now careful to keep my private opinion for the present to myself. . . .

Meantime telegrams are going daily to the King of the Hijaz begging him to send one of his sons. The functions of the Arab Ministers will be carried on by the Advisors (British). We have not yet received the telegram promised by Mr.

Churchill after he had consulted with the Cabinet; we are not therefore at liberty to make public that Faisal has H.M.G's consent to run as a candidate, but I felt sure that some announcement about the conference could not be delayed and I got Sir Percy to publish a preliminary statement. It contains nothing about the elections but it says that a general amnesty will be declared very shortly and this has been received with acclamation. . . . In a very short time therefore important new factors should have entered into the game : Faisal himself with his declared candidature, the pardoned leaders of last year's revolt, the Sharifian paper and the suspension of the Arab ministers . . . .

Meantime the general attitude of the country with regard to ourselves has immensely improved. There's a consensus of opinion that whatever happens they can't do without our guidance and help. Being Sunday, I rode down early this morning to Haji Naji and had breakfast with him on native bread, fresh unsalted butter, sugared apples and coffee. He is hand in glove with the Sharifians, thinks Naji, Nuri, Jafar and co., the best Mesopotamians he knows and is convinced that the overwhelming majority in the country is for Faisal. Said he with his customary wisdom, "Let the people do it themselves; the British Government need not interfere." It is so restful and delicious sitting with him under his fruit trees which were in flower when I left and are now loaded with green fruit. It was a heavenly morning and hot sun and a cool little north wind. . . . I'm happy in helping to forward what I profoundly believe to be the best thing for this country and the wish of the best of its people. . . .

To H.B.
BAGDAD, April. 25th, 1921.

Capt. Thomas who is a musician, carried up a piano with him to Shatrah and invited his Sheikhs to come and listen to the Pathétique sonata. At the end he asked what they thought of it. "Wallahi," said one "khosh daqqah." By God a good thumping.

To her Parents.
BAGDAD, May 2nd, 1921.

Yesterday, Sunday, their Excellencies took a party to Babylon with me as guide. We left at 7 a.m. and arrived by motor about 11, saw the Palace and Ishtar gate and had an excellent lunch—need I say since it was provided by Lady Cox in the German Expeditions-Haus. . . .

I've just had about 30 ladies to tea, quite a nice party in the garden, so that's that.

The office hours are now 7 a.m. till 1, which means breakfasting at 6:30. I think I shall rather like it. Later in the summer I shall come back for lunch and then have a rest in my house, but as yet it's not at all hot, an exceptionally cool pleasant spring. . . .

Good-bye my dearest beloved Father and Mother, I'm happy and interested in my work and very happy in the confidence of my chief. When I think of this time last year. . . .

To H.B.
BAGDAD, May 5th, 1921.

Your weekly letters are the greatest joy, I don't know what I should do without them. . . .

We are not having a very easy time. Persia is a doubtful quantity but so far remains quiescent.

In Angora, I think I told you, the extremists have got the upper hand, which from our point of view means that Turkish agitation continues on our northern frontier. . . .

My young Nationalist friends are alarmed at the activity of the Turks on the frontier and the existence of a large body of pro-Turkish feeling in this country. Their fear is that the return of the Turks would kill or indefinitely postpone their dearest hopes—namely the setting up of an independent Arab State. This is the sentiment which we want to foster, and as it is held exclusively by Sharifians, they are the people for us to back, as we decided at Cairo. Unfortunately there must have been many delays and Faisal who should have been here in the middle of May has not yet left Mecca. The League of Nations is holding up the mandate in deference to American prejudice and Mr. Churchill's statement in the House which ought to have taken place on June 2nd is again postponed. Sir Percy has urged that we should drop the mandate altogether and go for a treaty with the Arab State when it is constituted. It would be a magnificent move if we're bold enough to do it. It isn't the mandate which bothers us here—no Nationalist wants to shake loose from British help and control —but the word mandate isn't popular and a freely negotiated treaty would be infinitely better liked, besides giving us a much freer hand. We have always known that Faisal would ultimately insist on a treaty in place of a mandate—now we have the opportunity of making a 'beau geste' and giving of our own accord what we should certainly have had to give later at his request.

Meantime the amnesty is out and my friends are busying themselves in the constitution of a moderate Sharifian party with a definite programme- the latter was submitted to me. . . . Sir Percy has told them through me to go ahead and rely on his support. . . .

Captain Smith and I (you know he's the son of the Master of Balliol) went to another school function this week. It was a prodigious affair. 'Le tout' Bagdad was there—the Arab world. We were the only English, and it lasted the usual three hours. We sat in rows and listened to speeches, songs and poems and I really believe the audience liked it. There were parts of it which were quite remarkably long speeches (no speech lasted less than 15 minutes) about the light of education being the sole ray that illumines the world; but I must confess that there were also interesting moments. one was an ode by a half paralysed old poet, Jamil Zuhawi—there was 35 minutes of it, which is long for an ode, but nevertheless it was worth sitting through. He is not only a great poet but he is a very great 'diseur'. He began by tumbling off the estrade and having to be poked and pushed back on to it while everyone murmured "Allah!" Then he embarked on an invocation of some 20 couplets to the skies of the Iraq. He began very quietly with great throbbing lines which pulsed on to a glowing volume of sound. The whole audience took fire; they leant forward with their faces illuminated and time after time the falling couplet was revivified with a "Repeat! Repeat!" . . . Jamil Zuhawi was followed by another and rival poet, a man called Maruf. He is said to be one of the greatest Arabists living. I didn't understand the poem which was immensely applauded but I did understand the speech with which he prefaced it and I thought it first rate, very bold and liberal and full of good sense. . . .

We all had to get up at 5 next morning to go to the King's birthday parade which was held in the desert quite near my house. All the Arab magnates came and there were an astonishing number of troops; but this was a deception—we happened to have in Bagdad the regiments which have just come down from Persia and are going to India or England. It ended with a flight of 30 aeroplanes which was really splendid. The Coxes gave a dinner that night. . . . It was very well done. After dinner we sat on the terrace over the river. The trees were hung with coloured lamps and the lights of the town glittered across the river. It's a great asset having your river running through the heart of your city. . . .

To F.B.
BAGDAD, May 8th, 1921.

On Friday there was an immense tea party at the Persian Consul's in honour of the Shah's birthday—I wonder how many more birthdays the Shah will celebrate on his throne! Persian affairs seem fairly stable but there's a great pressure of opinion against the rich landlord class, most of whom are indeed in prison, the Shah only, who is the greatest landlord of them all, being spared. . . .

I was feeling so tired of sitting up and behaving that this morning, Sunday, I rode out early to Karradah and breakfasted with Haji Naji who is the salt of the earth. We gossiped pleasantly of all that was happening—he is eminently sensible—and walked about under the fruit trees where the apricots are just ripening. I ate the first to-day. This week, Ramadhan begins, which will put an end to tea parties, a thing I shan't regret. I go into the office at 7 a.m. come away about 3:30, and if there's a tea party to follow I haven't a minute all day in which to ride or rest or look about me.

Our politics are rather hanging fire. . . . A bewildered little Saiyid from Najaf way came to see me one day, and told me his hopes and fears. He was very shy. . . . He left me feeling that it wasn't astonishing that they don't know what we're up to. First we imprison them for saying they want Abdullah and then we encourage them to ask for Faisal! One of my best informants about affairs in Bagdad, when he relates the conversation with people who inquire what he thinks the British Government wants, generally gives as his share in the conversation, this answer: "Wallahi, my brother! who knows what is in their minds."

To H.B.
BAGDAD, May 15th, 1921.

Your letters have an almost too acute interest. . . . You speak of a possible settlement, but more than a month has passed without one. It is most interesting about the Defence Force and the miners joining it. It doesn't sound as if there were much bitterness in our part of the world. . . . I think of all our countryside at this beautiful time and wish I were there, nevertheless I'm happy in the work here and it ought to develop very soon in various directions. We haven't even yet got the amnesty out. It has been held up first by having to consult the French, then the Government of India. Nor has there yet been a pronouncement about the elections, but that is because we had to find out first what parts of the Kurdish provinces would come in to the Arab State. I hope that we shall know this week that most of them will. Answers are beginning to flow in from the Sharif in reply to the first telegram sent to him asking him to send one of his sons here. The answers are characteristically vague. . . .

Basrah opinion will carry a good deal of weight. They are trying to draw up a programme for the election which will be wide enough to embrace the greatest number of opinions. I've got the draft and it seems quite good. If one leaves them alone, giving them only the sympathetic encouragement they ask, they come to an agreement with one another, and that's the best. . . .

It strikes me that not many people of the upper classes are fasting this year. Even the Naqib, for the first time in his life, is not keeping the fast—for reasons of health. He would have died of it. . . . I wonder how long the fast will hold Islam—like the veiling of women it might disappear, as a universal institution, pretty fast. The women who have come back from Syria or Constantinople find the Bagdad social observances very trying. They have been accustomed to much greater freedom. As soon as we get our local institutions firmly established they will be bolder. They and their husbands are afraid that any steps taken now would set all the prejudiced old tongues wagging and jeopardise their future. Nevertheless these new men bring their wives to see me, which is an unexpected departure from Bagdad customs according to which a man would never go about with his wife, I welcome everything that tends in this direction, but, again one can do so little but give sympathetic welcome to the women. They must work out their own salvation and it wouldn't help them to be actively backed by an infidel, even if the infidel were I who am permitted many things here. . . .

Maurice must be having a time with his Territorials and the Defence Force, bless him.

To H.B.
BAGDAD, May 22nd, 1921.

I anticipated that things would happen much more quickly. But they haven't happened. They are, I may say, just beginning now, for the telegrams from Mecca . . . are making an appreciable effect. People are inclined to think . . . . that they are more or less inspired by H.M.G. or at rate imply a leaning in a Sharifian direction on the part of H.M.G. They are the natural result of our saying that a son of the Sharif would be regarded as a suitable candidate and might be approached as to whether he would stand. . . .

Naji Suwaidi has drawn up and submitted to me a programme for a moderate Sharifian party—which I showed to Sir Percy who thought it all right.

I'm very grateful to Naji for keeping me so closely in touch. . . . I've found Naji very sensible and capable as well as very patient under the prolonged delay. All this promises well for the future. . . .

We're debating what we can do to strengthen the foundation of Ctesiphon so as to save the great façade wall. There's no immediate prospect of its falling but it has a very marked list outwards. We have dug some holes down to the foundations and I went out early on Saturday morning with Major Wilson (the architect, you remember) to look at them. He proposes to put a big wad of concrete against the foundations underground, and I'm afraid we shall have to slope it off against the wall for about 10 feet of its height above ground, which won't be pretty, but ought to make the wall as safe as we can make it.

To H.B.
BAGDAD, May 29th, 1921.

It's too soon for a forecast but probably this turn of the wheel will mean that North Persia will fall once more under Russian domination- under the new Russia whose foreign policy differs not a whit from that of the old . . . . .

From Anatolia the news is not good. The extremists have got the upper hand at Angora, they will accept no compromise over Smyrna or Thrace; they are in for a prolonged struggle with the Greeks during the whole of which they will be bitterly anti-European. Our chief hope there is that if we get Faisal he may come to some settlement with them on our northern frontier.

The amnesty is out tomorrow, Heaven be praised. It will set free the hands of our Nationalists and they will get to work in earnest. Mr. Churchill's statement to the House ought to clear the air further, for he must, I take it, say something about Faisal's being a candidate acceptable to H.M.G. which will be widely regarded as indicating that he is the most acceptable.

I'm thinking of going to Sulaimaniyah at the end of the week for a few days—to Kirkuk for a couple of nights and so on by motor. Sulaimaniya has refused, on a plebiscite, to come in under the Arab Govt. and is going for the present to be a little Kurdish enclave administered directly under Sir Percy. . . . The population is wholly Kurdish and they say they don't want to be part of an Arab State. I've never been there and as we shall hear a good deal about it in the High Commissioner's Office I should like to get the colour and sentiment of it at first hand, so I spend my evenings rubbing up my rusty Persian.

To H.B.
BAGDAD, June 12th, 1921.

Things are at last beginning to move. Telegrams have come from King Hussain saying that Faisal leaves for the Iraq this week.

What everybody wants to know is our wishes and as soon as they get any kind of lead they will all, I think, come into line. Meantime, I receive many agitated visits from my young Sharifian friends asking for reassurances and for guidance, which I give to the best of my ability and according to Sir Percy's directions. He is a master hand at the game of politics; it's an education to watch him playing it . . . . .

I've just had this Sunday morning a long visit from two big Sheikhs, Fahad Bey of the Anazeh and Ali Sulaiman, of the Dulaim. Both came down from Ramadi to see Sir Percy and find out his views... So they have been told to stay here for a day or two when H.M.G. will make pronouncements.

I don't for a moment hesitate about the rightness of our policy. We can't continue direct British control though the country would be better governed by it, but its rather a comic position to be telling people over and over again that whether they like it or not they must have Arab not British Govt. . . .

To H.B.
BAGDAD June 19th, 1921.

We here are now launched on our perilous way. On Monday my old friend the Mayor came to my office and said that since Faisal was coming it was up to the notables of Bagdad to make a proper reception for him and not to leave it all to the young extremists. Faisal was a famous Arab and the son of a King and must be treated as such. I said I thought that view perfectly proper, he as the Mayor of the town, should make the arrangements.

The younger men have frequented my office this week. We had to settle on a temporary flag—I suppose the Constituent Assembly will have the final word there—and then there was the difficult question as to where Faisal should be lodged. If only we had got the official communiqué from home earlier everything would have been much easier ... I believe Faisal is statesman enough to realise that he must capture the older more steady going people while at the same time not chilling over much the enthusiasm of his more ardent supporters.

Well, to continue my tale . . . Here was Faisal arriving at Basrah on the 23rd and we still without any communiqué from home. . . . Meanwhile his partisans were growing naturally impatient and anxious to get busy. Sir Percy realised this and unofficially approved the project presented through me that they should summon the town to a big meeting on Friday, 6 days before Faisal's arrival. As soon as the invitations were out, in the name of Naji Suwaidi, clerics and others dropped in to my office to sound me as to whether they ought to go "Oh yes." said I "why not?" the meeting has the approval of H.E." On Thursday afternoon the Naqib . . . made a sound move. He informed the Council of Ministers that Faisal was coming and that they must make preparations to receive him properly and see that he was suitably lodged. Therefore they appointed a reception committee of 5 Ministers. I had been out after tea and on the way home I met the Secretary to the Council, who stopped me and told me this excellent news. I rode on much cheered and when I got home I found a letter from Sir Percy enclosing the long expected communiqué which he told me to get through to Jafar or Naji Suwaidi before the meeting which was to take place at 8 next morning. By good luck Jafar with his wife and sister were dining so I translated the communiqué to them and gave it to Jafar for the meeting. They were all delighted with it and indeed it was just what we wanted.

Next day Naji Suwaidi and the Mutasarrif, came to my office after the meeting to report. It had been a great success, everyone had been present and 60 people had been chosen to go down to Basrah to welcome Faisal—would I kindly make arrangements with the Railway. There remained the question of his lodging here which they proposed to solve by putting him into some rooms in the Sarai (the Government offices) which were now under repair, . . . if they could be got ready in time. Public Works declared that it couldn't be done. Jafar telephoned to me in despair on Saturday morning; I telephoned to Public Works, made suggestions for covering bare walls with hangings and finally the thing was arranged.

In the evening I went to the Naqib, whom I found receiving the report of the Reception Committee. Directly I got in he showed me a telegram which had just come to him from King Hussain couched in very suitable terms and announcing that he was sending his son Faisal to him. . . .

This morning, being Sunday, Mr. Tod and I rode before breakfast to Haji Naji . . . Haji Naji presently drew me aside and told me he thought of going with the party to Basrah only he was rather afraid of being lost in the ruck. I said I would give him a letter of introduction to Mr. Cornwallis, who is coming with Faisal, so that he might be treated with consideration. . . .

To H.B.
June 23rd, 1921.

Faisal arrives in Bastah to-day. . His adherents anticipate that his coming will be the sign for a great popular ovation. Heaven send it may be so for it will immensely simplify matters for us. Meantime there can be no question that it is regarded with anxiety by the Magnates. On Monday we had a strong deputation from Basrah bringing a petition in which they asked for separate treatment for the Basrah area. They were ready to accept a common King but they asked that Basrah might have a separate Legislative Assembly, a separate Army, police service and raise and spend its own taxes, making a suitable contribution to the central administration. They came to me on their way to Sir Percy and asked me to support their request. I said No; whatever H.M.G. decided would have my loyal support as a Government servant, but until that decision was given I must exercise my private opinion which was that what they asked was not in the interests of the country as a whole and would not prove to be permanently in their own interests... With that they went to Sir Percy who gave them a sympathetic hearing but said in general terms that he would not conceal from them that H.M.G. wanted to see a United Iraq. However a large degree of local autonomy would be consistent with that end and a compromise on these lines should be considered . . . . I have been elected President of the Bagdad Public Library . . .

The Reception Committee got their programme through the Council on Monday. Mutasarrif Rashid Bey, a strong Sharifian, brought it in to us for Sir Percy's approval on Tuesday. What they wanted to know was what part Sir Percy was going to take and above all whether he would provide a guard of honour. I promised to get the reply as soon as possible. But things don't go as quickly as that and yesterday morning, Wed., Rashid Bey turned up again and said they had no answer. Later in the morning I arranged that he and Majid Bey al Shawi should come in and have a personal interview. Meantime Nuri Said, who had been in Basrah, had seen me the previous evening and told me about the popular demonstration. He thought it might result in an immediate acclamation of Faisal as King, and asked me anxiously whether we should mind that. I answered in suitable terms that we only wanted to know the opinion of the country.... All this I reported to Sir Percy that night at a ball given by Lady Cox and it may have partly influenced his answer to Rashid Bey next morning. Anyway Faisal is to have his guard of honour both at Basrah and here....

I expect Faisal will come to terms with the Basrah magnates and satisfy them that Basrah will receive full consideration. Mr. Cornwallis is with him, a tower of strength and wisdom, I've sent him a letter explaining how the wind blows throughout the Iraq and as soon as he comes up here I shall be able to keep him posted in local politics....

Already the whole town is flying the Sharifian flag. I saw it to-day flying on every other shop in the Bazaar. The intention is good but the flag heraldically bad. I don't know if you know it. The red triangle colour comes over the black and green colour on colour, and therefore wrong isn't it....

Yesterday we had news of Faisal's arrival in Basrah and an excellent reception, heaven be praised.... Faisal has now gone off to Najaf and Karbala and gets here on Wednesday 29th. Half of my mornings have been spent in receiving visits from the Mutasarrif or exchanging messages with him on the telephone about the reception and festivities here. We have got it right at last I think. Mosul also is coming forward. A large deputation of all the leading people came down here last night and Nuri Said, whom I saw this morning, tells me that their line of argument is that they can't think why there's such division of opinion here and that far the best course is to proclaim Faisal King at once.... and said that if they hadn't had my constant help they could not have carried on, and I replied that I stood fast all the time in Sir Percy's unswerving purpose. But I have been useful to them all the same, these last weeks and I'm glad I've been here.

I'm told that Naji Suwaidi is in favour of a mandate rather than the proposed treaty, because a mandate gives us more authority! Faisal wants a treaty I know, so probably that's the way it will work out, and for my part I think its quite immaterial. You can't run a mandate without the goodwill of the people, and if you've got that it doesn't matter whether its a mandate or a treaty, but what rejoices me is the fulfilment of my dream that we should sit by in an attitude of repose and have them coming up our front door steps to beg us to be more active....

NOTICE TO ALL AUTHORS, PUBLISHERS AND BOOKSELLERS

The Salam Library, Bagdad, intends to issue a periodical publication—in Arabic and English—the object of which is to review books published in Oriental languages, Arabic, Persian, Turkish, Hebrew, Syriac, Hindustani, etc.;

and also books published in European languages, English, French and German, etc.

This publication will deal only with books presented to the library with a request from the publisher or author asking for a review or notice of the book.

It will also give an account of such manuscripts as may be found in the library or are to be found in local bookshops. Thus the Salam Library's periodical publication will be the best means for introducing European books to Orientals and Oriental books to Europeans and will serve as a means to facilitate the sale of books.

The Committee of the Salam Library is composed of Arab and British members who will undertake the publication of the periodical.

(Signed) GERTRUDE BELL, President, Salam Library. BAGDAD

[Gertrude sent copies of this notice to be distributed in England, together with a circular, addressed to English publishers, asking if they would care to send books to the Salam Library].

CHAPTER XXI
1921

BAGDAD

To H.B.
BAGDAD, June 30th, 1921.

It's being so frightfully interesting—there! There! Let me begin at the beginning. Where was I? It was Monday's vernacular paper which gave the first full account of Faisal's arrival at Basrah and the quite admirable speech which he made at a big function they had for him. Tumbling in on this came an agent whom I had sent down to Basrah to bring me a report of the temper of his reception and gave a very glowing account of the effort made by this speech which he said inclined all hearts towards Faisal. This was cheering and in the evening Naji Suwaidi and Nuri dropped in after tea; Naji back from Basrah with a rosy tale. Then we fell to talking of the next steps and agreed that we could not leave him here not knowing what his position would be for 6 or 8 weeks till the elections were over. Somehow or other the country must be got to declare itself. Sir Percy and I had already discussed this but I didn't feel at liberty to mention the fact to my two friends, so I only gave them comforting reassurances. But we don't want Faisal to come in by a coup d'état of the extremists—we must have something much more constitutional than that. . . . On Wednesday Faisal was to arrive at 7 a.m. Col. Joyce and I motored to the station together, going all the way up the big street to the upper bridge. The whole town was decorated, triumphal arches, Arab flags, and packed with people, in the streets, on the housetops, everywhere. At the station immense crowds. It was very well arranged with seats for the magnates all round, and all filled with magnates. Sir Percy and Sir Aylmer and a guard of honour and all. But we learnt there had been an 'éboulement' on the line—a telegram had been received to say he was coming by motor and hoped to arrive at the appointed hour. We waited, we talked, we shook hands all round—at least I did—we looked at the Arab levies and towards 8, paf! came a message down the line that he was in the train after all, couldn't get through and might be here at mid-day! Sir Percy quickly took command. Noon at the end of June is not an hour at which you can hold a great reception out of doors... He was accordingly asked to spend the day in the train and get in at 6 p.m. And so we all went home. I to the office where presently Nuri came in and assured me that the evening's reception would be better even than that of the morning. Then Haji Naji, up from Basrah, full of delight. Thanks to the letter I had given him to Mr. Cornwallis he had spoken to Faisal and he was the being they wanted and that was all right! . . . And so behold me at 5:30 again setting off for the station . . . And this time the train arrived.

Sidi Faisal stood at the carriage door looking very splendid in full Arab dress, saluting the guard of honour. Sir Percy and Sir Aylmer went up to him as he got out and gave him a fine ceremonious greeting, and all the people clapped. He went down the line of the guard of honour, inspecting it . . . . Sir Percy began to present the Arab Magnates, representatives of the Naqib, etc. I hid behind Mr. Cornwallis, but Faisal saw me and stepped across to shake hands with me. He looked excited and anxious—you're not a king on approbation without any tension of the spirit—but it only gave his natural dignity a more human charm. Then he was lost in the crowd and Col. Joyce and I stayed talking to Mr. Cornwallis who, poor dear, was so dried up with thirst that he could scarcely talk at all. But what he said was that up to now things hadn't gone well. The people were standing back. . . .

All the way up the story they had heard was, the High Commissioner is neutral, the Khatun and Mr. Garbett want Faisal and Mr. Philby wants a republic. . . . Naturally Faisal was bewildered—was the High Commissioner with him and if so why did his officers adopt a different attitude? All the more was he bewildered because he was told with equal frequency that if the local officers would lift a finger all the people would follow their lead. Why wasn't the finger lifted if that was the official policy? We explained all that had happened, and the long delay in getting the pronouncement from England, and that Sir Percy was absolutely sound and determined to carry the thing through. . . .

This morning on my way to the office I went to the Sarai and gave my card to Faisal's A.D.C. He said would I wait a minute, the Amir would like to see me; it was a little past seven, rather early for a morning call. I waited, talking to the A.D.C. and presently Faisal sent for me. They showed me into a big room and he came quickly across in his long white robes, took me by both hands and said "I couldn't have believed that you could have given me so much help as you have given me." So we sat down on a sofa. I assured him that Sir Percy was absolutely with him. . . .

Mr. Cornwallis came into the office later and I told him I had called on Faisal. He said (I must tell you because it pleased me so much) "That was quite right. All the way up he had been hearing your praise and he gave me a message for you in case he didn't see you to speak to to-day. I was to tell you how grateful he was. And my private spy the man I sent to Basrah tells me the people constantly say, "Is the Khatun satisfied. . . ."

The next event was that evening's banquet in the Maude gardens. It was really beautifully done. The place lighted with electric lights looked lovely.

Faisal carried on a little conversation in French with Sir Aylmer, but mostly he and I and Sir Percy, and Abdul Majid and I talked across the table. Faisal looked very happy and I felt very happy and so did Sir Percy. . . .

Then got up our great poet, of whom I've often told you, Jamil Zahawi, and recited a tremendous ode in which he repeatedly alluded to Faisal as King of the Iraq and everyone clapped and cheered. And then there stepped forward into the grassy space between the tables a Shiah in white robes and a black cloak and big black turban and chanted a poem of which I didn't understand a word. It was far too long and as I say quite unintelligible but nevertheless it was wonderful. The tall robed figure chanting and marking time with an uplifted hand, the darkness in the palm trees beyond the illuminated circle—it hypnotised you. . . .

But its not all smooth yet. We get reports about the lower Euphrates tribes preparing monstrous petitions in favour of a republic and of Shiah Alim Mujtahids being all against Faisal. I don't believe half of them are true but they keep one in anxiety. To-day I sent for one of the principal Euphrates Sheikhs. . . . He is a strong Sharifian and we talked the whole matter over. Before him I had had an influential group of Bagdadis saying that we must finish the business, we couldn't wait for elections. Somehow or other Faisal must be proclaimed King. I referred them to Faisal himself, knowing that he has discussed it with Sir Percy, and told them to take Faisal's orders. In the afternoon Faisal sent for me and told me his ideas which were very sound. I also gave him a few suggestions to bring before Sir Percy. . . . With that Faisal went off to see Sir Percy, so I should think things will happen. I'm beginning to feel as if I couldn't stand it much longer! One is straining every nerve all the time to pull the matter forward; talking, persuading, writing, I find myself carrying on the argument even in my sleep. But anyway Faisal's antechamber contains a good many of the right people and it's comforting to think that he can do the talking so well himself. We've got Bagdad and I'm pretty certain we've got Mosul the rest will fall into line.

TO H.B.
BAGDAD, Thursday, July 7th, 1921.

On Monday morning I was having a crucial interview. The leading Christian here, came in with the Mutasarrif and Naji Suwaidi to urge that once Faisal had come we couldn't afford to wait for election and must resort to referendum to place him on the throne. We were all fully aware of this, indeed Faisal had talked of it when I saw him on Saturday, but he added that the one thing he feared was a coup d'état, and we must continue to make the proceedings as constitutional as we could . . . Accordingly Sir Percy saw the Naqib and it was arranged that the Council shall consider how soon the elections can take place, since there is obviously urgent need to come to a settlement. Sir Percy has ascertained that we can't get the registration of electors through under two months. The local press has already began to talk about a referendum, without an inspiration. I read the four local papers every morning and if there's anything I think unsuitable I intimate the fact to the editors, directly or indirectly. To-day I had to do it directly; one enthusiast had published a violent attack on the French in Syria. I sent for him and proved to his satisfaction that they had better leave the Syrians to take care of themselves. . . .

What helps everything is that Faisal's personality goes three quarters of the way. He has been roping in adherents; they most of them come round to me to be patted on the back at which I'm getting to be an adept. It's a little more delicate when they are trembling on the brink but I then bring in the overwhelming argument that Sir Percy and Faisal are working hand in hand—it's really remarkable how completely satisfied they are if they know that Sir Percy approves. He has an extraordinary hold on the country.

Most of the towns—I think I told you—have sent deputations to greet

Faisal. With these I exchange visits.

Its rather a complication in all these festivities that the temperature is 120—at least that's what it goes up to by day.

One by one all the leaders of the rebellion are coming in to pay their respects. One came on Tuesday and got a fine dressing down first from me and then from Sir Percy. However he took it in good part and went away saying that he was delighted with Sir Percy! All the Sheikhs and Saiyids who fought against us are turning up also. I need not say that Sir Percy's handling of them is perfect. . . . This morning an opportunity presented itself in which I could both do the right thing and the thing that pleased me—a rare combination. There came in one of the leaders of the revolt, a horrid worthless man . . . . and I was more icily rude to him than I've ever been to anyone. He had evidently hoped to climb back into some sort of esteem by being allowed to see Sir Percy; I gave him firstly clearly to understand that Sir Percy could not receive him and he retired in disorder. It was a great satisfaction.

Friday, July 8th. Last night the Naqib gave a dinner to Faisal in his house opposite his own mosque. The English guests were Sir Percy and his staff. All the rest were the Ministers and Notables of Bagdad. Sir Percy took me. The streets were crowded with people as we drove up; the Naqib's family received us at the door and we climbed up two flights of stairs into a roof overlooking the mosque, a sort of wide balcony. it was carpeted and lighted; the mosque door opposite was hung with lamps and the minarets ringed with them. The Naqib was sitting with the Ministers; he got up and faltered forward to meet Sir Percy, a touching and dignified figure. The rest of the guests some 100 I should think, sat below us on the open gallery which runs round two sides of the courtyard on the first story of the house. A burning wind blew on us while we drank coffee and talked till the clapping of hands in the street announced the arrival of Faisal. The Naqib got up and helped by his personal physician walked across the whole of the carpeted space and reached the head of the stairs just as Faisal's white-robed figure appeared. They embraced formally on both cheeks and walked back hand in hand to the end of the balcony where we were all standing up. Faisal sat down between the Naqib and Sir Percy and after a few minutes dinner was announced. Faisal, Sir Percy, the C. in C. and I went down: then the Naqib with a servant on each side of him to help him. The long dinner table stood on the open gallery. Faisal sat in the place of honour opposite the Naqib with the C. in C. on one side of him and I on the other. . . . It was a wonderful sight that dinner party. The robes and their uniforms and the crowds of servants, all brought up in the Naqib's household, the ordered dignity, the real solid magnificence, the tension of spirit which one felt all round one, as we felt the burning heat of the night. For, after all, to the best of our ability, we were making history.

[The Naqib, so much honoured and esteemed, died in May 1927.)

But you may rely upon one thing—I'll never engage in creating kings again; its too great a strain . . . .

Sir Percy and I, as we drove home, felt we had jumped another hedge, but we agreed that we were in a very stiff country.

Again to-day the same sort of morning in the office—it's a morning which lasts from 7 to 1:30! Faisal was there interviewing Sir Percy even before I got there. . . . After lunch Sir Percy, Mr. Garbett and I drafted the crucial letter to the Council, and soon after 3 I came home and got to Faisal's house at four o'clock with all the tribal maps, to give him a lesson in tribal geography. Mr. Cornwallis turned up too. There it was cool for we sat in a big vaulted room, half underground, and for an hour we studied tribes and drank iced lemonade, after which we spent another hour discussing the formation of Faisal's first Cabinet and his very excellent idea of creating a sort of Privy Council of laymen and notables . . . Came Izzat Pasha with a request for an interview with Sir Percy which I got him at once... He had come to tell Sir Percy that he had seen Faisal and could bring in to him the Kurdish chiefs any time Sir Percy wished. . . . "Khatun," said he, "I've seen Walis and Sultans and Generals but I've never yet seen anyone like Sir Percy, and as long as he is guiding us I am satisfied." It is true that Sir Percy may easily be considered better than the average Wali, but Izzat's conviction that he was better than anyone was unmistakable. Isn't it an extraordinary position for any man to hold? The whole country waits for his word. What should we have done without him? . . .

I confidently expect that the Hindiyah tribes will roll up this week. That's what it's all like, they won't take a step till they asked the advice of some one of us whom they know. . . .

To H.B.
BAGDAD, July 16th, 1921.

The heat is terrific, day after day over 121 and the nights hot too... Sir Percy and I think we ought to put at end of difficult telegrams home: N.B. temp. 121.8. On the other hand, politics are running on wheels greased with extremely well melted grease and Sir Percy and Faisal are scoring great triumphs. On Monday the 11th the Council, at the instance of the Naqib . . . unanimously declared Faisal King, and charged the Ministry of the Interior with the necessary arrangements. I was dining alone that night and feeling anxious—the heat makes one not quite normal, I think. You may fancy what it was like to get to the office next morning and hear this news from Sir Percy, the moment I arrived. He added that he felt, good as this was, that it wasn't enough and that we must have an election by Referendum to be able to prove that Faisal really had the voice of the people. With that, one of Faisal's A.D.C.'s telephoned to me and asked me to go round. I found him radiant— very different from my first early morning visit the day after he arrived! but eagerly insisting on the need of a referendum through the machinery of the Ministry of the Interior which I was able to assure him was exactly what Sir Percy wanted too... His ante-chamber was a sight to gladden one—full of Bagdad nobles and sheikhs from all parts of the Iraq. I went back to Sir Percy to report. The thing we have been looking for seems to be in a fair way to fulfilment. Sir Percy and Faisal between them are making a new Sharifian party composed of all the solid moderate people. Faisal has played his part; he has handled his over-zealous adherents with admirable discretion. . .

The office of a morning is flooded with tribal sheikhs. Today they were sitting in rows on the ground under the awning of the courtyard. They come up to see Faisal and pay their respects to Sir Percy and incidentally to me. What they come to learn is whether Faisal has our support. They hear it first from me and then from Sir Percy and I think they go away satisfied. This week it has been the Euphrates; next week it will be the Tigris. To-night Faisal has fifty of them to dinner. Dinners! in this weather they really are a trial. The Coxes gave one to Faisal on Wednesday. I was well off for I sat by Air Marshal Sir John M. Salmond who has flown over from Cairo in 9 hours and says he never suffered so much as he has in being transplanted so rapidly from the temperate climate of Egypt to our torrid zone. . . .

To H.B.
Wednesday, July 20th, 1921.

Really these days are so packed with incident that I must quickly record them before one impression overlays another. In an atmosphere which has been uninterruptedly at a maximum of over 120 for the last three weeks—I may mention that for the first time in my life I've got prickly heat—not very bad however. Well—on Monday the Jewish community gave a great reception to Faisal in the Grand Rabbi's official house. The Garbetts and I represented the Residency and Mr. Cornwallis came with the Amir. The function took place at 7:30 a.m. in the big courtyard of the house—a square court round which the two storied house stands. It was filled with rows of seats, with rows of notables sitting in them, the Jewish Rabbis in their turbans or twisted shawls, the leading Christians, all the Arab Ministers and practically all the leading Moslems with a sprinkling of white-robed, black-cloaked Ulama. The Court was roofed over with an awning, the gallery hung with flags and streamers of the Arab colours. The Jewish school children filled it and the women looked out from the upper windows. They put me on the right hand of the chair prepared for Faisal—you know the absurd fuss they make about me, bless them. Faisal was clapped to the echo when we came and we all sat down to a programme of 13 speeches and songs interspersed with iced lemonade, coffee, tea and cakes and ices! It took two hours by the clock, in sweltering heat. . . . The Rabbi is a wonderful figure, stepped straight out of a picture by Gentile Bellini. The speeches on this occasion are all set speeches. . . . But yet they were interesting because one knew the tensions which underlay them, the anxiety of the Jews lest an Arab government should mean chaos, and their gradual reassurance, by reason of Faisal's obviously enlightened attitude. Presently they brought the Rolls of the Law in their gold cylinders, they were kissed by the Grand Rabbi, and then by Faisal, and they presented him with a small gold facsimile of the tables of the law and a beautifully bound Talmud. I whispered to him that I hoped he would make a speech. He said he hadn't meant to say much but he thought he must, and added "You know I don't speak like they do. I just say what is in my thoughts." Towards the end he got up and spoke really beautifully; it was straight and good and eloquent. . . . He made an immense impression.

The Jews were delighted at his insistence on their being of one race with the Arabs, and all our friends . . . were equally delighted with his allusion to British support. . . .

To H.B.
BAGDAD, July 27th, 1921.

I'm immensely happy over the way this thing is going. I feel as if I were in a dream. . . . On our guarantee all the solid people are coming in to Faisal and there is a general feeling that we made the right choice in recommending him. If we can bring some kind of order out of chaos, what a thing worth doing it will be!

Our great heat is over, the temp. has fallen to about 115 more or less which is quite bearable, and I'm very well.

To H.B.
BAGDAD, July 31st, 1921

I must now give you an account of our doings. Overshadowing all else was the display at Ramadi. Fakhri Jamil Zadah and I left at 4 a.m. but Faisal was a little in front of us. We caught him up at Naqtah, half way to the Euphrates and asked leave to go ahead so that I might photograph his arrival at Fallujah. Outside that village a couple of big tents were pitched in the desert and for several miles crowds of tribal horsemen gathered in and stood along the track as he passed. . . . Then we drove through Fallujah which was all decorated and packed with people. The tribesmen lined the road to the ferry some 6 miles—rode round, after and beside the cars (I was immediately behind Faisal) amid incredible clouds of dust. . . .

Under the steep edge of the Syrian desert were drawn up the fighting men of the Anazeh, horsemen and camel riders, bearing the huge standard of the tribe. We stopped to salute it as we passed. Ali Sulaiman the Chief of the Dulaim, and one of the most remarkable men in Iraq came out of the Ramadi to meet us. He has been strongly and consistently pro-British. . . .

We drove to the Euphrates bank where Ali Sulaiman had pitched a huge tent about 200 ft. long with a dais at the upper end and roofed with tent cloth and walled with fresh green boughs. Outside were drawn up the camel riders of the Dulaim, their horsemen and their standard carried by a negro mounted on a gigantic white camel; inside the tribesmen lined the tent 5 or 6 deep from the dais to the very end. Faisal sat on the high divan with Fahad on his right while Major Yetts and I brought up people to sit on his left—those we thought he ought to speak to. He was supremely happy, a great tribesman amongst famous tribes and, as I couldn't help feeling, a great Sunni among Sunnis. . . . Faisal was in his own country with the people he knew. I never saw him look so splendid. He wore his usual white robes with a fine black abba over them, flowing white headdress and silver bound Aqal. Then he began to speak, leaning forward over the small table in front of him, sitting with his hand raised and bringing it down on the table to emphasize his sentences. The people at the end of the tent were too far off to hear; he called them all up and they sat on the ground below the dais rows and rows of them, 400 or 500 men. He spoke in the great tongue of the desert, sonorous, magnificent—no language like it. He spoke as a tribal chief to his feudatories. "For four years," he said "I have not found myself in a place like this or in such company"—you could see how he was loving it. Then he told them how Iraq was to rise to their endeavours with himself at their head. "Oh Arabs are you at peace with one another?" They shouted "Yes, yes, we are at peace." "From this day— what is the date? and what is the hour?" Someone answered him. "From this day the 25th July (only he gave the Mohammedan date) and the hour of the morning (it was 11 o'clock) any tribesman who lifts his hand against a tribesman is responsible to me—I will judge between you calling your Sheikhs in council. I have my rights over you as your Lord." A grey bearded man interrupted, "And our rights" "And you have your rights as subjects which it is my business to guard." So it went on, the tribesmen interrupting him with shouts, "Yes, yes," "We agree . . . . . Yes, by God." It was the descriptions of great tribal gatherings in the days of ignorance, before the prophet, when the poets recited verse which has come down to this day and the people shouted at the end of each phrase, "The truth, by God the truth."

When it was over Fahad and Ali Sulaiman stood up on either side of him and said, "We swear allegiance to you because you are acceptable to the British Government." Faisal was a little surprised. He looked quickly round to me smiling and then he said, "No one can doubt what my relations are to the British, but we must settle our affairs ourselves." He looked at me again, and I held out my two hands clasped as a symbol of the Union of the Arab and British Governments. It was a tremendous moment, those two really big men who have played their part in the history of their time, and Faisal between them the finest living representative of his race—and the link ourselves. One after another Bali Sulaiman brought up his sheikhs, some 40 or 50 of them. They laid their hands in Faisal's and swore allegiance. . . . The afternoon's ceremony was the swearing of allegiance on the part of the towns. From Fallujah to Qaim, the northern frontier, all the Mayors, Qazis and notables had come in. The place was a palace garden. There was a high dais built up against a blank house wall which was hung with carpets. On this Faisal and the rest of us sat while the elders and notables, sitting in rows under the trees, got up, stepped to the dais and laid their hands in his. . . The beauty of the setting, the variety of dress and colour, the grave faces of the village elders, white turbaned or draped in the red Arab kerchief and the fine dignity with which Faisal accepted the homage offered to him made the scene almost as striking as that of the morning. . . .

We are now waiting for the Mosul and Hillah papers to come in to declare Faisal King. He may possibly be crowned next week. Isn't that very remarkable! 5 weeks work.

To H.B.
BAGDAD, August 6th, 1921.

We have had a great week. The plebiscite is nearly finished throughout the country. Many districts, Ramadi, Basrah, the Euphrates, Amarah, have added a rider to the papers, swearing allegiance to Faisal "on condition that he accept British guidance." . . .

I had a terrific day on Tuesday. I got up at 4:45 motored at 5:45 with Mr. Cornwallis to Ctesiphon—we took Faisal there—office 10:30 to 3:30, with an interval for lunch, home to wash and change; visit to the Naqib 4:30 to 6, library Committee 6 to 7, visit to Sasun's sister-in-law 7 to 7:30. Hamid Khan to dinner 8 to 10. It was too much; I felt tired all next day—however it was worth it.

The Ctesiphon expedition was an immense success. I invited Faisal and two of his A.D.C's, the Garbetts, Fakhri Jamil and Mr. Cornwallis, and I took Zaya, with an excellent breakfast of eggs, tongues, sardines and melons. It was wonderfully interesting showing that splendid place to Faisal. He is an inspiring tourist. After we had re-constructed the palace and seen Khosroes sitting in it, I took him into the high windows to the South, when we could see the Tigris, and told him the story of the Arab conquest as Tabari records it, the fording of the river and the rest of the magnificent tale. It was the tale of his own people. You can imagine what it was like reciting it to him. I don't know which of us was the more thrilled. I had a good audience too in one of his A.D.Cs. .

Faisal has promised me a regiment of the Arab Army—the Khatun's Own." I shall presently ask you to have their colours embroidered. Nuri proposes that I should have an Army Corps!

Oh Father, isn't it wonderful. I sometimes think I must be in a dream.

Sorry to say that it's desperately hot again. As regards climate this is being the devil's own summer.

To H.B.
BAGDAD, Aug. 14th, 1921.

The referendum is finished and we are only waiting for the last of the signed papers to come in from the Provinces, after which Faisal will be proclaimed King without delay. With one exception he has been elected unanimously. . . .

The difficulty this week has been the climate. Not that it has been so very hot—never over 119 I think—but it has been quite still with a lightly coloured sky. When you get up in the morning and see a cloud your heart sinks, for it means a close oppressive day like the half hour before a thunderstorm carried to the Nth. There were a couple of days at the beginning of the week when I seriously considered whether I could bear it. Now it is better. . . .

The other day a young gentleman from Mosul who designs to start a paper there asked me to draw him up some directions for the guidance of the press. I did it with a will, and produced a minor masterpiece—with the more pleasure because I sent a copy to Faisal who was delighted. .

I swam the Tigris—not much of a feat you will rightly observe, but the current is very strong in places. Sorry to say there are sharks in the Tigris; they haven't yet been reported higher than the mouth of the Diala where one bit an Arab boy this week.

To H.B.
BAGDAD, August 21, 1921.

There's no post in this week. I'm not only without letters but also without papers and books. However, thank God, I've got plenty to say. Wherein, as you'll note, I differ from my chief I heard a delightful saying about him the other day, quoted from the lips of one of the leading notables of Basrah. "Wallahi," he observed, "Sir Percy Cox has forty ears and only one tongue." I must tell you another nice tale about the Coxes. You know he is a great naturalist. He is making a collection of an Mesopotamian birds—sometimes they arrive dead and sometimes alive. The last one was alive. It's a huge eagle, not yet in its grown up plumage but for all that the largest fowl I've ever set eyes on. It lives on a perch on the shady side of the house and it eats bats, mainly. These bats are netted for it in the dusk when they obligingly fly across the river and over Sir Percy's garden wall. But the eagle likes to catch them in the morning, so the long suffering Lady Cox keeps them in a tin in her ice chest, and if ever you've heard before of an eagle that lives on iced bat you'll please inform me.

And since I'm telling you stories, I must tell you one about the Naqib. It hangs on what I was relating to you last week on the subject of al Damakratiyah. It was the Naqib, to his huge delight—he's by every instinct an aristocrat, and an autocrat if ever there was one—who gave currency to the word, by announcing in the Council that Faisal should be King of a constitutional democratic state. . . . The other day a Shammar Sheikh up from Hail, drops in to call. "Are you a Damakrati?" says the Naqib. "Wallahi, No!" says the Shammari, slightly offended. "I'm not a Magrati. What is it?" "Well," says the Naqib enjoying himself thoroughly, "I'm Sheikh of the Damakratiyah" (the Democrats). "I take refuge in God!" replied the Sheikh, feeling he had gone wrong somewhere. "If you are the sheikh of the Magratiyah, then I must be one of them, for I'm altogether in your service. But what is it?" "Damakratiyah," say the Naqib, "is equality. There's no big man and no little, all are alike and equal." With which the bewildered Shammari plumped on to solid ground. "God is my witness," said he, seeing his tribal authority slipping from him, "if that's it I'm not a Magrati."

Well now to the history of the Iraq.

Last Monday was the first day of the Id al Fitr, The Feast of Sacrifice, which is the great occasion of the Moslem year. It lasts four mortal days. At 7 a.m. on Monday, Mr. Cornwallis and I set out on a round of calls. . . .

That afternoon Faisal called on the Naqib to form his first Cabinet—a very very wise move. He's embarking on a promising political career at the age f 77. Good, isn't it?

That evening I had got so tired of sitting in the office that in spite of the heat I went out riding, and coming home along the river bank for coolness, I passed Faisal's new house, up-stream, a house they have rented for him which is being done up. I saw his motor at the door so I left my pony with one of his slaves and went up on to the roof where I found him sitting with his A.D.Cs. It was wonderful, the sun just set, the softly luminous curves of the river below us, the belt of palm trees, and then the desert, with Agar Quf standing up against the fading red of the sky. We all ate and talked. Faisal uses no honorifics: "Enti, thou" he says to me—it's so refreshing after the endless "honours," and "excellencies"—Enti Iraqiyah, enti badawiyah—you're a Mesopotamian, a Bedouin.". . . .

The Colonial Office has sent us a cable saying Faisal in his Coronation speech must announce that the ultimate authority in the land is the High Commissioner. . . . Faisal urged that from the first he is an independent sovereign in treaty with us, otherwise he can't hold his extremists. . . .

It is I suppose difficult for them to realise that we are not building. here with lifeless stones; we're encouraging the living thing to grow and we feel it pulsing in our hands. We can direct it, to a great extent, but we can't prevent it growing upwards. That is, indeed, what we have invited it to do. . . .

To H.B.
BAGDAD, August 28th, 1921.

We have had a terrific week but we've got our King crowned and Sir Percy and I agree that we're now half seas over, the remaining half is the Congress and the Organic Law. . . .

The enthronement took place at 6 a.m. on Tuesday, admirably arranged. A dais about 2ft. 6in. high was set up in the middle of the big Sarai courtyard; behind it are the quarters Faisal is occupying, the big Government reception rooms; in front were seated in blocks, English, Arab Officials, townsmen, Ministers, local deputations, to the number of 1,500.

Exactly at 6 we saw Faisal in uniform, Sir Percy in white diplomatic uniform with all his ribbons and stars Sir Aylmer, Cornwallis and a following of A.D.Cs descend the Serai steps from Faisals lodging an come pacing down the long path of carpets, past the guard of honour (the Dorsets, they looked magnificent) and so to the dais... We all stood up while they came in and sat when they had taken their places on the dais. Faisal looked very dignified but much strung up—it was an agitating moment. He looked along the front row and caught my eye and I gave him a tiny salute. Then Saiyid Hussain stood up and read Sir Percy's proclamation in which he announced that Faisal had been elected King by 96 per cent of the people of Mesopotamia, long live the King! with that we stood up and saluted him. The national flag was broken on the flagstaff by his side and the band played "God save the King"—they have no national anthem yet. There followed a salute of 21 guns. . . . It was an amazing thing to see all Iraq, from North to South gathered together. It is the first time it has happened in history. . . .

Sir Percy had been unwell but on the day of the Coronation he began to recover and is now quite fit again, so I who had kept all people off him for a week quietly arranged for the deputations to pay their respects to him. We had two days of it Friday and Saturday morning. It would be difficult to tell you how many people there are in the office one and the same time. It was immensely interesting seeing them—there were people I had never seen before and a great great many who had never seen Bagdad before. Basrah and Amarah came on Friday, Hillah and Mosul on Saturday; they were the big deputations, of these Mosul was the most wonderful. I divided it into three sections—first the Mosul town magnates, my guests and their colleagues, next the Christian Archbishops and Bishops—Mosul abounds in them—and the Jewish Grand Rabbi. . . . The third group was more exciting than all the others; it was the Kurdish chiefs of the frontier who have elected to come into the Iraq state until they see whether an independent Kurdistan develops which will be still better to their liking. . . .

After they had had their quarter of an hour with Sir Percy all in turn came down to me. The Kurds came last and stayed longest. The Mayor . . . said that they hadn't had an opportunity to discuss with Sir Percy the future of Kurdistan, what did I think about it? I said that my opinion was that the districts they came from were economically dependent on Mosul and always would be however many Kurdistans were created. They agreed but, they must have Kurdish officials. I said I saw no difficulty there. And the children must be taught in Kurdish schools. I pointed out that there would be some difficulty about that as there wasn't a single school book—nor any other—written in Kurdish. This gave them pain and after consideration they said they thought the teaching might as well be in Arabic, but what about local administrative autonomy . . . I said "Have you talked it over with Saiyidna Faisal—our Lord Faisal?" "No," they said. "Well you had better go and do it at once." I suggested. "Shall I arrange an appointment for you?" "Yes," they said. So I telephoned to Rustam Haidar and made an appointment for yesterday afternoon—I'm longing to hear from Faisal what came of it. Fun isn't it? Faisal . . . . asked me to tea.

We spent a happy hour discussing (a) our desert frontier to South and West and (b) the National Flag and Faisal's personal flag. For the latter we arranged provisionally this, i.e., the Hijaz flag with a gold crown on the red triangle. The red I must tell you is the colour of his house so he bears his own crown on it. Father, do for heaven's sake tell me whether the Hijaz flag is heraldically right. You might telegraph. Its a very good flag and we could differentiate it for the Iraq by putting a gold star on the black stripe or on the red triangle. The Congress will settle it directly it meets. Do let me know in time, Also whether you have a better suggestion for Faisal's standard. . . .

There's no doubt that this is the most absorbing job that I've ever taken a hand in. . . .

To H.B.
BAGDAD, Sept. 11th, 1921. \

Faisal's first Cabinet is formed. On the whole we are well satisfied. Out of the 9 Ministers, 6 are eminently capable men, well-fitted for their job. . . .

Faisal has got into his new house, on the river above Bagdad, it's small but its really very nice. On Wednesday one of the A.D.C's telephoned to me to ask me to dinner—I went up by launch. Have I ever told you what the river is like on a hot summer night? At dusk the mist hangs in long white bands over the water; the twilight fades and the lights of the town shine out on either bank, with the river, dark and smooth and full of mysterious reflections, like a road of triumph through the mist. Silently a boat with a winking headlight slips down the stream, then a company of quffahs, each with his tiny lamp, loaded to the brim with water melons from Samarra. "Slowly, slowly," the voices of the Quffahijs drift across the water. "Don't ruffle the river lest we sink—see how we're loaded." And we slow down the launch so that the wash may not disturb them. The waves of our passage don't even extinguish the floating votive candle each burning on its minute boat made out of the swathe of a date cluster, which anxious hands launched above the town— if they reach the last town yet burning, the sick man will recover, the baby will be born safely into this world of hot darkness and glittering lights and bewildering reflections. Now I've brought you out to where the palm trees stand marshalled along the banks. The water is so still that you can see the Scorpion in it, star by star; we'll go gently past these quffahs—and here are Faisal's steps.

And you still can't form the remotest conception of how marvellously beautiful it is. . . . I also rode with Nuri on Friday morning; we went down to breakfast with Haji Naji.

As we rode back through the gardens of the Karradah suburb where all the people know me and salute me as I pass, Nuri said "one of the reasons you stand out so is because you're a woman. There's only one Khatun. It is like when Sidi Faisal was in London and always wore Arab dress, there was no one like him. So for a hundred years they'll talk of the Khatun riding by."

I think they very likely will.

It may have escaped your notice that we are in the middle of Muharram. From the first to the fifteenth the Shiahs mourn for Hussain, the Prophet's grandson, who was invited over from Mecca by the Iraqis to be Khalif, and when he arrived got no support from them, was opposed by the army of his rival Muawiyah at the place where Karbala stands now, saw his followers die of thirst and wounds and was killed himself on the 15th. One small son escaped and from him Faisal is descended (so is the Naqib for that matter).

Incidentally when Faisal came, that story of his ancestor was in my mind. The parallel was so complete, the invitation, from Iraq, the journey from Mecca, the arrival with nothing but his formal following. If the end has proved different it's because I said "Absit omen" so often.

Well the Shiahs are mourning hard. It takes the form of processions every night, lighted torches, drums and beating of breasts. Some of the young men in our office invited me to dinner on Friday to see the processions. . . . Presently the wild drums drew near, the glare of torches filled the sky and the processions turned into the courtyards. Torches, and men leading horses in gorgeous trappings, and men carrying large banners, and men with trays of lights on their heads. And then a black-robed company which spread out in two rows across the court, and they were swinging chains, with which they beat their backs—the black robes were open to the waist at the back so that the chains might fall on their bare skins. They swing them very skilfully with a little jerk at the top of the swing so that the chains barely touched the skin, but the effect was wonderful—the black figures in the glaring torch light, swinging rhythmically from side to side with the swing of the chains and the drums marking time. Next came the breast beaters, naked to the waist; and they stood in companies and beat their breasts in unison to a different rhythm of drums. Each procession surged through the courtyards, swung their chains, beat their breasts and surged out into the street; and another followed it interminably. . . .

To F.B.
BAGDAD, September 17th, 1921.

I'm glad you take an interest in my letters, bless you. It's not at all true that I have determined the fortunes of Iraq, but it's true that with an Arab Government I've come to my own. It's a delicate position to be so much in their confidence. I'm very careful about not obtruding myself on them, I let all the "come hither" emanate from them. When they want to come and ask my advice I'm always there; when they're busy with other things I go about affairs of my own. . . .

Last Tuesday was the fifteenth of Muharram, the "Ashurah." It's the culminating day of mourning for Hussain, the anniversary of his death. . . . They enact the whole history of Hussain's death, the attack of Muawiyah's hosts, the little band killed one by one, the burning of their tents and the cutting off of the heads of the dead to send to Muawiyah. . . .

To H.B.
BAGDAD, September 25th, 1921.

We've had a hot week—temp. up again to 108—but suddenly it dropped yesterday to 92 and to-day, for the first time for five months, I'm sitting in my little sitting-room with doors and windows open and no fan. It was so heavenly this morning when I went out riding at 6 (it being Sunday) that I rode right across the desert to Fahamah, close on 2 hours away and breakfasted with my friend Faiq Bey. We sat in his garden, full of roses just breaking into their second flower, while I ate hard boiled eggs, native bread and butter like cream, and Faiq Bey talked. His face . . . . grew quite perturbed while he related to me the difficulties of cultivators nowadays—the labourers all gone off to better paid jobs in town, or taking up land of their own on the near canals; they think they do you a service for working for ten times their former hire and even so, Yallah, you're lucky if they come an hour after dawn, don't knock off more than four hours at noon, nor leave earlier than an hour before sunset. Poor Faiq Bey! It's progress of course; the country is getting richer and the inhabitants expect more, but it's very awkward for the old society, when progress steps in to dislocate it. And in the end it won't produce anything better than Faiq Bey; straight out of Arcady he steps, with his rosy apple face, his personal rectitude and his industrious days among his palms and orange trees and barley fields. . . .

To H.B.
Sept. 29th, 1921.

Sir Percy who is a very keen sportsman, has got two hawks which are being trained. Every morning there is a hawk party at the office. Our hawks invite their friends and when I come in of a morning I find two or three falconers each with a couple of hawks on his wrist waiting for Sir Percy to appear.

One of my daily jobs is to read and summarise the local papers. I have as assistant a capital little Soudanese as merry as a cricket. The more work you give him the merrier he grows. His Arabic is excellent and his English far from bad but very colloquial. His comments on the newspaper tosh, are a perpetual joy. Yesterday there was a literary piece by one of our local poets:

MAKKI: Oh, Lord! this fellow! This is a silly fellow. He talks to the moon.

G.L.B. (severely): It's frequently done. Go on Makki, see if there's anything political in it.

MAKKI (reading): My sorrows thou see'st, oh moon—Oh, Lord this fellow! No, its all general, nothing serious.

G.L.B. : Hurry up then, what's next? etc., etc.

To H.B.
BAGDAD, Oct. 2nd, 1921.

... I shall have to keep a sort of diary to you now for with fortnightly letters the intervals are too long. . . .

We send an immense amount of dispatches home by every Air Mail and the 14th and the 30th of each month are days of feverish finishing off of work. Added to which they are the days when my fortnightly report has to be finished, so that Sir Percy may see it on the 15th and 1st, before it goes to the press—I am doing little less than writing a history of Mesopotamia in fortnightly parts. I myself find it an invaluable record, but I've not heard what they think of it at home. The 1st of October saw the 22nd number. Each number is divided into the following parts : 1. Proceedings of the Council of Ministers (as you might say Hansard compressed). 2. Public Opinion—all significant events, or propaganda or newspaper campaigns. 3. Notes on Provincial affairs, the actual history of the provinces, tribal unrest, irrigation. 4. Frontiers.

It's a great work, it really is. It goes to all our provincial officers as well as to India, Aden, Jaffa, Constantinople, Jerusalem and London, also Teheran. If they don't know everything they ought to know about us it is not my fault. . . .

To F.B.
BAGDAD, Oct. 17th, 1921.

They really are wonderful, these young Englishmen, who are thrown out into the provinces and left entirely to their own resources. They so completely identify themselves with their surroundings that nothing else has any significance for them, but if they think you're interested they open out like a flower and reveal quite unconsciously, wisdom, tact, and patience which you would have thought to be incompatible with their years. . . .

My blue gown and cloak have arrived they are very nice indeed. I am so infinitely grateful for the trouble my kind family have taken about them. Lennox Gardens papers please copy. . . .

I've suggested to Sir Percy that it would be a pleasant change for me to set up as uncrowned Queen of Kurdistan. I don't want to stand in his way if he has a fancy for the job—we might perhaps toss for it. . . .

Yesterday, Sunday, I shook myself free and motored with Fakhri Eff. to his gardens above Baqubah. We started about 8 on a close hot morning . . . . and a more beautiful sight I don't think I ever saw. The dates are late in ripening this year and are still hanging in great golden crowns on the palms; below them the pomegranate bushes are weighed down with the immense rosy globes of their fruit and the orange trees laden with the pale green and yellow of ripening oranges— it was a paradise of loveliness; I walked about in a bewilderment of admiration. There was also a big stretch of vineyard where the last of the grapes were hanging on the vines—gigantic bunches of white grapes each sheltered from the sun by a little roof of liquorice stalks. Our lunch was cooked in the open air—excellent rice and chicken and stewed meats, with strained pomegranate juice to drink, and served to us in an arbour made of a woven roof of boughs. . . .

To H.B.
BAGDAD, Oct. 31st, 1921.

What an excessive amount of trouble you take about your children and we accept it all as a matter of course—more shame to us. At any rate I do realise from time to time what it is to have someone always watching and caring for one without the care having any relation to the worth of the object it's expended on. The object is worth less than you can guess. I think I may have been of some use here but I suspect I've come very near the end of it. . . .

To H.B.
BAGDAD, Nov. 25th, 1921.

I left Bagdad on the 22nd by train for Kirkuk.

Next morning I got off by motor at about 11, eastward to Sulaiman. The road ran at first through a broken country of little mud hills, confused and ugly because they lack all mountain architecture. Gradually the hillocks gathered themselves together and coalesced into an up and down country with broad gracious curves and grassy hollows where a tiny spring would rise cradled in purple-flowered mint. Before long we reached the summit and saw below us the Chemchemal valley with a range of real mountains beyond it, barren and rock built, and beyond that, range behind range, the Kurdish highlands up to the Persian frontier and further still to the N.E. the great massif of Kandil Dagh lifted its snowy flanks against the sky. Hills and valleys were almost alike, unpeopled and uncultivated; the sere grasses spread their white gold carpet to the rock, the rock rose stark to heaven and there was nothing else in the landscape except at our feet the tiny villages of Chemchemal, flat mud roofs clustered below an ancient Median mound. It is the country of the fierce Hamawand tribe, a living terror to the government and the scattered villages (which from their protective colouring and their site among the hill folds I could not see . . .) In the pass we met a buxom rosy Kurdish girl with a baby strapped on to her back and a loaded cow walking sedately in front of her—a strange pack animal. As soon as it saw us it took fright and attempted to scramble up the stony bank when, cow-like, it collapsed hopelessly under its load. The baby began to cry, the woman beat the cow and the cow struggled effetely till I thought it would break its legs—such a pother we had made in Kurdistan with our motor! So we flew to the rescue, unloaded the cow, set it on its feet, held the baby till the mother had tied up the loads again and went happily on our several ways. . . .

To H.B.
BAGDAD, Dec. 4th, 1921.
Faisal privately doesn't want the Congress to be convened (it's duty is to draw up the Organic law) until he has got the terms of the treaty satisfactorily settled and respective responsibilities of the British and Arab Governments defined. It's this question of responsibility which perturbs everyone; on it the position of the Advisors and indeed most other things rests. Roughly the skeleton of the problem is whether we can assume responsibility for defence if the country is attacked from without. . . . We must be able to satisfy the League of Nations that we can fulfil the international obligations with which the mandate entrusts us, and even if we drop the mandate and call it a treaty, that treaty must make certain reservations which the Arabs must accept. . . .

The word Mandate produces much the same effect here as the word Protectorate did in Egypt. . . .

But you mustn't think for a moment I have any part in settling these problems. I know about them because Sir Percy tells me about them in outline but I'm merely an onlooker and although Faisal is very friendly and agreeable he doesn't, quite rightly, consult me. I hadn't seen him for nearly 5 weeks what with his being away and my being away, and I very carefully abstain from offering advice in matters the delicate manipulation of which had much better be left to Sir Percy. All I can do and all I try to do, is to give as accurate an impression as I can of what people are saying and thinking.

I had a well spent morning at the office making out the Southern desert frontier of the Iraq with the help of a gentleman from Hayil and of Fahad Bey the paramount chief of the Anazeh. The latter's belief in my knowledge of the desert makes me blush. When he was asked by Mr. Cornwallis to define his tribal boundaries all he said was "You ask the Khatun. She knows." In order to keep up this reputation of omniscience, I've been careful to find out from Fahad all the Wells claimed by the Shammar. One way and another, I think I've succeeded in compiling a reasonable frontier. The importance of the matter lies in the fact that Ibn Saud has captured Hayil and at the earliest possible opportunity Sir Percy wants to have a conference between him and Faisal to state definitely what tribes and lands belong to the Iraq and what to Ibn Saud. . . .

Did I tell you that Sir Percy is building an extra room on to my house? It's causing me acute discomfort at the moment but it will be a great blessing when finished.

One of the joys of my new sitting-room will be that it has a fireplace. . . . To-day Percy Loraine arrived on his way to Persia. After lunch he and I retired to my office and had a real talk. I came home at tea-time to prepare for my own dinner party, the foundation of which was three of the Kirkuk delagates. I had just had time to get my room into some sort of order when at 5:30 (the time of the dinner party being 7:30) the first of my guests arrived. . . .

CHAPTER XXII
1922-23

BAGDAD

To H.B.
January 2, 1922.
 I've been having an exceptionally horrid Christmas, as I will now recount. Captain Clayton, Saiyid Hussain and I intended to go to Baqubah on Dec. 23. The day looked very threatening, however we decided by telephone that we would start. In the afternoon the weather looked so bad that we gave up our scheme altogether. So there I was landed with Christmas holidays with nothing to do and nowhere to go, disgustingly cold and wet weather and an increasing cold which gradually developed into the worst I've ever had. It's still very bad. Mr. Tod and Major Wilkinson came to lunch with me on Saturday, which was cheerful, and Nuri Said on Christmas day, after which I went to tea with the King—he lives a long way outside the town, up river, and the road was indescribable; however, I succeeded in getting there and we had the usual delightful talk ... On Wednesday the damnable holidays were over— but not my cold. I went to the office and made it so much worse that I had to spend Thursday indoors . . . I went to the office Friday morning and came back to lunch feeling unutterably ill. . . .
 It is so uncheerful sitting by one's self on New Year's Eve. They had an immense party for a Fancy Dress Ball to which I didn't go nor was I in fancy dress—unless to dine in one's fur coat is fancy dress. I didn't enjoy it very much because I was feeling so miserable, and when they went to the ball I went home. However, I can't complain of any loneliness of New Year's Day. My first callers arrived at 7:30 a.m. while I was still in bed. They were Haji Naji and a sheikh of the Dulaim. Accordingly I invited them to breakfast . . . I wish you could have observed even for a minute my breakfast party—I wrapped up in furs and they in their brown cloaks . . . After that I had an uninterrupted stream of visitors whom I regaled on coffee and chocolates until 1:15 when the last of them fortunately left, and I went out to lunch with the Joyces, feeling more dead than alive. After I came back the throng set in again till 6 o'clock when I closed my doors for a moment's breathing space before dinner. I dined with Sir Aylmer who had asked the King and the eldest son of the Naqib and Hadoud Pasha, Mr. Tod and some of the G.H.Q. staff and Sir John Davidson, a retired Major General and M.P.
 He is coming to have a heart to heart talk with me one of these days. The dinner was a huge success. Faisal took me in and I must say I enjoyed myself mightily too. It is so pleasant and friendly at the General's house—everyone is at their ease and he is such a kind and delightful host.
Jan. 6th.
I am a trifle better and though far from well I begin to think I may ultimately recover.

To H.B.
BAGDAD, Jan. 30th, 1922.

During the last fortnight I've taken my health seriously in hand. I really was dreadfully run down and nearly expired of fatigue at the end of a morning in the office so I've firmly come away at 1 p.m. or thereabouts, lunched at home or with Mr. Cornwallis, the Joyces or any one else I wanted to see and then gone out riding till tea time. The weather has been delicious and this programme has been just what I wanted for it has got me out every afternoon into the sun and air. Never in my experience of Iraq has there been such a spring . . . To-day I rode through the Dairy Farm and back by the gardens bordering the Tigris. Man and beast were rejoicing in the abundance of green—"By God, I've never seen the like!" I stopped to say to the shepherds. And they, "It is the mercy of God and your presence Khatun."

How I love their darling phrases: you know, Father, it's shocking how the East has wound itself round my heart till I don't know which is me and which is it. I never lose the sense of it. I'm acutely conscious always of its charm and grace which do not seem to wear thin with familiarity. I'm more a citizen of Bagdad than many a Bagdadi born, and I'll wager that no Bagdadi cares more, or half so much, for the beauty of the river or the palm gardens, or clings more closely to the rights of citizenship which I have acquired. . . .

An excellent Municipal Council has been returned at Basrah but what pleases me almost most is that at Kirkuk the former Mayor who is a great ally of mine, had an immense majority, though the Turkish party pulled every possible string against him, including an appeal to pan-Islamic sentiment . . . It will be very interesting to see what the Shah makes of it . . . .

My new room is so nice. It's also an indescribable blessing to have a real fireplace with a fire burning in it. My house has a wonderful feeling of spaciousness in a modest way. Rishan loves the fire even more than I do. You know, Father, I shall never be content till you come out again—I want you to see the King and my new room and everything. I think your next visit should be in the spring of 1923—I'll come to Aleppo to meet you, and take you here by motor. . . .

To H.B.
BAGDAD, Feb. 16th, 1922.

I want to tell you, just you, who know and understand everything, that I'm acutely conscious of how much life has given me. I've gone back now to the wild feeling of joy in existence—I'm happy in feeling that I've got the love and confidence of a whole nation, a very wonderful and absorbing thing—almost too absorbing perhaps. You must forgive me if it seems to preoccupy me too much—it doesn't really divide me from you, for one of the greatest pleasures is to tell you all about it, in the certainty that you will sympathise. I don't for a moment suppose that I can make much difference to our ultimate relations with the Arabs and with Asia, but for the time I'm one of the factors in the game. I can't think why all these people here turn to me for comfort and encouragement; if I weren't here they would find someone else, of course, but being accustomed to come to me, they come. And in their comfort I find my own. I remember your saying to me once that the older one grows the more one lives in other people's lives. Well, I've got plenty of lives to live in, haven't I? And perhaps after all, it has been best this way. At any rate, as it had to be this way, I don't now regret it.

To H.B.
BAGDAD, Feb. 16th, 1922.

The day after I wrote to you I went out with Mr. Thomson to see the Yusufiyah canal. We had a delightful day. We motored to Mahmudivah, half way to Hillah where we found our horses. Then with a local sheikh and a few outsiders we rode up the canal. It was an enchanting ride for this wonderful spring has covered the world with verdure . . . I must tell you the Yusufiyah is one of the oldest canals in the world. It was the Babylonian Nahr Malka, Julian sailed down it to Ctesiphon and the Abbassids re-dug it. Consequently there are great early Babylonian mounds all along it. Where we crossed by the bridge we were four miles from Tel Abn Habbah, which was Sippa and as we came back we rode up on to a wonderful mound called Tel Dair. It was completely covered with potsherds and bits of brick and I picked up a half brick with an inscription in early Babylonian characters—which was rather interesting because so far as I know nothing earlier than Nebuchadnezzar has been noted there. . . .

Faisal sent for me that day, but as I was out I telephoned a day or two later to ask if I might come to tea. We had a tremendous talk. He is most delightful and certainly often most amazing. I caught myself up in the middle of discussion and said to him that it was almost impossible to believe that while he had been born in Mecca and educated at Constantinople and I in England and educated at Oxford there was no difference whatever in our points of view.

Already the country is finding its feet. The stable people, the big sheikhs and nobles relying on our support of Faisal, are rallying round him and are combined. They are going to stand no nonsense from extremists and tub-thumpers. . . .

To H.B.
BAGDAD, Feb. 26, 1922.

I took the King to see the apricot blossom in Karradah. I hadn't warned Haji Naji beforehand and he unfortunately wasn't there, but the King and all his court were much impressed by the beautiful way the gardens were kept and very envious of the seedling fruit trees. One of Haji Naji's sons was there and said he would send him anything he wanted. The King's need for fruit trees is that he has bought a large bit of the Dairy Farm which he intends to make into a park. . . .

I'm very glad. First of all because it's evidence of his taking root and secondly because it brings him up against different sorts of people.

Mr. Cooke and I sat long talking over the fire and we agreed that there couldn't be anything in the world more absorbing than to be in the very heart of intellectual Asia—to be watching and encouraging the effort to overmaster secular prejudices. Heaven knows their wits are acute enough; it's moral courage that's lacking to throw off the long domination of the theocratic ordinance in human affairs which from a valuable referent has become a cord of strangulation. After all it has taken us Europeans centuries to win through. . . .

To turn to matters of minor importance, I'm largely living on delicious truffles. One usually gets them in from the desert at this time of the year but I've never known them in such abundance as in this extraordinarily beautiful spring. Daffodils, marigolds and wall-flowers are blooming in my garden and the rose trees coming into bud.

To H.B.
BAGDAD, March 12th, 1922.
I spent Tuesday afternoon with the King and we had an immense talk, partly owing to the nearness of general elections, about the formation of political parties. He was anxious—I really think that in this country it would be best—that people of different opinions should find a platform of agreement and start a single party with a combined policy for the election. I've unexpectedly been thrown into the thick of it during the last few days. On Thursday the extremists petitioned the interior for permission to form a party. . . .

It is pretty clear that the extremists are alarmed by the determined attitude of the moderates and I fancy they have every reason for being so. . . .

Sir Percy has just been in to give his advice on the question of the parties, namely that if the two parties can't come to an agreement the moderates are bound to go ahead on their own lines . . . It is deeply interesting but rather agonizing to be taking so decisive a share in all this. One feels that a wrong step may do a great deal of harm. . . .

It is just on the cards that I may have to come back here after our time together in Palestine, but I don't think it is very likely. You see my feeling is that I can't very well leave my friends here stranded at such a crucial moment, for at least I serve as a sort of clearing house for them. But in the course of the next few weeks things may have shaped themselves. . . . [Same letter continued.]

March 14th. The party question is still undecided and I haven't heard anything about it to-day. Meantime the wind is up in another quarter. For some time past letters have been passing between Sir Percy and Ibn Saud. The conquest of Hayil by the latter in November makes his frontiers continuous with the Iraq. Sir Percy is anxious to arrange a treaty between him and Faisal—on the basis that the desert edges into which our shepherds go down with their flocks in the spring shall be included in Iraq—Ibn Saud wants to claim all the desert as his and has recently been exacting tribute from our shepherds.

Finally matters came to a head on the 11th when Ibn Saud's people attacked in immense force a camel corps recently organised by the King to protect our frontiers and routed them. To-day the Akhwan fired on an aeroplane reconnaissance and orders were issued that their camp was to be bombed. Ibn

Saud may of course repudiate the action of his followers; that's the best that can happen, for otherwise we're practically at war with him. Life in this country is not lacking in incident . . . .

Thanks to your sending me the cutting from the Times by air mail, my letter was published in one of the vernacular papers to-day and was the subject of much rejoicing to-night at the palace. It has made a good effect and I hope will restore my credit a little with the extremists who, I hear, regard me as exceedingly severe. Well, if it's severity to try and stop them from pitching headlong into a gulf of wild nationalist ambition, I am.

To H.B.
BAGDAD, March 30th, 1922.

During the last fortnight I have come definitely to the conclusion that I can't go on leave this summer. Things are too much in the melting pot ... I'm not going to telegraph to you because it might prevent you from coming out and I not only want dreadfully to see you but also the little holiday will be immensely to the good. I shall very likely fly over on the 29th April, but you are not to mention this to anyone. Also it's not certain. I may come by motor via Aleppo in which case I should make to be in Jerusalem a day before you so as to welcome you. If I fly back I should leave Ramleh on May 27th so that I should come down to Egypt with you and see you off. Since I made up my mind I've been feeling rather homesick but I haven't any doubt I'm doing what I ought to do. We've put our hand to this plough and at any rate Sir Percy thinks that I'm some help to him in his difficult furrow. I'm perfectly well and I shall go up to Sulaimani for a month in the middle of the summer. I might possibly come home for a bit in the autumn so that it would only be six months difference. I hope you and Mother and Maurice won't be much disappointed. I do love you so much and I hate staying away so long.

Well now we come to the sordid but serious question of clothes—of course, I've made no provision for the summer. I've written to Marte (78 Grosvenor Street) by this mail, telling her that if she is in time to catch you, she is to send out by you two washing gowns, an evening gown and a hat . . . if, however, you have left before this letter arrives Mother will open it and will tell Marte to post things I've asked her to send me as quickly as she can so that I may find them here if possible when I get back. But please if you possibly can bring a hat. Elsa might choose it if the combination with Marte fails—she is on the telephone, by the way—a ribbon hat, black or mauvy blue and mushroom in shape. There! You'll do your best, I feel sure, and if you can't do anything I must just wear the topee I shall come over in. . . .

I've received a lovely photograph of Hugo's wedding. I think that is partly what made me feel homesick. You all look such darlings and my two sisters so especially delightful.

[Hugo's marriage to Frances Morkill took place on November 24th, 1922, at Kirby Malham in the West Riding of Yorkshire.]

To F.B.
BAGDAD, April 28th, 1922.

I have just telegraphed to Father at Jerusalem telling him that I'm coming over by air on the 29th and suggesting that he should meet me at Amman on that day....

[This meeting with her father took place most successfully, as arranged. He had arrived at Jerusalem, and then gone on to Amman, where he received a telephone message to say that the two official aeroplanes, in one of which Gertrude was flying, had left Bagdad at 9 a.m. and were due to arrive at Ziza between 11 and 12. He at once motored to Ziza and stood with the officials who were awaiting the aeroplanes, looking out into the Eastern sky. It was an exciting moment when two small specks first appeared on the horizon and then came to a pause over the heads of the expectant group. The planes landed beautifully, Gertrude alighted and fell into her father's arms. For a little while she was dizzy, and unable to hear, then in a short time she completely recovered. Her father then told her that he and she had been invited to dine with Abdullah King Faisal's brother, the Emir of Transjordania, who was then encamped near Amman, but that he had declined as he did not suppose that she would feel able to do so after her long flight. But Gertrude entirely repudiated the idea of refusing, got out her evening clothes, and they went to dinner with the Emir and enjoyed themselves very much.]

To F.B.
JERUSALEM, May 10th, 1922.

I can't tell you what a wonderful time we have had. The joy of being with Father in these surroundings and of having his amazingly acute and perceptive mind to help one in coming to conclusions! Was there ever anyone who combined as he does such wealth of experience with so fresh and vital an outlook on all and everything that he encounters? And isn't he the most delicious companion with his humanness and his charming humour and his appreciation of beauty and history and birds and flowers and all that ever was the biggest thing to the least. I shall so dreadfully miss him when we part and I do very much regret that I'm not coming home to you, Maurice and my sisters. It's an extraordinary sense of rest, peace and understanding that one gets when one is with one's own family and it's just that which I miss so much—the intimacy and confidence in our love for one another. But though I feel so much drawn to home and you, I know I couldn't have left Iraq happily at this moment. I should always have felt that I had left my job at a moment when I might and very likely would be needed if anything untoward had happened, though I know I couldn't have made much difference, I should have imagined that just the little I could have done might have helped to turn the scale....

Marte sent me the most excellent clothes, bless her—lovely embroidered muslin gowns to wear during the summer

To H.B.
BAGDAD, Thursday, May 18th, 1922.

    We did the journey in six hours, coming down at For amadi a quarter of an hour to refill. It wasn't really quite as comfortable as Vickers-Vimy though so much quicker. . . . the wind being slightly in the North was very battering on the left side. Guided, however, by the gesticulation of my charming pilot, Mr. Brunton, I succeeded in following the motor track across the desert and keeping count of the landing grounds, so that I knew exactly where we were all the time. . . . We flew very high, 6,000 to 7,000 feet and very fast, 100 to 110 miles an hour. Just before we reached Ramadi it rained a little, and when we got in we found it quite cool. Our whole journey was most agreeable and I fear I've become the confirmed aviator. . . .

    I went to tea with the King. I took him your letter with which he was very much pleased, and told him all about Abdullah and Palestine and Syria. He talked very delightfully about his feeling that as long as he had our confidence nothing mattered. I said that I had come back with the conviction that we were the only Arab province which was set in the right path, and that if we failed here, which I hoped was unthinkable, it would be the end of Arab aspirations.

    If I'm not mistaken, public opinion is crystallizing hard in our favour and I believe if H.M.G. would put the issue openly and clearly the large majority would declare for us on any terms.

To H.B.
BAGDAD, June 2nd, 1922.

    Yes, there wasn't one moment of our fortnight in Palestine that was not perfect. Everything helped—the lovely country and the nice people, but they were only the setting of the picture, which was you. There's no doubt that being with you is the most enjoyable thing known. Haven't you got your niche in the East . . . .

    The Minister of the Interior telephoned to tell me that a group of extremists were planning a big demonstration against the mandate for the afternoon. The King had ordered it to be stopped and did I know where Mr. Cornwallis was? With that, Mr. C. came in and I left him to deal with the Minister. At five Mr. Cooke and I went out on another round of visits and got through some ten notables or more. There was a good deal of talk about the attempted demonstration and very plain speaking as to how this kind of thing could not be tolerated.

    It was a horrible day that Tuesday of the Id. A south wind which scorched you and even at night was extremely hot. It has been better since, but summer has set in and you can't mistake it. Yesterday there were races to which I went—rather late in the afternoon, sat in the King's box and had a most cheerful talk with him. He was rather pleased with himself and I hastened to assure him that he had every reason for gratification. The extremist papers have been outrageous, describing the Sunday business as an immense popular demonstration.

The High Commissioner gave a Garden Party for the King's birthday. I had prepared the Arab list—all officials and nobles quite apart from their political opinions. They all came—trust Lady Cox for that!—and we hobnobbed with most of the people who led the rebellion two years ago. Sir Percy told me to look after the King and wallahi I did it well! First of all I took him round all the groups of Arab officials and notables. He made the circle, saying the right thing to everyone—he plays his part. Then we got him established in a corner of the lawn and I brought up all the wives of Advisors so far as I could catch them, and gave each one a short audience with him. Also the new French Consul and his wife, the eldest son of the Naqib and any one else whom I thought he ought to speak to....

Faisal has hitched his wagon to the stars. . . . At the bottom of his mind he trusts us and believes that one or two of us would go to the stake for him and that's the strongest hold we have of him. . . .

Oh, darling, isn't the human equation immensely interesting. I feel as if I and all of us were playing the most magical tunes on their heart strings, drawn taut by the desperate case in which they find themselves. Can they succeed in setting up a reasonable government? Can they save themselves from chaos? Their one cry is "Help us." And one sits there, in their eyes an epitome of human knowledge, and feeling oneself so very far from filling the bill! Poor children of Adam, they and we! I'm not sure (but perhaps that's because of my sex) that the emotional link between us isn't the better part of wisdom, but I wish I had a little more real wisdom to offer. However, Sir Percy has plenty. . . .

To-day the vernacular press was full of Lord Apsley [who had come over as representing the Morning Post) gratitude for the part the Morning Post had played in the Palestine question and hope that he would now direct his attention to that of Iraq. The leaders of the people will meet the Lord and expound to him the position, in which no doubt he will be deeply interested.

At five I took the Lord to tea with the King. I told him all that there was in the papers and he replied that he was to meet all the extremists to-morrow at Kadhaimain. I gave him the lie of the land and I've no doubt he will do extremely well. For in conversation with the King he was quite admirable—I'm free to confess that I translated like an angel! . . . . We talked over the whole mandate question with complete amity. Lord A. developed the reasons for which we had to have recourse to a mandate—a means of obtaining the consent of the powers to our treaty and of persuading the British Nation that we had accepted a responsibility and were bound to fulfil it etc. The King asked whether he saw any objection to a combined protest on the part of ourselves and the Arabs to the League of Nations against the mandatory relation once the treaty was an accomplished fact. Lord A. said on the contrary the Morning Post would do all it could to help us, but they must get the treaty through first otherwise all our enemies would declare that the Arab nation did not want us. The King enthusiastically agreed.

At the end, Lord Apsley, who really is a diplomat of the highest order, said that now he wanted to come to something really serious. They all pricked their ears—"Yes," he said "a thing of real importance—when are you going to have a polo team?" They were delighted. . . .

In that we took our leave and I'll wager that a very pleasant impression remained with us. It was one of the most useful talks I've ever heard at the palace and I'm infinitely grateful to Lord Apsley for the skill with which he conducted it. I confided to him that I had been a very good interpreter, to which he replied that the Mufti of Jerusalem had told him that he had never heard better Arabic than mine on the lips of a foreigner. I was gratified by this. . . .

To H.B.
BAGDAD, June 22nd, 1922.

On the Sunday after I last wrote (June 11th) Mr. Cornwallis, Captain Clayton, Major Murray, Captain Ashton and I went to swim in the Diala. It wasn't a very well chosen day. There was a tempestuous south wind and we, motoring in the teeth of it, felt as if we were motoring through Hell. We hit the Diala in the wrong place, found it full of people bathing and had to go hunting for a better. I don't remember to have yet performed my toilet so completely in the open, it was merely by the mercy of providence that cows and women were the only spectators—had our swim in the dark—the Diala was running very strong still—and then sat on the high bank very peacefully and ate our cold dinner oh, above all drank our cold drinks! The wind dropped, night hushed the chattering in some Arab tents close by, the river hurried below us and a late moon lifted its distorted shape out of the East and spread a soft light over the interminable miles of desert thorn. We lay there till past nine talking of the Iraq and the Arabs and the things we are doing. . . .

Next day I went to tea with the King and had one of the most interesting talks I've ever had with him. . . .

When if ever we come up to eternal judgment, you may be very sure that we shall ultimately be graded according to the very highest point we have been able to reach. . . . Faisal on that day will come out very high. He surges up a long long way across the heavenly strand; the tide goes down again, but he has been there and left his little line of sea gold on the shore.

On Thursday I took Mrs. Wilkinson to tea with some Arab ladies—I'm always taking some of our nice Englishwomen out to tea like that; it's such a help.

In the evening I had an evening party in my garden 9/11:30. Coffee and ices and talk under my lanterns. I asked about ten Arabs and five Englishmen. It was quite brought off and I shall do it again and again. . . . This afternoon there is a very important meeting of Council—the treaty will be laid before the Ministers. I've been getting at Ministers this morning in the interval of writing to you and I suppose nothing more can be done. If it doesn't come out quite straight it will be up to Sir Percy, that great weaver of destinies, to put it right again.

Elsa will be gratified to hear that the parasol has come and excites the deepest admiration at Court!

Perhaps someday you might send me a Bridge Box—I haven't one. Also possibly some patience cards?

To H.B.
BAGDAD, July 16th, 1922.

I must begin by a really remarkable observation on the weather. They are repairing something to do with the electric current and in consequence it's off till 1 p.m. and no fans. Nevertheless on this mid July Sunday morning as I am sitting, in a thorough draught it's true, between door and window, but quite cool enough to write to you with comfort, the temperature can't be over 100 degrees. I don't think we've had it over 110 this year, and generally, as to-day, a jolly north wind. My office is unfortunately the worst spot in Bagdad; it's sheltered from every breeze and exposed to every ray of the sun. My house, on the other hand, is wonderfully cool.

The King and the Naqib have proclaimed to the listening Universe that they will never, so help them God, accept the Mandate. H.M.G. have replied that they can conclude no treaty except by reason of the right to do so given to them by the League of Nations—i.e., the mandate.

I think I've said before, but anyway I'll say right here, that I'm convinced that no country in the world can work a mandate. . . . The Arabs won't submit to any diminution of their sovereign rights such as being placed in tutelage under the L. of N. They are ready to exercise those rights in such manner as to bind themselves by treaty to accept advice in return for help.

We had a great function later in the afternoon—the opening of our Anglo-Arab Club. Sir Percy was there and was perfectly delightful to everyone. It's a man's club but I was asked to the party though I'm not a member. And our dashing Euphrates sheikhs were there, half a dozen of them, all up here to see the treaty put through, if they can. It remains to be seen whether the club will be a success—it is designed to be a common meeting ground. . . .

Oh, we're up against such problems—the formation of political parties is the first. The extremists are already in the field and I'm pushing and dragging the others into the open.

Here is an engaging picture of the General Staff of the Iraq Army having their new drill. Jafar Pasha appears saliently on the extreme left.

July 17th Yesterday's experiences were as usual remarkable. Feeling very energetic for once, I got up at five and rode out to Karradah to breakfast with Haji Naji on scrumptious roasted fish. While I was sitting in his summer house a curious episode occurred. There strode in a youngish man in the dress of a dervish who announced that he had come as a guest. Haji Naji replied that he was busy and bade him begone. The man blustered a little, looked sharply at me and said he had just as much right to be a guest as others and finally went out and sat down just outside a mat-walled summer house. Haji Naji called the servants and one of his sons and told them to send the man away. They failed to make him move. Presently he began to read out the Koran in a loud voice. This was more than I could bear and I went out and told him, by God, to clear out. He said "I am reading the Holy Book." I replied I know you are—get out or I shall send for the police." He replied irrelevantly "I rely on God." I said "God's a long way off and the police very near," and with that I picked up his iron staff and gently poked him up. He made up his mind that he was beaten and saying "Because you are here I shall go", picked up himself and his Koran and made off. . . . If I hadn't sent the man away Haji would have been absolutely helpless. A man who sits down on your threshold to read the Koran can only be regarded, in theory, as a blessing—you can't lift him. Curious, wasn't it? I shall tell the police to keep an eye on any dervish wandering about in Karradah. . . .

10 P.M. I've just heard by telephone that the Ministers passed the treaty at this afternoon's meeting. . . .

We're having a heat wave—I think the temperature must have been up to 120 degrees to-day. One knows at once when the thermometer runs up by the intolerable hotness of everything one touches. Mr. Cooke, Major Wilson and I accepted the invitation of Sabih Bey, Minister of P.W.D., to bathe from his house in Muadhdham. It was an ideal place. A delightful house with two courtyards full of flowering oleanders; you undress like a lady in Sabih Bey's bedroom, climb down the wall of his house by a ladder and so by a steep sandy bank straight into deep water- -so swiftly deep that you can dive in off the bank. You swim lazily down in the soft warm water under the high fortress-like walls of Muadhdham river front, after which, if you're me, you come to shore and run up the bank to your starting point, but if you're Mr. Cooke you swim gallantly up against the current. That over, we drank many glasses of grape juice and so motored home. . . .

To-day the King ordered me to tea and we had two hours most excellent talk. First of all I got his assistance for my Law of Excavations which I've compiled with the utmost care in consultation with the legal authorities. He has undertaken to push it through Council—he's perfectly sound about archaeology, having been trained by T. E. Lawrence—and has agreed to my suggestion that he should appoint me, if Sir Percy consents, provisional Director of Archaeology to his government, in addition to my other duties. I should then be able to run the whole thing in direct agreement with him, Which would be excellent.

To H.B.
Bagdad, July 30th, 1922.

I left off in the beginning of a heat wave which I trust is now nearly over. The day after I wrote to you, the 21st, I got so tired of being hot that I thought I would try and mend it by being hotter so I went out riding about. I didn't go very far but before I got home I felt more like having a heat-stroke than I've ever felt in my life and when I looked in the looking glass my face was scarlet all over. I put my head quickly into iced water and recovered at once. I had a party in my garden that night—it was far too hot and I'm having no more until it gets cooler. . . .

To H.B.
BAGDAD, August 15th, 1922.

We are having a very exhausting time, physically and politically. Physically because of the incredibly horrible weather. It's not very hot, never much over 110, but heavy and close beyond all belief. Every two or three days I get up in the morning wondering why, instead of getting up, I don't lie down and die. At the end of the day one feels absolutely dead beat. Then for a day or two one is better, for no special reason, and then again moribund. It's not only me; everyone is the same. . . .

On Sunday 6th the King invited us to a picnic. I walked with the King through the wonderful palm gardens and out to the desert. For the sixth time I've watched the dates ripen. Six times I've seen the palms take on the likeness of huge Crown Imperials, with the yellow date clusters hanging like immense golden flowers below the feathery fronds. . . . The King took us back in his launch and as we slipped past the palm groves he and I laid plans to write the history of the Arab revival from first to last, from his diaries and my knowledge. It would be a remarkable tale.

Father, you do realise, don't you, how the magic and the fascination of it all holds one prisoner? . . . .

Yesterday in a perfectly infernal climate and feeling fit to die I worked from 7 to 1:30 in the office, came home and lunched and worked uninterruptedly from 2:30 to six, after which I went to a Committee meeting and then to a dinner at the French consulate where we played Bridge till midnight. I came home feeling like a horrible spectre.

The High Commissioner has telegraphed home that he doesn't see any advantage in Faisal's going to England. He recommends that we should publish the treaty, say that we're all agreed upon it and that the sole point of difference is the mandate. On that point the electors of the Iraq must decide; if they decide against it we will evacuate to-morrow. The King is delighted with this proposed solution.

But will our Government accept this suggestion? That's what we want to know, for being all away grouse shooting we can get no answer to any telegrams however urgent. . . .

August 16th. This was one of the moribund days, nevertheless I've been extremely busy. Any quantity of Sheikhs came in this morning. . . . I really believe they are getting to work. They have parcelled out the whole country according to administrative divisions. There's a head branch in every divisional headquarter and sub-branches in every district; the sheikhs are going back to organise them. Their tails are up sky high. They declare they'll bring in the whole country. . . . And the sheikhs from further afield are trooping in to register themselves as members. They are the people I love, I know every Tribal chief of any importance through the whole length and breadth of Iraq and I think them the backbone of the country.

One has to take one's courage in one's hands when a wrong decision may mean universal chaos.

Meantime all these internal hostilities that are so gravely preoccupying us may well be obliterated by the growing menace of the Kamalists of our northern frontier. . . .

Now I come to think of it I can't imagine how you can bear to wade through all these reams of Iraq politics—can you bear it

August 18th, 1922. As there's an immense cryptic telegram from home—not deciphered yet. No doubt it contains the answer which we think will decide our fate.

I can't see any prospect of getting away this autumn, unless the whole thing blows up—a possible contingency. If it doesn't we shall be in the thick of a general election and the Constituent Assembly should be meeting towards the end of the year. But Iraq and everything else may go to the dogs before I stay here another summer. I should not be telling the truth if I did not observe that my disappearance from the scene at the present juncture would fill the breasts of my tribal sheikhs with dismay. . . .

To H.B.
August 27th, 1922.

On Sunday evening August 20th we escaped from politics for a happy hour or two. The King came out bathing and picnicking with us and we had the usual party. It was my picnic and I did it beautifully. We roasted great fishes on spits over a fire of palm fronds—the most delicious food in the world—I brought carpets and cushions and hung old Bagdad lanterns in the tamarisk bushes where we kept simple state in the rosy stillness of the sunset. "This is peace," said the King. We lay on our cushions for a couple of hours after dinner while he and Nuri and Mr. Cornwallis told stories of the Syrian campaign—I have seldom passed a more enchanting evening.

Next day we were back in the turmoil.

Wednesday was the anniversary of the accession, August 23rd. I rode with His Majesty before breakfast on Tuesday morning to see his cotton farm. . . . It is a tremendous cavalcade when the King goes out riding— A.D.C.'s behind us and four lancers of the body guard bringing up the rear. . . .

With that we stopped talking and played bridge. So we came to August 23rd. . . . We were due at the Levée at 9:45.

I went across to the Residency by boat, all in lace clothes and miniature orders, the first time I had worn the miniatures; they are the greatest comfort— and we started off in a procession of two motors for the levee, the High Commissioner and his staff. When we got to the Palace the courtyard was packed with people, three or four hundred under the King's stair, and numbers of white-robed persons on the balcony, apparently addressing them. The police had to clear a way for the High Commissioner's car. As he walked up the stair, a very striking figure in his white uniform and orders, a voice in the crowd called out something which he did not hear and I did not catch, upon which came a storm of clapping. It was almost as though they were clapping his appearance, and much perplexed we went into the audience room. The King seemed rather nervous but the conversation quickly got into easy channels—the morning's review and so forth—and after a quarter of an hour we came away. The court was empty.

As soon as we were back in the office the High Commissioner told me to get on to it at once and find out what had happened. I did, and within an hour I had the information we wanted. It was a demonstration on the part of the two extremist political parties, no doubt arranged to take place at the hour of Sir Percy's audience.

It was now Sir Percy's turn to get busy. He waited until the anniversary was over and on the following morning (24th) sent the letter and received the answer. . . . At noon on the 24th we heard that the King was down with appendicitis, in the evening his temperature was up, at 6 a.m. next day, five doctors, two English and three Arabs, were debating whether an immediate operation were necessary, at 8 they decided it was and at 11 it was successfully over

The King has made a rapid convalescence. On Sunday he was allowed to see a selected body of notables. This was thought advisable because a rumour had been spread that he was dead. On Monday the Officers of the Iraq army offered him their congratulations on his recovery. To-day Mr. Cornwallis saw him—in the presence of notables and the A.D.C.'s. There was no mention of politics. . . .

The extreme right is just as subversive of the policy of H.M.G. as the extreme left. The one is opposed to the King and the Arab Government, the other opposed to British assistance. How are we to combine the two sharply conflicting schools of thought? I myself believe that if the King refuses to accept Sir Percy's action the majority of the Iraq will request him to abdicate. You'll understand that immediate preoccupations block out the firmament. If I don't specifically answer your letters it's not because I don't like having them. They are like an escape to another world. But waking and sleeping I am absorbed by what lies to my hand and the countless interviews which I conduct daily with turbaned gentlemen and tribesmen and what you please, seem to me to matter more than anything else in the world. . . .

To H.B.
BAGDAD, September 8th, 1922.

I spent the afternoon with the Davidsons. She is going home next week to my great sorrow. I shall miss her dreadfully. I do hope Aurelia Tod will be back this winter—it's nice to have a female friend.

At the beginning of September we had an unusual drop in the temperature, a month earlier than usual. I promptly caught cold—but I've also promptly got rid of it. You can't think how difficult it is to tackle the first on-coming of cold. You would think it absurd to speak of it as cold. The thermometer often goes up to 110 in the afterday, but it drops to 70 before dawn. You're just too hot without a punkah when the temperature of your room is 90 and just too cold with it.

September 10th. This Sunday morning while I'm writing to you Sir Percy and Mr. Cornwallis are having a momentous interview with the King, at which

Sir Percy is asking him to endorse all he has done, and to give certain undertakings for the future. . . .

Sept. 14th. Now I must tell you that the King's momentous conversation with Sir Percy passed off very satisfactorily. He accepted and endorsed all that Sir Percy had done. . . .

To H.B.
BAGDAD, September 24th, 1922.

Our next excitement was the arrival of Amir Zaid, H.M.'s youngest brother to whom he is devoted. He arrived last Sunday the 17th. There was a great reception for him at the station to which we all went— notables and advisors and Arab Army and everyone you can think of. . . .

The Mandate has been much softened for them since Mr. Churchill has agreed to announce that the moment Iraq enters the League of Nations it becomes a dead letter. Now one of the clauses of the treaty is an undertaking on our part to get Iraq admitted as quickly as possible. . . . . .

September 28th. A new planet has arisen in the shape of Sir John Salmond, Air Marshal, who takes over command of all British Forces on October 1st. . . . He is alert, forcible, amazingly quick in the uptake, a man who means to understand the Iraq and our dealings with its people. He dined with me last night to meet Mr. Cornwallis—just we three for I wanted him to get into instant touch with the Iraq government to which Mr. Cornwallis belongs. We had the most enchanting evening for Sir John is delightful to talk to on any subject.

To H.B.
BAGDAD, October 8th, 1922.

As usual a great many things seem to have happened but for the most part we have had our eyes fixed on Chanak. . . . We, however, seem to have found a man in General Harington.

I wrote to you on the 29th. The 30th was the first of their Autumn races. We began the day, the Joyces and I, by taking the Amir Zaid to Ctesiphon. . . . He is so eager to find out and learn about everything—as quick and appreciative as the King. I took our breakfast which we ate under the shadow of the great walls, while I told Zaid of all the battles that had been fought there, 637 and 1914. In the afternoon we went to the races as H.M. was going. I went to Sir Percy's box and he put me next the King. After we had talked a little Sir John Salmond strolled over from his box, so I took him into H.M.'s box and we three had an hour's talk, I interpreting. The King went straight to the heart of things, asking the A.V.M, what he could do to protect us from attack, how much he could do if at the worst we could ask for more help and so on. The Air Vice Marshal answered with as much directness and produced, as he does, a great feeling of confidence. . . .

Major Noel lunched with me yesterday and returned to Sulaimani last night. He described a situation in which he is hourly risking his life as a very interesting experience. He is what would be called at Eton mad—an enchanting adventurer, an immense understanding of the Kurd, and flawless courage

The main thing is to get the extremists and moderates to work together. At present the one is always on the alert to break the head of the other—I use the Arab idiom. It's very much on the principle of 'ôte-toi que je m'y mette'—there's often nothing else behind it....

I've been getting at the moderate party telling them they are quite disgracefully inactive....

I hear the King is overjoyed at the signature of the treaty. I went up and wrote my name with respectful congratulations yesterday but I haven't yet seen him. To-day I've been translating his really beautiful proclamation which will be published in English and Arabic to-morrow together with the treaty. I wish I had more time to do it properly; it demanded better work than could be put into the twenty-five minutes allowed me....

To H.B.
BAGDAD, October 24th, 1922.

As for you and Uncle Lyulph you are the most remarkable people I know. I love to think of his trundling off to Perth, and I long to hear of your visit to Frankfort. Yes, your railway negotiations are not unlike things of which I have intimate knowledge and after all human affairs seem to be much the same all the world over....

The Cabinet at the request of the King, has appointed me honorary Director of Archaeology—there didn't seem to be any other way of keeping the place warm till we could afford a proper Director. The department to my great satisfaction, has been placed in the Ministry of Public Works, so that I am directly under my friend Sabih Bey and shall have the help of the architect Major J. M. Wilson, whom you remember pupil of Lutyens. I went over to the Ministry on Tuesday morning to have my first conference with the Minister about the Law of Excavation, which I've drafted....

Now that the treaty is signed the King is out to defend every line of it from the slightest breach of criticism. His own proclamation and his telegram to King George accurately reflect his state of mind. The Iradah for the holding of elections has been issued; registration of Directors begins this week and will last about six weeks—what with the somewhat cumbrous system of electoral colleges we shan't have the Constituent Assembly sitting till about January.... The King is determined that it shall be an Assembly which will ratify the treaty and I think it will be.

October 25th. The news of the Cabinet appointments reached us last night. I'm so enchanted to have the Duke [of Devonshire] as our Minister that I've written to tell him so....

Registration of primary electors began yesterday.... When I got in at six o'clock I found an urgent message from the King bidding me to dinner. Jafar, Nuri and Zaid were the party. We had a very merry dinner, during the course of which H.M. described the glories of Chatsworth, and played a game of Bridge afterwards, I teaching the Amir Zaid. I like him more and more—and I never met anyone with such exquisite manners. Incidentally, I was wearing a new gold and white gown . . . . so I had a modest triumph too. . . . I've had a terribly busy day. I was out, as usual, at six, riding (I came in past the Iraq Army parade and receive the salute of the units which happen to be drilling there) and when I got into the office at 8:15 I found Sir Percy champing for a draft of a telegram he wanted to send home, pointing out the disastrous effect that would result from the re-cession of Mosul to the Turks. So I proceeded to write it for him while he was at breakfast. I've no doubt he'll improve it in detail but the general lines were, if I may say, masterly. Having got that done I had to write the report for the Secretary of State, which goes fortnightly by air mail . . . . our successes against the Turks on the Kurdish frontier, the reception of the treaty and the King's plans. With an interval for lunch it took me till four o'clock, when I walked home and at once addressed myself to letters for the mail. I won't say I'm as active as you but still I do take my part in the affairs of the world, don't I?

To H.B.
BAGDAD, November 1st, 1922.

I'm beginning this letter very early and shall close it early because the day after to-morrow I'm going to Mosul for a few days. It's this way: there has long been a promise that I shall personally conduct Major J. M. Wilson to Hatra. Round this kernel have solidified Capt. Clayton and Major Murray (just back from leave and posted to Mosul, to the regret of Captain Clayton and me) and we will set out on Friday night. We sleep a night at Shagat with the Arab Army as hosts, motor next day to Hatra where we spend the night à la grâce de Dieu (we have camp beds with us and the Shammar of Ajil al Yawar are in that neighbourhood and will, we hope, provide us with a sheep roasted whole and coffee) and then motor back to Qaiyarah where if we arrive late we may spend another night . . . . .

I've been figuring in my capacity as Director of Archaeology. Mr. Woolley arrived on Sunday. He is a first-class digger and an archaeologist after my own heart—i.e., he entirely backs me up in the way I'm conducting the department. He has come out as head of a joint expedition organised by the British Museum and Pennsylvania University and they are going to dig Ur, no less, and are prepared to put in two years' work. After lunch Sabih Bey and I went to a meeting of the Cabinet which I attended for the first time to explain and defend the Law of Excavations which I had drafted. The Naqib and the Ministers made me affectionately welcome.

We passed to my law through which we laboured, clause by clause, for two hours I got it passed in principle but certain verbal alterations are still to be made in the Arabic text. When we had done I bowed myself out and went to a committee meeting of the Salam Library where it was my agreeable duty to present to them some 40 pounds worth of books, the response to my appeal to Sir Frederick Macmillan. Isn't it generous of him! . . . . I confidently expect that the Salam Library will soon be one of the best institutions in the East. . . .

A deputation is coming down from Sulaimani to discuss the Kurdish question with H.E. and H.M. It has missed its train, as it naturally would, but it may possibly arrive tomorrow. . . .

November 2nd. The deputation has come, fourteen in all, including their followers, and all armed to the teeth. They've put up at one of the smaller Hotels, from which they promptly ejected all other occupants. The landlord wilted and vanished into the cellar. Yet according to Major Noel their views are quite reasonable—not that he is a great judge of reasonableness, bless him— they are explaining them to Sir Percy this evening.

To H.B.
MOSUL, November 10th, 1922.
. . . . We motored straight across a heavenly rolling desert, across which I had ridden in 1911 to Hatra. As we drew near we saw the Arab flag flying from the high vaults of the ruined palace and in the huge courtyard where the Arab Prince, liegeman of the Parthian kings, had sheltered his flocks in times of stress. . . .

Hatra twice makes its appearance in the history of the world, the first time in 116 when Trajan besieged it twice, capturing it the first time and failing to take it the second after it had revolted from him. Then in 196 Septimus Severus in his turn besieged it twice and it held out against him both times. From that date it disappears from the ken of historians until Layard revisited its amazing ruins last century. . . . At sunset I lay on the highest wall under the shadow of the Arab flag. I'd watched the light fall and fade across the universe of desert. Below me the camels and horses of Ajil's bairak strayed through the court and beyond the city wall the blue smoke from among the tents of a Shammar camp. It was a scene in which past and present were so bewilderingly mingled that you might have looked down upon its like any evening for twenty centuries. . . . We left about nine and motored across the desert to the Mosul road which we joined at Qaiyarah, and so on through clouds of dust to Mosul. . . .

There came to dinner Col. Rogers, O.C. of the Rajputs stationed here, and his Major named Johnson, both very nice, and Major Maclean (Arab Army), a charming person whom I already knew.

Next day, November 6th, I went down with Captain Flaxman to the Sarai and called on the Mutasatrif. . . . He was chiefly preoccupied with the news from Zakho, on the extreme northern frontier, whence the Kaimmakam had the day before been sending alarmist telegrams to say that a Turkish and tribal attack was imminent and if more soldiers were not sent immediately he begged to resign. We did not feel very anxious because we knew that the new Inspector General of Levies, Colonel Dobbin, had arrived at Zakho the previous evening and that if there had been anything very serious he would have telegraphed. However Major Murray, Major Wilson, Captain Slater and I determined to pull on our chain armour, shoulder our muskets and go out next day to reinforce the Kaimmakam. And who so pleased as I?

So on November 7th we made a fairly good start about eight. . . . An hour or two out we met Colonel Dobbin with his A.D.C. Unfortunately he was the bringer of bad news—the battle was off! . . . .

The Kaimmakam was all of a twitter-obviously not the man for a frontier post. Major Murray promised guns for the levy camp above the town, they've now gone and I trust the Zakho valley reverberates with the sound of their practice. I've urged on Sir Percy that we shouldn't allow the Turks the advantageous position of heads I win and tails you lose. The guns they've heard; the Levies are ready, and behind them - aeroplanes enough to obscure the light of the sun.

It was near sunset when we reached the Levy Camp which lies in a cup on the top of the foothills with the British flag flying on it. . . . I occupied the hut of our host Captain Merry, a simple, cheerful, self-reliant young officer. . . . We were waited on by four Assyrian boys, in full native dress—striped embroidered trousers, scarlet and yellow tassels flung over their shoulders under the white felt zouave jacket, white peaked caps with a white or scarlet feather at the side. . . .

Before we left next day I inspected many of the huts—spotlessly clean, the women all dressed up in their best in anticipation of a visit, but their feathers are not so fine as those of the men. I went away much impressed. Truly we are a remarkable people. We save from destruction remnants of oppressed nations, laboriously and expensively giving them sanitary accommodation, teaching their children, respecting their faiths, but all the time cursing at the trouble they are giving us, and they're cursing us, not infrequently, for the trouble we are giving them with our meticulous regulations. And then behold, when left to themselves they flock to our standards, our Captain Merrys for their chosen leaders, our regulations their decalogue. . . . And on all this we gaze without amazement. It's the sort of thing that happens under the British flag, don't ask us why, we don't know. . . .

On the 15th I caught the train at Qaraghan and reached Bagdad on the 16th without incident except that the train was some six hours late, you know our ways. I arrived to find a political crisis, for which I was partly prepared by letter. The Naqib has resigned. It has happened quite simply and without anyone's feelings being hurt-the Cabinet has just died of inanition. So now they are busy Cabinet making as hard as they can go and with luck I think they may have a much stronger lot than before. . . .

To-night Sir Percy goes off to the Persian Gulf—a long postponed conference which I hope will end in the conclusion of a satisfactory treaty between Nejd and Iraq but it's rather agitating to have Sir Percy away when so many things are happening. We've had, however, very reassuring telegrams from home about the attitude they are going to take up with the Turks in defence of the Iraq frontiers. . . .

November 23rd. The new Cabinet is formed and is, I think very good. Yasin Pasha goes to Public Works so I shall do my Archaeological dept. with him which I shall like. H.M. and the Cabinet are determined to take a strong line. It's needed, for the Shiah mujtahids have issued fatwahs forbidding people to take part in the elections. . . .

To H.B. . . .
BAGDAD, December 4th, 1922.

Do you know-apropos of nothing at all-that I've been four times mentioned in dispatches for my valuable and distinguished services in the field! It came to me as a surprise—indeed it is singularly preposterous—when I counted up the documents in order to fill up a Colonial Office form. I hadn't realised there were so many. Apparently one of the fields I distinguished myself in was Palestine, for I was mentioned by Sir Reginald Wingate. . . .

I sent you by post the yearly report to the S. of S., a very silly sort of Xmas present. I wrote all the first general chapter and the next on administration, then the chapters on refugees and foreign relations. The other bits came from the respective departments. Mr. Slater's financial chapter is interesting and Mr. Davidson's judicial chapter. It was a tidy job putting it all together, but interesting.

To F.B.
BAGDAD, December 5th, 1922.

Isn't it a shocking thing that four years after the armistice we should still see the world in such confusion . . . . .

But I would not have done what I'm doing here. I often wonder whether it is very selfish of me to have gone on with it. Life here has drawbacks, of course; there are long moments when I feel very lonely, but the work has been so interesting that as far as I am concerned I couldn't have experienced better or even as good, a destiny. My present plans are to come home on leave in May, arriving towards the end of the month. If Sir Henry Dobbs wants me to return I should probably like to do so for another winter at any rate, but of course that's for him to say.

I can't think what it would have been like not to have had you and father taking such an interest in our doings, but this I know that you have added immensely to the pleasure of them. To write to you about them has been half the battle and you never seem bored however much I write.

December 7th. Sir Percy is still dallying in the Persian Gulf, not without profit, however, for he has got the Nejd-Iraq treaty ratified which Ibn Saud had refused to do. I knew I.S. would come round directly Sir Percy put the matter to him. What an amazing influence has my chief.

A very happy Xmas and all good things. The love of your children is always with you and I can't think that any of them can love you more than your daughter, Gertrude.

To H.B.
BAGDAD, December 16th, 1922.

Sir Percy came back on the 11th with treaties all signed and finished in his hands. Ibn Saud is coming to the Iraq in the Spring to visit the King under Sir Percy's auspices. Sabih Bey, ex-Minister of Works, who went with Sir Percy as the King's representative told me that the matter is finished, that Sir Percy was magnificent and that Ibn Saud is convinced that the future of himself and his country depends on our goodwill and that he will never break with us. In point of fact the treaty is on exactly the lines that Sir Percy stipulated. I was glad to see him. It makes an immense difference having him back. . . .

To H.B.
BAGDAD, December 18th, 1922.

Major Young asked me whether I would accept appointment as Oriental Secretary, with the rest of Sir Percy's staff, till Oct. 1923 (which is to be the date of Sir Percy's own appointment). I said I would. So that's how matters stand. I shall hold the appointment till Sir Percy leaves at any rate. Major Young suggested that his successor might like me to stay on for a bit so as not to make a complete change all at once. I said, other things being equal, I should probably be able to do that, but of course it would depend largely on who the successor might be, and at that we left it. It has turned out very much as I should have wished because it's they who have asked me to stay and not I who am clinging on. I made it very clear to Major Young that I wasn't clinging on if they did not want me. What a strange political career I've had, to be sure. . . . Oh for peace—peace at any price, I could almost say. I wonder if any generation was so weary of strife as we are. Jafar Pasha dropped into the office this morning for a talk. I wish there were more people of his integrity and moderation. . . . Jafar's fidelity and devotion to the King are really beautiful. I know the man in every aspect and he is equally delightful in his affectionate chivalry towards his womenfolk, his adoration of his children and his fervent loyalty to Faisal, whom he regards (as indeed, I do also) as the one man who can lead the Arab cause to success.

We've another problem looming on our Southern borders. You know that Ibn Saud has captured Hayil, thereby changing the balance of Arabian politics. His frontier now runs with that of the Iraq and it's as yet an undefined frontier. Sir Percy has invited him to come into conference with himself and Faisal at the earliest possible moment, and I've been laying out on the map what I think should be our desert boundaries. There's nothing I should like so much as to attend that conference of Kings but I don't suppose for a moment that Sir Percy will take me. . . . . . .

The conquest of Hayil will have far-reaching consequences. It will bring Ibn Saud into the theatre of trans-Jordanian politics and probably into the Franco-Syrian vista also—it's difficult as yet to see with what results. I should, however, feel much greater anxiety if I weren't so certain of Sir Percys power to guide him. It's really amazing that anyone should exercise influence such as his. . . . I don't think that any European in history has made a deeper impression on the Oriental mind. . . .

To H.B. . . .
BAGDAD, December 31st, 1922.

[Gertrude gives an account of a shooting party consisting of Mr. Davidson, Mr. Cornwallis and Major Murray besides herself.)

Our destination, the Shamiyah channel of the Euphrates, which runs parallel to the Mishkhab . . . We poled up the river, stopping at any likely place on the banks to get out and shoot.

The Shamiyah Channel is much more beautiful than the Mishkhab. Willows and Euphrates poplars fringe the river, their red gold and amber frothing round the stiff green palms. The little straw villages lie closely in these woods and the white sails glitter down the river. Over all was a glorious sun shining through fresh keen air and we, plunging through the willows and the russet scrub, jumping over or into innumerable water courses, felt again the vigorous enchantment of that delightful place, the world. . . .

At 4 a.m. we were up again and after a hasty cup of tea jumped into our boats and paddled down to the Hor. It was wonderful in the still night. The only sound was the talking of the geese, whom we were out to kill. But we didn't kill them—they were a great deal too many for us. Dawn was just beginning to break as we reached the Hor, the flocks of geese were rising with immense chatter and disturbances, stringing out in long beautiful patterns across the pale sky, but ever so far above our heads. In the cold dawn we jumped out of our boats on to a wide desolate island in the middle of the Hor. There we scattered and finding what cover we could, lay and watched the geese alighting. They were never really within shot, but that didn't make any difference to the beauty of it and for my part I couldn't tire of seeing the kingfishers hunting for their breakfast in their delightful fashion. . . .

Christmas day was perhaps the best day we had, weather and sport and good spirits. We went by boat down the river, shooting all the way, till we got to the mouth of a loop canal, the Abu Tibn (Father of Straw) on which lives the paramount Sheikh of the Khazail. . . . What we wanted to do was to shoot duck on the Hor, not to speak of geese, and we went out in tiny canoes. . . . It was a delicious Hor full of beautiful flowering reeds and alive with water-birds—not much less alive after our visit I'm sorry to say. We got to the other side after sunset. The geese and ducks were flighting in thousands but all in the top of the sky. Nevertheless it was enchanting coming back under the moon and stars across the quiet Hor. The reeds brushed your boat softly, a sleepy goose raised his voice, a coot bustled over the water with noisy awkward flight and you lay in your boat and listened and wondered. . . . And at mid-day on Thursday 28th, we were back in Bagdad, disgracefully sun and wind burnt, cheerful, fat and healthy. . . .

To H.B.
BAGDAD, January 16th, 1923.

The chief news is that Sir Percy is going home by this air mail to help the Cabinet to come to a conclusion about Iraq policy. . . . It is far more satisfactory that he in person should go and put the whole case to the authorities, for you see, even if they don't want to shoulder the burden they have got to learn that it's amazingly difficult to let it drop with a bump. Even the evacuation of Mosul would mean, I am convinced that we should be faced with the problem of sixty to seventy thousand Christian refugees. . . .

It is almost impossible to believe that a few years ago the human race was more or less governed by reason and considered consequences, before it did things. I don't feel reasonable myself—how can one when political values are as fluctuating as the currency? . . . At the back of my mind I have a feeling that we people of the war can never return to complete sanity. The shock has been too great; we're unbalanced. I am aware that I myself have much less control over my own emotions than I used to have. I don't really feel certain about what I might do next and I can only hope that the opportunity for doing impossibly reckless things won't arise, if it did I should probably do them; at least I can't be sure I shouldn't. . . .

It will be dreadfully flat when I return to London, not to be consulted about all Cabinet appointments!

Next came Sir Henry Dobbs for a good talk for which we really hadn't yet had an opportunity and we discussed Mesopotamia and history since the early days of the Occupation.

On Tuesday 9th I went to Diwaniyah with Major J. M. Wilson and Major Jefferies. Our object was to see the mound of Niffar which we did on the following day. . . . Niffar is by far the most striking site I've seen here. It's so enormously big and the temple pyramid soars so high above the plain. Moreover you get a very clear impression of the topography of the town, from the old Nil canal, the forerunner of the Dagharah, cut through it, and it's easy to picture the huge temple with its library and divinity school on one bank and the commercial city on the other . . . . you see in section age after age of civilization extending over a period of three or four thousand years. It's amazing and rather horrible to be brought face to face with millenniums of human effort and then to consider what a mess we've made of it, as I remarked above. . . .

I got back to my house feeling as if I had travelled in nightmare trains for 10,000 hours at least.

I've been pretty busy these last two days picking up threads, writing reports for the mail and preparing things which Sir Percy wants to take with him. It's always the greatest pleasure to work for him and the fact remains that whatever I may do in the future I shall never have a chief whom I serve more whole heartedly than I serve him. The sense that one has gained his confidence, is I think the thing that I'm more proud of than anything else. He has, you know, been an angel of kindness and consideration to me. . . .

To-night as I was coming back from the office very dirty and tired, I met Sir John Salmond and Air Commodore Borton on their doorstep and they dragged me in to a very merry tea. . . . I'm much attached to the Air Force; they have the same sort of charm that sailors have, they are so keen and so busy with their job, and it's a job that they are always at, just as sailors are. And they are so amazingly gallant. The things that they've done in this country without anything said about them, might be a theme for epics.

To H.B.
January 18th.
. . . . I'm very glad to gather from your letter of Dec. 27th that there's every prospect of my predeceasing you, which is what I should wish to do. The world

would be a poor place without you. I must have a talk with Sir Henry one day about plans. As at present arranged I've engaged berths for Marie and me on a ship that leaves Bombay on May 5th. . . . Meantime I must break to Sir Henry that I'm going on leave and find out whether he wants me to come back. I don't like going just as he takes over but apart from seeing my family I think three consecutive summers here is enough. . . .

To H.B.
BAGDAD, January 30th, 1923.
. . . . Seven years I've been at this job of setting up an Arab State. If we fail it's little consolation to me personally that other generations may succeed, as I believe they must. . . .

I've been rather busy with archaeology. First I had long reports about Ur to write for my Minister and for the local papers and next I've had to tackle the Oxford University expedition to Kish—I was promised a field worker and an epigraphist and on that agreed to ask my Minister for a concession, and lo and behold, one solitary man turns up. . . .

I feel convinced that no one, however good, can undertake single handed so big a work as the excavation of Kish, so I've held up the concession and telegraphed for the advice of the joint Committee which is the highest archaeological authority at home—for convenience, I'm a member of it. . . .

To H.B.
BAGDAD, February 13th, 1923.
The relations between the Arabs and the British General Staff are most satisfactory. In times of stress like the present, Sir John takes supreme command of all forces and they work together without the slightest friction. . . .

It was a delicious soft spring day yesterday and I rode out. To-day it has poured steadily almost all day, the heaviest rain we have had this month and very welcome though I tremble to think of the mud to-morrow. The streets were lakes this afternoon. And I had to run round with the Committee of the Salain Library and put off a performance we were going to have at the Cinema to-morrow for the benefit of the Library, because we felt sure that in this mud no one would come. . . .

To-day, the roads have at last recovered from the rain. I rode down to Karradah and found the first apricots in flower in Haji Naji's garden. I have a bunch of flowering branches in my room now. . . .

To H.B.
BAGDAD, March 1, 1923.
Will you please do something for me. The King (with whom I've just been having tea) is in perplexity as to how to furnish a big room in the little palace that has just been built—a reception room. It's an awkward shape for it was meant for a dining room—170 paces long by about 70 wide with a monumental fireplace on one of the long sides. I've suggested that it must be somehow

broken up in furnishing it and that he ought to make a central sitting place in the middle, opposite the fireplace, with three big handsome sofas, the middle one the most imposing. In this dusty country it's better to have furniture rather simple in pattern as otherwise it's difficult to clean, and we think that if we had some good drawings or pictures we could make it here. So could you perhaps send us a selection of catalogues or drawings from some of the best London shops by next air mail? We could get chairs and tables out of them too and make something that would do for the present. . . .

I went to Ur with Major Wilson. They are closing down for the season and we had to go in person and divide the finds between the diggers and the Iraq. . . .

It took us the whole day to do the division but it was extremely interesting and Mr. Woolley was an angel. We had to claim the best things for ourselves but we did our best to make it up to him and I don't think he was very much dissatisfied. We, for our part, were well pleased. The best object is a hideous Sumerian statue of a King of Lagach, about three feet high but headless.

It has a long inscription across the shoulder in which they have read the King's name, but it will go back to London to be completely deciphered and then return to us. . . .

To H.B.
BAGDAD, April 10th, 1923.

Thank you a thousand times for all the trouble you took about the King's furniture. He is delighted with the pictures. Major Wilson and I are going to have a great talk with him to-morrow and decide what he shall order . . . .

Sir Percy arrived safely on the 31st . . . . We're satisfied he thinks Parliament will agree to the scheme of the Cabinet Committee and that we can pull through on that though the economic conditions will be very difficult for the first few years. It's also settled that I should come back in September. I hate going away while the thing is still so much in the melting pot, but apart from my wish to see my family, I don't think I ought to stay a fourth summer on end and I shall come back more competent, we'll hope, to carry on the job. . . .

Talking of archaeologists, isn't it terrible about Lord Carnarvon. And so extraordinarily tiresome that people should be given an opportunity to say it's a curse. . . .

The floods have gone down, but it will be months before the desert East of Bagdad is dry. It is still a great sea of muddy water. They are digging a great cut in to the Diala to drain it off. . . .

April 11th. We had a terrific day yesterday beginning with a great rush of work in the office, then at 12:30 an enormous lunch given by the Iraq Army. There were sports afterwards, but I got away early following H.M. who had commissioned Major Wilson and me to come and talk about the furniture. . . .

To F.B.
BAGDAD, April 24th, 1923.

I went to Hillah for the night on the 14th with Major Wilson and Dr.

Herzfeld. We stayed with the Longriggs that night and next morning motored out about an hour to the East to see the excavations at Kish—I was inspecting, you understand. We found that Mr. Mackay had done a great deal of work at one of the mounds—the one for which I had got him a permit—but it was almost certainly not the oldest part of Kish which lies under another mound about a mile away. This second mound is covered with very ancient plans—convex bricks and very ancient pottery. I'm getting permission for him to do some preliminary work there. . . .

Haji Naji gave a luncheon party in his garden last Sunday to Sir Percy. In spite of its being Ramadhan several of the Ministers came—scarcely any of them are fasting. It was a very charming little function and Haji Naji's sorrow at parting with Sir Percy goes to my heart. But fortunately he has made great friends with Sir Henry.

The hot weather has come in with a burst the last two days. The entertainments to Sir Percy continue. Yesterday we had in immense tea party in a garden—it was given by the Indian Mercantile community. . . . . To-day there's a dinner of 200 people given by the civil community of Bagdad of whom I'm one. I'm one of four who propose the health of Sir Percy, Sir Henry, the A.V.M. and Col. Slater being the other three. How he'll hate our all talking about him.

All this time rather tears the heart strings, you understand, it's very moving saying good-bye to Sir Percy. . . . We had the annual election of members of the Library Committee this Week. I came out top. Last year I was third. They never elect any other European. That's the sort of thing that makes it difficult to leave.

To F.B.
BAGDAD, May 9th, 1923.

This is I fear going to be a very scrappy letter for I'm rather overcome with departure. . . .

Last week Sir Percy left—a very moving farewell. . . . What a position he has made for himself here. I think no Englishman has inspired more confidence in the East. He himself was dreadfully unhappy at going—40 years service is not a thing one lays down easily.

To F.B.
HAIFA, May 21st, 1923.

The Samuels [Sir Herbert Samuel was High Commissioner in Palestine] were extraordinarily kind. I had some interesting talks with them and felt great admiration for his breadth of view and honesty.

CHAPTER XXIII
SEPTEMBER 1923 TO JUNE 1924

BAGDAD

To F.B.
BAGDAD, Sept. 11, 1923.

Here's an interesting experiment: I am going to post this to-morrow by the overland mail, i.e. by car to Damascus. Will you tell me how many days it is on the way, for if it proves a success I shall write to you weekly instead of fortnightly.

I'm suffering from a violent cold in the head which I've caught from everybody else—there's a plague of colds. Mine began two days ago and to-day I hope to have nearly settled it by staying in all day. That seems absurd with the temperature at 100, but if I had gone out at all I should have had to dine with the King and sit under a punkah all the evening. So I made my excuse and he has kindly put me off till Friday. I was sorry not to go to-day because I haven't yet had a real good talk with him, other people being there when I dined with him before. However it doesn't matter much since things are going quite reasonably well.

Captain Clayton came down from Mosul on Thursday, the day I posted my last letter, with the Amir Zaid. He and Mr. Thomson and I dined with Haji Naji on Friday. That was a very delightful occasion, an excellent dinner spread on his roof over which nodded the tops of the mulberry trees—such broiled fish and such a lamb roasted whole and such figs from our host's garden! We dined about 7 and getting back early, the other two spent the rest of the evening with me. I had had a dinner party the night before, the Lloyds (he is Mr. Cornwallis's assistant in the Interior and I like both him and his wife) Mr. Jardine from Mosul, Assistant Inspector, and a nice man called Mackay in the A.P.O.C. I enjoy seeing them all again.

On Saturday I rode out to see the Arab Army play polo. Mr. Thomson plays with them and all their British officers; they are getting quite good. But it's sad to ride out over that great stretch of desert which had been converted first by our army into a wonderful farm and was then taken over by the King. The floods of last spring have sent it back to desert, the roads are blotted out, the irrigation channels half filled in and the young trees which the King planted in hundreds, all killed or uprooted. And all the desert which was under water is horrid to ride on, covered with a cracked mud surface and full of holes.

I've had a fearful brawl in my household—not the fault of my household fortunately. You remember Mr. Thomson dismissed my gardener, Mizhir, and installed a brother in his place. When I came back Mizhir turned up at once expecting to be reinstated. I refused and finding him a day or two ago making claims to draw water at my pipe I forbade him to come into my garden. Yesterday while I was at the office and Zaya and the new gardener, Jaji Marzuq, were out being inoculated for cholera (doubly inoculated to show 'bonne volonté') did Mizbir and two other brothers come in and beat Haji Ali, my inestimable cook, over the head. Haji Ali quite rightly hauled Mizhir off to the police station next door and I who was lunching at home because of the cold in my head telephoned to a British Inspector. And then I heard shouting and screaming in the street and behold there was Mizhir let out and one of his brothers struggling in the arms of some privates of the Levies with the evident intention of renewing their proceedings with me or any other victim. So I had the police up at once and clapped all three into the police station. So I hope that's happily concluded.

I've been spending such part of the day as was not taken up in telephonic communication with the police in writing an article about the Iraq for the Round Table. They don't want it in till the end of October however, so I shall have to let it lie for a bit till I can tell of the result of the elections and see how the preliminary negotiations with the Turks are going.

Sept. 12. I'm better and have come into office—now I must go to the Minister of Justice to discuss the law with Mr. Drower.

To H.B.
BAGDAD, Sept. 17, 1923.

It's been rather hot since I wrote, temp. up to 110 daily and the heavy mugginess which we generally get in September. However, it's needed to ripen the dates which are very late this year and still hanging quite unripe on the trees. I love to see them, it's the nicest part of dates, the great yellow crown of bunches, and as far as I'm concerned they may remain unripe as long as they please.

It's been very touching the welcome I've had from the big tribal people. Several of them have come in from as far as Diwaniyah on purpose to see me and I don't think one could mistake the fact that they're glad of my return. I feel rather ashamed of the immense confidence they place in one when I consider how little any of us can do really. They trust us as they never trust their own people and they think we have behind us the concentrated force of Great Britain entirely at our disposal, in any matter connected with the Iraq. . . .

To H.B.
Sept. 25th, 1923.

I'm again going to write by the overland mail. . . . The Waring and Gillow furniture has come—it's rather lighter in build than I expected and some of our Iraqis are weighty people. . . .

On Saturday there was a huge dinner party at the Palace in honour of Sir Henry's accession to the High Commissionership. I sat by Zaid who next morning sent me two guinea pigs as a present—I felt as if I had retired into my remotest childhood as I installed them in a cage in my garden. . . . And last night, we spent a delicious evening. Saiyid Hashim, the Naqib's son, invited Mr. Thomson, Ken and me to dine in the Turjmaniyah garden—away towards the Diala. It was a full moon and we loved motoring down and arriving in the peaceful coolness of the garden. We dined on the roof with the famous eucalyptus trees towering over us, and the sweet silence broken only by the gentle ripple of talk. . . .

We're having great dealings with the Ministry of Pious Bequests in the matter of our library. It's finances are in a bad way and I can't go on struggling to get money for it, so we've conceived the idea of offering ourselves bodily to Auqaf and are now in negotiation with the Minister who favours the suggestion. We discussed it at length at a Committee meeting yesterday, after which I went round to call on Mina Abdud, a wealthy Christian lady. And there dropped in an old Christian of high repute who is a member of the central electoral committee. With him came the Director of Health, and then Jafar Pasha, and we sat gossiping till it was time for me to go away.

You know I do enjoy myself here. I like being in the middle of this Arab world and on the terms I'm on with it, but I confess even now I have moments of amazement at finding how much we're in the middle of it—for instance when I looked round Sheikh Ali's luncheon table at all those turban-murbans on either side of me!

To H.B. and F.B.
BAGDAD, Oct. 1st, 1923.

All the R'ton doings sound very pleasant, it's curious to have been so lately part of them and now to be so rapt again in to the life of Iraq. But I am immensely happy here, there's no doubt of it. . . My work in the office grows more interesting—I've got all the tribal questions into my hands now. . . .

J.M. is full of his furnishings and decorations and I send you separately a drawing of a bit of the King 's throne for which we want a bit of stamped leather. Would you be so very angelic Father or Mother, to order it for me?

I'm so very sorry to see the death of Aubrey in the telegrams, I feared he was spinning a bad cotton when I saw him in London.

Oct. 4th. We had a terrific orgy last night! The dinner was excellent, Marie having supplied her best sauces and afterwards we played a preposterous game of cards invented by Capt. Clayton with pistachios, for counters. Ken Cornwallis kept the score and so well that at the end everyone was proved to have won. Unfortunately no one could pocket his winnings as there was no one to pay, so we ate the pistachios and separated in peace.

The temp. is rapidly falling—it's been down to a maximum of 95, very pleasant.

To H.B.
BAGDAD, October 13th, 1923.

My article for the Round Table has also been approved by Sir Henry so it goes to Sir Percy by this mail. It's rather lifeless, I think, but at any rate it puts our case and it's a very encouraging story. On Friday I had a perfectly charming dinner with the Prime Minister en famille. The Minister of Justice and his wife were also there. All the women are Turks of C'ple. They scarcely talk Arabic—

Muhsin's wife talks none but his sister-in-law and her pretty daughter have learnt some. N.'s wife was very prettily dressed in a blue crêpe de chine gown. It was very agreeable and friendly. . . .

I had to work 8 solid hours that day on a despatch Sir Henry had asked me to draft for him no less than a comprehensive statement of the whole Iraq case for the frontier negotiations. I was very glad H.E. asked me to do it and it interested me immensely. Moreover he is pleased with it. It will now have to be shown to the King and the P.M. . . .

I've been spending most of the morning at the Ministry of Works where we are starting—what do you think? the Iraq Museum! It will be a modest beginning, but it is a beginning . . . .

To H.B.
Oct. 30th, 1923.

The Naqib, the last time I saw him, expressed the hope that you had observed in what superior Arabic his letter was written. Few, he said, would have produced one like it. I replied that I had called your attention to the fact. There was a glorious stormy sunset and the tallest rainbow I've ever seen. It went on long after the sun was below the horizon, lifting itself higher and higher above the earth till it nearly touched the zenith. Light rains now are very beneficent. The weather has become delightful, a temperature rarely above 89 and cold dawns. . . .

My household is in a great jig about the King's coming to dinner and Marie has quickly made a complete new set of lovely shades for the electric lights! . . . It has begun to rain—it has been showery for the last two days. It's nice and early for rain; all the desert tribes will go out to pasture and keep quiet. . . .

To H.B. BAGDAD, Nov. 7th, 1923. I seem to have been socially very busy. On Friday morning we had the formal inauguration of the American School of Archaeology. There's no concrete school as yet because there's no money and no Director and no nothing. But I made the acquaintance of a charming man, Dr. Hewett, head of the American school in Mexico. He and his wife came to see me in the evening. . . . On Sunday, the weather being heavenly, I got on to a pony at 10 o'clock and rode off to Fakhamah, 10 miles above Bagdad to see an old friend of mine, Faiq Eff. He greeted me with open arms and insisted on giving me lunch; very good it was, a ragout, sour curds and burghul, a sort of crushed wheat. While it was being prepared we walked in his date gardens and he told me of his recent journey to Syria to see a boy of his who was at the American College at Beyrout and has now gone to England to study. I've written to Professor Denison Ross about him. . . . .

Did I tell you that Rishan has been missing for nearly a fortnight? He turned up today, very thin and very explanatory. But he doesn't say where he has been.

To H.B.
BAGDAD, Nov. 14th, 1923.

On Sunday I had Ken to dinner to meet Dr. and Mrs. Hewett. He's head of the American school in Mexico and told us most interesting things about American archaeology and anthropology. I expect you know—I didn't— that while they have all the ancient beasts they haven't ancient man. He didn't develop there and America was peopled from Asia via Behring Straits—at quite a comparatively late period.

The Hewetts have now gone to Mosul. They're charming people, both of them. When they come back I'm going to take her to see an Arab family. She has never been in the East before and is deeply interested in everything.

Thank you both a thousand times for your kind shoppings and writings. In reply to Mother, I'm afraid the brocades will be too expensive but I long for the patterns to arrive.

To H.B.
BAGDAD, Nov. 21st, 1923.

The Hewetts left. He wants me to come and lecture in America, but I shall not; think of the newspaper interviews! . . .

Sir Henry is in Basrah, meeting Lady Dobbs; I'm looking forward very much to her coming. It will be very amusing to have someone so alert and intelligent.

Nov. 22nd. Major Maclean tells us there's a new race game which everyone in London is playing. That would be the very thing when I have sticky dinner parties with people who don't play Bridge. Would you be very kind and send me this apparatus if it's not expensive. . . .

To H.B.
BAGDAD, Nov. 29th, 1923.

My chief news is the arrival of Lady Dobbs. We all went to meet them at the station on Friday and found that Sabih Bey had spontaneously arranged an elegant reception, carpets on the ground and a police guard, the King's chief A.D.C. and all the officials. Poor Lady Dobbs was rather taken aback.

She has with her a little cousin, Miss Miller, very bright-eyed and alert; she is learning Arabic for all she is worth. The meeting over I hurried home—it was 2 p.m. and found the magnates of the wilderness waiting in my garden by appointment—I had arranged to photograph them. Audah Abu Tai, Nuri al Shalan who is Fahad Bey's opposite number in Damascus—head of the western—and Ali Sulaiman of the Dulaim, our Dularn of the Euphrates.

I shall now stop photographing for I have done my masterpiece with Audah and I shall not be able to approach it. I'll send you a copy next week— it's a magnificent engraving. But then he's a fine subject, the old eagle.

On Saturday afternoon we all went to the races, H.M. and Their Exs. It was Lady Dobbs' introduction to our world and she was much entertained. Lady D. is an angel to me.

We were all rather beaming on Saturday because the Cabinet had just been finally settled quite satisfactorily. . . . Things are going almost incredibly well. . . .

To H.B.
Dec. 6th 1923.

I was having tea with H.M., it was the loveliest oriental scene. He was sitting in his garden near a fountain in full Arab dress, the white and gold of the Mecca princes. And by him, sitting on the stone lip of the fountain, were three of the great chiefs of the desert. . . . Every where round them, tossed over the fountain edge, lying in swathes in the garden beds, gold and orange marigolds—waves and waves of them, with the white and yellow of chrysanthemums above them, echoing the King's white and gold. And the low sun sending long soft beams between the willow birches and the palms, brushing the gold and the orange the white and yellow into a brighter glow. Such a talk we had, too, of the desert and its secular strife. . . .

To H.B.
BAGDAD, Dec. 11th, 1923.

I've made a new friend, the Director of Operations at the W.O. General Burnett Stuart, who has been out to have a look at us. I sat by him at dinner at the Air Marshal's on Thursday and told him things a General ought to know—all through dinner from beginning to end. . . .

The new railway crosses Euphrates by the Barraya and runs through the lovely gardens that gird Karbala. We got in about noon, glorious weather and an enthusiastic reception. I send you a picture of H.M. after he had cut the ribbons across the track, waiting for the trains to steam into the stations. Next to him is Sir Henry, then Col. Tainsh, Director of Railways, then H.M.'s chief A.D.C. then me. The Iraq flag flies from the engine. Then we went under a tent awning, gaily embroidered with carpets spread beneath, where the King received all the notables and sheikhs—he did it with a charming grace. So we sat down in rows, I between H.E. and the Mutasarrif on H.M's right hand and all the sheikhs in their brown robes and the turbaned gentlemen in their black and white; and a cinched, black-visaged Shiah got up and made a speech about the hope of Arab union resting in the King and his family. . . . Next a boy scout read a poem in honour of the King and at the end coupled "Long live the King" with "Long live the High Commissioner." And after another poem from a school boy, H.M. got up with a fine reply in thanks, his best manner, ending with a great phrase in which he expressed his assurance of success "because we walk hand in hand with the mightiest Power in the world."

To H.B.
BAGDAD, Dec. 31st, 1923.
(They go for a shooting party.]

We collected beaters in the little village at bridge head and walked down the right bank of the arm of the Euphrates called Abu Shorah for 3 hours. It was glorious. The sun grew hotter and hotter as we walked through the poplar thickets and the green tamarisk scrub and thorns where the partridge lie. We got 55 brace to three guns—Rasim is nothing of a shot and that day didn't hit a bird.

At the last we reluctantly decided that we must turn back, crossed the river and shot a gorgeous island, at the end of which the birds rose in great coveys. Unfortunately we had neglected to take any food with us, so having shot 3 hours down we shot 3 hours up and were rather hungry and thirsty before we got back to the cars. Not that it mattered; we had had such tremendous fun that nothing mattered. Also Mr. Yapp deserves a testimonial, for he had made me such a fine pair of boots, lacing up to the knees, that though, as a rule, my skin comes off if you so much as look at it, after 6 hours hard walking I wasn't even rubbed. My costume, I must tell you, was a most successful creation—brown boots up to the knees and a brown tweed tunic down to them. We got back to Babylon an hour after sunset, washed, dined and went to bed. The whole 6 days we were there we never saw Babylon by daylight. We were off an hour before sunrise—aided by a full moon, and home after nightfall.

We shot for another hour after lunch and then motored home. It was a good Xmas Day spent with friends. Altogether I think no more delightful expedition has ever been made in Iraq.

Now everyone but me has gone to a fancy dress ball and I'm ending the year by writing to you,

I must tell you a curious problem that arose—I hope you'll think I decided rightly. To-morrow Sir Henry gives an official dinner to the King, Cabinet and Advisors, a male dinner. He told me about it before I went to Babylon and I made no comment except approval. When I came back I found an invitation to myself and I went to him and asked him, as man to man, whether he wanted me to come. He said "yes of course if you won't feel smothered." I said I thought, as a high official in his office, I was sexless and that I ought to come and would. Sir Percy, on these occasions (levees and so on) always treated me simply as an official and I don't think there's any other way. So I'm going,

Jan. 3, 1924. I spent New Year's Day from 10 a.m. to 5 p.m. receiving visitors. It was fatiguing but I felt rewarded when one of my guests observed with satisfaction "the habits of the Khatut, are like ours—she sits at home on the Id to receive congratulations."

The dinner party at the Residency was a very small affair. I wore my best gown, our diamond tiara, Mother, and all my orders. Don't wish me back too much, life is being so interesting.

To H.B.
BAGDAD, Jam 9th, 1924.

. . . . I don't think I quite agree as to the possibility of submerging civilization. We're too self-conscious, too analytical and we've got too many means of exposing our views. We've broadcasted civilization in a way the Romans couldn't—I think it has sown too many seeds. Nevertheless your letter was very interesting. I'm not the least sorry that Labour should come in. They'll learn that it's not an easy thing to govern a large empire and they'll learn, I hope, that they don't know the nature of team work and that govt. as far as the individual is concerned is always a compromise. No one permanently has things exactly his own way of thinking except the dictator or the tyrant, who is 'ex-hypothesi' excluded. But is he?

To H.B.
BAGDAD, Jan. 9th, 1924.
. . . I am planning on my way down to Ur a two days' jaunt by myself in the desert. I hope the scheme will come off. I want to feel savage and independent again for two days instead of being a Secretary in a High Commissioner's Office.

Mr. Woolley at Ur has been making wonderful finds and has written urgently to me to go down. So I'm going next Sunday, taking Kish en route— And I've a great scheme for visiting some mounds this side of Nasiriyah which I hope will come off.

To H.B.
BAGDAD, Jan. 22nd, 1924.
I'll tell you the human details of my tour of inspection. I left Bagdad on Sunday 13th with J. M. Wilson and we went by train to Hillah. It was grey stormy weather and there had been rain in the night. We arrived at Hillah about 2 p.m. and found a taxi to take us the 12 miles into the desert to Kish.

We began our adventures by falling into the first canal, just outside the railway station—at least our front wheel was well over the narrow bridge. However, I called up support from the station and we pushed the car over. As we went on it behaved in a fashion madder and madder. Finally when the car in the open plain, began to spin round like a teetotum J.M. declared that he would not risk his precious life any longer. On examination it was proved that the sole connection between the steerage and the front wheels was a wire which had snapped; I wandered off to look for help. Sure enough I found a boy walking from Hillah to Kish. I bade him go back to Hillah, tell the Administration Advisor or the Mutasarrif to send us a relief car, gave him an eye glass case to serve as an identification badge and relieved him of his cloak and kerchief full of pomegranates which he was carrying so that he might run quicker. He set off at a fast trot and I returned to J.M. We walked for an hour and a half through rain and mud, to Kish where we were welcomed by Professor Langdon and Mr. Mackay. No car subsequently turned up and consequently no baggage. We spent the time before dinner in looking at their wonderful finds, and after dinner in discussing ancient Babylon sites with Professor Langdon. And then we went to bed in tents and slept soundly—at least I did anyway.

Next morning there was a thick white mist which gradually cleared into bright sunshine. The boy turned up and said the Mutasarrif would send out no car until he heard further from me and he reclaimed his cloak and pomegranates. Accordingly I despatched another boy with a letter. We spent 3 hours walking over the site and examining the excavations. When we got back to the tents at 11 o'clock there was no car, so I climbed to the top of the zigurrat, hailed in 4 horsemen and requisitioned their horses, on two of which J.M. and I mounted and prepared to ride into Hillah. But we hadn't gone ten minutes when we espied two cars, in one of which was the baggage. J.M. had by this time missed his train to Bagdad, but I had time to catch mine; so I jumped into the car and arrived without accident at Hillah.

Next day Tuesday 15th, my carriage was slipped at Khidhr Station before dawn. After an early breakfast I went down to the river, crossed in a ferry to Khidhr village and presented myself at the house of the Mudir, who provided me with a horse and escort to ride to Warka, which is Erah, the great Babylonian capital of the South. When we reached the mound we found quantities of people digging and rounded them up. They all screamed and cried when they saw me, but I gave them the salute and they were comforted. I said "Have you any anticas?" "No," they answered, "by God no." I observed, "What are those spades and picks for? I'll give you backsheesh for anything you have." At that a change came over the scene and one after another fumbled in his breast and produced a cylinder or a seal which I bought for the museum at a few annas. The people came from a little village, Hasyah, about a mile away and I sent them off to bring all that was there while I examined the mounds. They returned while I was lunching on the zigurrat and I bought a quantity of terracottas. I rode to the village and then back to Khidhr and back to my carriage.

In the night I was carried down to Ur junction where I arrived at dawn on Thursday and walked out to Ur mound in the bitter cold of the early morning, to meet Mr. Woolley just coming back from the excavations to breakfast—a meal of which I partook heartily.

We spent the morning looking at their finds and at the excavations and the afternoon examining the Tall al Ubair site which gave me the greatest sensation, I think, which in archaeology I have ever experienced.

I left Ur on Friday night, got to Bagdad on Saturday afternoon and spent the whole evening up to 1 a.m. in writing my report.

On Sunday J. M. took me to the Ministry, where I deposited all that I had brought in the Museum.

Then I went to the house of Madame Jafar Pasha to attend a meeting of a women's club which is just coming into being. I am wholly in favour of it—it's the first step in female emancipation here.

Lionel Smith came to dinner to pour out his woes and be comforted by my tales of what happened to mankind 6,000 years ago. When you see their immensely old things your own troubles don't seem to matter.

We're longing to know who is to be S. of S. But already I find myself writing to him shadow-cast-before reports and despatches quite different from those I used to write to His Grace. It is curious—one insensibly finds oneself wanting to bring out different points, better ones often. I believe I shall feel at home with a Labour Government. I have written quite a good despatch to-day about Anglo-French relations I do hope Sir Henry will approve of it.

To H.B.
Feb., 1924.

This time Mother's letter has missed and I have yours of Jan. 22. Very interesting about the rly strike; I long to hear what you think of the settlement. Also a delightful analysis of your children, only the second thing that I am I can't read, so I remain only an Imperialist. Well, if I am, I contend that it's in the best sense for I've directed all my efforts to detaching a large kingdom—for the good of the Empire! Anyhow, you're sorely tried, to be sure, but I'm glad you're fond of us.

On Sunday I spent the morning at my museum editing the labels. This sort of thing: I pick up a little marble fragment of a horse's neck and mane and find it labelled thus "This is a portion of a man's shoulder, marble object."

"But," say I "does a man grow a mane on his shoulder?" "True, by God," murmurs the Chalabi.

I forget what day it was that I was overtaken by an idea, but it came about this way. Col. Tainsh, Director of Rlys, came one morning to ask me who could possibly write a little account of all the places of interest you could get to by his railways—in view of the tourists who will come by car from Damascus, you understand. So I said I could, which was what he wanted. And thinking over it, I said (to myself) damn it all! Why shouldn't I write Murray's Guide for the Iraq. I began it that day, but I haven't so far gone on, except to write to John Murray about it. It's a good idea but I'm now rather taken aback to think of the amount of writing and writing that it will mean. What do you think?

Oh dear, I wish I weren't so cold.

To H.B.
Feb. 13th, 1924.

On Tuesday afternoon I pursued my explorations round Kadhimain. This time I was looking for a house described by Herzfeld with an Assyrian statue on its roof. I found the house, standing outside the town, but nothing on the roof. But as I rode round it I espied half an elephant planted on the top of the courtyard wall over the door. It's unusual to see half an elephant standing on a wall—it may be a hippopotamus; I don't think I can distinguish between the hindquarters of an elephant and a hippopotamus except by the size and this one was only 3 feet high—so I rode into the court and asked who lived there. It was a very tumbledown place and the proprietor, or rather caretaker, was to match; but when he appeared he greeted me with joy and announced that he had been the servant of Miss Cheesman and had often seen me before. He evidently thought that I had come to ask if I could do anything for him. I asked if there were an idol in the house. "Oh, yes," he said, and taking me into the inner court, lifted up a mat, and there was the Assyrian statue. It's very roughly blocked out but so like a statue of Semiramis that was found at Assam that Herzfeld thinks it may be no other than she. It is said to have been brought from Babylon. Only the upper part remains, down to about the waist. It seems to have bobbed hair; Sir Henry says it must be Semiramis as a flapper. But I must have it for my museum. This may be easy for the house belonged to the late Sir Iqbal al Daulah, a British subject, and I understand that we administer his property.

(I shall have the elephant; it was brought from India 60 Years ago by Sir

Iqbal).

I rode home by the river through the gardens of Kadhimain, over the ground on which stood the palace of Harun al Rashid, but I wasn't thinking so much of him as of the fact that spring had come (Haji Naji sent me apricot flowers last week) the grass growing so beautifully green along the water channels and the buds showing on the pomegranates. And this naturally made me want to grow and open too, things almost impossible to do in an office.

So that evening, I being at dinner with the King—the party Ken and me, the Joyces and Col. Vincent and Yasin Pasha—Zaid began arranging to go out shooting tomorrow, I said I would come too. We go in the afternoon by car to a place near Baquba where Zaid sends out tents, shoot the evening flight of ducks and the morning flight at dawn next day, and then anything we can get all day long and the evening flight at night; sleep in net tents again and motor back at dawn. Doesn't it sound nice.

It's rather warmer today. When I came in at 4 from the office I found Marie sitting in the garden looking like a female St. Jerome, with a needle for a book, a slughi dog for a lion and a tame red-legged partridge standing solemnly beside her instead of a quail.

To H.B.
BAGDAD, Feb. 20th, 1924.

On Sat. I had a hard day in the office—8:30 to 6 as hard as I could go. But you know, Father, I really am glad I'm not one of the unemployed. I can hold up my head and tell people that I do an 8-9 hours' day. That's what I have been doing these days—there has been a fearful amount of work.

Unfortunately, as soon as I got out of the sun, the cold came back. I stayed in all Sunday and did a lot of work. . . . A very cheerful evening only I felt rather ill. . . .

However, Monday was the day for writing the report to the Sec. of State, so I had to be early and late in the office. . . . Yesterday again there was a terrific rush at the office.

Today I felt really ill—I'm better this evening so don't be anxious. I spent the morning at the office writing eloquent memos and came home after lunch to write to you. Now I've got to draft before dinner H.E.'s despatch to General —

Goodbye, I lead a life almost as full as yours and I can't say better than that.

To H.B.
BAGDAD, February 27th, 1924.

The sensation of the week is the elections, the results of which are coming out daily. Bagdad was declared on Monday. On the whole very good and such other reports as are in are good too. . . .

I went with my minister to see the Bagdad orphanage. It's a very touching place, 85 boys from 6 to about 14 whom they've picked up in the streets. And there they all are, dressed as boy scouts, clean and tidy and being taught. The subscription lists are really wonderful.

Not money only is given—a bag of rice, a plate of cakes, people give what they can. And it's the first time it has ever occurred to any one in Bagdad to support a public institution of this kind and not to expect that dim entity, the Govt., to do it for him. They made a tremendous fuss about our coming, of course.

There were perturbations about my Sunday dinner party. I had asked a perfectly charming French traveller, Laurent-Vibert, a Lyonnais. He is going to translate Amurath into French—so he says.

To F.B.
BAGDAD, Feb. 28th, 1924.

Would you be so obliging as to buy me a sun helmet. It's not as easy as you think because I'm very fussy about them. I scarcely feel the sun and only use a helmet for riding and I like it exceptionally small and light. I've now found the place to go for it, Woodrow, 46 Piccadilly. It's to be covered with cream-coloured tussore—I hate drill . . . . .

My guide book is being so exciting. The part I shall not like is writing the introduction about the coinage being rupees and annas, and that kind of thing. However I haven't got to that yet.

Confidential. This is what Sir Henry has written to the Col. Office about me in his annual report on his officers:

It is difficult to write of Miss Bell's services both to the British and Iraq Govts. without seeming to exaggerate. Her remarkable knowledge of this country and its people and her sympathy with them enable her to penetrate into their minds, while her inextinguishable faith prevents her from being discouraged by what she sometimes finds there. Her long acquaintance with the tribes and sheikhs makes her advice in the recurring crises in tribal affairs invaluable and her vitality and width of culture make her house a focus of all that is best worth having in both European and Arab society in Bagdad. She is in fact a connecting link between the British and Arab races without which there would be dislocation both of public business and of private amenities.

To H.B.
BAGDAD, March 6th, 1924.

Oh dear, I've been so busy that I haven't written any letters and to-morrow is the mail. On Friday after lunch J. M. Wilson and I took the so-called express and went to Ur to do the division. We arrived at 5:10 a.m. on Sat. and Zaya having omitted to wake me, I had a bare half hour to get up and pack my bed and things. So I jumped up and put on my clothes, neither washed nor did my hair, and J.M. and I, with old Abdul Qadir, my curator walked out to Ur in the still dawn. It's about a mile. We arrived before sunrise, found no one up and went off to the Zigurrat to see the uncovered stair. It's amazing and unexpected, a triple stair laid against the Zigurrat with blocks of masonry between the stairways. It's latest Babylonian—Nabonidus, after Nebuchadnezzar—and must cover an Ur 3rd dynasty stair of which as yet we know nothing. We climbed up it to the top and watched the sun rise over the desert which was green with grass and covered with flocks and tents. By this time the workmen began to arrive, saluting us as Pasha (I'm going up in rank); and next Mr. Woolley, so we marvelled at the stair and all the rest and I went back to the house to wash, summarily and do my hair. By 8. 15 when breakfast was ready I felt rather as if I had been up since the creation of the world, or at least since the time of Nabonidus. However that wasn't what we had to think about. Before 9 we started the division (it began by my winning the gold scarab on the toss of a rupee) and we carried on till 12:30, when I struck. It's a difficult and rather agonizing job, you know. We sat with our catalogues and ticked the things off. But the really agonizing part was after lunch when I had to tell them that I must take the milking scene. I can't do otherwise. It's unique and it depicts the life of the country at an immensely early date. In my capacity as Director of Antiquities I'm an Iraqi official and bound by the terms on which we gave the permit for excavation. J.M. backed me but it broke Mr. Woolley's heart, though he expected the decision. I've written to Sir F. Kenyon explaining.

I took very little of the bronze; we can't preserve it properly, and I gave them their choice with the door post stones.

By this time it was 3 p.m. J.M., poor dear, retired to bed with fever, and Mr. Woolley and I, undaunted, went on alone. We finished after 5 p.m. and I went to tea feeling so broken that all I could do afterwards was to play Patience with Mr. Newton till 7 when I left to catch my train....

On Sunday I spent the whole day in the train writing the guide book to Bagdad, which I finished. I wrote 11 foolscap pages and then for the last 2 hours buried myself in a novel. We got in at 6:15, only 11 hours late.

On Monday I had to write the fortnightly report for the Sec. of State which took from 8: 15 till 5. So that was that.

I had a dinner party in the evening to meet a Mrs. Harrison, an American traveller and writer and an exceptionally brilliant woman.

[The following extract from a long article written by Mrs. Marguerite Harrison in the New York Times, shows, on the other hand, the impression made on her by Gertrude.

"When I was first in Bagdad in 1923 I had the privilege of seeing Gertrude Bell on many occasions and of having several long talks with her. The first time I met her was by appointment at her office in the Administration building of the High Commission near the British Residency—across the Tigris from the present City of Bagdad....

"After waiting for a few moments I was ushered into a small room with a high ceiling and long French windows facing the river. It was the untidiest room I had ever seen, chairs, tables and sofas being littered with documents, maps, pamphlets and papers in English, French and Arabic. At a desk piled high with documents that had overflowed on to the carpet sat a slender woman in a smart sports frock of knitted silk, pale tan in colour. As she rose I noticed that her figure was still willowy and graceful. Her delicate oval face with its firm mouth and chin and steel-blue eyes and with its aureole of soft grey hair, was the face of a'grande dame.' There was nothing of the weather-beaten hardened explorer in her looks or bearing. 'Paris frock, Mayfair manners.' And this was the woman who had made Sheikhs tremble at the thought of the Anglez!

"Her smile was completely disarming as was the gesture with which she swept all the papers from the sofa to the floor to make room for me . . . ."]

To H.B.
BAGDAD, March 12th, 1924.
. . . .Saturday the 15th was the anniversary of the Nahdhah, the Arab Awakening, i.e. of their joining in the war in 1916, and the ceremonies fixed for it were (a) a review of Iraq troops, (b) the laying of the foundation stone of the central building of the University of Al al Bait, (c) the opening of the Divinity School of that University, Faisal having laid the first brick two years ago.

Mr. Cooke dashed in on Thursday evening and asked me to write the leader for the papers about it. So I jumped up at 5:30 a.m. on Friday and complied. It was very important to get the right note. The functions were wonderful; for the first time I felt that we really had wakened up and become a nation. The review was at 9 on the Arab polo ground. Ken and I drove out and as we went saw the boy scouts marching along to line the roads. The whole town turned out, and the King taking the salute and looking so happy, Sir Henry, Sir John Salmond and all their staffs and all the notables, and Fahad Bey our great nomad sheikh, standing as close as possible to the King and Zaid. The troops were wonderful—as smart as could be, and all our soldiers said that they had accomplished a miracle in the last year.

When that was over, we went on to the Al al Bait. It's in a charming spot, barley growing under palms and nabk trees—thick evergreen trees- and the road running through the middle to the great dome of your imagination. . . .

Then the King came, walking down on the carpeted path under the palm trees, between rows of clapping people. Presently they went up onto the platform and I slipped after them and not only got my photograph but heard what was said. And it was memorable, for after H.M. had laid the stone, Saiyid Mahmud, the Naqib's son, read a prayer in the name of King Faisal son of H.M. King Hussain ibn Ali Amiral Muminin and Khalifat al Muslimin. I must say my heart gave a jump—the Khalifat back to the Arabs!

Next came the opening of the Divinity School; the police were wonderful; the place was packed with cars and carriages and we all got away without any difficulty at all. Ken's chauffeur was on the look out for me, caught me and packed me into the car. We drove back together rejoicing, oh rejoicing so much. We agreed the time hadn't quite come to say our Nunc Dimittis, but we thought it would be appropriate to embark on the opening verse of some song of thanksgiving or other.

What do you think, we spent a riotous evening being taught Mah Jong by Capt. C.! We loved it and mean to go on with it when we've time. Wasn't it lucky I had it.

On Sunday Ken took us with him to the Sarai, for I was going to my museum, and there I fell into one of the worst passions I've ever been in. I found old—mending the flowers from Ur with huge blobs of plaster of Paris so that the stone petals quite disappeared in them. I told him he was never to mend anything again and sent for a friend of mine, an antiquity dealer to repair the damage which he has done.

After that feeling rather upset, I came home and arranged flowers and played in my garden. . . .

Next day, March 17th, was St. Patrick's day and the Enniskillings gave a splendid show, trooping the colour. We all went. They kept murmuring "Beautiful, beautiful! habu, habu!" And "This is an army," they said. I reminded them that we had been at it a long time and the Iraq army 3 years and suggested, to cheer them, that we might smarten the latter up by putting the big-drummer into a leopard skin. "Yes," said Zaid, delighted, "we'll kill the King's leopard and dress him up in it."

I did like that morning—and what fine folk we are, to be sure. . . .

I didn't get back from the trooping of the colour till 11:30 and had a terrific day's work writing the Intelligence Report for the mail. It was finished about 5 by dint of letting no one interrupt me.

To F.B.
BAGDAD, March 18th, 1924.

Send me out some mules (not for riding, for wearing on the feet). You get them at the Galerie Lafayette in Regent St. Black and gold, red and gold and blue and gold brocade are what I should like, one pair of each.

To H.B.
March 27th, 1924.

Well, my doings are not without moment. First Kish. We found an atmosphere of electric gloom and learnt afterwards that they had expected to find us such that in the first half hour Prof. Langdon would close down the excavations and Mr. Mackay would find himself without a job. So I, unknowing, while eating a scrap of lunch, explained that my object was to leave, as far as possible, the tablets to them for they should be at the disposition of students. On the other hand, they would have to make up by parting with some other fine objects. "Who decides," said the Professor, "if we disagree?" I replied that I did, but he needn't be afraid for he would find me eager to oblige. I said "Come on, Professor, you'll see how it works out." So we went to his tent where all the tablets were exposed. There was one unique object, a stone tablet inscribed with what is probably the oldest known human script. The Professor positively pressed it on me; he said he had copied it and read it and didn't mind what happened. So I took it. Then we went to a little room where all the other objects were, and began on the beads and jewels. There was a lovely pomegranate bud earring, found in the grave of a girl, time of Nebuchadnezzar, and he set against it a wonderful copper stag, early Babylonian and falling into dust. It was obvious that we here could not preserve the latter, as I explained. I took the pomegranate bud and he was pleased. So we turned to the necklaces, and we picked, turn and turn about. And thus with all the rest. The Professor grew more and more excited. It is very amusing to do I must say. And isn't it fantastic to be seeing pots and things four to six thousand years old! I got a marvellous stone inlay of a Sumerian king leading captives and not being at all nice to them, and a mother of pearl inlay of a king and his wives—inscribed with his name. The Professor got, what he longed for, a mother of pearl inlay representing a milking scene— you see I have my milking scene in the great plaque from Ur.

We worked from 1:30 to 10:30, with brief intervals for tea and dinner, choosing and packing, till I felt absolutely broken with fatigue—so tired that I couldn't sleep and when I slept dreamt restlessly. I was up at 7 and out to see the zigurrat where I met J.M. We began work again at 8 and went on till 11, by which time all was finished and packed except 3 huge Hamurabi pots which J.M. and I carried home on our knees. We went out, before we left, to see the palace—amazing! a niched and columned court (it's 4000 B.C. or thereabouts) with a stair leading up to an audience hall, unexcavated as yet. . . .

Oh dear, I've just seen the first mosquito of the season

The deputies are all pouring in and most of them pour through my office. . .

Out in the afternoon to see Haji Naji M.P. and had a very consoling and soothing talk with him. He's a fund of loyal good sense. And, Father, he wants another pair of pruning scissors. Will you get one for me? Not too big. Oh, but the really important thing I forgot—in the morning J.M. telephoned to me that Professor Sayce was "loafering" about the Museum and would I come at once. So I rushed up in a launch and there he was, looking exactly the same as when I lunched with him in Edinburgh 10 years ago. He had arrived from Damascus the day before by car, and he is 80. But he is not nearly as young as you physically though for wits he is bad to beat. I fell into his arms and showed him our treasures with which he was unspeakably thrilled.

I had tea with A.V.M. Higgins who had just arrived. I happened in the course of conversation to quote Herbert [Richmond] and he mentioned that in all the three services there was no one whose opinion he valued so highly. That was nice, wasn't it.

I'm writing in the middle of the night, being unable to sleep.

To H.B.
BAGDAD, April 1, 1924.

Well, the Assembly. The King came in looking very wonderful in full Arab dress. The Ministers followed him and sat down on either side, he sitting on the dais. He was tremendously clapped. Then he read his speech from the throne, a very fine bit of oratory and most moving. I think I have never seen him so much agitated; his voice shook. After it his procession reformed and he left.

Then they elected their President—a moment of breathless excitement. They all wrote their choice on bits of paper and dropped them into a box.

The annual lunch and sports of the Iraq army, a spring festival in the Maude gardens, this year swelled by all the deputies. It was really great fun, H.M. and Zaid, H.E., the Air Marshals and all the male world, and me in my official capacity. Such an atmosphere of goodwill and gratification too. At lunch I sat between two ministers with the President of the Assembly opposite. They do their lunch very well, it is quite simple and good Arab food, sheep roasted whole, with rice, and a sweet and fruit, and it's quite short. The reports were very amusing, full of 'entrain,' and they only lasted an hour. H.M. gave the prizes and we all got away by 3 p.m.

I'll give you an outline of the next few days: tomorrow a garden party at the Residency to meet the deputies; Friday a lunch at Kadhimain to say goodbye to J. M. Wilson who is going on leave, and an official dinner at the Palace to Sir John. Saturday I'm going to see H.M. cut the first sod (if u can call it a sod) of a new canal at Najaf. And on Sunday Ramadhan begins, thank goodness. At 6:30 Ken and I were at the station, prepared to travel in the Royal train to Karbala. We got to Karbala at 10:30 and found a crowd at the station. H.M. was most enthusiastically received.

This over we hustled into motors, Ken and I and Col. Tainsh together— we were the only Europeans there. And motored through dust and a high hot wind, just like summer, for an hour and a quarter down the Najaf road. We alighted in an arid wilderness where the King lifted the first spadeful of sand of the first canal which is to supply Najaf with water.

To H.B.
BAGDAD, April 9th, 1924.
...... So we motored back to Karbala and while the King went to make a pilgrimage in the two mosques, we repaired to the bazaar where I bought shoes with turned up toes, yellow, red and blue.

To F.B.
BAGDAD, April 10th, 1924.
...... And will you please do a commission for me next time you are in London, no other than to buy me a new every morning hat. The one I have has faded so dreadfully. I enclose a picture of a Woolland hat which seems to me nice, together with the approximate colour of the straw—the trimming should be a shade darker .....

Summer has begun lamentably early this year. I like the present temperature—80 to 90—but it has come a month too soon. I expect we're in for a scorching time.

I must tell you something which has pleased me. I sent Mr. Scott, of the Manchester Guardian, my article about the Al al Bait university and he telegraphs asking for plans and photographs which I'm despatching this week. I hope he intends to put a very friendly article into his paper.

I woke up this morning at 3 a.m.—it's now 4 and I have just heard the gun which announces the beginning of the day's fast. The Muezzin next door to me is chanting the call to prayer in his tiny mosque.

To H.B.
BAGDAD, April 15th, 1924.
.... Yes, of course I think that there is a rationalizing spirit abroad in the East just as much as in the West, and do you know I think it will go much quicker here than it did with us because we have broken down the barriers and set the example which they will be eager to follow.

[She tells that she had a dinner party where one of the guests was a somewhat enterprising storyteller.)

One of the stories I will tell you—I laughed at it too. "How would you punctuate this sentence—Mary ran out into the garden naked?" Ken said: "with a full stop, I hope." "No," said Sir - "a dash after Mary."

On Sunday morning I went to my Museum where I had various visitors including Ken. It really is fun showing people over the museum; there are such wonderful things to be seen in it.

I've never had so many roses in my garden before—it blushes with them. And lovely carnations, stock, larkspur and things as well.

To H.B.
BAGDAD, April 21st, 1924.
When I left the office I motored out to Kadhimain to see a very interesting woman, who is the mother of the Agha Khan and manages all his vast businesses, secular and religious, while he is in Europe. She is on pilgrimage here and is going on to Mashhad in Persia and so back to India via Seistan!—something of a journey, but she seems to take it in her stride. . . . .

. . . . I dined with Nigel Davidson to meet the very nice Colonel of the Inniskillings, Col. Ridings. . . .

In this phantasmagoria of a week we all went off to the circus.

It was a Belgian circus. Now I don't think I've been to a circus since the age of 6 but I shall never lose an opportunity of going to every one I can. It was delicious, so funny and so clever and so amazing. It was composed of every race under the sun; there were Japanese and Indians and Sudanese and Belgians who spoke broken English and yet more broken Arabic. But the nicest thing of all was the elephants on a seesaw. The elephant bumped the see-saw down and jumped the acrobat into the air, so high that he alighted on the elephant's head and slipped down his back and his tail. Then the audience were invited to participate and a lot of Arab coolie boys ran into the arena. Some were white with fear at being confronted with so large an animal; but the elephant loved it. He bumped them up and they fell all ways some onto the plank and some on to the ground, till at last one, more by good luck than by any skill, succeeded in falling on to the elephant's head. And we rocked with laughter—all except the Kurdish deputies who sat together in a box and never moved a muscle the whole evening. I suppose they thought it beneath their Kurdish dignity to laugh at elephants and coolie boys. . . .

After lunch I rode up to the hospital to visit the Sheikhs. It wrung my heart. Addai whom I adore looked so white and tired. Salman with two compound fractures in the arms and a bullet through his leg declaring roundly that it was of no consequence. I sat with them not more than five minutes and they sent a boy running after me to beg me to hurry on the work. It is their blood which has hurried on the work!

Darling, I tell you all these things about my sheikhs and people and I daresay you think them very silly. I know I'm not seeing to scale, but my heart is in it—I live and die for it. Nothing else matters. . . .

To H.B.
April 29th, 1924.
. . . . In the evening I dined alone, and had dined early—by luck, when at 8 p.m. came a telephone message to say the King wanted me. I motored up to the Palace—he sent me a car. The little Palace in the Garden. It was a strange sight in Ramadhan. In the lighted rooms of the Pavilion I caught a glimpse of long robed figures saying their prayers. . . .

In the long saloon I found the King in full Arab dress, white and gold and black. There may be (I don't say there are not) more momentous affairs elsewhere, but there is nowhere I'll be bound where they are presented to you in such a setting. That night was unforgettable. The praying tribesmen, the King in white robes, the riot of flowers around the pavilion, and the sandflies goading you to distraction, while you try to think straight.

Your letter of April 15th: I'm not one of those whom Iraq keeps or sends away. I'm on the High Com.'s staff as long as there is a High Com. and a British Government servant. All you say on wages and economics is most interesting and most sound—but hard for general understanding.

To F.B.
BAGDAD, April 30th, 1924.
. . . Summer has come and I find I want another lace gown to wear in the evenings. I would like a black one for I have a silver 'fourreau' which it will go with. so will you please send me four and a half yards of black filet lace two and a half inches wide. And the great thing is to get a lace covered with pattern as much as possible, not with a big stretch of blank net at the top if you understand me.

I forgot to tell Father that my picture for the King has come, in a gorgeous frame. I sent it to him yesterday but have not yet heard from him.

I had a very nice dinner party on Friday. The Colonel of the Inniskillings, Col. Ridings, (he knows the eldest Dorman and has stayed with him). He brought a charming Captain Vaughan, very keen about antiquities. There were also delightful Major and Mrs. Gore, such nice people, and Captain Braham, my beloved doctor. We sat in the garden after dinner for the first time, with Bagdad lanterns hanging in the trees and they thought it a half acre cut out of Paradise. It did indeed look lovely.

Today I went to the Museum in the morning where Sir Henry, Esme and Captain Vaughan visited us. I burst with pride when I show people over the

Museum. It is becoming such a wonderful place. It was a great morning because there were 6 boxes from Kish to be unpacked—the remainder of our share. Such copper instruments as have never before been handed down from antiquity; the shelves shout with them

To F.B.
May 5th, 1924.

Could you please send me a bit of lace like the enclosed to renovate a muslin gown. This is exactly the quantity I want and it must be very good otherwise it washes to a rag. This was very good but you see how it is worn out. I think this kind is best.

To H.B.
BAGDAD, May 14th, 1924.

I'm waiting for two old Turbans. I hope they'll come soon for I want to ride before dinner.—They came, nice old things.

In the matter of the hat I'm most grateful. The mules have come and are exactly what I want.

To H.B.
BAGDAD, May 20th, 1924.

Your letters are almost always delivered on Saturday afternoon—9 days post—and I've now made an arrangement with the office by which they send them over. So you may think of me happily reading them on Saturday evening when I come in from riding or what not. And indeed they are a great solace.

Meantime, I've ceased to worry. I tell all who come to see me that I'm thinking how nice it will be to go back to live at home.

To H.B.
BAGDAD, June 11th, 1924.

We beat Cinderella by half an hour—the Treaty was ratified last night at 11:30.

To H.B. [who was in Australia]
BAGDAD, June 25th, 1924.

I suppose it's the reaction from the unholy excitement in which we have lived for the last few months, but whatever may be the reason, I'm feeling shockingly dull and depressed. So I'm afraid this letter won't be up to standard.

First a little bit of business—since you say that the quickest way of writing to Ceylon is via London, I don't see why I shouldn't send my letters to you to mother, for her to read and forward. It will be a great simplification for me, for I shall not have to write the general news twice over—which I really cannot do—and I can write her a little extra note about the things I generally confide to her private ear. So, unless you raise objections, that is the course I shall pursue. And in order that I may not be deterred from keeping you informed as to the history of the Iraq and of your daughter, would you think it worth while to present me with some more writing paper like this? What you gave me four or three years ago has lasted till now, but it is very nearly finished. I think, as far as you are concerned, I've put it to good use—don't you agree?

At present we really are the happy nation which has no history. The Assembly is passing the Organic Law... Now there is a solid block in the Assembly—the upholders of the treaty—who, having learnt wisdom from the vagaries of the only representative body they have known, are determined not to weaken the powers of the throne. There's a fund of good sense in the Arab, of real value.

I have not done much this week. I swim a good deal and every Sunday the usual party of us goes up by launch to near Muadhdham where we swim and dive on the river bank. I have a little reed mat hut there to undress in and another at the swimming place, opposite the King's palace, where we go when we want to be back for dinner. Yesterday the King and Zaid joined us—and I'm now going to let them know whenever we go up so that they can come across and swim with us.

To F.B.
BAGDAD, June 25th, 1924.

I have been swimming so vigorously that my bathing costume is wearing out and already has to be darned. Will you please get me another. The kind I like is in two pieces, drawers and jumper, and I like it black with a coloured border of some kind round all the edges. I prefer silk tricotine to silk and I like best a square or V-shaped opening at the neck. As to colour if you see something nice in a variegated tricotine (vide enclosed—but this particular one is in silk not tricotine and I don't like that so much) it might be a pleasant change from black. But the colours should show a general tendency to dark blue or green if you understand me.

Bathing clothes are so exiguous that I think it might be sent by letter post by overland mail—they don't normally take parcels.

Ever your very affectionate (but tiresome) daughter, GERTRUDE.

[This particular order for clothes certainly was tiresome, for it was completely baffling. There were no bathing costumes to be found in two pieces, there were none to be found in tricotine, variegated or otherwise: there were very few in black or dark blue, or green, and of these none had a coloured border. Most of the costumes obtainable were in one piece, usually of bright coloured silk, with a design in gaudy embroidery on back or front, sometimes on both.

One of the least impossible of these garments was finally despatched to Gertrude. It did not give entire satisfaction, as will be seen from a subsequent letter.]

CHAPTER XXIV
BAGDAD

JULY 1924-DECEMBER 1924

To H.B.
BAGDAD, July 2nd, 1924.

As for my annals, they are now becoming very tame, I'm glad to say! The Assembly is duly passing the Organic Law: which ought to be through before Sir Henry goes on leave on the 14th. Did I tell you he was going on leave? He will be away for about 2 months, leaving Nigel Davidson in command. I think it is a good plan. He needs a little rest and also it will be an advantage his seeing the authorities in London and impressing his views upon them. I entirely agree with Lord Cromer who used to say that a big official should take leave every year if possible as much for the sake of H.M.G. as for his own sake. And so far as I can see we shall be very peaceful for the next two months.

The most interesting thing which happened during this week was a performance by the R.A.F., a bombing demonstration. It was even more remarkable than the one we saw last year at the Air Force show because it was much more real. They had made an imaginary village about a quarter of a Mile from where we sat on the Diala dyke and the two first bombs dropped from 3000 feet, went straight into the middle of it and set it alight. It was wonderful and horrible. Then they dropped bombs all round it, as if to catch the fugitives and finally fire bombs which even in the brightest sunlight made flues of bright flame in the desert. They burn through metal and water won't extinguish them. At the end the armoured cars went out to round up the fugitives with machine guns.

I was tremendously impressed. It's an amazingly relentless and terrible thing war from the air. . . .

To F.B.
BAGDAD, July 2nd, 1924.

(She writes of her father who had gone to Ceylon to see the Richmonds. Vice-Admiral Richmond was now Naval Commander-in-Chief, East Indies.]

Isn't it really a good thing that he should be so full of vitality and the power of enjoyment. How delightful it will be for Elsa and Herbert to have him! He is, we may admit to one another, like no one else in the world. I can't think how other daughters can bear not having him for a father.

I have been reading a bunch of modern plays published by Benn. Some of them seem to me to be very good and to strike a very real and human note. What do you think of The Fanatics? It took me by the throat as an expression of what, in general terms, I also think. I'm not sure that it is a play, in the sense that it could be good on the stage. I have sent for two new plays by O'Neill—if there's anything else you think remarkable, you might tell me. One is apt to miss even outstanding things when one is guided only by reviews.

I read when I come home after lunch. I've had six and a half steady hours of work and I'm tired, and besides it's too hot to do much. So I read myself to sleep, if I can, for an hour, and then go on reading till it's time to swim. On Saturday evening I get my mail, just before dinner—that's an exciting and delightful evening.

To F.B.
BAGDAD, July 9th, 1924.
. . . . . We picnic every Sunday on the river bank after swimming and that is unfailingly delightful. We take a great fish which the servants roast over a wood fire, excellent food, a cold chicken and joint, and we don't get back till after 10. I look forward to Sunday evenings. Besides that I swim two or three times a week between tea and dinner. The water is quite warm now with the temperature up to 116. You can stay in as long as you like. I love it. Otherwise I do very little. Office 7 to 1:30 lunch with Sir Henry and then home. On Sunday I have an advisor or a minister to lunch as a rule. Not an eventful life—one estivates, you can't do anything else—with the heat closed down round you like a wall. I'm quite well though. But I would give no small thing for a fortnight at Rounton.

Saturday evenings I look forward to also for its then the mail comes in and the delightful letters of my family, I dine alone and read them several times over. They're not wasted I assure you. . . .

To H.B.
BAGDAD, July 9th, 1924.
This is a very cleverly conceived letter designed to catch you at Port Said. . . .

Do you know, I have a great admiration for Sir Henry. He is extremely good at his job; I admire his despatches home immensely—they are very courageous and very illuminating. He is a considerable administrator. He goes on leave next week and will be away 2 months.

To H.B.
BAGDAD, July 16th, 1924.
I can't say I had a nice birthday, indeed it was one of the most infernal days I ever remember. The temperature had jumped up to 121 with a raging furnace wind. It was so bad that Sir Henry, who was to have started off for Ramadi by air, on his way home, failed to get off at 6 and again at 10 and came back sadly to lunch. Finally he left at 5 and with considerable difficulty landed safely at Ramadi after dark. To-day I hope he is in Egypt. To-day the temperature has dropped again to something reasonable, round about 110 and I'm hoping that you won't be too hot in the Red Sea.

Nigel Davidson is left in charge and is living at the Residency, where I lunch with him. We're hoping that no 'orrible crisis will occur while the H.C. is away.

To F.B.
BAGDAD, July 16th, 1924.
. . . . I think I told you in one of my letters what I do every day. I get up at

5:30, do exercises till 5:45 and walk in the garden till 6 or a little after cutting flowers. All that grows now is a beautiful double jasmin of which I have bowls full every day, and zinnias, ugly and useful. I breakfast at 6:40 on an egg and some fruit, interview my old cook Haji Ali at 6:45 when I order any meal I want and pay the daily books. Leave for the office by car at 6:55, get there at 7. I'm there till 1:30 when I lunch with the High Commissioner—now with Nigel.

The first thing I do in the office is to look through the three vernacular papers and translate anything that ought to be brought to the notice of the authorities. These translations are typed and circulated to the H.C., the Advisers in the Arab offices, and finally as an appendix of the fortnightly reports to the Secretary of State. By the time I've done that, papers are beginning to come in, intelligence reports from all the Near East and India, local reports, petitions, etc. The petitions I generally dispose of myself; the local reports I note on, suggesting if necessary memoranda to the Ministries of Interior or Finance (mostly Interior which is the Ministry I'm most concerned with) or despatches and letters. Sometimes I write a draft at once, sometimes I propose the general outlines and wait for approval or correction. In and out of all this people come in to see me, sheikhs, and Arab Officials or just people who want to give some bit of information or ask for advice, if there's anything important in what they have to say I inform the H.C. At intervals in the daily routine, I'm now busy writing the Annual Report for the League of Nations. I usually get a clear hour or two before lunch.

I get home about 2:30 and do nothing till 5. I don't often sleep, but I lie on a big sofa under a fan and read novels or papers. All the windows are shut and the room is comparatively cool. After 5 I go out swimming or I take a little walk or people come to see me. I very seldom ride in the summer, it's too hot in the evening and I haven't time before going to office. I dine about 7:30 on some iced soup or a bit of fish or some fruit and sometimes if I'm feeling unusually energetic I do an hour's work or I write letters. Generally I read again till about ten and then go to bed on the roof, and that's the hot weather life. And now it's time to go and have my bath before dinner. Now I come to think of it, it seems rather a hermit programme. It is. I hate dining out or having people to dinner in the hot weather.

To F.B.
BAGDAD, July 23rd, 1924.

About the bathing dress. It was my fault. I ought to have left you carte blanche about the material. Probably no one wears tricotinc now— something else is the vogue. The one you sent is rather baggy but I shall be very glad of it when my present one goes into holes.

Nigel and I are getting on famously. Of course I'm rather a Person now that we are so short handed. I hope I shall not make any dreadful mistakes—but there's always Nigel to stop me. He is very cautious.

I've been bathing and it's now after dinner and I have two despatches to draft so I must turn to them.

To H.B.
BAGDAD, July 30th, 1924.

I have had a good deal of work this week. And there have been two or three very complicated and important administrative propositions which I have had to study and prepare for Nigel Davidson's decision. We are so shorthanded in the office, you see, that at this moment the greater part of the two other people's work comes to me. It's very interesting, however; I don't mind doing it. And in the summer it's well to be pretty fully employed. It keeps you from brooding on being a dog.

For once in my life I really am almost indispensable, someone has to do the routine work in the office and there literally isn't anyone but me to devil for Nigel the political and administrative things . . . . .

To F.B.
Aug. 5th, 1924.

It is deadly hot and I'm as thin as a lathe—I can't eat anything in the heat. But I have a glass of iced soup at 11 a.m. and find that it makes all the difference. There is another month of extreme heat and then it begins to tail off.

M— made a malady last week—fortunately she's well again. Do you remember Richmond Ritchie writing "My wife and family have influenza. The cook, thank God, is spared." I felt I knew what he meant.

There is really a great deal of work in the office; to-day I spent from 9 to 1 just over routine work—memoranda to write to the Ministries, office notes explaining papers and proposing action for Nigel, translating the papers, dealing with petitions. I didn't get down to my own work, reports, etc. till the morning was nearly over.

But I like having plenty of work; it keeps one alive. However as I began life at 5:30 and have been ceaselessly at it and it's now 10 p.m. I shall end this letter.

To H.B.
BAGDAD, Aug. 13th, 1924.

We have come to the end of Muharram without incident, yesterday was the last day. I'm glad it's over. Every night for the last 10 days the air has been uneasy with the wailings of the processions mourning for Hussain, their cries and the dull throb of the chains with which they beat their breasts. It is savage even from far off and it makes one feel disturbed. There is a little Shiah mosque a few hundred yards away behind my house and on the first nights of the month, when the moon was young, the glare of the torch flickered through my windows. The people work themselves up into such a state of frenzy that it's amazing some outburst of fanaticism doesn't occur, but it never does here.

To F.B.
BAGDAD, Aug. 13, 1924.

Thank you for the two books—The Adding Machine and Men and Masses. Modern literature is very queer isn't it, but it's also extremely interesting. One has to get oneself accustomed to entirely new forms— that which they embody is as old as the world because it is a variant of the human story! I thought both those books—I can't call them plays—very striking and I'm so grateful because that is just the kind of thing I miss, not knowing about them. Yes, I've read St. Joan, this week. I thought it wonderful; I wish I had seen it on the stage. It is so clever of him to have made her a bluff—not to say rough—country girl. Of course so she was, with the mysticism threaded separately through her.

To H.B.
BAGDAD, Aug. 20, 1924.

I dined with Haji Naji on his roof It was a nice cool evening for once and we sat on the roof with the full moon so bright that we wanted no other light and the tops of the mulberry trees waving round us. Presently I glanced up and saw the moon looking a very odd shape and found that it was a total eclipse! You saw it too I expect. It's a sinister thing, an eclipse, isn't it. As we motored back the shadow spread over the moon, deepened and left the world in a threatening darkness. The people in the houses were beating pans and firing off revolvers to frighten the whale which was devouring the moon. This they ultimately succeeded in doing, but not without great trouble. It was a very long eclipse.

. . . Bathing in our favourite pool opposite the King's palace. To us a party of shining ones, the King, Zaid, jafar, Nuri . . . all the King's pals. They had come, some of them to bathe and all of them to picnic on the bank. Do you know it's difficult to make a curtsey with grace when you're wet in a bathing dress.

On Sunday morning I went to the Museum which I had promised to show to some teachers from Mosul. They were very much impressed and said many complimentary things about the service I was rendering to the Iraq. But what pleases me still more—since I'm blowing my own trumpet so loud—is that I have a letter from Sir F. Kenyon saying that he holds up the Iraq Department of Antiquities as the model for the manner in which the division of finds is made between excavators and the local Government and that as long as things remain in my hands he will be perfectly satisfied. I am very much relieved for I feared they would never forgive me for taking the milking plaque which was by far the best thing they found. I could do no other and I am so glad they recognized it. They have been most reasonable.

To H.B.
BAGDAD, Sept. 17th, 1924.

And what do you think I was doing this morning? I was taking a friend of yours to Babylon, Mr. Tom Griffiths. This is how it came about. Two Labour members and a Unionist, Mr. Griffiths, Dr. Williamson and Mr. Davies are here for three days on their way to Muhammarah and on to India. It is a tour arranged by the A.P.O.C., whose guests they are—a bit of propaganda. Lionel Smith and I took them to Babylon. We started, I may mention, by trolley on the railway, at 5:20 a.m. Mr. Griffiths conceived a high opinion of me when I told him I was your daughter and it wasn't diminished when he heard that I was sister-in-law to Charles. "We call him Charlie" he observed affectionately; "Our Charlie." I hope you like Mr. Griffiths; I think him such a nice man (like Mr. Terrapin) and certainly I never had a better audience at Babylon than I had today.

. . . It was quite cold going down in the early morning and not too hot at Babylon, but coming back, from 10 to 1, it was infernal. There was a wind that scorched you. I had to take refuge on the floor to get out of that blast. I still feel like a cinder. . . .

To H.B.
BAGDAD, Sept. 30, 1924.
. . . The evening he arrived (Thursday) there was an official dinner at the Residency. He at once greeted me as sister and after dinner he came and talked. Lord Thomson is certainly very pleasant socially. Next day the King asked me to tea to interpret for him, but there was a circle of Ministers sitting round and the talk was quite on the surface. On Saturday Lord T. flew to Mosul, Sunday all round the N. frontier, Arbil and Kirkuk where he spent the night. On Monday he flew to Sulaimani, had two hours there, flew back to Bagdad and was at the Residency at lunch. Wonderful isn't it! In the evening there was a staff banquet at the Palace —it was amusing, as much as such things can be. The King had his talk afterwards in the garden; Sasun interpreted. Sir Henry told me that Lord T. had been very sympathetic. . . . Lord T. had a tremendous reception at Sulaimani. All the Kurdish chiefs came in to see him with hundreds of followers, sheeted in ammunition belts with revolvers and daggers sticking out from them. The procession was so long that before they had finished the round of the town they were treading on their own tail—a difficult question of precedence arose! Lord T. said he felt like a minor Roman emperor and was conscious that there should have been a man riding by his side to remind him that he must some day die. He flew away this morning.

The King has acquired an estate near Khanaqin and he invited me to motor up with him today as he wanted to choose a site for a shooting cottage. I have arranged with Sir Henry to go up by tonight's train, arriving about 6 a.m., spend the day with H.M. and return by tomorrow night's train, getting back to the office on Thursday morning. I shall like having a day out of doors—H.M. is in tents—and today for the first time for a month there's a little north wind. I really think the weather may be going to cool down. It has been a very hot, still September. . . . . .

I've reverted now to a regular Sunday dinner party and bridge. I expect I shall be able to get away very little. But George I shall send up to Mosul with Lionel Smith the week before the Richmonds come. The A.V.M is going to fly Herbert all round the frontiers and I shall show Elsa and George, and Herbert when he is here, the local sights.

I'm very much engrossed in the Cambridge Ancient History which certainly is a very remarkable achievement. Its first two volumes have got down to 1000 B.C. It gives one a wonderfully universal idea of the beginnings of history, a fascinating book. I'm writing the Mosul part of my guide book, in and out of my work. I wish I had time to go steadily at it. I've wholly failed to discover who now publishes Murray's Guides—could you find out for me and put me into touch with the publishers? It is not either Murray or Stanford, so don't try those blind avenues.

To H.B.
BAGDAD, Oct. 15th, 1924.

I have letters from you and Mother of October 1, all about your Free Traders. You are thick in the election and I'm longing to know your views. Upon my soul, I think I would vote Labour if I were in England. The turning out of the Government at a time when the peace of Europe is still on such thin ice seems to me to be such a mean party trick. And the programmes of the Conservatives and Liberals are poor, hackneyed stuff, don't you think?

[In October of this year Gertrude had the great pleasure of a visit from the Richmonds, Elsa and her husband Vice-Admiral Herbert Richmond and their daughter Mary. They were on board the flagship Chatham on one of its official cruises and came up to the Persian Gulf to Basrah and then to Bagdad. This coincided with a visit from George Trevelyan, Molly's elder son who was on his way to stay with the Richmonds in Ceylon and spent a week at Bagdad on the way. His arrival was a great joy to Gertrude. It is worth including some extracts from her letters for the interest of seeing that she who had cared so much for her younger sisters when they were children was ready to welcome their children as if they had been her own.]

To H.B.
BAGDAD, Oct. 29, 1924.

I have been a very poor thing this week with a touch of bronchitis—entirely my own fault for going out to dinner when I had a bad cold. However, at last, thank goodness, I'm better and have been doing short hours in the office for the last three days. The disappointment was that I was still in bed when George arrived and could not have him here. I was really crumpled up and Sinbad said I wasn't fit for company, so George went to the Residency, coming to see me every evening after tea. I have written to Moll about him. He is the most enchanting creature. He went off with Lionel Smith to Mosul on Monday night and will be away about a week. The Richmonds arrive next Monday, by which time I hope I shall be quite well.

There was a heavy fall of rain on Monday night, heavy for the time of year, for we scarcely ever have rain till November. It has cleaned the world wonderfully and made the temperature drop to a reasonable autumn level. To-night, for the first time since February, I have a fire in my sitting room. Summer has passed so rapidly into winter this year that I never wore any intermediate clothes but passed straight out of the thinnest muslin gowns into heavy woollens. It is a difficult climate to tackle. You can't at first believe that you really feel cold.

The excavations at Kish and Ur are opening—Kish has already begun and Mr. Woolley arrived last Saturday and goes down to Ur to-morrow. We are all frightfully thrilled by the discovery in India by Sir John Marshall of seals which are exactly like Sumerian seals here. I have written to Sir John Marshall asking him for impressions of his seals. I do hope they will have a good season at Ur this year.

I've so little to write about because I have been seeing so few people. But oh I'm thankful to be getting well again! I do get so dreadfully bored when I'm ill.

To her sister.
BAGDAD, October 28th, 1924.
DARLING MOLL,
George arrived safely on Saturday at 1:30. I was delighted to see him.
We sat hand in hand talking breathlessly.
He is immensely eager to know and understand and so intelligent and quick in the uptake. He went off after dinner with Lionel Smith to Mosul.
He is so outgoing and so eager, besides being so charming to look at. I am very proud of having him for a nephew. it was a great disappointment not being able to take him about myself, but next week when he comes back I hope I shall be all right again and we will go about with the Richmonds.

To the same.
BAGDAD, November 12th, 1924.
    We had the most delicious days all together when George joined us after his Northern tour . . . . .

    He is wildly interested in everything. He used to sit and listen when Herbert talked of India and I of the Iraq asking us now and then of things he had not understood. He is not going to waste his time on this journey, he will come back full of new impressions and experiences and now the East looms so very large it is worth while to know something about it. . . .

    Well, I hope I have made a new friend with him. I should always like to be in close touch. Last year in England I made a new friend in Pauline and now I've got George. Isn't it nice. Kitty must be next. . . . [Pauline and Kitty Trevelyan.]

    The Chatham sailed from Basrah this morning at ten. I do feel rather flat without them. All my servants adored them and one of them wept when they left.

To Charles Trevelyan.
BAGDAD, December 3, 1924.
    MY DEAR CHARLIE, . . . He may be too young to appreciate to the full all that he is seeing but I do not doubt that you and Moll have done well to let him make this journey. He may miss a good deal but he will understand a good deal more especially with such a guide as Herbert.

    I do love him very much and I think he has got the makings of a fine and generous creature. . . .

To H.B.
BAGDAD, Nov. 5, 1924.

As you may imagine, we have been having rather a rushing time, complicated by the fact that I had only just got out of bed. But I'm really beginning to feel well now.

The Richmonds all arrived on Saturday. My car broke down on the way to the station so that I didn't succeed in meeting them, but after telephonic communications, they all turned up in my office at 10:30. I took them to the Sarai, showed them the Museum, at which Herbert was thrilled; after which we called on several of the Ministers. We all lunched together at my house, and Elsa and I spent the afternoon lying in the garden and talking while Mr. Cooke took Herbert and Mary on some wild round, which they appear to have loved. I had the Prime Minister to dinner, Sasun Eff. and J. M. Wilson—most successful. Elsa and Herbert are universally loved.

On Sunday we sat about in the sun in my garden till noon, when I took them for a little sightseeing in the town and out to Kadhimain to lunch with the Mayor, Saiyid Jafar—you had tea with him—a nine course lunch. We saw as much of the mosque as one can see. The Sinbads were also of the party and came home to tea. Jafar dined and my Minister, Muzahim, and my ex-Minister, Sabih Bey.

On Monday morning they went to Ctesiphon and I to the office. We all lunched at the Residency. Esme is back and is being kindness itself, putting her car at our disposal and so forth. After a tea party with the King, the Richmond family dined with the A.O.M., where Herbert is staying, but I didn't go as I felt still rather shaky.

On Tuesday Herbert flew to Kut and back. Elsa and Mary went shopping carpets with Elsie Sinbad and Mr. Cooke, and we all lunched with the Sinbads. Then I gave a tea—party attended by 10 ladies and two of their daughters, at which Elsa and Mary shone. I hear it is likely to be the talk of the town for the next month. They dined with Jafar—I didn't go.

This afternoon Elsa, Mary, the King, the Amir Ghazi, Sabih Bey and I all had tea with Haji Naji and walked about his garden—a delicious entertainment. Saiyid Hussain Afnan and his wife are coming to dinner to play Mahjong. Herbert has flown to Mosul and won't be back till Friday. George arrives from his northern tour to-morrow morning and is being put up at the Residency.

I feel as I did when you were here that it is almost incredible that they should actually be in Bagdad. It is also incredibly delightful. Elsa is so delicious always. She is picking up Arabic and delights everyone with her efforts to talk it. Isn't she wonderfully quick and intelligent! And it has been so endlessly enjoyable to have her to talk to. I feel as if I had got things off my mind that had lain on it for months and months. She is amazingly well—never tired, eats enormously and is amused by everything.

Now I must go and dress for dinner.

Ever your very affectionate daughter, GERTRUDE.

To F.B.
BAGDAD, Nov. 12, 1924.

. . . To act The Verge [acted by Sybil Thorndike in London] really does seem to me to be a supreme adventure. All these modern plays are eagerly borrowed by my colleagues so that I scarcely have time to read them myself. . . .

I continue to think Elsa perhaps the nicest person in the world—don't you.

To H.B.
BAGDAD, Dec. 3, 1924.

. . . . After lunch, while I was sitting in my garden, there rolled up an American, adviser or ex-adviser to the U.S.A. on the subject of irrigation engineering and he had just been the guest of the Australian and Indian Governments! As he shook hands with me on the garden path, he observed: "I greet the first citizen of Iraq." Gratifying, wasn't it. He then proceeded to talk as ceaselessly as Americans do, but I got a word or two in edgeways. Finally, he said that J.M. (who had sent him to me) had told him I was going to see the King and might he come and present his respects! I was going on my way to a Library Committee so I took him there (it was conducted in Arabic which must have left him cold) and then on to H.M. who received him very graciously and gave him tea, after which he left.

. . . I wonder who he really is. He was all superlatives he had the deepest admiration for and confidence in my great nation; he was convinced that the future of the Iraq as one of the leading cotton growing countries was assured; he could scarcely believe that he was really having the honour of spending an hour with me, etc., etc.

On Monday—Forget what did, as we used to put in our diaries when we were small. . . .

To F.B.
BAGDAD, Dec. 14, 1924.

I'm going to try to get a letter through by the special Xmas mail though I doubt whether I shall succeed, for it's raining hard this evening and I don't think cars will run to-morrow. Anyhow, if it does get through, this is to wish you all a merry Xmas.

I've just had the little Amir Ghazi to tea, with his tutor and governess. The train and soldiers I had ordered for him from Harrod's had arrived last mail and were presented, with great success. Especially the train. He loves all kinds of machinery and in fact was much cleverer about the engine than any of us—found out where the brake was and how to make the engine go backwards or forwards. We all sat on the floor and watched it running along the rails, following it with shouts of joy. Fancy a little Mecca child introduced to the most lovely modern toys! . . . .

To H.B.
BAGDAD, Dec. 10th 1924.

Your most beloved letter of Nov. 26th—I was glad to have it—it made me feel quite warm inside. I'm perfectly aware that I don't merit so much love, but the nicest thing about love is that you can have it without merit. You mustn't bother, darling, about my health. You are not reckoning with the immense elasticity which comes of being everywhere sound. I shall always be thin—an inherited characteristic; and I would rather anyhow. I don't like fat people. I really did have a very hard and lonely summer and I suppose it temporarily sapped my powers of withstanding heat. But now all my own friends are back it's very different and if we get out shooting at Xmas I shall walk eight hours a day without turning a hair.

[I am told that Lionel Smith after one of the said shooting parties in which Gertrude was included said that she had outlasted them all in the matter of walking, and was as fresh at the end of the day as when she started.]

To H.B.
BAGDAD, Dec. 23rd, 1924.

Yesterday a very interesting thing happened—I went to see the Queen. She's charming, I'm so happy to say. She has the delicate, sensitive Hashimi face (she's his first cousin, you know) and the same winning manner that he has. She had on a very nice, long tunicked brown gown made by the nuns, a long long string of pearls, and a splendid aquamarine pendant. I saw the two eldest girls who are just like her, rather shy but eager to be outgoing, one could see.

Will you tell Geoffrey Dawson next time you see him that it was a great pleasure to meet Mr. Peterson whom I thought singularly level and unprejudiced. I've no doubt you will see some articles from him in the Times. They will be worth reading.

Oh dear! isn't it a difficult world.

I've a growing conviction, Father, that I shall not come on leave next year. Don't be disappointed.

[These are two of the annual testimonials about Gertrude's work sent to the Colonial Office in 1925.)

To describe Miss Bell as a complete and accurate encyclopaedia on all matters concerning this country would be true—but inadequate. Her extensive and detailed knowledge of past happenings and existing personalities is sufficient in itself to make her an invaluable colleague. But beyond all this, her keen intellect and her unfailing sympathy for the struggles of the infant Iraq state enable her to play a part that could not be played by anyone else, in ensuring not only the closeness but also the cordiality of the relations between this High Commission (the officials, be they Iraqi or British) and the Iraq Government. I cannot adequately express my gratitude for the assistance I receive from her. B.

BOURDILLON.

Miss Bell's extraordinary abilities and sympathies need no further testimony from me. But I realise them even better than I did last year and am still most grateful to her for all that she has done during the critical time through which we have been passing. H. DOBBS.

CHAPTER XXV
1925

BAGDAD-ENGLAND

To F.B.
BAGDAD, Jan., 1925.

. . . . I'm turning over in my mind whether I will or I won't write the Iraq book for Benn's Modern World Series. In a wild moment I promised Herbert Fisher nine months ago to do the volume of the Arab States. A month ago I wrote and said I wouldn't. . . . Whereat far from being discouraged they replied that that was all right and wouldn't I write a book about the Iraq only. So I'm rather caught for they have already advertised me . . . . and I feel some reluctance as to letting them down entirely—though far greater reluctance to write the book. Lionel is urging me to do it, and I'm feeling that I haven't enough time energy or knowledge. I'm postponing decision for a week.

To H.B.
BAGDAD, Jan. 7th, 1925.

I've had a week with the Queen and her court, culminating in her first reception to-day. On Saturday morning I went up to talk to her about it and on Saturday afternoon I took Esme to see her.

What with this and with preparing reports for the League of Nations delegation, I've been busy. But I did have a holiday last Friday—the only one of the season. We all went out shooting, Baqubah way—Bernard and Ken and I, Col. Joyce and Major Maclean. We started at 6:30 in freezing bitter cold and when we got out into the country it was still colder, the whole world white with hoar frost and all the waters frozen. But we enjoyed it tremendously—it looked so lovely, the green palm gardens against the white frost. We ran to the beats to keep ourselves warm and we returned 12 hours later with a bag of 150, geese, duck and snipe.

On New Year's Day, in the intervals of receiving the visits of Ministers, I made a little account of the year's expenditure. I have spent in all some 560 pounds over and above my salary. Of this, 230 (in round figures) is the cost of living here above my salary and another 79 is goods from England—also cost of living, therefore. 90 for books, papers, seeds and bulbs for my garden and various little odds and ends of that sort, and 160 for clothes—that is to say, gloves, shoes, hats, silks or stuffs for Marie to make up, for I have had no new clothes from home. On the whole I don't think it has been an extravagant year—do you?

In the afternoon Iltyd Clayton and I went to call on two Syrian families, friends of his, one Christian and one Moslem, but they all live together. It is very interesting, the little group of Syrians here. They are almost all in Govt. employment, like Hussain Afhan—a good many of them are teachers in the schools. They are making a little social revolution of their own, for the women, even if they are Moslems, are educated and behave as far as they can like European women. It is the thin edge of the wedge and I need not say that I am all in its favour.

I feel at this moment that I am a little tempted of discouragement, as the monk said of St. Francis.

I shall love to hear about your Xmas party which was just assembling when you wrote.

It is still dreadfully cold and freezing at nights. My office is icy and I sit and work in a fur coat, which doesn't keep my feet warm.

To F.B.
BAGDAD, Jan. 15th, 1925.
. . . But you know, though I love hearing of it, I don't feel that I should fit into an Xmas party. I've grown too much of a recluse. After all such years and years as I have had of being alone are bound to alter one's character. Not for the better, I admit and fear.

But there it is; if you have children and grandchildren growing up round you it is very different. I haven't had that, more's the pity. . . .

To H.B. BAGDAD, January 15th, 1925. I have had rather an unsatisfactory week, the icy cold of the reception added to the daily freezing cold of my office having been finally too much. So I stayed indoors solidly for 4 days, bored to tears, and am now practically all right. There's a great deal too much doing to have anything the matter with one at this moment. . . .

The Frontier Commission arrives to-morrow. . . .

To H.B.
BAGDAD, Jan. 21st, 1925.
This is going to be a very scrappy letter I fear, for I have too much to say and too little time to say it in. It's the Commission which is running us all to death. They arrived on Friday. . . .

On Saturday Sir Henry sent for me, he sent me straight up to the King. I found H.M. in the charming domed room he uses as an office, sitting in full Arab dress before a blazing fire (it's still very cold). I gave my message to which he listened attentively. . . .

As I motored back I found the Kotah bridge cut and stood in the crowd to watch the big launch pass up with Sir Henry and the Commission. . . .

I dined at the Residency—a biggish party and a tail—all English. The Dobbses are being admirable, they are always cheerful and apparently amused, and all their arrangements go beautifully. They had an enormous reception on Saturday afternoon for the Bagdadis to meet the Commission . . . .

January 22nd We were 58 at dinner last night! All the Iraqis appeared without a fez, the first time I had ever seen many of them bareheaded. It was a protest against the Turkish head dress—I wonder if they now intend to abandon it altogether.

To F.B.
BAGDAD, Jan. 28th, 1925.
. . . .We are still having an amazing bout of cold weather. It has frozen almost every night since Xmas and for the last three nights the temp. has been down to 18. By day it's little above freezing point with an excruciating north wind which cuts you like a knife. The sheep are dying like flies, the benyon trees and sweet limes are all killed (I shan't wear mourning for the latter) and all the young orange trees are dead. The people suffer horribly; the price of food has doubled and trebled, and they are not clad or lodged in a manner to resist cold. Lots of people in the desert and the villages have died. In the north we hear that there is deep snow. They say there has not been such prolonged cold for 40 of 50 years. Anyhow, I hope it won't happen again in my time for it is extremely disagreeable even if it is salutary for those who have furs and fires like me. I live in a fur coat except when I'm sitting before the fire in my sitting room. It's rare in this country to be longing for a little sun and warmth.

We are living through a very agitating time, feeling all of us that our destinies are in the melting pot. If good comes out of the Frontier Commission it will be mainly due to Sir Henry's extraordinarily tactful handling and the charming courtesy with which he and Esme treated them. . . .

The Bagdadis played up splendidly. On Thursday there was a great Boy Scout function to which I went. We were in the teeth of an almost unendurable north wind. There were 1500 Iraqi Scouts and all the Scout Masters were Iraqis. It was in the Sarai, the old Turkish military head-quarters. All the balconies were crowded with people and the great open square too—there were some 5000 spectators. Besides the ordinary Scout exercises and tent pitchings—which they did extremely well—they took the opportunity of introducing a little nationalist propaganda. They made the Iraq flag in living boys dressed in the national colours, and they drew in chalk over the square a huge map of the Iraq, with frontiers formed by a line of boys—stretching north, I need not say, far beyond the present boundary!—and boys with Iraq flags indicating the three towns, Basrah, Bagdad and Mosul.

At the end they hoisted the Iraq flag on a tall standard. It was wonderfully moving. Some boys ran forward with the flag staff and set it up; then all the boys who carried the various scout flags ran up and formed a circle round it, while the other boys crowded in in a huge semi-circle, with the spectators crowding in behind them. When the chief Scout Master broke the flag a huge roar went up from the boys and the crowd and after it had died down the Scout Master cried out "Three cheers for King Faisal the First!" Even out of doors they made a great sound. . . .

To H.B.
BAGDAD Feb. 4th 1925.
It is a trifle less cold. It no longer freezes at night and the sun is hot in the middle of the day, but the wind is still bitter. I walked out this afternoon, fetched a round outside the town and finally called on my dear Mistress of the

Ceremonies to discuss a mourning party which the Queen is to give. It appears that you ought to be given the opportunity to express your sympathy and ask how she is. As soon as the French nuns have made her a plain white gown—white is Hijazi mourning—we're to issue the invitations.

To H.B.
BAGDAD Feb. 11th 1925.

    This isn't going to be a very bright letter for I am suffering under the shock of a domestic tragedy with which I feel sure you will sympathise— the death of my darling little spaniel, Peter, and of his mother, Sally, who was Ken's dog. I don't know which of them I loved most, for Sally was with me all the summer while Ken was on leave. But I shall now miss Peter most—he was always with us, in the office and everywhere, and he adored me, and I him. Sally had a cold a few days ago and as Ken was going out shooting with the King I offered to take her—we neither of us, nor the vet, had any idea that it was distemper which it really was, the very worst kind that ends in pneumonia. Peter caught it and died after agonies of stifled breathing at 4 a.m. this morning—I had been up with him all night—and Sally died after the same agonies at 5 p.m. Ken and I were both with her. So you will understand that I am rather shattered. My whole household was affected to tears—they all loved them. One should not make trouble for oneself by unnecessary affections, should one, but without affections what would life be? It is difficult to know where to draw the line.

    Well, that's that. They are both buried in my garden. . . .

    I hope you are feeling a sense of relief at getting out of the rush. Your time on the sea will be very good for you, and how nice it will be seeing Elsa—my dear love to her. Tell her about Sally and Peter; she will be sorry for me, I know.

To F.B.
BAGDAD Feb. 18th, 1925.

    Thank you so much for the Cross Puzzle book. I have cracked my brain over it a little, with much amusement, and I'm going to bring it out on some suitable occasion at my parties. . . .

    We have had very heavy rain and on Friday afternoon I came home to find my sitting room more like a shower bath than anything else. You who live in solid houses don't know what the vicissitudes of the weather really mean. However, the sun came out on Saturday and the world has dried up wonderfully fast. It is beginning to feel like spring though it is still very cold at night. . . .

To H.B.
BAGDAD Feb. 18th 1925.

    . . . . It did rain! On Friday my roof, having been opened up by the frosts, gave up the game and I came home after lunch to find my sitting room more like a shower bath than anything else. However, fortunately the rain ceased about 5 and next day there was sun in which to dry the carpets. The world has dried up wonderfully fast. . . .

I have been feeling dreadfully mopish about my poor little dogs, specially Peter, because I miss him dancing round me all day. Everyone has been most kind and sympathetic. . . .

To H.B.
BAGDAD, Feb. 25th, 1925.
. . . .Even though I have been a govt. servant for 9 years I continue to be disappointed by the slowness with which official wheels grind. . . .

To F.B.
BAGDAD, Feb. 25th, 1925.
. . . .I went to the Palace and first of all we looked at the children— Ghazi in a fearful jig because he had his first lesson in developing photographs in the developing box I had given him. He really is a nice little boy. He rushed and brought me a chair and said in English "Please sit down." The two girls were having a music lesson. And then we went to see Ghazi having a writing lesson in his own little house. He is making a garden, digging and planting in it himself and much pleased with it. Altogether I had a very pleasant impression. . . .

Sunday was a delicious spring day. We lunched in the sun on the river bank. The peasants were all planting their summer vegetables. The whole family turns out for the day; the babies lie in the furrows and the dogs sit by. [A dinner followed by Bridge.] I introduced the Cross Puzzle book and Iltyd became so wrapped in it that he could scarcely remember what was trumps. It is very entertaining.

To H.B.
BAGDAD, March 4th, 1925.
I got in from Ur at 6 a.m. this morning and not having slept in the train, I slept all this afternoon till 6. . . .

Our excavations this year, without being so sensationally exciting as they were last year, have been extremely good and there were some wonderful objects to divide. The division was rather difficult but I think J.M. and I were very fair and reasonable—I hope Mr. Woolley thinks the same.

I do miss my Peter so. I longed for his little cheerful presence when I went to Ur. He would have loved that boring journey—so many dogs to look at out of the window. . . . .

H.M.G. has appointed the Financial Commission to enquire into the finance of Iraq—Hilton Young and Mr. Vernon (the latter financial adviser to the Col. Office). They arrive on March 15th. Excellent, we think, and it really looks like business. Our spirits are all going up.

To F.B.
BAGDAD, March 4th, 1925.
. . . . It has been a good season, though not so sensational as last year, but still there were some wonderful finds, rather more difficult than usual to divide.

This year I left the great piece to them—it is a huge stele with amazingly interesting reliefs, but as it was all in fragments and needed a great deal of careful reconstruction, which we can't do here, I thought it was in the interests of science to let it go to some big museum —the British Museum or Pennsylvania—where it can be properly treated. . . .

To H.B.
BAGDAD, March 11th, 1925.
. . . .Upon my soul I almost wish there weren't a desert route—it brings silly females, all with introductions to me. . . .

To F.B.
BAGDAD, March 12th, 1925.
. . . . I spent Sunday morning rearranging the Museum in a horrible dust storm which prevented J.M. and me from making a brief archaeological expedition by train that night. It was lucky we decided not to go as the train was held up by floods which wrecked the line and it never got anywhere. . . .

Esme leaves next week to my great regret—she does make such a difference. We all love her. Sir Henry and she and I went for a little walk yesterday along the river bank where it was not too muddy, and it was so nice. It's a great pity that Esme won't be here to entertain the secretaries of state.

To H.B.
BAGDAD, March 18th, 1925.
. . . Hilton Young has come bringing me a letter from Moll. He was to have dined with me the day after his arrival, but the High Commissioner pinched him. He is coming next Sunday. Everyone likes him, I hear, but he is gravelled to invent any way to make our budget balance for the next few years. . . .

To H.B.
BAGDAD, March 25th, 1925.
Uncle Lyulph's death came in Reuters yesterday—I feel very sad about it. It makes a great hole in the family, doesn't it. . . . [This was Lord Sheffield.]

J.M. and I had a pleasant night at Kish, did our work and got safely back without motor accidents, contrary to our habit. The digging this year has been rather disappointing—nothing but grave finds, good of their kind but not specially important. One gets blasée about small Sumerian objects which were once so exciting and I do wish the ancients hadn't used so many copper pins. They are very dull in a museum. I spent most of Sunday morning arranging them, with Madame La Caze to help me. . . . .

On Sunday afternoon Ken and I took Hilton Young out to some marshes near the Baquba road to see birds. That was very nice. The birds played up and I brought out tea—partly in your thermos which is still one of the mainstays of existence—and Hilton Young was delighted and delightful.

Chiefly we are busy preparing for the Secretaries of State who arrive to-morrow. There are to be no end of functions for them.

To F.B.
BAGDAD, March 25th, 1925.
. . . .The Secretaries of State arrive to-morrow and we seem to spend our time in the office making arrangements for their parties and sightseeing. I hope they will be as nice as Mr. Hilton Young, who is charming. We all loved him. Tell Molly. . . .

J.M. and I had a pleasant night at Kish. The finds aren't very good, at least, they are good of their kind but it's rather a boring kind, nothing of any great importance. I have a feeling that Kish is not going to yield much and I am sorry for the excavator, Mr. Mackay, who is looking very well and carefully without much to reward him. . . .

Yes, I'm sure the snapdragons will be nice [at Rounton] if the peacocks don't sit on them.

To H.B.
BAGDAD, April 1st, 1925.
I feel that I have been addressing myself to the winds and waves for a long time; I wonder when I shall get your first letter from Australia.

We have been remarkably busy with secretaries of state. They arrived last Thursday and I met them at lunch on Friday and carried off Mr. Amery in the afternoon to look at birds. . . . They are all very sympathetic and I do like Sir John Shuckburgh so much. . . .

On Monday we began again with an official dinner at the Residency to meet the Secretaries of State and the Cabinet. . . . And on Tuesday everyone flew away to Mosul except Sir John who has stayed to study our difficulties and see what he can do to help. . . .

To F.B.
BAGDAD, April 1st, 1925.
. . . .The description of Uncle Lyulph's funeral was so touching and beautiful. I can't yet picture the difference that his death makes in the family—I did care for him so much.

I have had rather a rushing week. The Ministerial party came back from their northern tour on Saturday. The Prime Minister gave an official dinner for them that night. I had a dinner for Sir John Shuckburgh on Sunday and another for Mr. Amery on Monday. . . .

To-morrow we go off for a three day Easter jaunt, Ken and Lionel and I, to Ukhaidhir. J.M. was to have come but can't get away. Mr. Cooke is coming in his place. I haven't been to Ukhaidhir since 1911.

The Secretaries of State flew down to Basrah to-day. I feel sure that their visit has been very useful and advantageous, but I shan't be sorry to relapse into a more humdrum existence when they go next week. . . . Naturally, I have had nothing to do with their conferences; I have only heard the hopes and fears which they evoked in subsequent echoes.

There was a terrific dust storm last week after which the temperature fell to lower than it should normally be and we all shivered.

What a tale about Father's nearly missing his boat at Ceylon! Haven't heard from him yet from Australia—it's a terrific way off, isn't it.

To H.B.
BAGDAD, April 8th, 1925.

I seem to be much busier outside the office than in it and I'm going to write to you this morning while I'm waiting for more files to turn up. The Secretaries of State were to have come back from their northern flights last Friday, but the whole country was wrapped in the most terrific dust storm, like a yellow London fog, we worked in the morning by electric light—and they were delayed in Kirkuk. . . .

Mr. Amery's knowledge is encyclopaedic—he acquires it with extraordinary speed and never forgets what he has once acquired. He is not the least a pedant; what he knows, he knows quite naturally and simply. . . .

To H.B.
BAGDAD, April 15th, 1925.

[The "Easter jaunt" to Ukhaidir to which she had been looking forward.] It made me feel rather ghostlike to be in these places again, with such years between, and I was glad I wasn't there alone. Next day we motored back to Bagdad, lunching on the bank of the Euphrates under willow trees.

The Secretaries of State also returned from Bastah that day but I did not see them on Sunday, which I spent partly at the Museum in the morning and riding after tea, with the usual Bridge party at night.

Yesterday morning the Secretaries of State flew away in clouds of dust and glory and we all went down to the aerodrome to bid them farewell. And then, though relieved, we felt a little flat! But there's no doubt that their visit has done good. I love Sir John and Mr. Amery. The latter distinguished himself by conversing in Turkish which he hadn't done since 1898

To F.B.
BAGDAD, April 16th, 1925.

The Secretaries of State left on Tuesday. I went with Mr. Amery to the Museum on Monday morning and on the way back he said very satisfactory things. He said he had been much struck by the admirable relations between the British officials and the Arabs, and thought the former had done wonderful work and that the whole administration was much better than he expected. I was very glad because I felt that he was giving praise where it was due. . . .

I really am surprised that The Verge was a success on the stage—I should have thought it would have been too bewildering. . . .

To H.B.
BAGDAD, April 22, 1925.

I am very much interested by your accounts of the fifth continent and its inhabitants, but what you say confirms my feeling that I should never want to go there or to see them at home. But I like hearing about them from you. It must be horrid to have to cook one's own dinner always—it would be horrider to eat always the one I should cook, I'm bound to say.

As for my plans, I'm thinking of coming home for a couple of months towards the end of July, so as to have two peaceful months at Rounton. If I drop into the end of a London season, I rush about so and it's not very restful. So barring accidents, that is what is in my mind. . . .

In the evening we were mainly engaged in canvassing the merits of a little black and white puppy which Col. Prescott had offered me. She ought to have been a spaniel but she has got mixed up with an Airedale and has the oddest little ugly pathetic face and very apologetic manners. I've got her so far on appro. She is singularly intelligent and already has a passion for me. The servants all call her Peter so I've called her Petra—my poor Peter!

We have been having odd weather—violent dust storms at the end of last week and on Sunday night a terrific thunderstorm and heavy rain which sent the temperature down with a bump. Very nice that was. J.M. and I had got permission from the AN.M. to go up to Kirkuk by air mail in order to see a little excavation which is being done there under the auspices of the Museum. We went yesterday morning and came back this morning—two and a half hours up and two hours down, with a following wind. I like flying. The only 'contretemps' was that they forgot to put my little valise into the plane and I arrived with nothing. However, my hostess, Mrs. Miller (Capt. Miller is Administrative Inspector) lent me brushes and combs and things, and once you have made up your mind that you have no luggage, it is rather an exhilarating feeling.

We got in about 10:30, saw some things in the town that we wanted to see and after lunch went out to the dig which is being very well done by a certain Dr. Chiera, an Italian professor of Assyriology at an American University. It's a villa, a house belonging to some wealthy private person who lived about 800 B.C. Chiera has found masses of tablets from which we hope that we shall ultimately piece together the story of the family. It's a comfortable house with a bathroom, hot and cold water laid on, so to speak (we found and traced the drain while we were there), nice big reception rooms, a paved court and all you could wish. It was very interesting and the country round Kirkuk looked so agreeable with scarlet ranunculus on the edges of the green barley fields. It was delightfully cold too. . . .

The King has asked me to go out to his farm near Khanaqin for a couple of days during the holidays at the end of Ramadhan. They begin on Friday or Saturday but as H.M. wants to leave on Friday afternoon I expect they will continue to see the new moon on Thursday. I shall go, I think; a couple of days out of doors would be good and it doesn't look as if it would be too hot.

To H.B.
BAGDAD, April 29th, 1925.

We had some emotions as to the beginning of the Id. on Thursday night no one knew whether the moon had been seen nor whether there was an Id and a levee and a departure to the King's farm (for me) next day. At 11 p.m. the guns announced the Id, for they had managed to get the moon seen at sunset but it had taken the Qadhi all those hours to make sure that the witnesses had spoken true.

I hopped up at 6 to get Zaya and my baggage off to the station and at 8 behold me at the King's levee. I then in the course of an hour visited all the Ministers and the Naqib, went home and got into country clothes and at 10 was picked up by H.M. at the station near my house. We went up by trolley—the party was H.M., Naji Suwaidi, a Chamberlain and an A.D.C. The King's farm is a little to the N.W. of Khanaqin. We got to the nearest point to his tents at 2, having had an excellent lunch in the trolley, found horses waiting and rode up through the fields to the tents, about 20 minutes away. It was so heavenly to be riding through grass and flowers—gardens of purple salvia and blue borage and golden mullein, with scarlet ranunculus in between. After tea we went out for a walk through the crops, H.M. rejoicing over his splendid hemp and barley and wheat—they were splendid, I must say. And then we sat in the pleasant dark till dinner, after which we all went to bed. Zaya had arrived by this time and I had all my camp furniture in an enormous tent—unfortunately I shared it with innumerable sand flies. Petra had come with me; she enjoyed herself enormously and behaved not too badly for one so young. She is going to be a nice little dog.
. . .

We left after dinner, Iltyd, J.M. and I riding for half an hour to the station through black night on a path which played in and out of the irrigation canals. I had Petra on my saddle bow—she proved an excellent rider but it was fright rather than pleasure which kept her quiet I think. We succeeded in catching the train after missing our way several times and got safely to Bagdad next morning. It was a very nice Id.

Hilton Young has presented his report and gone. I read the report this morning. It's admirable. There are no miracles, just good sense —and helpful advice to both Governments, but if it is followed we ought to get on to our feet in a year or two. . . .

To F.B.
BAGDAD, April 29th, 1925.

Your visit to Newtimber sounds delightful but it wasn't nicer than my visit to the King's farm last week. . . . It was so delicious, grass and wild flowers everywhere; you can't think what that was like after the arid desert round Bagdad. The farm is just under the Persian hills with lovely views in all directions. On Saturday morning Iltyd Clayton arrived by train and on Sunday J. M Wilson, so we made a regular house-party. We walked and rode and motored, looked at all the crops, settled where the house is to be built (he is still in tents) and where the roads are to be made and we were very peaceful and happy. It is very delightful being with the King up there: he is a perfect host and he puts politics out of his head and becomes the country gentleman very contentedly. It is excellent for him that he should have a place of his own to go to and when the little house is built it will be even better. For though it is very pleasant to be in tents at this moment, in another week or so it will be too hot. Even to-day I had a fan in my office for the first time. We got back on Monday morning and were very sorry that it was over. . . .

Now I must go up and see the Queen about her washing silk dresses. Those sent by Moll are a great success. I've written a long rambling letter to Father about the visit to the farm thinking it would beguile him on the ship and that's why this one to you is rather scrappy. I shall be glad when my parents are happily reunited! I daresay they will too.

To F.B.
BAGDAD, May 6th, 1925.
. . . . Yes, I think clothes are frightful, or at least they offer vast opportunities for frightfulness. . . .

To F.B.
BAGDAD, May 13th, 1925.
. . . .There has been a nice, very young Guardsman here, Mr. Codrington. I have just been showing him some of the sights of the town. . . .

To F.B.
BAGDAD, May 13th, 1925.
We have had a week of very disagreeable weather, not hot—not for us; it's rarely 100—but south wind and cloud and heaviness and dust. It takes all the stiffening out of you. On Saturday night it suddenly became wonderful fresh for a few hours and we made the most of them by going out to the Karradah gardens and dining on Haji Naji's roof, Ken and Iltyd and Lionel and I. He gave us a very good dinner—roast fish and chicken and rice and all the different kinds of vegetables he grows on his farm, and fruit. After dinner we lay on his cushioned benches under the moon and talked to one another while Haji Naji and a friend bubbled with narghilehs. . . .

To F.B.
BAGDAD, May 20th, 1925.
The chief news this week is that which you already know, namely that the Council of the League will not receive the report of the Frontier Commission till the Autumn session. . . .

Last night just as night fell we were enveloped in a raging dust storm; the subsequent night was disgusting, the wind so hot that one couldn't sleep out of doors and the house so stuffy that one could scarcely sleep inside. Weather of this kind cannot be described; it must be experienced.

So far as heat goes, it has not been bad—only once over 100 I think— but south wind and dust storms have been unusually frequent and they take the stiffening out of you more than heat. . . .

I'm not writing to father this week. It is a comfort he is coming nearer. Australia is dreadfully far away isn't it. Thank heaven, I hear that Cook is opening an office here so that I shall no longer be the sole agent for tourists. . . .

To H.B.
BAGDAD, June 10th, 1925.

We are in the thick of elections and so far the results are more than reasonably good. The electors choosing decent, solid men. I don't think the House will meet till the autumn; the budget is not ready and cannot be prepared until a decision on the Hilton Young report has been taken by both governments, so there's nothing for it to meet about. . . .

Now I'm going to swim. Petra is a great swimming dog and loves it. She is a clever little thing but not as nice as Peter. Are you glad to be home and to see so many of your family?

You didn't say whether you saw Elsa in Ceylon this time.

To H.B.
BAGDAD, June 17th, 1925.

. . . On Monday the Queen asked me to come and take a stroll on the bank opposite the palace. I arrived about 5:15 and we spent half an hour in desultory talk. Then I suggested that we should cross over the river, but their launch was out of order so at 6 I insisted on going over in a boat. Mme. Jaudat, the Mistress of the Ceremonies had meantime arrived with her little boy, and we all went over, the two girls, Ghazi, Miss Fairley, H.M. and I. On the other bank I found that leisurely preparations for a large meal were going on, including a pile of fish waiting to be roasted . . . . and finally about 7 a sort of high tea was ready, sandwiches and roast fish and cakes. And as it was a very pleasantly cool evening it was agreeable to sit there and eat. . . .

To H.B.
BAGDAD, June 24th, 1925.

It was very nice to get your letter home of June 11th and Mother's of June 10th in which she says she is suffering so from the heat. I know what will happen—by the time I get home it will be icy and will remain so for the two months of my leave. And probably rain all the time. However perhaps that will be a pleasant change.

I was cut to the heart about Anthony. [Brig. Gen. Hon. Anthony Henley, who had died suddenly in Roumania.] I hope you will give me some news of Sylvia.

An interesting man came to see me on Monday, one Pernot. He is editor of the Revue des Deux Mondes and is making an exhaustive enquiry for it and for the Débats into the state of Moslem feeling towards the West . . . .

Politically we are in full crisis . . . . On the whole the country is all in favour of stability. It's a pity that here as elsewhere the economic stringency presses . . . . so greatly. Trade is at a low ebb and a bad harvest has made things especially difficult.

Goodbye, dearest. There's a despatch waiting to be written for Sir Henry.

[Gertrude came on leave this year and arrived in London on July 17th. She was in a condition of great nervous fatigue, and appeared exhausted mentally and physically. Sir Thomas Parkinson, M.D., our old and valued friend as well as our doctor said that she was in a condition which required a great deal of care and that she ought not to return to the climate of Bagdad. Dr. Thomas Body, M.D., of Middlesbrough who saw her when she went north took the same view. On Gertrude's way through London she saw Mrs. W. L. Courtney, who came to dine one night at 95 Sloane Street with her and her father. She had a few minutes private talk with Mrs. Courtney and asked her to suggest something that she could do if she remained in England. Mrs. Courtney wrote a few days later suggesting that Gertrude should stand for Parliament. The following letter is the reply.]

To Mrs. W. L. COURTNEY.
ROUNTON GRANGE, NORTHALLERTON, Aug. 4

YOU DEAR AND BELOVED JANET, No, I'm afraid you will never see me in the House. I have an invincible hatred of that kind of politics and if you knew how little I should be fitted for it you would not give it another thought— though it is delightful of you, all the same, to think of it. I have not, and I have never had the quickness of thought and speech which could fit the clash of parliament. I can do my own job in a way and explain why I think that the right way of doing it, but I don't cover a wide enough field and my natural desire is to slip back into the comfortable arena of archaeology and history and to take only an onlooker's interest in the contest over actual affairs. I know I could not enter the lists, apart from the fact that it would make me supremely miserable.

I shall hope to see you in London before I leave—that will be about the end of September. For I think I must certainly go back for this winter, though I privately very much doubt whether it won't be the last.

Goodbye, my dear, and don't forget that I'm ever your very affectionate
GERTRUDE.

[Gertrude came to Rounton, for a while, much enjoying her own gardens, and grew gradually better there. She then went to stay in Scotland with Mr. and Mrs. Lionel Dugdale at their shooting box, where the affectionate solicitude with which they surrounded her went far to complete her cure.

We all felt after this last visit of Gertrude to England that she had never seemed more glad to be with us all, never more affectionate and delightful to all her Yorkshire surroundings. It was a solace to her when the time came for her return to Bagdad at the beginning of October to have the company of her cousin Sylvia (Hon. Mrs. Anthony Henley) for whom she cared very much.]

To F.D.
October 2nd, 1925.

. . . . You must think of us as very happy together—I can't be too glad that I've got Sylvia. She is an enchanting travelling companion. I read the Great Pandolfo in the train yesterday and began Black Oxen—both very good. . . .

To H.B.
Monday. Oct. 5th, 1925.

. . . . Sylvia's delight in everything has been such an added zest—she has never been on a sea voyage before and her interest culminated when Captain S. took us on to the bridge last night and showed us the stars through a sextant. . . .

To H.B.
HAIFA, October 9th, 1925.

Here we are nearly at the end of a rather tiresome slow journey which would have been more than tiresome if it had not been for Sylvia's delight in all the places we touched at. . . . .

[They go on shore at Jaffa].

. . . We went on shore after breakfast and drove out to the new Jewish suburb, the inhabitants of which subsist I understand on taking in one another's washing. It looked a poorish place—on the outskirts gaunt new houses were being run up on the sand. These are let out room by room, at exorbitant rates, to Jewish immigrants. Gladly we drove back to Jaffa which is however, also submerged by Jews. At last we got out of them to a delightful little Palestinian hotel by the sea at the extreme southern end of the town—is to the north. We lunched happily on a balcony and on our way back walked through the old Arab town, a tiny medieval place with narrow streets, half arched over, climbing up and down a hill. It was the first really Eastern place which Sylvia had seen and she loved it. So did I. That night we played bridge with a brother and sister called Kennedy—he is in Posts and Telegraphs here. Before parting we arranged to meet on shore at 3 p.m. to-day so that he should take us in his car on to Mount Carmel. Accordingly we stayed on board till after lunch, but when we proposed to go on shore we found that we had not got the necessary documents for landing, the Customs Officer having disappeared before we were up. The policeman left in charge doggedly refused to allow our boat to put off—we were a long way from the shore. However, I cajoled the Arab boatmen and they took us away under the very eyes of the indignant policeman. On the pier we met the Kennedys and between us persuaded the English Customs House man to give us our permits and forgive our boatmen. We had a delightful drive on Carmel and from the top saw the heights of Gilead, across Jordan. On the way back we stopped at the Monastery and at that moment a Carmelite monk came out of the door. "That's Father Lamb," said Mr. Kennedy, "the Father-Superior." With that I went boldly up and said who I was—of course he had heard of me from the Carmelites at Bagdad. Our success was complete when Sylvia announced herself to be the niece of Monsignor Algernon [Stanley]. Nothing would satisfy

Father Lamb but to take us all about himself, into Elijah's cave, into the garden (where Sylvia made him pose for a picture with the monastery behind him) and finally up to the guest rooms to give us a glass of Carmel liqueur. We parted in warm friendship and the Kennedys drove us back to the port where we found our boatmen waiting. . . .

[They finally land at Beyrout].

BEYROUT,
Oct. 10th. 1925. The French C.G.S., Commandant Deutz, has telephoned to ask if he may come and see me. I met him at Bagdad, a very intelligent, liberal-minded man. . . .

We went to the American College—exquisite place. The Dodges were out, but I introduced myself to one of the professors and we ran to ground Sabah son of Nuri Pasha, who rushed to greet me as soon as he saw me and asked me to take a letter to his father. While I was waiting for the letter to be written Sylvia went to see the hospital. Several other Iraq boys came and greeted me— one the nephew of the Naqib. They all came over ten days ago and the road is quite safe.

Then we went to the Museum where I sent in my card to the Director. He came and showed us over and opened for us the safe which contains the famous golden treasure of Byblos —about 1300 B.C. Most interesting, but what interested me more were the sarcophagi with Phœnician inscriptions said to date from the 4th millennium B.C. That's as early as our earliest inscriptions from Ur. . . .

Oh it's fun to be me when one gets to Asia—there's no doubt of it . . .

. . . . Got to Bagdad at 1:30, in thick winter clothes with a temperature of 90. S. went straight off to the Residency and I home where I was greeted rapturously by my servants. Marie performed prodigies of unpacking and by one o'clock I had had a bath and got into a cotton gown. . . .

This is very much potted news I have no time for more except to say that the Iraq and its government are being models of orderliness and wisdom and that Sir H. still hopes to get home on leave at Xmas.

To H.B.
BAGDAD, October 14th, 1925.

It has been so wonderful coming back here. For the first two days I could not do any work at all in the office, because of the uninterrupted streams of people who came to see me. "Light of our eyes," they said, "Light of our eyes," as they kissed my hands and made almost absurd demonstrations of delight and affection. It goes a little to the head, you know—I almost began to think I were a Person.

Sylvia also came to dine . . . . On Friday she moved over to me. She has Marie's room which we have made very comfortable and Marie sleeps in the garden room—the sitting room when you were here. My household are thrilled to have her and put themselves in four to serve her. . . .

On Saturday afternoon we annexed Mr. Warner (our travelling companion who is on his way to the Teheran Legation) and took him off to call on Haji Naji. Haji Naji took us through all the orange gardens, loaded us with fruit and flowers and gave us tea and coffee. It was so delicious—Sylvia loved it. . . .

I called on all the Ministers, found them all in their offices and had a most satisfactory talk with each one of them: they are worn to a shadow what with having to sit in Parliament all the morning, get through their office work between 12 and 4 and then attend a meeting of the Government party to settle the line which is to be taken next day in the house. But the system is working excellently. . . .

They have almost got through the work of the preliminary session (the budget) and hope to adjourn next week. The new session meets on November 1 but their scheme is to open it formally and then prorogue for a month or 6 weeks. I devoutly hope they will for I find the compilation of the parliamentary reports from the very bad reports in the vernacular papers a most exhausting business. One begins by reading all the papers through and then one compiles a composite report drawn from all four.

On Sunday afternoon Sylvia and I went to the races. It was excessively hot—it has been over 90 every day since we came back—and S. wasn't feeling very fit, though she would not hear of not going. . . .

She was looking quite enchanting in a black and white muslin gown. She creates a sensation in Bagdad society whenever she appears. H.E. brought us back and sat talking for a bit. Sylvia then went to tea and read while I tackled some of my gradually diminishing pile of papers. At 7:30 I went in and found her very unwell and in great pain. I sent at once for a Doctor; Sinbad is still away but I got hold of Woodman whom we both like very much. Her temperature was 104

To H.B.
BAGDAD, October 14th, 1925.

On Monday morning S. was better. I saw her Doctor before I went to the office and heard that he considered her malady to be nothing but the usual sort of internal upset that almost every newcomer goes through before they settle down to Bagdad. I've no doubt the unaccustomed heat had something to do with it . . . . .

[After this, Sylvia had ups and downs of health, although able at intervals to join in seeing the people and the sights of Bagdad all of which she enjoyed very much. It was finally decided that she ought not to remain in the East, and she returned to England in November, 1925, to Gertrude's great disappointment.]

Sir Henry has written a quite admirable report on the history of the country since 1920—taking it up where my white paper left it. The C.O. is going to publish it and you must read it at once. There is a really beautiful page about Sir Percy with a very graceful mention of me at the end. For once in my life I have liked being mentioned by name as part of Sir Percy's material. . . .

. . . . no, railway discussions can't be very cheerful at this juncture. I do wish you hadn't such horrid things to do—I feel a real compunction at having such nice ones to do myself.

. . . . On Sunday morning I didn't go out—far from it. I had breakfast in bed and tried to make believe that I wasn't an overworked Oriental secretary. I wrote a remarkable memo. on tribal customs, the second. I had spent all Saturday morning over the first at the office.

. . . . In spite of all I have said of my activities in the office you must please remember that I am not a Person. . . .

To H.B.
BAGDAD, Nov. 17th, 1925.

On Sunday the King at last arrived. Ken took Sylvia and me to the aerodrome where all high dignitaries and notables were assembled. We waited there for about three-quarters of an hour but it was very amusing talking to all the people. At 11 H.M.'s great plane came in sight, convoyed by 9 little planes, a most beautiful spectacle, and made a perfect landing, drawing up exactly opposite the reception tents. H.E., Zaid and Ghazi went forward to greet him as he stepped out, the Ministers, Advisers and I followed, and out he came looking very well and very much pleased while the British guard of honour played the Arab national tune. It was immensely effective and has made a deep impression here on the Arab mind.

Having made my curtsey I retired into the background while H.M. sat in his tent and received the notables. S. and I drove behind his procession with Ken to the end of the town to see the decorations and the crowd. There is no doubt he has come back with a large and shining halo. . . .

To H.B.
BAGDAD, Nov. 25th, 1925.

. . . . The two Americans dined with Mr. Edwards who is a very eager amateur. After dinner we three examined pottery which they had picked up on the tells near Khabu, a northern tributary of the Euphrates. I'm going to bore you by telling you that a lot of it was our oldest Sumerian stuff which we have got both in the Southern Delta and round Kirkuk, all of which means that the earliest Sumerian civilization (circa 3300 B.C. a date well within the margin) covered the whole area of the two rivers. Some other pottery they had obviously much later, which they could not place. I had a vague idea that I knew it. I got down one of the Hertzfeld's great Euphrat-Tigris Gebiet volumes and there it was! exactly, exactly the same in his pictures late classical or early Byzantine. I may add that the Americans jumped (too hastily) to the conclusion that they had met in me the first authority on Mesopotamian pottery. . . .

. . . . My hat what a social asylum bridge is

. . . . Next day Sunday, I went to the Museum where I had an assignation with the two Americans. We spent a glorious hour over early pottery and all of us learnt a good deal—I know I did. On the way home I showed them a couple of mediaeval buildings and an 8th century marble mahrab, the oldest monument in Bagdad. They were thrilled and so was I. We went to the Diala and walked along the bank in palm groves, most lovely, though why a bit of desert and a stretch of river and a few palms and a sunset should have been so lovely I don't know. It was only God's bright and intricate device I suppose. . . .

To H.B.
BAGDAD, Dec. 9th, 1925.

To-day I have worked like a beaver all the morning—Bernard being away I had to do a lot of his work. . . . I have a terrific amount to do—the annual report and an article for the Encyclopaedia and I don't know what more.

To H.B.
BAGDAD, December 30th, 1925.

I've had some adventures myself. Following the example of everyone in Bagdad—nearly—I had a terrific cold in the head last week and when I wrote to you I had been indoors for two days, but I didn't tell you "not wishing to trouble you." Bernard was in bed with a cold too so it was all most inconvenient. . . .

On Sunday I put on more clothes than I have ever worn before, and with a hot water bottle on my knees, went up with the King and Ken and Iltyd in a closed trolley to Khanaqin. We got to the farm about sunset, found some of the new furniture arrived and spent a happy time arranging it, the King and I began then to feel very tired and went to bed immediately after dinner. Next morning I felt rather bad; they all came in to see if I wanted things and were in favour of not going out shooting. However I shoo'd them off and Zaya looked after me till 5 when they came in. I felt rather better and had them in before dinner to play a game of Bridge with me in bed. But the next day I was pretty bad so Ken sent for the very good local doctor only to find that he was spending Xmas away and immediately, without telling me, telegraphed to Bagdad for a doctor. By that time I wasn't taking much notice, except that I had a general feeling that I was slipping into great gulfs . . . . Finally at 6 arrived Dr. Spencer. He brought with him a charming nurse, Miss Hannifan, who sat up with me all night. They were both of them convinced that I had got pneumonia, but not a bit of it. Next morning it was clear that it was no worse than pleurisy and a pretty general congestion. So they delayed the departure of the morning train by an hour, thus do we behave with our railway management, and took me down to Bagdad . . . . They sat a good deal in my compartment and amused me, I had a very comfortable journey. An ambulance met me at the station and took me straight to hospital, I told Ken to go and sit on my letters for I didn't think I could bear them while I felt so weak, but he did far better, for he found your telegram of the 24th in my house and sent it straight down to me. So by the 27th I was feeling that acute anxiety was over—I hope I am right.

[This refers to Hugo. See last paragraph of this chapter.]

I have spent two very quiet days in bed. Marie comes in the morning and Ken and Iltyd to tea. The Prime Minister paid me a visit this morning and Sayad

Afhan came the morning before, and Elsie Sinbad to-day before lunch. Sinbad came in yesterday coming as soon as he got back to see how I was going on. Otherwise, —with the strong backing up of Dr. Spencer, I've refused to be flooded with visitors after the Arab fashion, and I'm quickly getting well. I have had a night nurse up to now, but I feel sure I shall not need her after to-night— Miss Isherwood, I like her very much too, but Miss Hannifan is a nurse who almost makes it worth while to be ill. And lest you may think that I'm tottering about on edges of graves, I may tell you that Drs. Spencer, Woodman and Dunlop all declare that if I hadn't the most remarkable constitution I should certainly have now been dangerously ill with pneumonia.

[This December and January were overshadowed for Gertrude by the deep anxiety which she shared with us about her much-loved brother Hugo. He contracted typhoid on his voyage home from South Africa with his wife and children in the autumn of 1925, and when they arrived in England on December 11th, he was desperately ill. Hope was almost abandoned. In the third week of December, however, his condition improved, and at Christmas and the New Year the cloud seemed to be lifting. Then he had a relapse. He died on February 2nd, 1926.]

CHAPTER XXVI
1925-1926

BAGDAD

To Hon. Mrs. HENLEY.
BAGDAD, Dec. 9th, 1925.
. . . I am anxious about Hugo. My parents write me that they hear by wireless that he has pneumonia on board ship coming home and I know no more. If anything happened to him it would be such a terrible blow . . .

To the same.
BAGDAD, Dec. 23rd, 1925.
. . . . You can't think what a memory you have left with me, of courage and delicious companionship, and of distinguished wit and high character. I often think about you and I always think how fortunate I am to have you for a cousin and a friend.

You will realise that I am terribly unhappy about Hugo. . . . My heart aches for my darling mother and father and for his poor wife. Isn't it all tragic. If it weren't for love and friendship the world would be a bitter place, but thank God for them, and I will try to make my corner warmer and kinder. I feel I have so much more than I deserve.

To the same.
BAGDAD, Jan. 15th, 1926.
. . . .I don't suppose you can imagine how often I have missed you and how much. Not only to talk to for myself. . . . we seem to have left such a lot of things untalked about, we must have wasted our time—but also when there are other people here, to throw the ball so that we may catch it and throw it back. Mr. Cooke says "she woke us all up" and that's perfectly true, but being awake to what companionship can be like it is hard to have it snatched from me. I keep seeing in imagination all your darling ways and your charming grace and hearing echoes of your delicious voice—but there it is. . . .

To H.B.
BAGDAD, January 6th, 1926.
I can't tell you how I've enjoyed reading the "Confessions of a Capitalist." It's a book everyone should read and I'm now going to lend it to all my friends. It contains as much good sound sense as there are sentences to the page. I did rejoice over it—things like the fallacy involved in profit sharing, you remember. I can't say that any of it is exactly new to me (except Pareto's law which I hadn't heard of before) for I have been brought up so well that I could hear you saying most of the things I was reading in the book. But he has put it well together and in fact what I really meant to say was "God bless my soul! how any" etc. That's what I feel. I hope it will be widely read, that book, and that it will cause a storm

of controversy over which its author will sail joyously with his good heavy facts for a keel. Anyhow, you see you gave me a most successful present and I've been talking about it to everyone who comes to see me . . . . . are all scrambling for it and I'm only wondering which of them will read it quickest so that I may get it on to more people still.

That and the 3rd vol. of the Cambridge Ancient History which has just come out, have been the staples of my days, but if you want to laugh feebly I can tell you a silly ass book which will help you—"Bill the Conqueror"; I forget the name of the talented author, but he nearly gave me a relapse and I'm sure you would feel that way too. Lionel is now seeking round Bagdad for the rest of his books. "Bill the Conqueror" was supplied by Ken. For good simple nonsense he is not easy to beat.

To F.B.
BAGDAD, January 6th, 1926.

I've been having a little quiet illness of my own but it's nearly gone. I was quite bad for a day or two, but now they all saying that they really wouldn't have bothered if they had known the kind of person they were dealing with. For three nights I had the most preposterous sort of nightmares, mostly about Iraq and the treaty and so on, but I'm pleased to remember that one was about flints, which I've been hearing about lately. You'll scarcely believe me but someone (in the nightmare) gave me a flint which had a fossil shell in it and I was so fearfully angry at anyone being such an idiot as to think that a flint could have a fossil shell in it, that I had to wake myself up and say what I thought about it. I found myself saying it and afterwards thought that, 'mutatis mutandis,' it was just the kind of thing that Father would do when he was ill. . . .

To H.B.
BAGDAD, January 13th, 1926.

My convalescence has been happily spent reading a great deal of archaeology and writing an article for the Encyclopaedia on the Iraq. The article would have been better if I had not been forced to compress so fearfully. Even as it is, I don't think it is so bad, but it has to be vetted by the Colonial office and perhaps they will take the spark of life out of it. I'm now embarked on the Annual Report for the League and am (if the truth were known) postponing my return to the office in order to break the back of it. For it is a terrific effort to get through a big piece of work while one is involved in the daily drudgery. I am, however, quite well, sleep, eat and go out walking daily. Indeed I think that the ten days of enforced idleness has done me a great deal of good.

The Iraq Cabinet has accepted the new treaty and I don't think there will be any difficulty about it in our Parliament. . . .

. . . . You need not be alarmed about our 25 years' mandate. If we go on as fast as we've gone for the last two years, Iraq will be a member of the League before five or six years have passed, and our direct responsibility will have ceased. It's almost incredible how the country is settling down. I look back to

1921 or 1922 and can scarcely believe that so great a change has taken place. . . . It's all being so interesting. Archaeology and my museum are taking a bigger and bigger place. I do hope this year to get the Museum properly lodged and arranged. It's such fun isn't it, to make things new from the beginning. . . .

Did I tell you I was now started off on flints, the most enthralling study. We have nothing as yet in the Iraq earlier than historic times (4000 B.C. downwards, roughly) but I'm going to set the oil geologists to find the oldest iron terraces and see if we can't pick up palaeolithic flints on them. If you could send me any short and handy treatise on flints I should be much obliged. I gather that, as a mineral, they are not very old, not what geologists call old. . . .

To H.B.
BAGDAD, January 20th, 1926.

I'm afraid that this will be a short and dull letter for the truth is that I'm being overworked! I have the rather tedious 'corvée' of the annual report upon me and to fit it into the ordinary office routine and take a little necessary exercise is about all I can do. I hope to get through it in the next fortnight and then to go to see the excavations at Ur and Kish which will be very refreshing. . . .

You will please note that the Iraq is the only eastern country which pulls together with Great Britain and the reason is that we have honestly tried out here to do the task that we said we were going to do, i.e., create an independent Arab state. . . .

Your letter and Mother's of Jan. 6th gave such a satisfactory account of Hugo and I also had a most delightful letter from Frances. It is to me more and more miraculous that he should be alive, isn't it to you? To have been so terribly ill under such unfavourable conditions and to have recovered is almost incredible. It is so comforting to think that now every circumstance is favourable. . . .

What a good plan that Herbert should go with you to Italy. He will be the most delightful addition to the party.

I did so love Mother's letter of Jan. 6 with the account of Xmas doings and I'm only not writing to her this week because, as I told you, my fingers are worn to the bone!

To H.B.
BAGDAD, January 27th, 1926.

. . . . It has been bad weather and I have done very little but work. The horrible annual report can't make the League of Nations yawn more than I have over it. It's the dullest thing I've ever written. It's so much more interesting to write about wicked people than good ones, and the same applies to states. The better we get the duller we shall be.

Incidentally I have read the enchanting volume of Page's "Letters to President Wilson." Do you remember when Lichnowsky accuses the U.S.A. of putting off the evil day in Mexico, and Page replies "What better can you do with an evil day than put it off?"

Now do you know, that is what I feel about leaving here. I simply can't bear to think of it, and I don't. . . .

To F.B.
BAGDAD, 3rd March, 1926.

I feel sure you will be glad to hear that I have got the building I wanted of all others for my museum. After addressing the Prime Minister in exalted terms, His Excellency came hurrying into my office, replete with promises. He advised me to get hold of Ken whose Ministry disposes of Government buildings. What could be easier! I hauled Ken off to the place and found him the more easy to convince because it was he who first gave me a secret hint that it might be obtainable and be is now full of satisfaction that his idea has turned out so well. So we settled it all in half an hour and to-day its former occupants have almost all turned out, and I have been settling about repairs, etc. Ken observes with complacency that the Ministry of Interior, when it once gets going, sticks at nothing and indeed I am amazed at the promptness with which it has been done. Government offices don't usually move fast. I am going to lodge the Library of the American School, which will be a great advantage to us, besides being very gratifying to them, and have heaps and heaps of room to show off all our things. At present you must tumble over one in order to have a glimpse of another. Oh dear, how much I should like you to see it! It will be a real Museum, rather like the British Museum only a little smaller. I am ordering long shallow drawers in chests to hold the pottery fragments, so that you will pull out a drawer and look at Sumerian bits, and then another and look at Parthian glaze, and another for early incised, then Arab incised (which I can pick up in quantities a quarter of an hour from my door) and Arab glaze and all. Won't it be nice? It is also nice to think that I shall clear the cupboards of my house of a mass of biscuit tins full of dusty fragments. . . .

To H.B.
BAGDAD, March 3rd, 1926.

. . . . My chief concern, at present, is that I have got the place I wanted for a museum and to-day I have been round it with the Civil Engineer of Bagdad and arranged about needful whitewashings and repairs. It is an excellent building which will give me ample space and allow me an office for the curator and an office for myself, which I ought to have, room to house duplicates till I can dispose of them and a big, fine room for large exhibits. When I come back from Ur, where I am going next week for the division of the objects found this year, I shall be able to begin getting in to it, I hope. I shall take great pride in making it something like a real museum. I always feel, when I'm back to archaeology, that I am nothing better than an antiquarian at heart.

I had Vita Nicolson [Hon. Mrs. Harold Nicolson] with me for two days. She arrived on Saturday morning for breakfast and left on Sunday night after an early dinner. . . . She was most agreeable.

[I reproduce here, by Mrs. Nicolson's permission, a chapter from A Passage to Teheran describing her brief visit to Gertrude.]

Gertrude Bell in Bagdad, by V. Sackville-West.

". . . . Anyone who goes to Bagdad in search of romance will be disappointed. It is a dusty jumble of mean buildings connected by atrocious streets, quagmires of mud in rainy weather, and in dry weather a series of pits and holes over which an English farmer might well hesitate to drive a waggon. I confess that I was startled by the roads of Bagdad, especially after we had turned out of the main street and drove between high, blank walls along a track still studded with the stumps of palm-trees recently felled; the mud was not dry here, and we skidded and slithered, hitting a tree-stump and getting straightened on our course again, racketing along, tilting occasionally at an angle which defied all the laws of balance, and which in England would certainly have overturned the more conventionally minded motor.

"Then: a door in the blank wall, a jerky stop, a creaking of hinges, a broadly smiling servant, a rush of dogs, a vista of garden-path edged with carnations in pots, a little verandah and a little low house at the end of the path, an English voice—Gertrude Bell.

"I had known her first in Constantinople, where she had arrived straight out of the desert, with all the evening dresses and cutlery and napery that she insisted on taking with her on her wanderings; and then in England; but here she was in her right place, in Iraq, in her own house, with her office in the city, and her white pony in a corner of the garden, and her Arab servants, and her English books, and her Babylonian shards on the mantelpiece, and her long thin nose, and her irrepressible vitality. I felt all my loneliness and despair lifted from me in a second. Had it been very hot in the Gulf? got fever, had I? but quinine would put that right; and a sprained ankle—too bad!—and would I like breakfast first, or a bath? and I would like to see her museum, wouldn't I? did I know she was Director of Antiquities in Iraq? wasn't that a joke? and would I like to come to tea with the king? and yes, there were lots of letters for me. I limped after her as she led me down the path, talking all the time, now in English to me, now in Arabic to the eager servants. She had the gift of making everyone feel suddenly eager; of making you feel that life was full and rich and exciting. I found myself laughing for the first time in ten days. The garden was small, but cool and friendly; her spaniel wagged not only his tail but his whole little body; the pony looked over the loose-box door and whinnied gently; a tame partridge hopped about the verandah; some native babies who were playing in a corner stopped playing to stare and grin. A tall, grey sloughi came out of the house, beating his tail against the posts of the verandah; 'I want one like that,' I said, 'to take up into Persia.' I did want one but I had reckoned without Gertrude's promptness. She rushed to the telephone, and as I poured cream over my porridge I heard her explaining—a friend of hers had arrived—must have a sloughi at once—was leaving for Persia next day—a selection of sloughis must be sent round that morning. Then she was back in her chair, pouring out information: the state of Iraq, the excavations at Ur, the need for a decent museum, what new books had come out? what was happening in England? The doctors had told her she ought not to go through another summer in Bagdad, but what should she do in England, eating out her heart for Iraq? next year, perhaps . . . . but I couldn't say she looked ill, could I? I could, and did. She laughed and brushed that aside. Then, jumping up—for all her movements were quick and impatient—if I had finished my breakfast wouldn't I like my bath? and she must go to her office, but would be back for luncheon. Oh yes, and there were people to luncheon; and so, still talking, still laughing, she pinned on a hat without looking in the glass, and took her departure.

"I had my bath—her house was extremely simple, and the bath just a tin saucer on the floor—and then the sloughis began to arrive. They slouched in, led on strings by Arabs in white woollen robes, sheepishly smiling. Left in command, I was somewhat taken aback, so I had them all tied up to the posts of the verandah, till Gertrude should return, an array of desert dogs, yellow, white, grey, elegant, but black with fleas and lumpy with ticks. I dared not go near them, but they curled up contentedly and went to sleep in the shade, and the partridge prinked round them on her dainty pink legs, investigating. At one o'clock Gertrude returned, just as my spirits were beginning to flag again; laughed heartily at this collection of dogs which her telephone message (miraculously, as it seemed to me) had called into being, shouted to the servants, ordered a bath to be prepared for the dog I should choose, unpinned her hat, set down some pansies on her luncheon-table, closed the shutters, and gave me a rapid biography of her guests.

"She was a wonderful hostess, and I felt that her personality held together and made a centre for all those exiled Englishmen whose other common bond was their service for Iraq. They all seemed to be informed by the same spirit of constructive enthusiasm; but I could not help feeling that their mission there would have been more in the nature of drudgery than of zeal, but for the radiant ardour of Gertrude Bell. Whatever subject she touched, she lit up; such vitality was irresistible. We laid plans, alas! for when I should return to Bagdad in the autumn: we would go to Babylon, we would go to Ctesiphon, she would have got her new museum by then. When she went back to England, if, indeed, she was compelled to go, she would write another book. . . . So we sat talking, as friends talk who have not seen one another for a long time, until the shadows lengthened and she said it was time to go and see the king . . ."

To H.B.
BAGDAD, March 10th, 1926.

Last Thursday night I went up to Khanaqin to spend Friday with the King . . . . In the morning, a carpenter and I were busy laying down linoleum and arranging furniture. . . .

We lunched early, went a few miles down the line on a trolley to a place in the farm where we found horses waiting, and spent the afternoon riding about. . . .

When we got back, the drawing room and two of the bedrooms were finished. I whipped the furniture into place and the drawing room looked like a nice comfy room in an English country house. Not all the furniture is covered yet—I have now bought supplementary chintzes and silks in the bazaar to finish it off.

After dinner I left, an A.D.C. taking me to the train. The motor car, characteristically, hadn't enough petrol to reach the station, so we had to get out and walk. But there was no danger of missing the train which would have been kept waiting for me, till I turned up, unlike the North Eastern. . . .

To H.B.
BAGDAD, March 16th, 1926.
. . . .We got to Ur in the early morning, after about 18 hours' journey and left at five in the evening, catching the mail and getting into Bagdad at 7 a.m. So I had a very busy day dividing the things. Nor was it very easy. I had to take the best thing they have got, a small but very perfect statue of the goddess Ban who presided over the farm-yard and has two geese by her throne and two under her feet. As we walked up to Ur from the train, the sky was black with geese flighting north, and talking as hard as they flew. I felt the goddess had been well supplied with them in her time.

I relinquished the lovely little head of the Moon goddess which was published in "The Times," and very reluctantly I relinquished two very early plaques showing sacrificial scenes. . . .

I'm getting much more knowing with practice. I now can place cylindrical and other seals at more or less their comparative date and value, so that I don't choose wildly according to prettiness.

The goddess Ban is worth a great deal of money. Lionel was so anxious lest we should be robbed of her that he carried her about in his 'rucksack' and I fancy used her as a pillow, like a crossed Foreign Office Bag. I took her away when we reached Bagdad, kept her in my house for a day and on Sunday deposited her in a safe.

To F.B.
BAGDAD, March 23rd, 1926.
. . . . I went to tea with the Queen on Sunday to say goodbye to the little Ghazi heir apparent who is going to England to be educated. I was so sorry for her. It must be hard to send your only little boy far away into conditions of which you haven't an inkling.

I have been spending the afternoon to-day trying to learn a little about arranging a museum. Oh dear! there's such a lot to be learnt that my heart sinks. However, I know what I shall do. I shall concentrate on exhibiting the best objects properly and get the others done little by little. Meantime the new museum building has to be re-roofed, for the present mud and beams could be cut through almost by a penknife held by a determined thief. So it will be some time before I get in to the upper floor, but I shall shortly be able to begin on two downstairs rooms . . . . .

To F.B.
BAGDAD, April 6th, 1926.
 . . . .In 30 years I don't suppose there has been such a spring—slopes and rivers of scarlet ranunculus, meadows of purple stock and wild mignonette, blue lilies, black arums and once a bank of yellow tulips. These and commoner things made the world look like a brilliant piece of enamel. . . .
 . . . . I went to Public Works and saw the measured drawings for my museum cases. Mr. Woolley and I (chiefly Mr. Woolley) have standardized wall cases and table cases so that one drawing does for all and the size suits the new building. But there were a good many points which hadn't been understood and the drawings needed careful revision. In the museum afterwards I found Squadron Leader Harnett who takes a deep interest in archaeology and will be very helpful when it comes to arranging the things in the cases. We sat each on a Sumerian gate socket and drew up a scheme for numbering. You see, every object must have a running museum number besides its number in its particular room—the latter for making a catalogue easily usable by the public. As yet we have only the excavators' numbers, Ur 1 to 4000, say, and Kish ditto; while objects that don't come from an excavation have no number at all. The new arrangement will be chronological not geographical, except in the downstairs rooms where all the big, heavy stone objects too heavy to carry upstairs, will stand—a Babylonian room, an Assyrian room and an Arab room are what I shall begin on downstairs when the necessary fittings are made. I foresee that I shall be very boring about Museums for some time to come! Also that I shall make innumerable mistakes. . . . . . .

To F.B.
BAGDAD, April 14th, 1926.
 Our chief preoccupation during the past week has been water. The two days of south wind, of which I spoke with disgust in my last letter, were being more disgusting than I knew. They were melting the snows in the northern mountains and on Thursday we were in for a terrific flood. The river was already so high that no cars or cabs were allowed to cross the bridges and one walked to office hoping devoutly that one would also be able to walk back. In fact the bridges have stood. On Thursday evening the river was almost lapping over its left bank and everybody was busy sandbagging his garden terrace lest the water should come in. After dinner, I sent my gardener round to Ken's house to help and went there myself for a better look at the flood. It was rumbling and sulking past; as we stood on the terrace it sounded as though it were pushing into the foundations under our feet. On Friday the Tigris dyke broke on the left bank—my bank—above the King's palace which it flooded. He was away at Khanaqin and his family had to be moved hastily into a house in the town. The water rushed over the eastern desert, lapping along the torn dyke and from then until now we have never been sure that it would not break through and flood the low lying parts of the town, which include my quarter! I think that risk is over now, unless the Tigris again does something very perverse, but the possibility of

having 6ft. of water in one's house hasn't been pleasant. How dreadfully annoyed I should have been, to be sure. It has been difficult to think of anything else. They have brought in thousands of peasants and propped the banks with reed mats and sand bags, but the worst is when the water begins to drip in through rotten places in the lower parts of the dyke. They have electric light all along and people watching and looking night, and day. The big railway station on the east bank is under water and enormous quantities of merchandize waiting to go up to Persia spoilt. . . .

The Arabs are so incurably careless; they won't shut their channels when the flood is coming down and then it finds a way in and breaks through. . . .

This is a country of extremes. It's either dying of thirst or it's dying of being drowned. Bagdad can never be made really safe, it lies in such low ground; but I expect that after this experience, following on that of 1923, they will do a great deal to make it safer. The whole desert to the east is under water for miles and miles; now the Euphrates is beginning and it's to be hoped that it won't lay under water the whole desert to the west! Anyhow it can't destroy my house, which is something.

This is only a flood letter I'm afraid.

I'm so sorry for the King—his nice house all spoilt. And poor Iltyd, who is in Mosul. . . .

To H.B.
BAGDAD, April 21st, 1926.

I ought to have told you about it and also to look for the Arabic graffiti on the columns, in the doorways of St. Mark's. I could not read them but they obviously must have been written before the columns were carried off from the east. I liked the general aspect of St. Mark's less when I saw it again, and some of the details more. . . .

We are now safe from floods—as safe as we can be, for as Mr. Bury observes, Bagdad cannot ever be safe unless it is rebuilt in another place. Fortunately the Diala did not rise too high so that the Tigris water began to flow off into it. But the Baquba road is for two miles under water—they have managed to get a temporary road open across the desert three or four miles to the south. The breach in the Tigris was closed on Friday by throwing sandbags between rows of wooden piles. It did not look very solid but they are now building a strong earth dyke behind. The King's palace is not so bad. They got all the furniture out, though most of it will have to be recovered, and the water has now run off. But the big house on the river bank where the Queen and the family live is cracking and probably means to fall into the Tigris. The bank is undermined. . . . The King means to get back by day into his own little palace and offices as soon as he can. Isn't it horribly boring for him.

I also find it boring, for all the desert where I used to ride and walk is a lake. . . .

The Prime Minister, I can't think why, has asked me to serve on the Government Committee for distributing relief to the peasants who were washed out above Bagdad. There's a meeting to-morrow. . . .

Iltyd is away in Mosul where he received a telegram thus worded "On approach of the water your house fell down" from one of his Arab officers. His house has in fact collapsed into the flood but he had moved all his clothes and things into the brick barracks nearby before he left, and these are safe. All his furniture was washed away and lost.

The only other thing I have done was to dine with Ken on Monday to meet the King, who was very cheerful considering all his troubles. But as we were six we had to play Vingt et Un (a very dull game I think) instead of bridge.

I was exceedingly sorry to hear of Will Pease's death—it was in the papers. I've written to Ernest.

We have all been imprisoned by very heavy rain. It's over now. On Saturday there wasn't a room in the office through the ceiling of which the rain wasn't dripping. On Sunday morning I went to the Sarai and did a lot of work in the Museum and then had a long gossip with the police about Bolsheviks, etc. An American came to lunch, he is the representative of the American school this year. We looked at pottery and flints collected by him on the southern mounds; we looked at them till four, I learnt something, I think, but he learnt more, for he knows much less about pottery than I do, which is saying that he knows very little. However, he had found some interesting inscribed bricks and these he did know about. The net result of his labours is that we don't yet know the site of an ancient Babylonian city called Isin, for he has got Isin bricks out of another mound. It's negative but it's better not to think we know when we don't.

This afternoon I went into the desert which was fairly dry and now I'm going to pack for I go to Ur to-morrow.

Iltyd and I are going to a little music party given by the Vernons to-night. I like the Vernons.

To H.B.
BAGDAD, May 5th, 1926.

[This is during the Strike in England.] Everything else is swallowed up in the thought of what is happening to you. The scanty news in Reuter gives one some impression of the terrible upheaval. One peers into the future much as one did at the beginning of August, 1914—absit omen! . . . .

On Saturday night I had a bridge party to while away the time before my train left which wasn't till 11:30. . . . It was rather a hot journey down to Ur, just hot enough to do nothing but laze and read a novel, but I restored the balance by unusual activity on arrival. There was a lot of pottery belonging to us left at the Expeditions Haus. I had brought 4 cases to pack it in and my museum clerk to help. The capable station master provided us with men to carry the cases out across the desert and soon after 6 o'clock we were busy packing up by the light of a lantern and with the willing assistance of the Arab guards. It took us about two hours, after which we walked back in the night over the deliciously cool desert. . . .

The King arrived from Basrah about 5:30 a.m. on Monday. We were all ready to receive him, the Mutasarrif, Administrative Inspector, sheikhs, I, etc. When he had finished with salutations we decided to go off at once to the excavations and come back to breakfast after. H.M. and I stepped into the Mutasarrif's car and the others followed in taxis, a Minister and a varied lot of officials who were with H.M. It was a most successful visit; the King was much interested—we got through before 8, when the sun was just beginning to be a little hot, having seen all that Kings need see. Then breakfast in the King's car with a couple of Ministers and nice Mr. Bury (irrigation). Subsequently I returned to my own compartment. It was a special train and we stopped nowhere but at Diwaniyah where we moved into a restaurant car for lunch (I lunched with a Minister and two Saiyids, one a Senator, one a Deputy) and again at Hillah where the King sent for me to have tea with him. It was now cool again and H.M. and I, a Minister and a courtier played bridge till we reached Bagdad at 6:45 p.m. on April 3rd. There I learnt that the strike had begun—Ken came in before dinner with the news. Since when we have all talked of little else.

Telegrams continue to come from the Colonial Office we suppose that Sir John Shuckburgh is transported thither in a government lorry.

We suppose and we wonder and we wish we knew more. Incidentally I don't know whether letters will reach you or how long they will be delayed, so I shall not write any other than this.

To H.B.
BAGDAD, May 11th, 1926.

Your letter of April 28th, written on the eve of the strike reached me by last mail; I wonder whether letters will have got through in the first week and fear that the next letter may be delayed. We have no news but Reuter and you may imagine how eagerly we await it. Indeed anxiety is never out of my mind; there has been word of disturbances at Middlesbrough and to-day there are railway accidents. These things don't make one feel easier. You ask about my plans for the summer. This doesn't seem to be the moment to make any plans which involve expenditure, for I don't know whether I shall have any income or whether any of us will. My duty to the museum is of the first importance. I can't go away and leave all those valuable things half transferred and the work goes very slowly. It will take months and months, I think. I have made a little headway this week. The alterations in the building itself are finished and a few simple fittings in one of the lower rooms were ready so on Sunday morning I called on Squadron Leader Harnett to help and we placed all the big gate sockets (dull things but valuable) on the bench along the wall that had been made for them, or rather we superintended the placing of them by porters. In the middle of the wall I had had a solid cement pedestal set up and onto this we hauled (I didn't) a great roughly blocked out Babylonian statue. When we had done, we were quite pleased with the look of it, but we have not got any further for we are waiting for a wooden pedestal for a statue which is to stand in the middle of the room and some shallow boxes in which to set some broken bits of relief in cement. In one corner I am going to reconstruct the tomb of a deified king of

Ur which was found this year, and as that is about all which the room will hold for the present (I mean, I have nothing more for that room), it ought not to take very long to get it finished. It will look, no doubt, rather home-made, but even now it is beginning to look like a museum. When it is ready, I want quickly to make a catalogue of it—no great task—and then get the King to open it so as to show people that we are doing something. . . .

To F.B.
BAGDAD, May 13th, 1926.

I don't see how I can possibly make any plans for the moment so of course keep the pageant where you like. I think it is extremely unlikely that I can afford to come back and out again this summer—it's a very expensive business. It would be worse to finish the museum and then be told not to come back here if I thought that the best course which I probably shall. Bernard is going on leave in about 3 weeks and when he is away Sir Henry rather leans on me, not so much to do things as to talk them over. He is full of plans for big administrative work, which doesn't in fact touch me. They interest me very much, his schemes and I think them on the whole very good.

Oh dear, I wonder what it is all like with you—what it will be like after, if there's any sort of an "after." . . . .

To H.B.
BAGDAD, May 18th, 1926.

I had scarcely posted my letter last week, when we got news of the ending of the general strike, but that doesn't mean the ending of difficulties and you are still in the thick of them. Indeed, I don't know whether your worst difficulties are not just about to begin. . . .

I have been very busy with my museum, but it has not got far yet. I go in at 7 a.m. and spend a couple of hours there before I go to the office. On Sunday we can work until it gets too hot and fortunately it is being remarkably cool weather. In a day or two I shall have my own workroom with an electric fan which will make things easier. . . . As for cases, tables and things, they have not begun to materialize yet and for the moment I am occupied with the big stone objects which do not need to be behind glass.

I forget if you know Sir John Cadman. He is, or is going to be, Chairman of the A.P.O.C. He was here a year and a half ago and brought a letter to me from Willie Tyrrell. He passed through again last week on his way back from Persia, where he had been to represent the A.P.O.C. at the coronation of the Shah. During the 4 days he spent here he succeeded in getting through the agreement with the Iraq Government for the working of the oil at Khanaqin which has been hanging fire for three years or more. I met him every day, lunching with Sir Henry, and was thrilled to hear his account of the way matters were proceeding. If all goes well—and there's no reason why it should not—the Iraq ought to begin to draw royalties next year and to have cheap oil from the Khanaqin refinery. On Sunday, the night before Sir John left, Sir Henry gave a large dinner party to meet the King. Sir John was sitting between H.M. and me and they spent most of the dinner in exchanging sentiments of gratitude and hopeful anticipation. As they had no common tongue, it fell to me to interpret for them. I felt I earned my dinner.

Sir John had with him as secretary a young Bridgeman, son of the First Lord of the Admiralty, a nice boy. He, and a very attractive and intelligent young soldier in the Iraq army, Captain Edwells, came to tea with me on Saturday, after which I took them sightseeing.

Iltyd is going to Mosul for a month, which is very tiresome. He dined with me on Tuesday and we played piquet afterwards. He is such a pleasant companion—I miss him very much when he is away. Lionel is also a great stand by. He comes in frequently to tea on his way back from office and we walk together to his house at Alwiyah about a mile away, through what you might almost call fields. But now that the barley is being cut they are gradually relapsing from fields into desert. . . . Ken and I dined with him last night and had an agreeable evening. We caught some huge hawk moths. Lionel is rather good at lepidoptera. and Ken is an expert. Between us we are getting quite a collection. It is an amusing way of passing the time.

I lunch always with Sir Henry and we discuss the affairs of the day, public and private, and then, if I have been early at the Museum, I go to sleep for a bit when I get home; in the evening if I am alone I read Babylonian history or books about seals and things so that I may know a little better how to arrange the Museum. It sounds rather a monotonous existence, but it is inexpensive and peaceful which, I am afraid, is more than can be said for yours.

To F.B.
BAGDAD, May 26th, 1926.

Your letter of May 11th was the very first news I had of your doings during the general strike. You don't sound as if you were living in a strike at all, but it is wonderful how little difference it made, even in London, I gather from Elsa. But if the coal strike drags on and on, it will be very dreadful and it must end in dislocating life. Molly hasn't written since just after she was ill.

I am sure that Maurice must have been admirable at Middlesbrough but there were anxious moments, weren't there. Oh dear, isn't it a horrid world.

I hope you won't think I'm wrong in saying that I can't go away yet and leave all my antiquities unarranged and unguarded. I have been writing to father about it. I'll see later how things go on, but it's so very expensive to return home and then come back here that I think I would rather finish and then go away. It isn't because I don't immensely want to see you and father, but I know you will understand that it means a very great deal to leave everything that I have been doing here and find myself really rather loose on the world. I don't see at all clearly what I shall do, but of course I can't stay here forever; already I feel that when Bernard is here, and Sir Henry, I'm not at all necessary in the office.

I would have liked to stay in the Department of Antiquities if I could come home every year, but I don't feel justified in asking the Iraq Government to give me anything like a permanent post. The Director here should know cuneiform and be a trained museum official. What I can do is just to tide them over. . . .

All the same I feel very much torn. Tell me what you think, will you please.

To H.B.
BAGDAD, May 26th, 1926.

I received by last mail your letters of May 5th and 11th and read them with the deepest interest. Also letters from mother and Elsa, of May 11th, so that I had a good all round view of what things were like. Your forecast as to the duration of the general strike was very good and I was particularly glad that you gave me a resumé of dealings with the colliers because Sir Henry is always asking me about it and your outline was so clear. I am going to have it typed for distribution to my colleagues. . . . Anyhow, I take it that we shall have very little income this year.

That is not the only reason, though it's a very good one, for my wanting to stay here this summer. I hope you won't be very much disappointed. What I vaguely think of doing (but don't talk about it) is to stay with the High Commissioner till Bernard comes back in the autumn; then to resign and ask the Iraq Government to take me on as Director of Antiquities for six months or so. (I'm only Hon. Director now, you know.) I should not in any case stay much longer with the H.C.; it has really ceased to be my job. Politics are dropping out and giving place to big administrative questions in which I'm not concerned and at which I'm no good. On the other hand, the Department of Antiquities is now a full time job. I am trying to get the Cabinet to let me deal with all the things the Germans left at Babylon as I should deal with a new excavation. Privately, I have put up the Deutch Orient Gesellschaft to make the proposal and they have suggested sending out Andrae, who dug at Shergat, to arrange and catalogue the objects, after which I would make a division. I know Andrae very well and like him; the fact that I was working with him would make everything go smoothly and the Iraq Government has complete confidence in me as Director and would not question anything I did. But all this would mean far too much work to be treated as a secondary employment. Yale is nibbling at the biggest mound in the Iraq, and if I have three excavations on my hands besides Babylon and the Museum it is very certain that I cannot do anything else. I am waiting to see how all this turns out, but already I know that I ought to have all my time for the Museum. As it is I now go there from 7 to 8:30 or so every morning and get to the office about 9. That has meant a pretty strenuous four and a half hours but I find that I can just get through the work, sometimes taking papers home to read in the evening. The weather has been beautifully cool. On Sunday (Whit Sunday) I worked from 7 to 1 in the Museum without any fans. Monday was a holiday in the office though I could not take it all as I had a report to write, but by doing some of it on Sunday afternoon I got from 7 to 1 in the Museum. One big room downstairs, the Babylonian Stone Room, is now finished and I am only waiting for the catalogue, which I have written, to be translated and printed, to ask the King to open it—just to show them that we are doing something. But this is the easiest of all the rooms, big objects not under glass, it is when I come to the upstairs rooms and all the little objects that the difficulties begin. The mere cataloguing and numbering of them is terrific. The cataloguing of things from Ur and Kish for the past three years has been done and I have now nearly finished the things of this year. But the serial number of the Bagdad Museum has to be put onto everything and until each object is in the catalogue we can't number it. There are a mass of things from other places than Ur and Kish which we have not begun on. Then will come the arrangement in cases—none of which have begun to come in yet. I have moved about half the things from the old room into the new Museum and they are lying about, some on tables, some on the floor, a desolating spectacle. In the course of the next ten days it will be even worse, for by that time I hope I may have got almost everything moved over. I don't think I could possibly leave it like this. If in the middle of the summer I felt tired or seedy, I might have got things into enough order to come away for a bit, but it's very expensive to come as far as England as I have Marie to take too. I'll see later.

The afternoons, after tea, hang rather heavy on my hands. . . . We can't swim yet because the river is so high and the current so strong. This last week I have sometimes gone into the Museum at 5, but it will soon be too hot to do that with any comfort and it is not really a good plan because one gets no exercise. I did it in order to finish cataloguing the Ur and Kish things of this year. . . .

To F.B.
BAGDAD, June 2nd, 1926.
. . . . Lionel and I yesterday were busy discussing the programme he is drawing up for a university curriculum. Sir Henry is pressing for a faculty of Fine Arts. Lionel's idea is to combine languages and literature—at least French and English—with history, political economy, all in a three years' course. . . .

I suggested that, in special historic subjects Babylonia and Assyria should be included. I should like to lecture on that myself, but I don't think the scheme will materialize for a long time . . . . .

Nevertheless, Sir Henry does put a great deal of vitality into things and I always stand amazed at his general capacity.

To H.B.
BAGDAD, June 2nd, 1926.
I can't refer to the Times because I have had no papers since the general strike. I can't think why they didn't come last week. Anyway the last Times I received was that of April 28th while your letter from Mt. Grace was dated May 18th. The 'sécateur' for Haji Naji has arrived, however. I have not taken it to him yet because I have been so busy in the Museum. Profiting by remarkably cool weather I've been there between tea and dinner as well as in the early morning. I know he will love it. I will try to take it down to him on Sunday. There is a little basket of fruit from him on my dining room table most mornings.

To-morrow we have a holiday for the King's birthday and I shall have a whole day for my Museum. That enthusiast, Squadron Leader Harnett, is coming too. We have been engaged in taking down a beautiful late Abbassid inscription (not brick) which was dropping out of the ruined building in which it stood. . . . It is coming out very well and Squadron Leader Harnett is now going to clean it and build it up against the wall of the big Arab room. We spent a long peaceful morning on Sunday cataloguing cylinder seals. . . . He is certainly a great asset and he seems to be amused with what some people might consider a very tedious job. I don't, for there is an indescribable attraction about these fine little things. The worst of it is that I can't extract the furniture out of the railway people so we don't get to anything final.

I haven't told you about the floods for a long time. The Euphrates, after threatening to cover the country up to the embankment of the Hillah railway, thought better of it. The Tigris is definitely going down, but one of the deputies told me the other day that the cellars of his house in the middle of Bagdad, a good deal below the river level, are 4ft. deep in water. . . .

To F.B.
BAGDAD, June 9th, 1926.

I unfortunately overslept myself this afternoon and the King is coming to dinner. I hope you will like the picture postcards I sent to Father of two of the exhibits in the Museum. They do rather fill me with pride. I haven't got any of my cases or tables yet for the upper rooms and I don't know when they will begin to come in. Meantime, with the help of S/L Harnett and occasionally Mr. Cooke, I am getting on with the numbering of all the objects. This year's finds have all been catalogued and numbered and all the cylinder seals are done—we could arrange them at once if we had the cases. That will be an absorbingly interesting task.

I have an extremely nice Indian foreman who is deputed to do all the odds and ends of jobs that arise—such as building up Bur Sin's shrine. He is so capable and so pleasant. And I shall be very much interested to see what the Arab bigwigs think of the lower room which the King opens next week. The one or two who have dropped in to see us at work have been much impressed.

To H.B.
BAGDAD, June 9th, 1926.

. . . I am enclosing the catalogue of the Babylonian Stone Room of the Museum and two picture postcards of the exhibits. No. 7 is the thing I am proudest of—there is nothing like it in any museum in the world. I forgot to mention in the catalogue that the bricks which form the pedestal of the statue (No. 1) are blue glazed bricks from the top of the Ziggurrat at Ur, remains of an upper chamber built or restored by Nabonidus the last king of Babylon. We brought away a lot of fragments and built them up into a pedestal—it is most effective. The King is going to open this room on Monday. It is the easiest of all to arrange because it consists only of a few large objects but it looks extremely well and I hope it will impress the Ministers! It has indeed all the appearance of a Museum. . . .

Thursday was a very nice day for I had the whole morning there (in the Museum) and came back to lunch and a good rest. There was a state dinner party for the King's birthday and a reception of about 500 people in the garden afterwards. The party was very interesting. All the deputies and senators and everyone one had ever known in Bagdad were there, the Ministers and most of the Arab civil servants in ordinary European evening dress and hatless and the religious leaders in robes and turbans. There was a wonderful diversity. . . .

On Sunday S/L Harnett and I had a good morning in the Museum. After tea Ken and I went out to Karradah and caught four exquisite swallow tail butterflies, the first we had seen. We were much elated.

Haji Naji is delighted with his knife and sends you a thousand messages of thanks.

To-night the King comes to dine and play bridge. . . .

To H.B.
BAGDAD, June 16th, 1926.

My principal news you have seen in the papers—the Turkish treaty. It is almost too good to be true. . . .

I had a nice little ceremony on Monday when the King opened the first room of the Museum. It was open to the public for the first time to-day and as I came away at 8:30 this morning, I saw some 15 or 20 ordinary Bagdadis going round it under the guidance of the Arab curator—very gratifying. Everyone agrees that it looks like a Museum. All the other rooms are still chaos, but S/L Harnett and I are forging ahead with the numbering and cataloguing and I actually hope to add a couple of small cases this week. But it is such a stupendous job that without the support of the admirable S/L Harnett I should certainly succumb. Fortunately it is being quite comparatively cool.

To F.B.
BAGDAD, June 16th, 1926.

. . . Decidedly a pageant is a much bigger undertaking than a Museum. I wonder if you sometimes think, as I do, that you will never get through with it! But it was a great satisfaction this morning to see the public actually looking at the room which the King opened on Monday. It is only open two days a week for a couple of hours because all my staff (an old Arab curator, a very intelligent Jew clerk and an odd man) is so busy. We are now beginning to see daylight through the preliminary task of numbering the objects—between three and four thousand of them.

It is being a very grim world, isn't it? I feel often that I don't know how I should face it but for the work I'm doing and I know you must feel the same. I think of you month after month as the time passes since that awful sorrow, and realize all the time that the passage of the months can make little difference. I wish I were coming home this summer but I feel sure that when I leave I shall not want to come back here and I would like to finish this job first—indeed, I feel that I must finish it, there being no one else. But it is too lonely, my existence here; one can't go on for ever being alone. At least, I don't feel I can. . . . . .

To H.B.
BAGDAD, June 23rd, 1926.
    We are labouring under the difficulties presented by the four days' holiday of the big Id when all the Arab offices are closed and one can't get anything through. A holiday at this time of year is no good as far as holiday making goes, for it is too hot to go out on any expedition. By luck—and the vagaries of the moon—it didn't begin till Monday, so that I had Sunday morning in the Museum. I have to give my staff a holiday and I shall not be able to work there again till Saturday which is a bore. However, I brought back some cases of cylinder seals at which I have been working of an evening. . . .
    We had a terrific day on Monday. It began with a levee at the palace at 6:10. I was within an ace of going without orders, but I discovered their absence as I was waiting for the High Commissioner at the end of the Maude Bridge and dispatched a Kavass hotfoot to fetch them. The H.C. being fortunately late, they arrived in the nick of time.
    I then came home, breakfasted and did an hour's work, after which I set out again on visits. First the Naqib, then the Ministers, then selected notables and finally the Queen and Ali and his family. . . .
    It has been extremely mild for Bagdad, rarely over a hundred and the nights quite cold; but after dinner my house is stuffy and I am glad when it is time to go to bed on the roof. We are going to begin swimming which is the only agreeable form of exercise at this time of year. . . .
    I am being much enthralled by the study of seals. In the scenes of worship and domestic life depicted on those tiny cylinders I constantly find pots and things which I have actually got in the Museum. Then I suddenly place them with a much greater sense of reality. Just as I placed the mace heads in the shrine of Bur Sin—I have found them on quantities of seals standing in the shrines of other gods. That is rather thrilling, isn't it. . . .

To H.B.
BAGDAD, June 30th, 1926.
    . . . . What an enormous waste and loss two months' coal strike must mean. It's so amazing that the world seems to go on just the same—Ascot and balls and parties are what I read of in the Times—or, rather, I see they are there—and extraordinarily little about things that really matter.
    We are now well into the hot weather—temperature at 113—but I am feeling it scarcely at all. Partly, I think, because we have begun bathing though the river is still very high and the current strong. It makes such a difference. We go up by launch to a place above the town where I have a little hut to undress in and get back after seven feeling both exercised and refreshed. . . . It is too hot

now to dine indoors and play bridge and much pleasanter to lie out on the river bank and come home by launch about 10.

I often wonder how the old Babylonians with whom I now feel such a close connection, passed their summer. Much as we do, I daresay, but without our ice and electric fans which add immensely to the amenities of existence. The moment of the day I don't like is going home after lunch at the hottest moment, but there is no way out of it.

In the Museum S/L Harnett and I are engaged in classifying seals. I have read books and books about them. The really important ones are usually plain sailing; one is pretty certain of their period, but there are dreadful backwaters of decadence when one is never sure whether the thing is very early or just very bad late work. Also the authorities are not in entire agreement and one has to make up one's mind whom one will follow. Still on the whole, I don't think I shall be very much out. . . . . Next week I hope to have my seal case and by that time we shall have got all the seals fairly well grouped and ready to be put in. . . .

Faisal has given me a bronze bust of himself by Feo Gleichen to put in the Museum. I shall set it up in the big Arab room. There, now I must go to lunch. My letters are extremely dull, but there is really nothing to recount.

To H.B.
2nd July, 1926.
. . . . I don't see for the moment what I can do. You see I have undertaken this very grave responsibility of the museum—I have been writing about it ad nauseam for months. I had been protesting for more than a year that I must have a proper building; this winter one fell vacant and they gave it to me together with a very large sum of money for fittings, etc. Then first I had to re-roof it and next I was held up at least two months by the floods and the work they entailed which prevented work being done for me. Now all the very valuable objects— they run into tens of thousands of pounds and incidentally they would never have been taken out of the ground if I had not been here to guarantee that they would be properly protected, have been transferred pell-mell into the new building and there is absolutely no one but I who knows anything about them, since J. M. Wilson left. It isn't merely a responsibility to the Iraq but to archaeology in general. I could not possibly leave things in this state except for the gravest reasons. I work at it as hard as I can, but it's a gigantic task—of course I love it and am ready to give all my spare time to it. But I can't resign from my post as Oriental Secretary. And as I am a civil servant, I have only about 2 months' leave owing to me, which means a little over 9 weeks in England.

That is the whole position. In a couple of months or so I may be beginning to see daylight in the museum or at any rate a condition in which I could safely leave it for a little. Let us wait for a bit, don't you think, and see how things look.

You do realise, don't you, that I feel bound to fulfil the undertakings I gave when, at my instance the Iraq Government allowed excavations to be begun 4 years ago. The thing has grown and grown—it can't do otherwise—and whereas until last autumn I had J.M. to help me, I now have no one. All the plans that were begun before Hugo was ill even, are now bearing fruit and I'm rather overwhelmed by them. Anyhow, father, give me a little time to get things into some kind of order and then if you want me to take what leave I can I will do so. But in that case I think I should have to come back for next winter or part of it.

Except for the Museum work, life is very dull.

To H.B.
BAGDAD, July 7th, 1926.
. . . . It had been very hot in the morning in the Museum but we have now changed into a north room and had a fan put into it which makes it comparatively luxurious. We can work there quite comfortably without a fan on week days when we leave at 8:30, but on Sundays when we stay until 1, it is essential to have a cool room. I have got a few standard cases and hope to have the seal case this week. But there is so much to learn; one constantly finds that the things don't exactly serve one's purpose and they have to be modified. However both we and the carpenters are learning gradually.

I have been having very busy mornings, lots of dispatches to write and long things to do. Sir Henry is delightful to work with, but he is most careful of detail and one has to pay great attention to what one is doing.

Darling I must stop now; summer does not conduce to the writing of very long letters.

To F.B.
BAGDAD, July 7, 1926.
. . . . photograph of you and the little boys. They are darlings. Is not the eldest one like Hugo? In this photograph I see a great likeness. . . . . . .

I am so glad you like the pictures of my museum, and when in return will you give me the text of the Pageant? I want so much to read it. I wish I were at the point of having photographs of the upper rooms taken, but they are still in chaos—not so chaotic as they were, however for most of the objects are roughly classified and ready to be put into cases. But I find arranging cases very difficult. Even the two tiny ones which I have done so far take an enormous amount of thought and re-arrangement till one puts them approximately right. And then the writing of labels! Fortunately my Arab clerk writes them beautifully so I only have to give him a list of what has to go on each one and leave him to do it during the rest of the morning while I am in the office. . . .

[These two letters of July 2nd and July 7th were the last she wrote home. They reached England after her death.

Her strenuous self-imposed work in the museum, in the terrible heat of a Bagdad summer, added to the daily round of her duties in the office, proved too much for her slender stock of physical energy. She had never really recovered from her illness in the winter.

She died quite peacefully in her sleep, in the early morning hours of Monday July 12th, 1926.

CHAPTER XXVII

CONCLUSION

THE tidings brought an overwhelming manifestation of sorrow and sympathy from all parts of the earth, and we realised afresh that her name was known in every continent, her story had crossed every sea. There had clustered round her in her lifetime so many fantastic tales of adventure, based on fact and embroidered by fiction, tales of the Mystery Woman of the East, the uncrowned Queen, the Diana of the Desert, that a kind of legendary personality had emerged which represented Gertrude in the imagination of the general public, to the day of her death.

When the crowning sequel came to those times of desert adventure, when she saw her dreams of the Arab resurgence turn into reality, she was one of those who helped to achieve it. She was at the throbbing centre of the events which lead to the dramatic leap into history of the Kingdom of Iraq with an Arab prince on the throne.

During the years that followed, when she became a servant of the State, her abilities were again conspicuously displayed in what was to her the entirely new field of official life. But her officialdom was always tinged with ardour and romance, and it was an unceasing interest to her that her congenial Post as Oriental Secretary to the High Commissioner enabled her still to keep in close touch with the Arabs of the desert as well as with the increasing number of their kinsmen in the town.

At the news of her death messages were received at the High Commissioner's office from all parts of Iraq, from Bagdad, from the desert, from officials and representatives—and most of them seem to be no mere formal condolences, but to have in them a note of real sorrow.

I quote here a sentence from a moving letter from Haji Naji, for whom Gertrude felt such warm friendship, and whose garden was always her delight:

"It was my faith always to send Miss Bell the first of my fruits and vegetables and I know not now where I shall send them."

I wish I had space enough to reproduce here many other letters from Gertrude's Arab friends.

In her own country there was a widespread expression of regret. Telegrams and letters, all seeming to convey a sense of personal loss, poured in from every layer of the social scale. They came from the highest in the land, they came from people of distinction in the world of letters, the world of art, the political world, the social world, from the villages of her Yorkshire countryside, who were so proud of her, from the Works where she had so many friends; and her family felt that however different the senders might be from one another, and however differently they expressed themselves, they were all saying and meaning the same thing—they all really cared.

Their Majesties sent the following message:

"The Queen and I are grieved to hear of the death of your distinguished and gifted daughter whom we held in high regard.

"The nation will with us mourn the loss of one who by her intellectual powers, force of character and personal courage rendered important and what I trust will prove lasting benefit to the country and to those regions where she worked with such devotion and self-sacrifice. We truly sympathise with you in your sorrow.

"(Signed) GEORGE R. I."

The Colonial Secretary, Mr. Amery, paid her the great tribute of a statement in the House of Commons, recapitulating her devoted service, in answer to a question from Mr. Runciman.

Sir Valentine Chirol, who, as shown so often in the letters, was one of her closest friends, wrote an obituary notice of her which appeared in the Times the day after she died. It was a striking portrait, written with the most profound sympathy and understanding. Sir Arnold Wilson, the "A.T." of her letters, under whom she served, wrote in the Times a generous appreciation of her work; so did Mr. Woolley, who shared her work in archaeology, so did also Dr. David Hogarth, her friend and counsellor, whose wide and learned experience of the East, added to his steadfast friendship, was always to Gertrude such a support. So did M. Salomon Reinach (writing in the Revue Archéologique) from whom Gertrude learned so very much.

Some of the letters we received were written by people who went to her house once, perhaps, as they passed through Bagdad, and record the vivid and ineffaceable impression she made on them.

The High Commissioner wrote the following letter to Gertrude's father about the Museum she founded in Bagdad, now called the Iraq Museum—how she would have preferred that name to any other!

6th June, 1927.

HIGH COMMISSIONER'S OFFICE, BAGDAD.

My dear Sir Hugh, King Faisal some time ago wrote to the Prime Minister of Iraq suggesting that one of the principal rooms in the Bagdad Museum should be named the "Gertrude Bell Room," and I understand that this has been accepted by the Iraq Cabinet.

A meeting of Gertrude's friends later decided to associate her name with the whole Museum by putting in a prominent position a brass plaque with a suitable inscription, which was to be submitted to you for approval. After you had approved it they thought of asking J. M. Wilson to design the plaque... Yours very sincerely,

H. DOBBS.

GERTRUDE BELL Whose memory the Arabs will ever hold in reverence and affection created this Museum in 1923, being then Honorary Director of Antiquities for the Iraq. With wonderful knowledge and devotion she assembled the most precious objects in it and through the heat of the summer worked on them until the day of her death on 12th July, 1926.

King Faisal and the Government of Iraq, in gratitude for her great deeds in this country, have ordered that the Principal Wing shall bear her name and with their permission her friends have erected this tablet.

It is a source of deep satisfaction to Gertrude's family that King Faisal, who honoured her with his friendship and to whom she was so loyally devoted, should have suggested that her name should be associated with the Museum and should have consented to the placing of the beautifully worded plaque.

Gertrude was buried in the afternoon of July 12th, in the cemetery outside Bagdad, with the honours of a military funeral. "A huge concourse of Iraqis and British," we were told were present. The High Commissioner and the whole of the British Staff, civil, military and Air Force, the Prime Minister of Iraq and the members of the Cabinet, and a great number of Arab sheikhs from the desert. The troops of the Iraq army lined the road, and an enormous crowd paid a last homage to one who was honoured throughout the length and breadth of the land."

Her coffin was borne from the gate of the cemetery to the graveside by the group of young men on the High Commissioner's staff, whose names recur so often in her letters, her intimate friends and comrades, to whom her house was always a beloved centre, a meeting place and haven. Her death had come to them as an unbelievable catastrophe.

The High Commissioner, Gertrude's chief, issued an official notification of her death, in which a sense of acute grief is felt to underlie the dignified and restrained wording. I quote from it two sentences which seem to me to sum up all that can be said about her services in the East.

"She had for the last ten years of her life consecrated all the indomitable fervour of her spirit and all the astounding gifts of her mind to the service of the Arab cause, and especially to Iraq. At last her body, always frail, was broken by the energy of her soul."

"Her bones rest where she had wished them to rest, in the soil of Iraq. Her friends are left desolate."

But let us not mourn, those who are left, even those who were nearest to her, that the end came to her so swiftly and so soon. Life would inexorably have led her down the slope—Death stayed her at the summit.

Lightning Source UK Ltd.
Milton Keynes UK
12 November 2009
146160UK00001B/99/P